MIDORI DAYS™

MIDORI DAYS
Action Edition
Volume 1

STORY AND ART BY KAZUROU INOUE

English Adaptation/Fred Burke
Translation/JN Productions
Touch-up Art & Lettering/James Gaubatz
Cover and Interior Design/Izumi Evers
Editor/Ian Robertson

Managing Editor/Annette Roman
Director of Production/Noboru Watanabe
Vice President of Publishing/Alvin Lu
Sr. Director of Acquisitions/Rika Inouye
Vice President of Sales and Marketing/Liza Coppola
Publisher/Hyoe Narita

Printed in the U.S.A.

Published by VIZ Media, LLC.
P.O. Box 77010
San Francisco, CA 94107

10 9 8 7 6 5 4 3 2 1
First Printing, July 2005

store.viz.com

PARENTAL ADVISORY
MIDORI DAYS is rated T+ for Older Teens. Contains strong language and sexual themes and nudity. Recommended for older teens (16 and up).

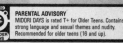

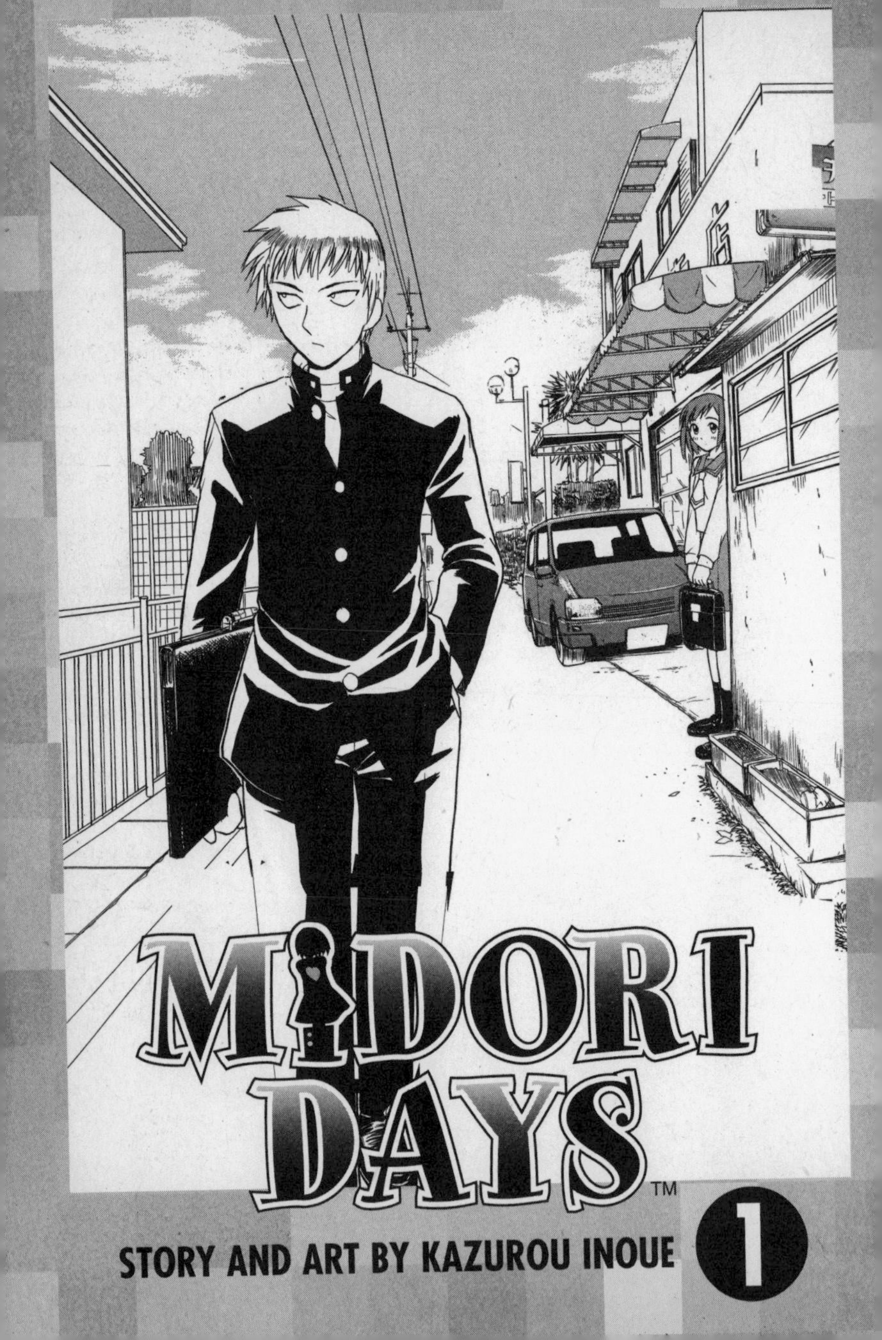
MIDORI DAYS™

STORY AND ART BY KAZUROU INOUE

1

Contents

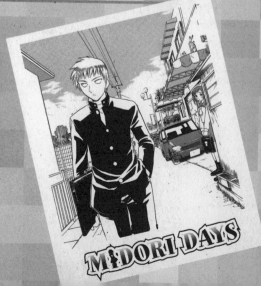

MIDORI DAYS

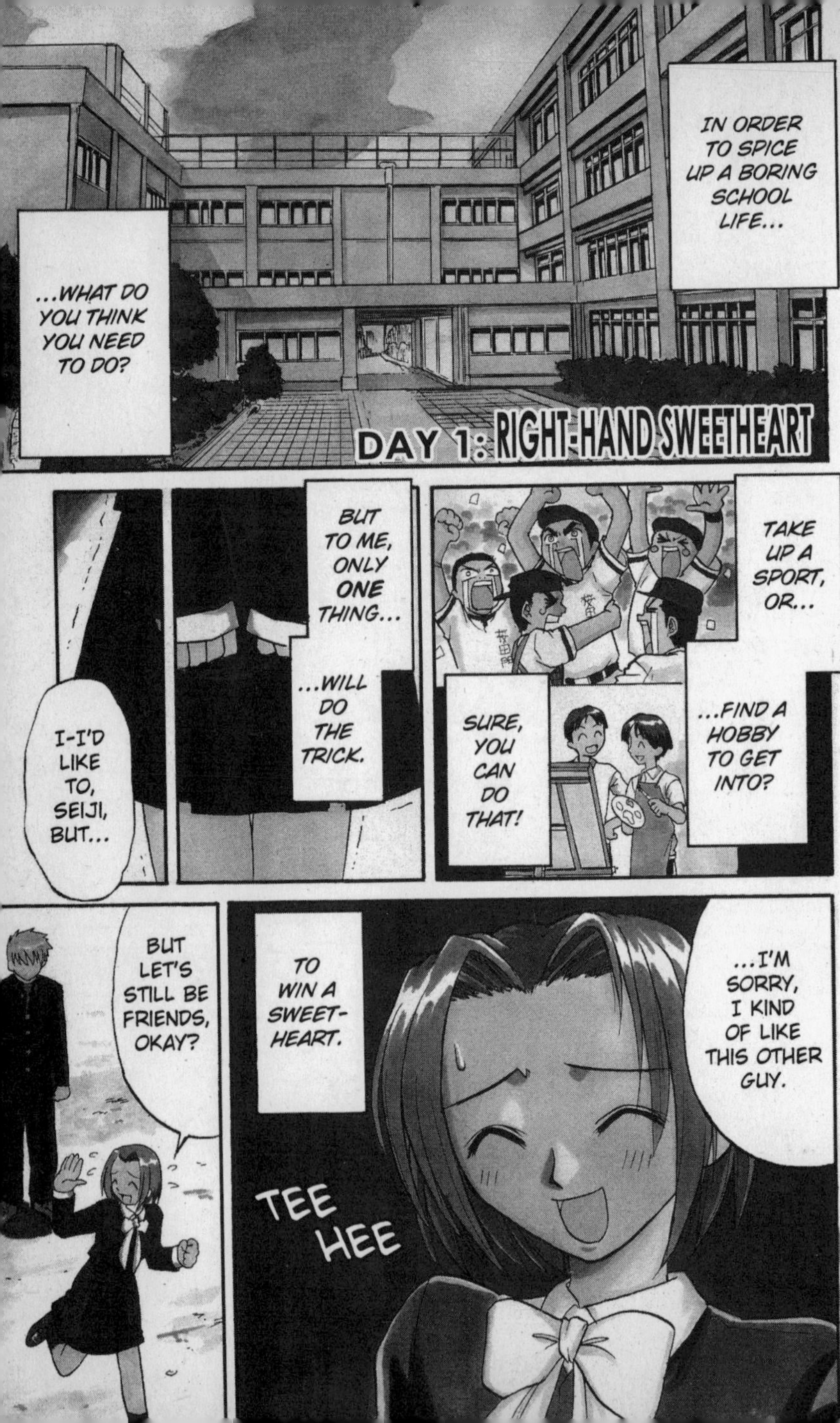
IN ORDER TO SPICE UP A BORING SCHOOL LIFE...
...WHAT DO YOU THINK YOU NEED TO DO?
DAY 1: RIGHT-HAND SWEETHEART
TAKE UP A SPORT, OR...
...FIND A HOBBY TO GET INTO?
SURE, YOU CAN DO THAT!
BUT TO ME, ONLY ONE THING...
...WILL DO THE TRICK.
I-I'D LIKE TO, SEIJI, BUT...
...I'M SORRY, I KIND OF LIKE THIS OTHER GUY.
TO WIN A SWEET-HEART.
TEE HEE
BUT LET'S STILL BE FRIENDS, OKAY?

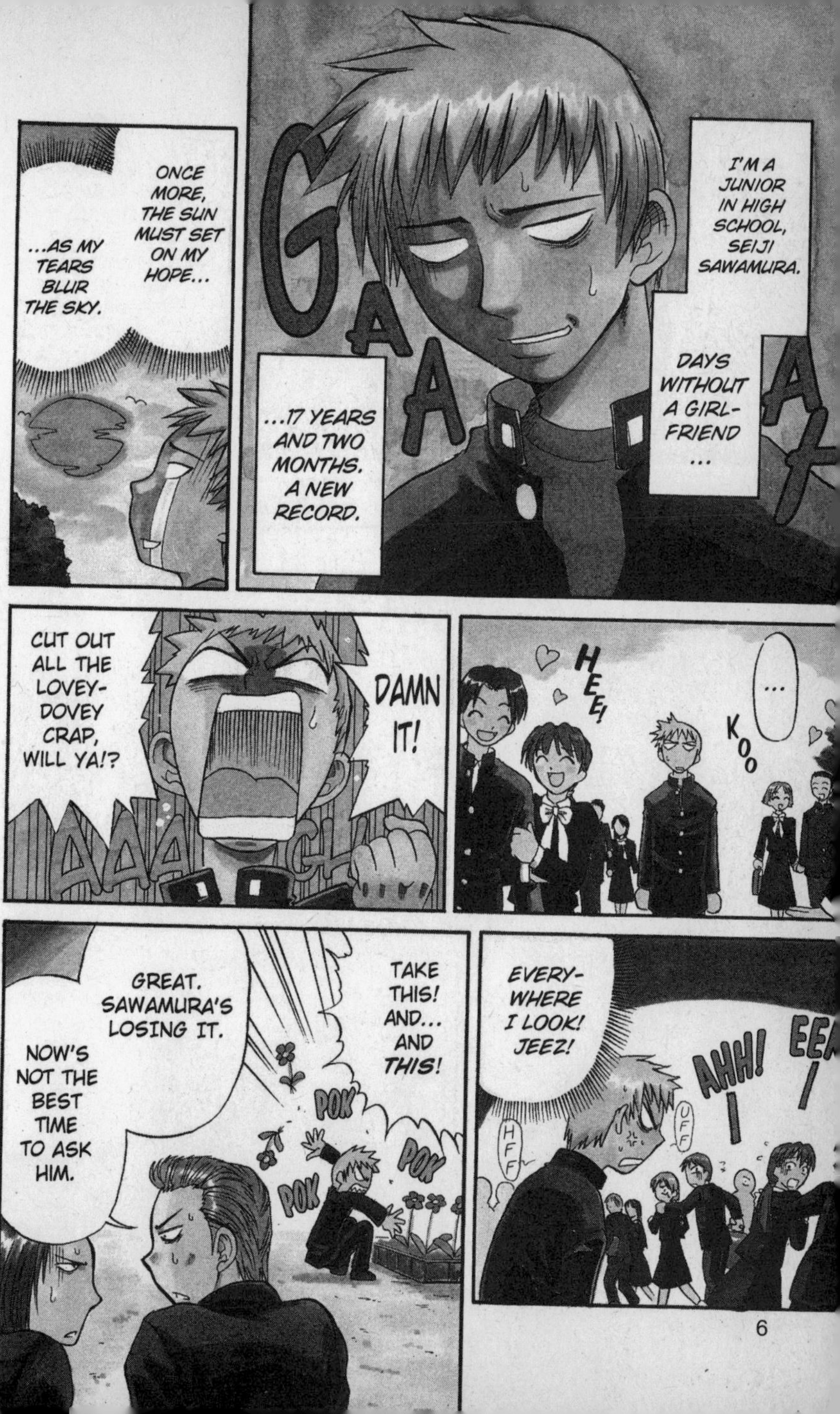
I'M A JUNIOR IN HIGH SCHOOL, SEIJI SAWAMURA.
DAYS WITHOUT A GIRL-FRIEND ...
...17 YEARS AND TWO MONTHS. A NEW RECORD.
GAAAA
ONCE MORE, THE SUN MUST SET ON MY HOPE...
...AS MY TEARS BLUR THE SKY.
...
HEE!
KOO
DAMN IT!
CUT OUT ALL THE LOVEY-DOVEY CRAP, WILL YA!?
AAAGH
EVERY-WHERE I LOOK! JEEZ!
AHH!
EEA
HFF
UFF
TAKE THIS! AND... AND THIS!
POK
POK
POK
GREAT. SAWAMURA'S LOSING IT.
NOW'S NOT THE BEST TIME TO ASK HIM.

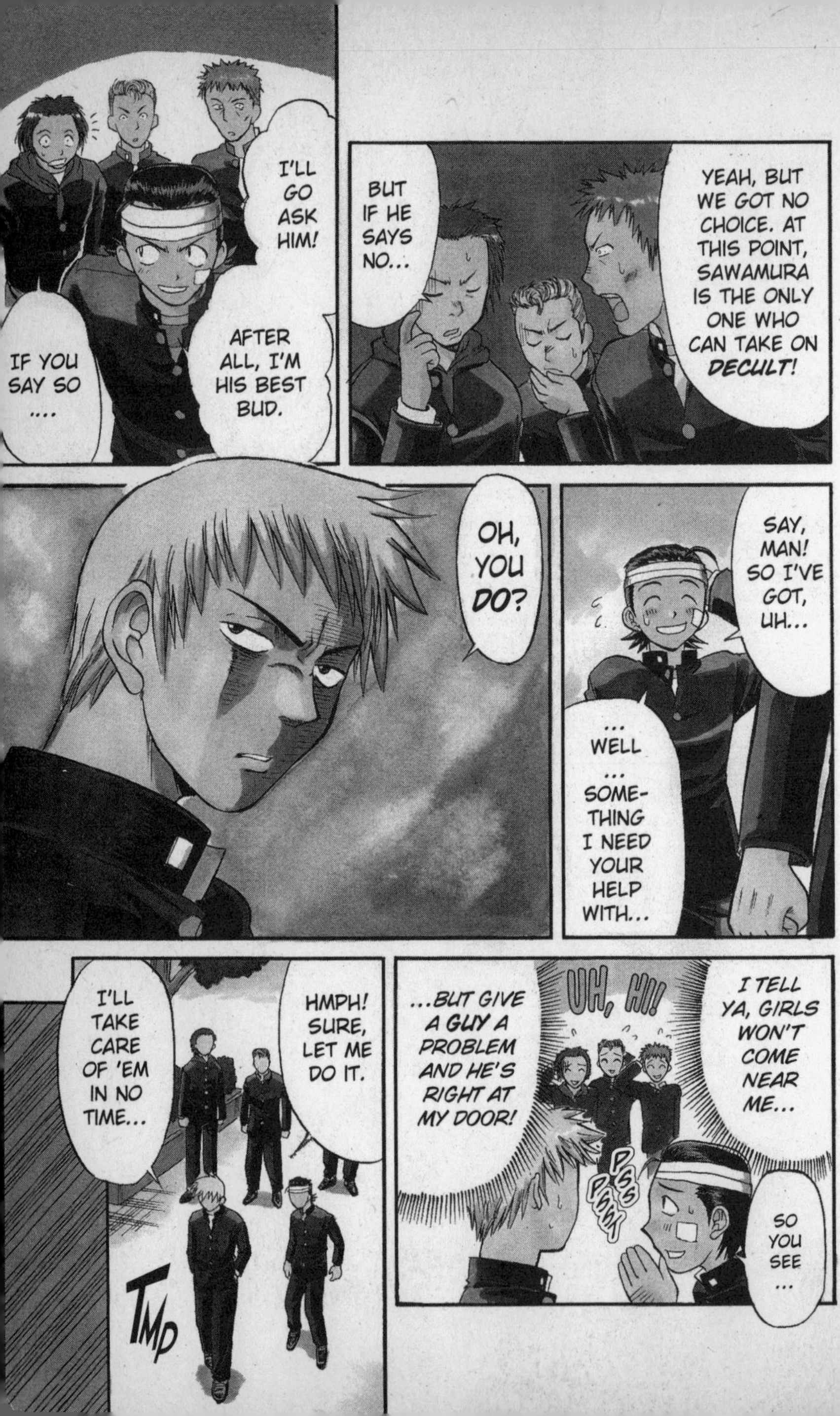
YEAH, BUT WE GOT NO CHOICE. AT THIS POINT, SAWAMURA IS THE ONLY ONE WHO CAN TAKE ON DECULT!
BUT IF HE SAYS NO...
I'LL GO ASK HIM!
AFTER ALL, I'M HIS BEST BUD.
IF YOU SAY SO ....
SAY, MAN! SO I'VE GOT, UH...
... WELL ... SOMETHING I NEED YOUR HELP WITH...
OH, YOU DO?
I TELL YA, GIRLS WON'T COME NEAR ME...
UH, HI!
...BUT GIVE A GUY A PROBLEM AND HE'S RIGHT AT MY DOOR!
PSS PSSt
SO YOU SEE ...
HMPH! SURE, LET ME DO IT.
I'LL TAKE CARE OF 'EM IN NO TIME...
TMP

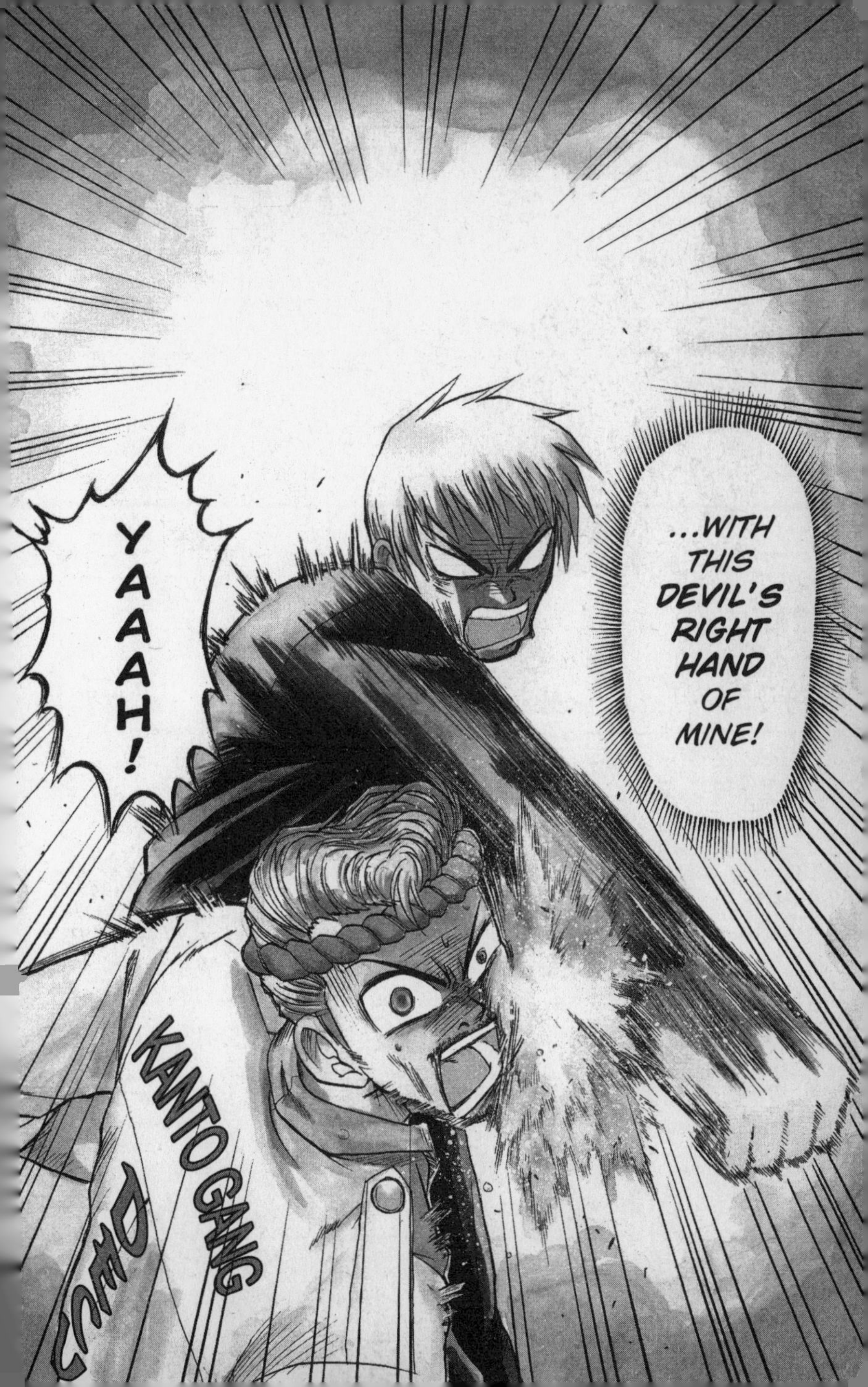
...WITH THIS DEVIL'S RIGHT HAND OF MINE!
YAAAH!
KANTO GANG

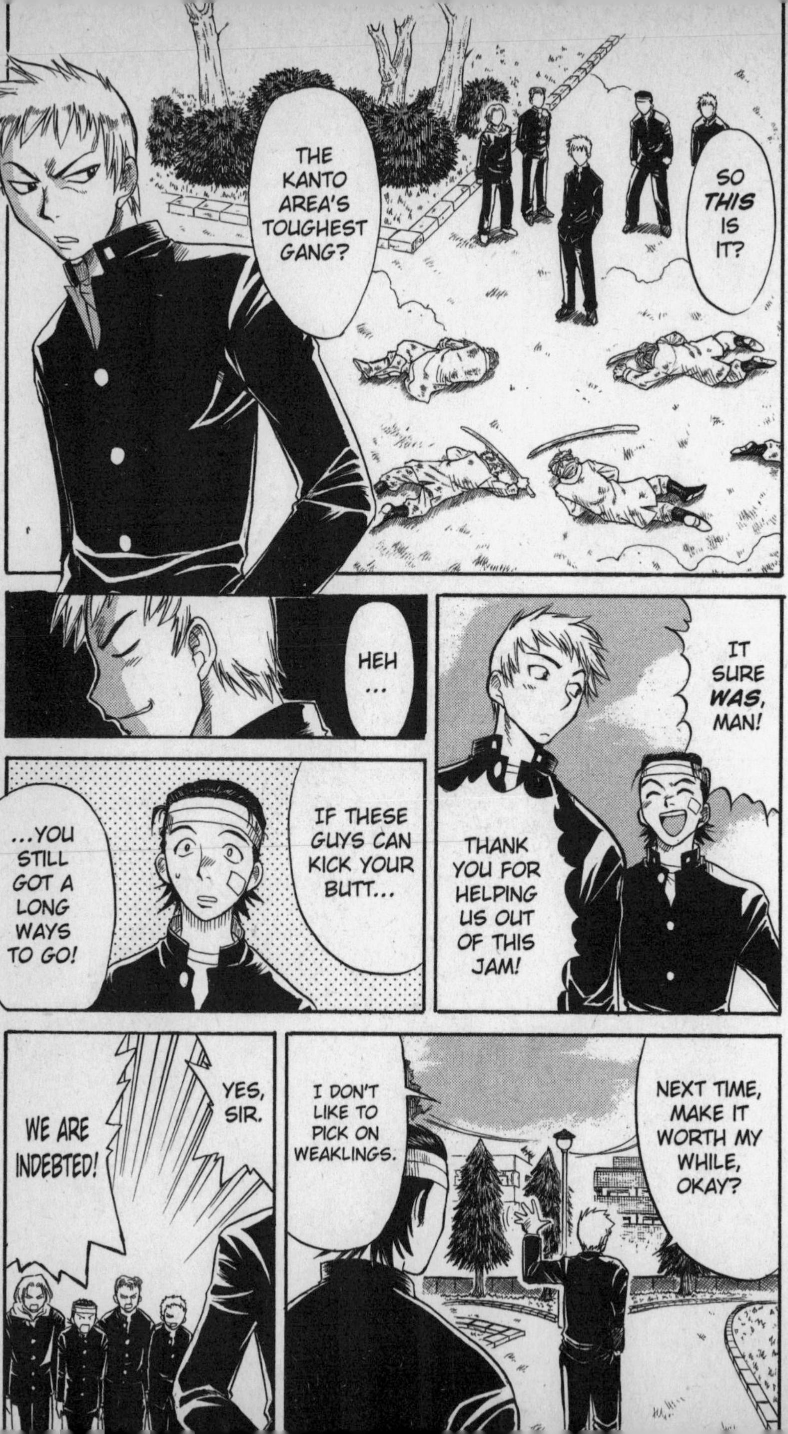
SO *THIS* IS IT?
THE KANTO AREA'S TOUGHEST GANG?
IT SURE *WAS*, MAN!
THANK YOU FOR HELPING US OUT OF THIS JAM!
HEH...
IF THESE GUYS CAN KICK YOUR BUTT...
...YOU STILL GOT A LONG WAYS TO GO!
NEXT TIME, MAKE IT WORTH MY WHILE, OKAY?
I DON'T LIKE TO PICK ON WEAKLINGS.
YES, SIR.
WE ARE INDEBTED!

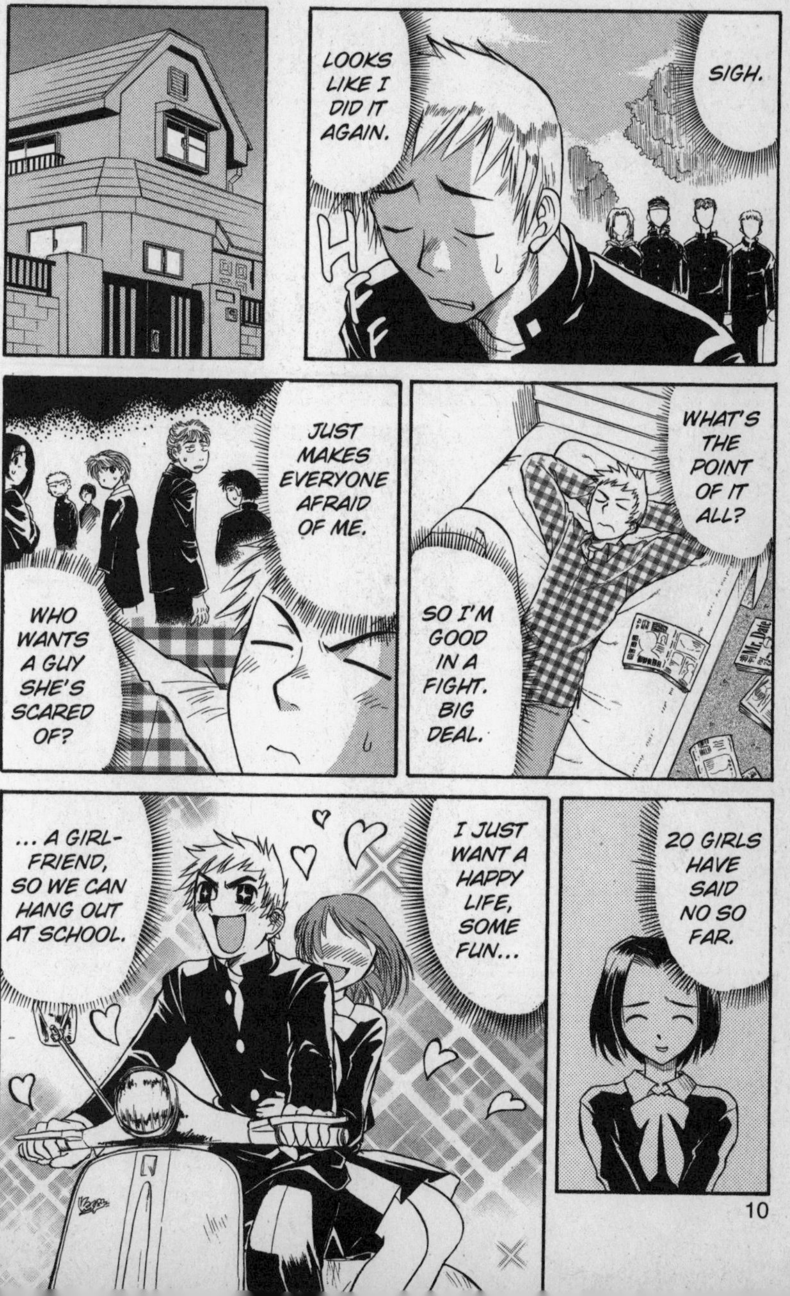
SIGH.
LOOKS LIKE I DID IT AGAIN.
HFF
WHAT'S THE POINT OF IT ALL?
SO I'M GOOD IN A FIGHT. BIG DEAL.
JUST MAKES EVERYONE AFRAID OF ME.
WHO WANTS A GUY SHE'S SCARED OF?
20 GIRLS HAVE SAID NO SO FAR.
I JUST WANT A HAPPY LIFE, SOME FUN...
... A GIRL-FRIEND, SO WE CAN HANG OUT AT SCHOOL.

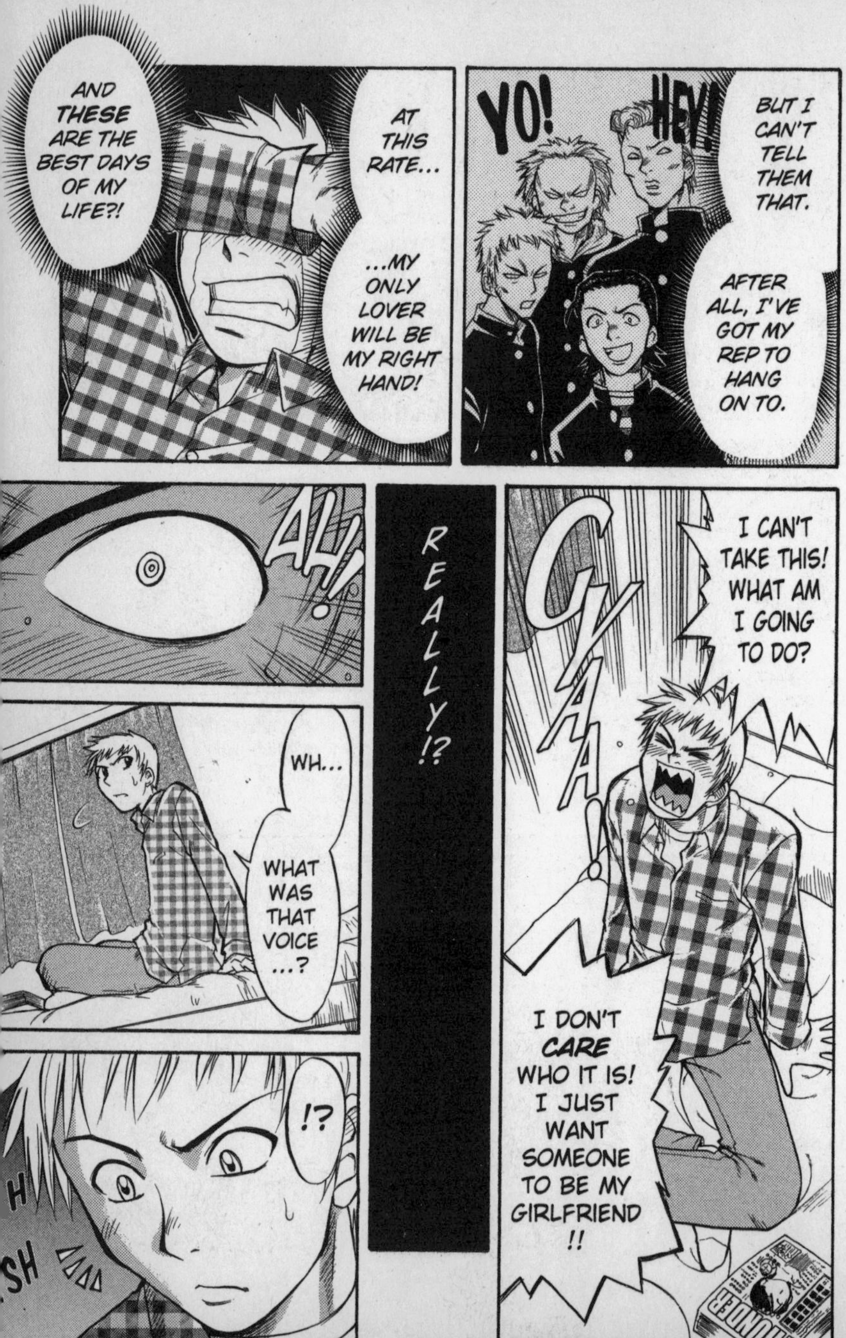
BUT I CAN'T TELL THEM THAT.
YO!
HEY!
AFTER ALL, I'VE GOT MY REP TO HANG ON TO.
AT THIS RATE...
...MY ONLY LOVER WILL BE MY RIGHT HAND!
AND THESE ARE THE BEST DAYS OF MY LIFE?!
I CAN'T TAKE THIS! WHAT AM I GOING TO DO?
GYAAA
I DON'T CARE WHO IT IS! I JUST WANT SOMEONE TO BE MY GIRLFRIEND!!
REALLY!?
AH!!
WH...
WHAT WAS THAT VOICE...?
!?

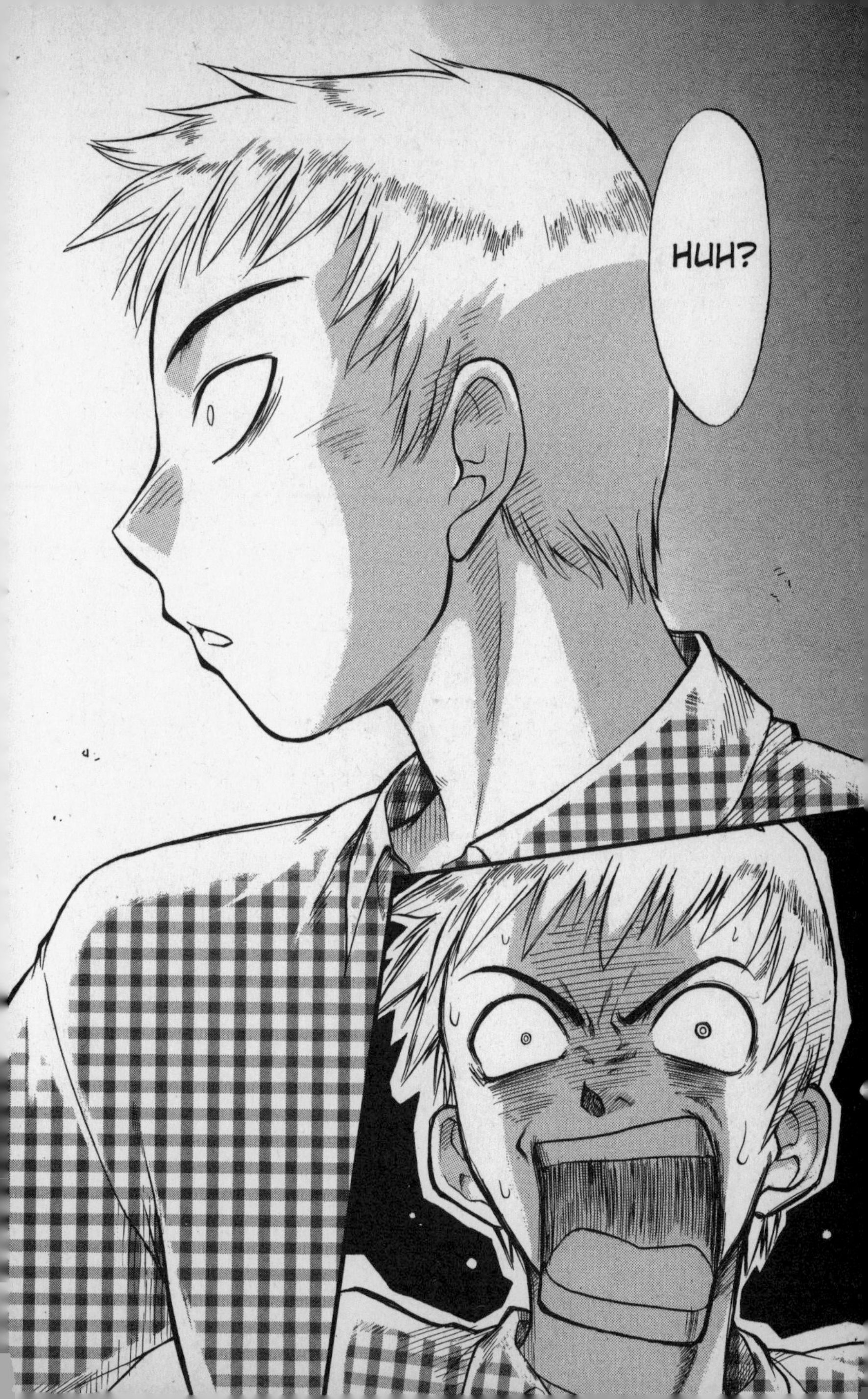
HUH?

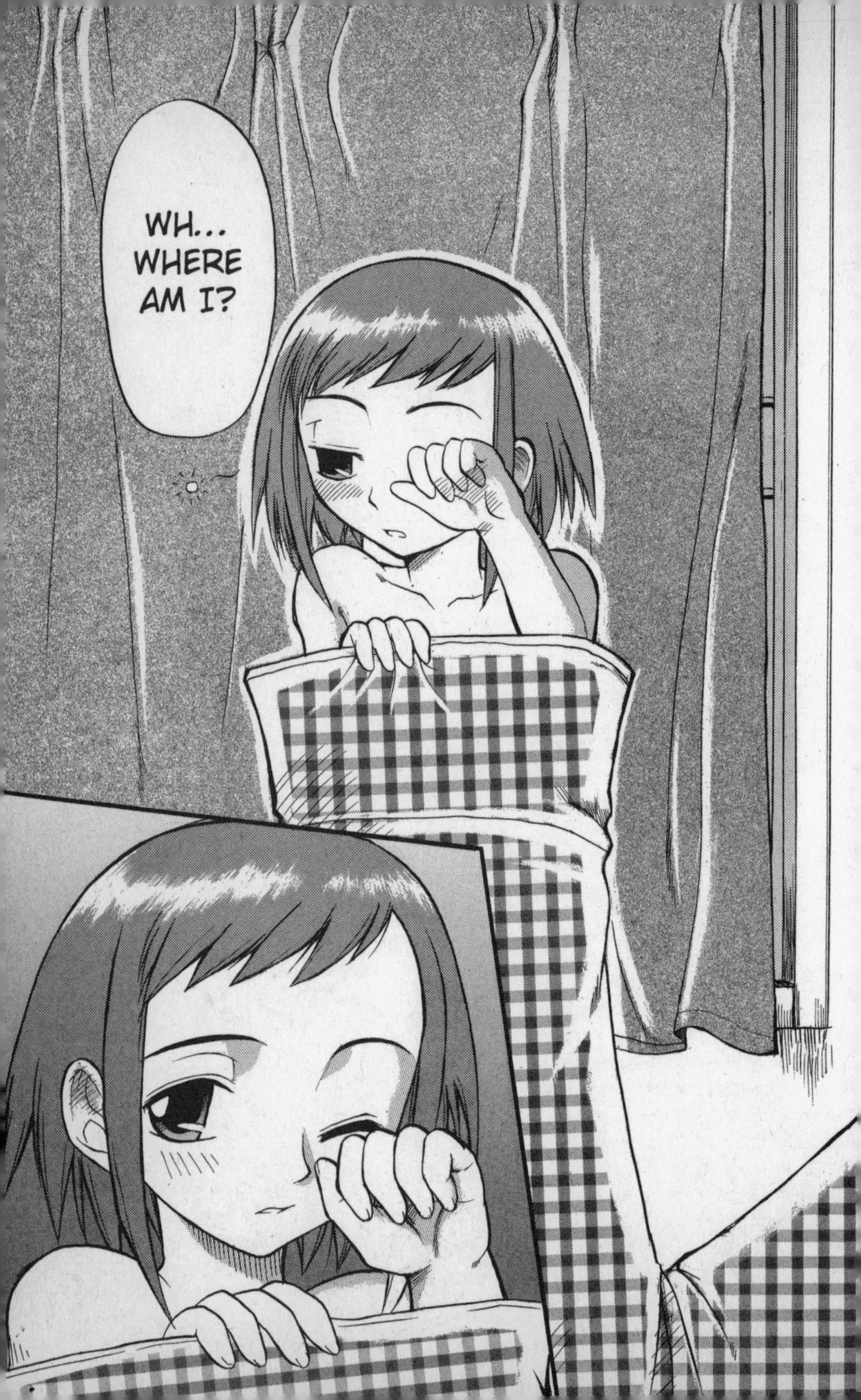
WH... WHERE AM I?

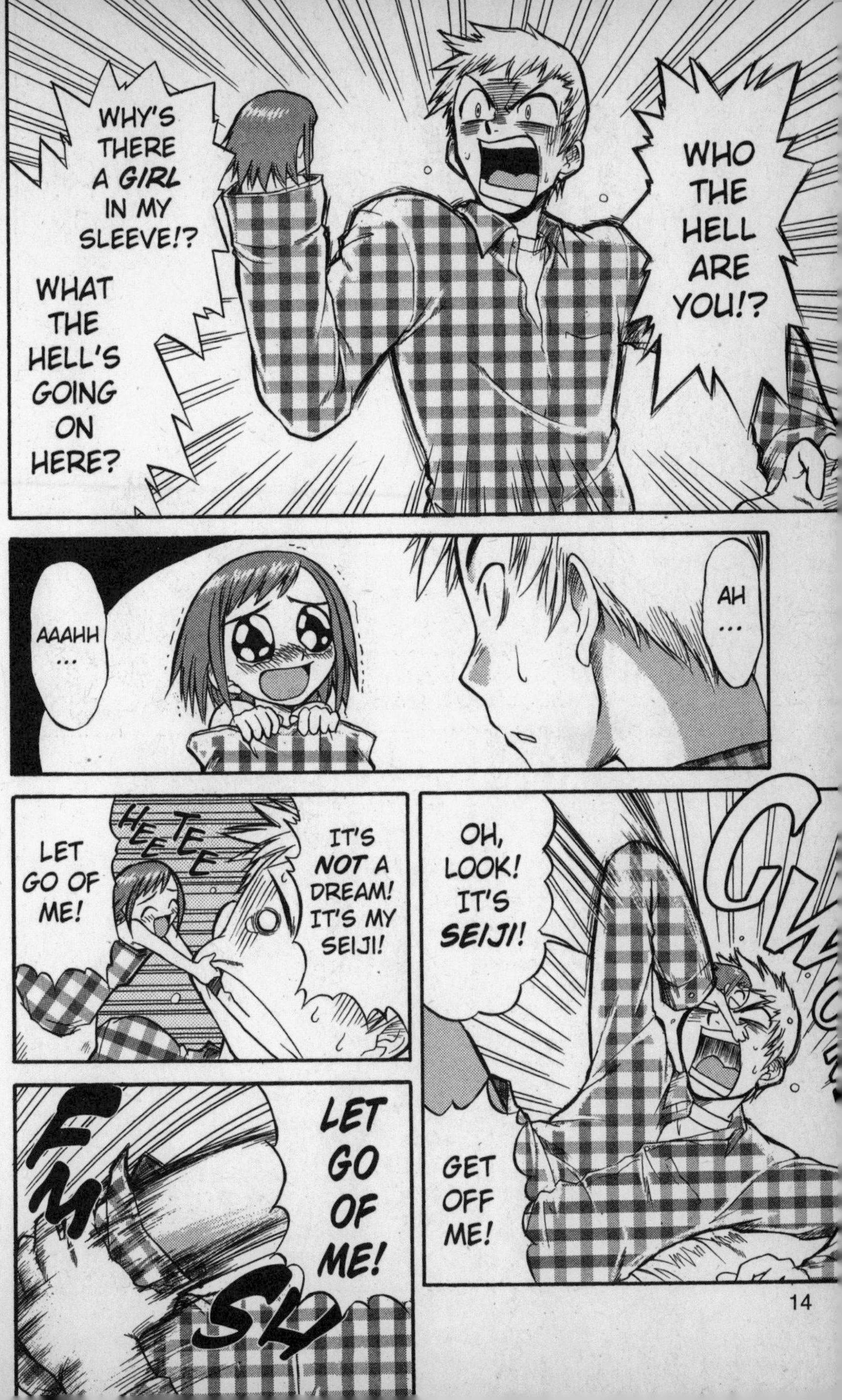
WHO THE HELL ARE YOU!?
WHY'S THERE A *GIRL* IN MY SLEEVE!?
WHAT THE HELL'S GOING ON HERE?
AH ...
AAAHH ...
OH, LOOK! IT'S *SEIJI*!
CWO
GET OFF ME!
IT'S *NOT* A DREAM! IT'S MY SEIJI!
HEE TEE
LET GO OF ME!
LET GO OF ME!
FMSH

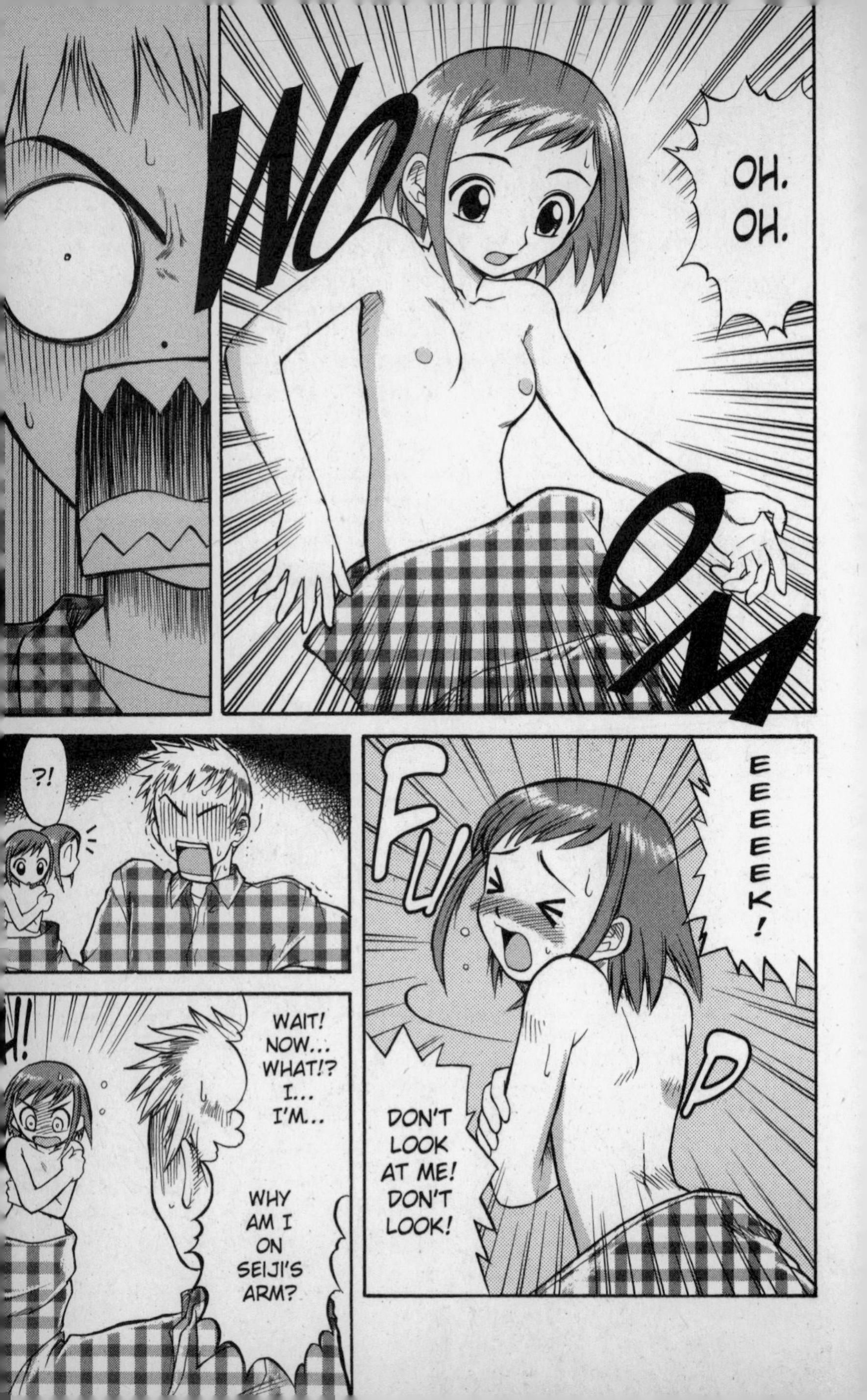
OH. OH.
WOOM
EEEEEK!
DON'T LOOK AT ME! DON'T LOOK!
?!
WAIT! NOW... WHAT!? I... I'M..
WHY AM I ON SEIJI'S ARM?

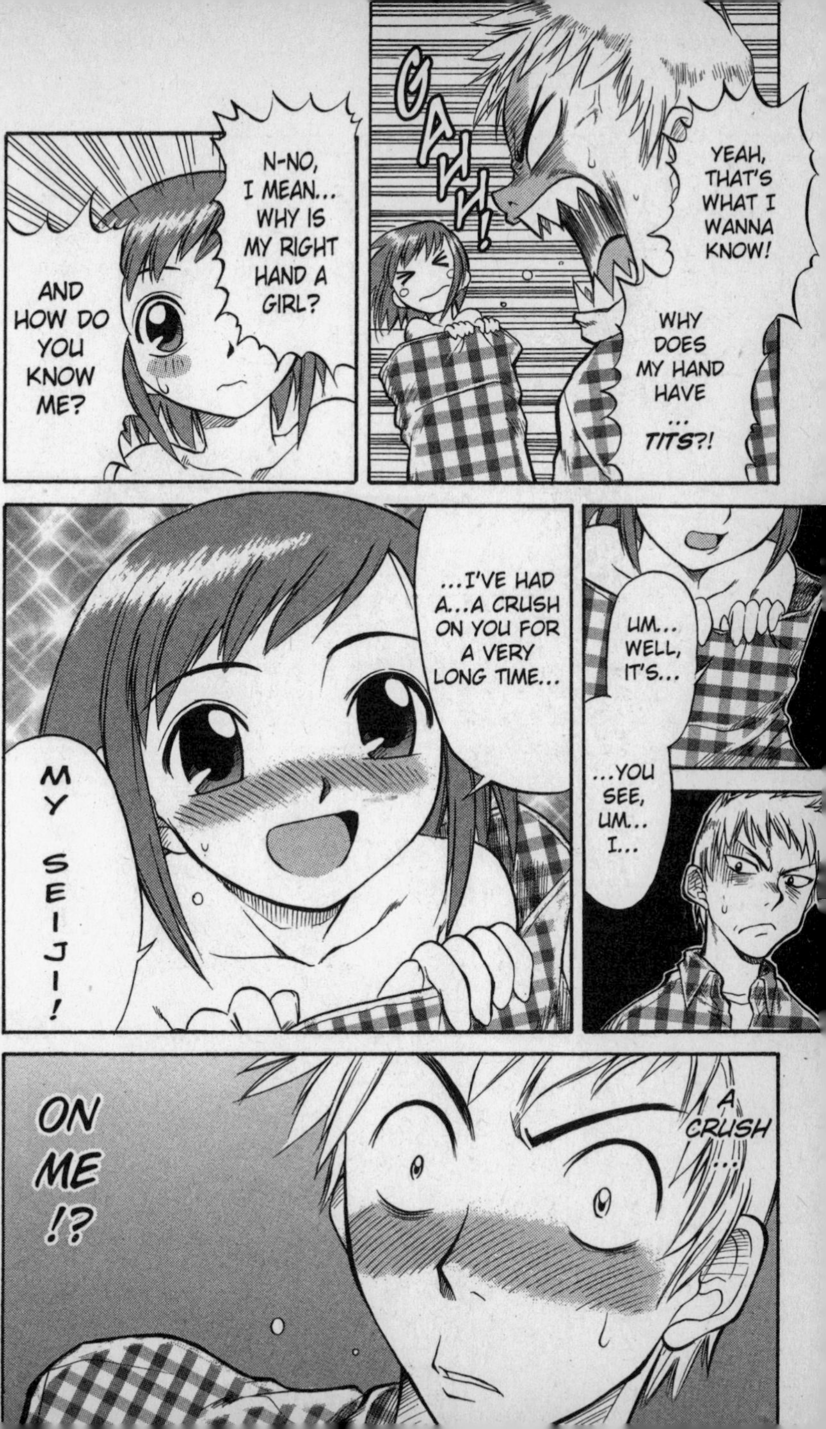
YEAH, THAT'S WHAT I WANNA KNOW!
GAHH!
WHY DOES MY HAND HAVE ... *TITS*?!
N-NO, I MEAN... WHY IS MY RIGHT HAND A GIRL?
AND HOW DO YOU KNOW ME?
UM... WELL, IT'S...
...YOU SEE, UM... I...
...I'VE HAD A...A CRUSH ON YOU FOR A VERY LONG TIME...
MY SEIJI!
A CRUSH...
ON ME!?

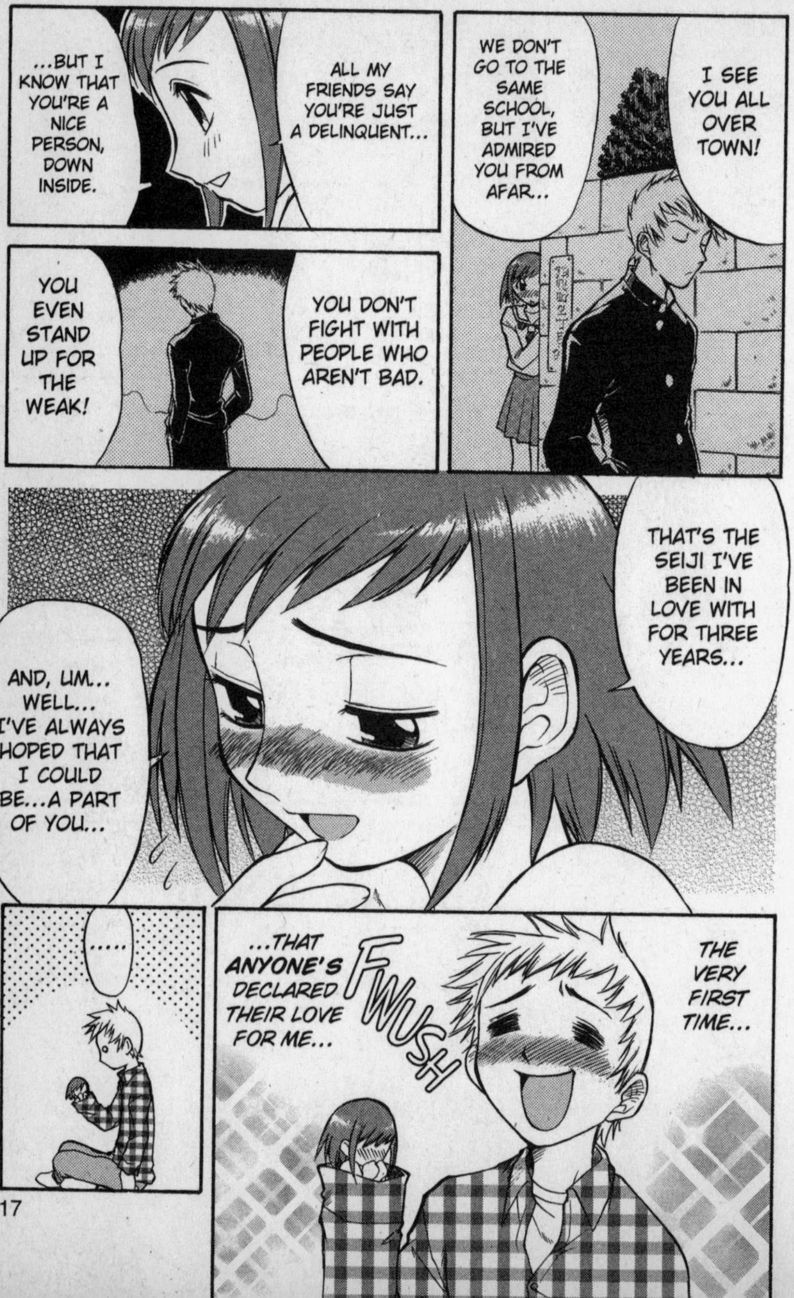
I SEE YOU ALL OVER TOWN!
WE DON'T GO TO THE SAME SCHOOL, BUT I'VE ADMIRED YOU FROM AFAR...
ALL MY FRIENDS SAY YOU'RE JUST A DELINQUENT...
...BUT I KNOW THAT YOU'RE A NICE PERSON, DOWN INSIDE.
YOU DON'T FIGHT WITH PEOPLE WHO AREN'T BAD.
YOU EVEN STAND UP FOR THE WEAK!
THAT'S THE SEIJI I'VE BEEN IN LOVE WITH FOR THREE YEARS...
AND, UM... WELL... I'VE ALWAYS HOPED THAT I COULD BE...A PART OF YOU...
THE VERY FIRST TIME...
FWUSH
...THAT ANYONE'S DECLARED THEIR LOVE FOR ME...
......

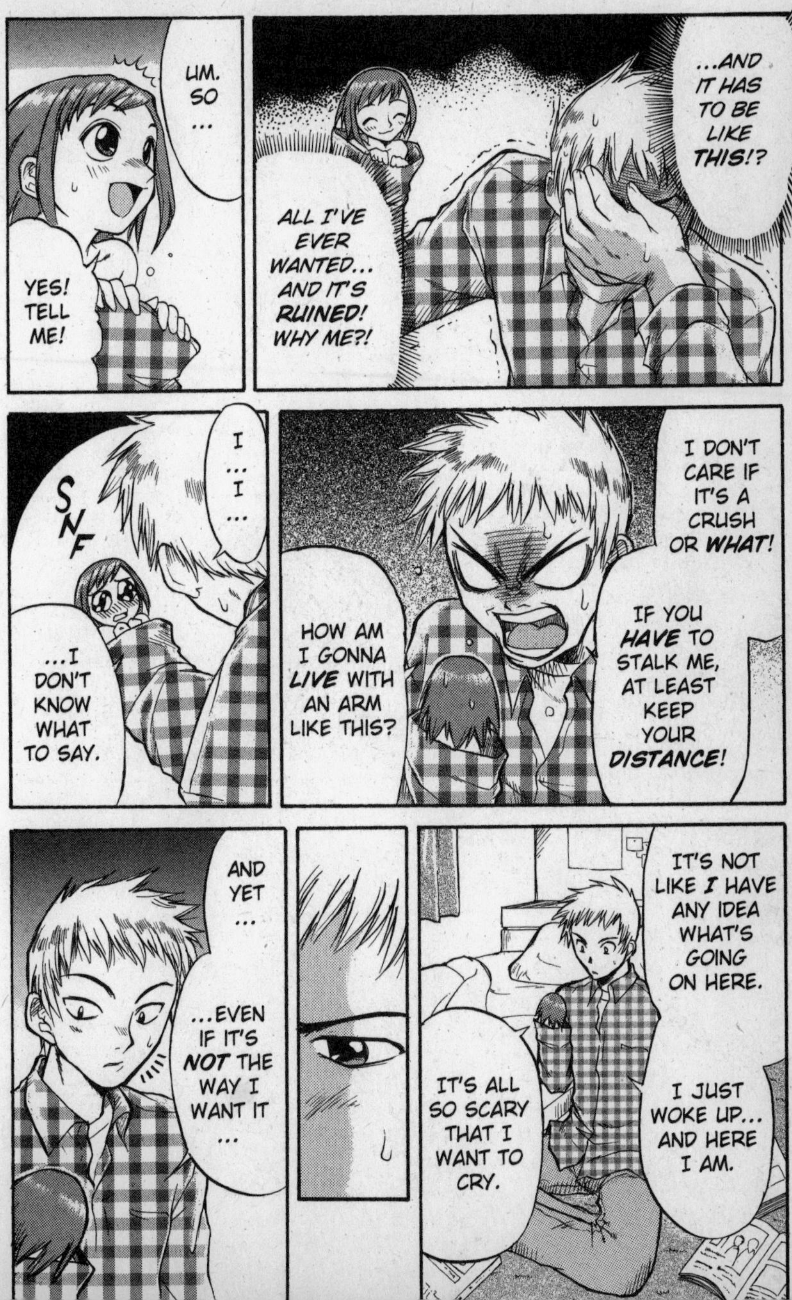
...AND IT HAS TO BE LIKE THIS!?
ALL I'VE EVER WANTED... AND IT'S RUINED! WHY ME?!
UM. SO ...
YES! TELL ME!
I DON'T CARE IF IT'S A CRUSH OR WHAT!
IF YOU HAVE TO STALK ME, AT LEAST KEEP YOUR DISTANCE!
HOW AM I GONNA LIVE WITH AN ARM LIKE THIS?
I ... I ...
SNF
...I DON'T KNOW WHAT TO SAY.
IT'S NOT LIKE I HAVE ANY IDEA WHAT'S GOING ON HERE.
I JUST WOKE UP... AND HERE I AM.
IT'S ALL SO SCARY THAT I WANT TO CRY.
AND YET ...
...EVEN IF IT'S NOT THE WAY I WANT IT ...

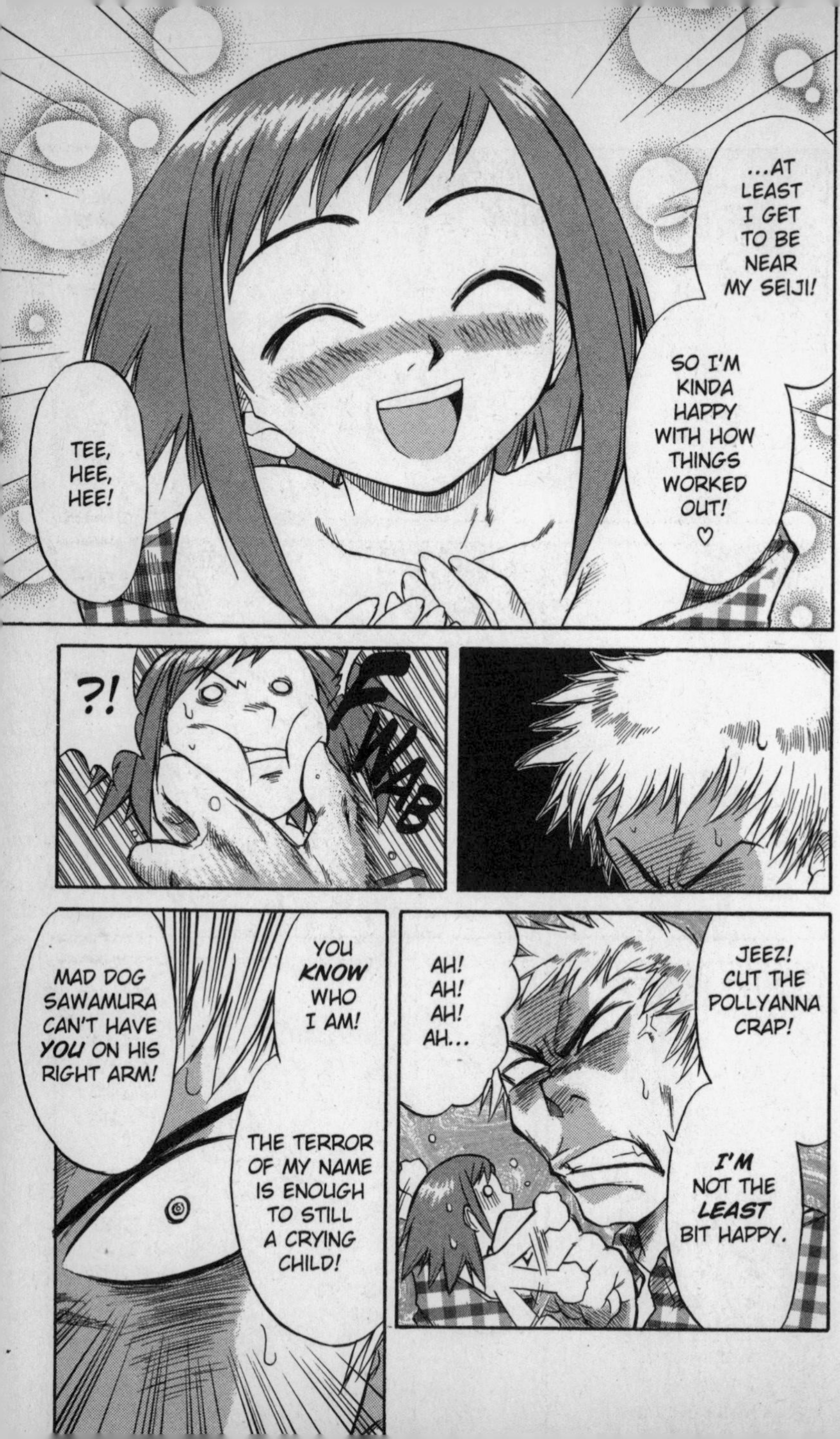
...AT LEAST I GET TO BE NEAR MY SEIJI!
SO I'M KINDA HAPPY WITH HOW THINGS WORKED OUT! ♡
TEE, HEE, HEE!
FWAB
?!
JEEZ! CUT THE POLLYANNA CRAP!
I'M NOT THE LEAST BIT HAPPY.
AH! AH! AH! AH...
YOU KNOW WHO I AM!
MAD DOG SAWAMURA CAN'T HAVE YOU ON HIS RIGHT ARM!
THE TERROR OF MY NAME IS ENOUGH TO STILL A CRYING CHILD!

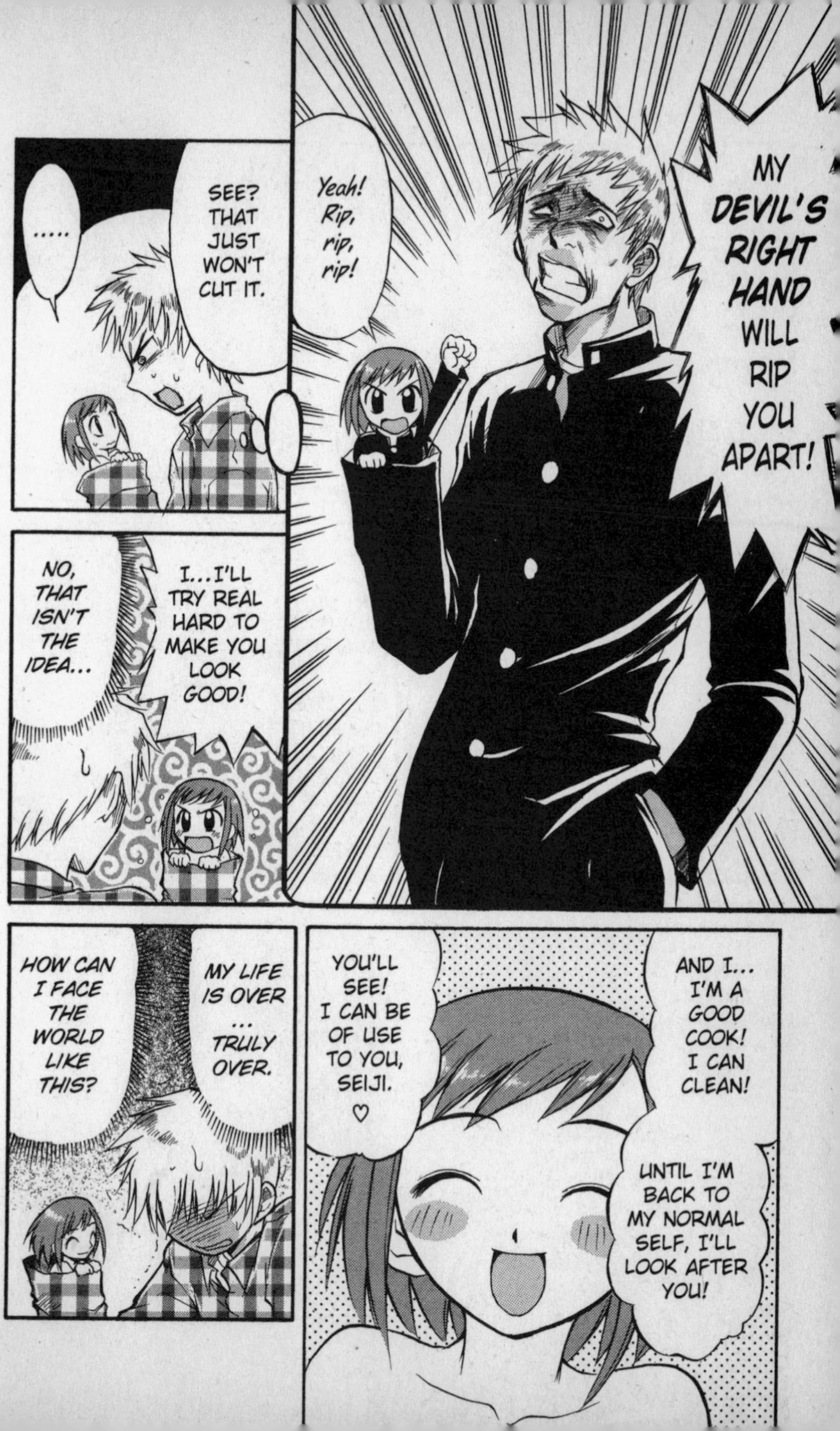
MY DEVIL'S RIGHT HAND WILL RIP YOU APART!
Yeah! Rip, rip, rip!
SEE? THAT JUST WON'T CUT IT.
.....
I...I'LL TRY REAL HARD TO MAKE YOU LOOK GOOD!
NO, THAT ISN'T THE IDEA...
AND I... I'M A GOOD COOK! I CAN CLEAN!
YOU'LL SEE! I CAN BE OF USE TO YOU, SEIJI. ♡
UNTIL I'M BACK TO MY NORMAL SELF, I'LL LOOK AFTER YOU!
MY LIFE IS OVER ... TRULY OVER.
HOW CAN I FACE THE WORLD LIKE THIS?

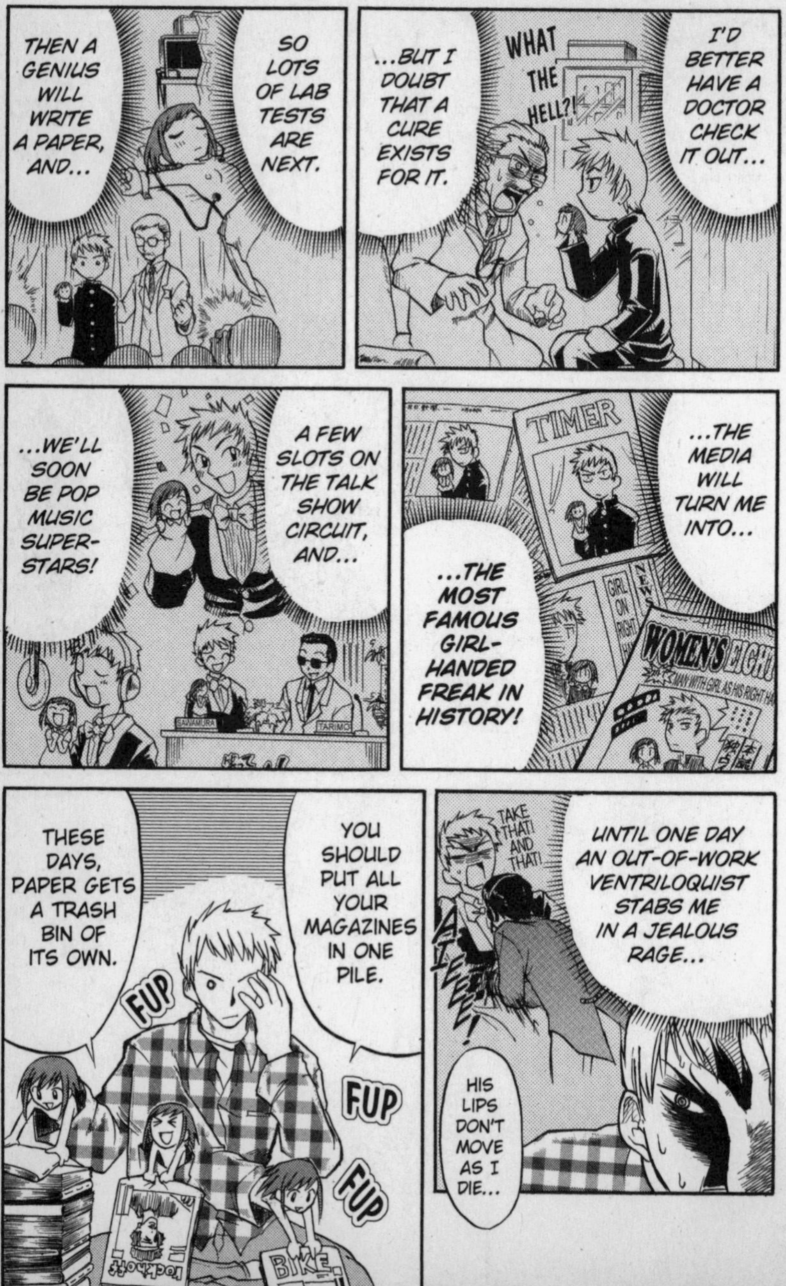

I'D BETTER HAVE A DOCTOR CHECK IT OUT...
WHAT THE HELL?!
...BUT I DOUBT THAT A CURE EXISTS FOR IT.
SO LOTS OF LAB TESTS ARE NEXT.
THEN A GENIUS WILL WRITE A PAPER, AND...
...THE MEDIA WILL TURN ME INTO...
TIMER
...THE MOST FAMOUS GIRL-HANDED FREAK IN HISTORY!
A FEW SLOTS ON THE TALK SHOW CIRCUIT, AND...
...WE'LL SOON BE POP MUSIC SUPER-STARS!
SAWAMURA
TARIMO
UNTIL ONE DAY AN OUT-OF-WORK VENTRILOQUIST STABS ME IN A JEALOUS RAGE...
TAKE THAT! AND THAT!
AIEEEE!
HIS LIPS DON'T MOVE AS I DIE...
YOU SHOULD PUT ALL YOUR MAGAZINES IN ONE PILE.
THESE DAYS, PAPER GETS A TRASH BIN OF ITS OWN.
FUP
FUP
FUP
BIKE

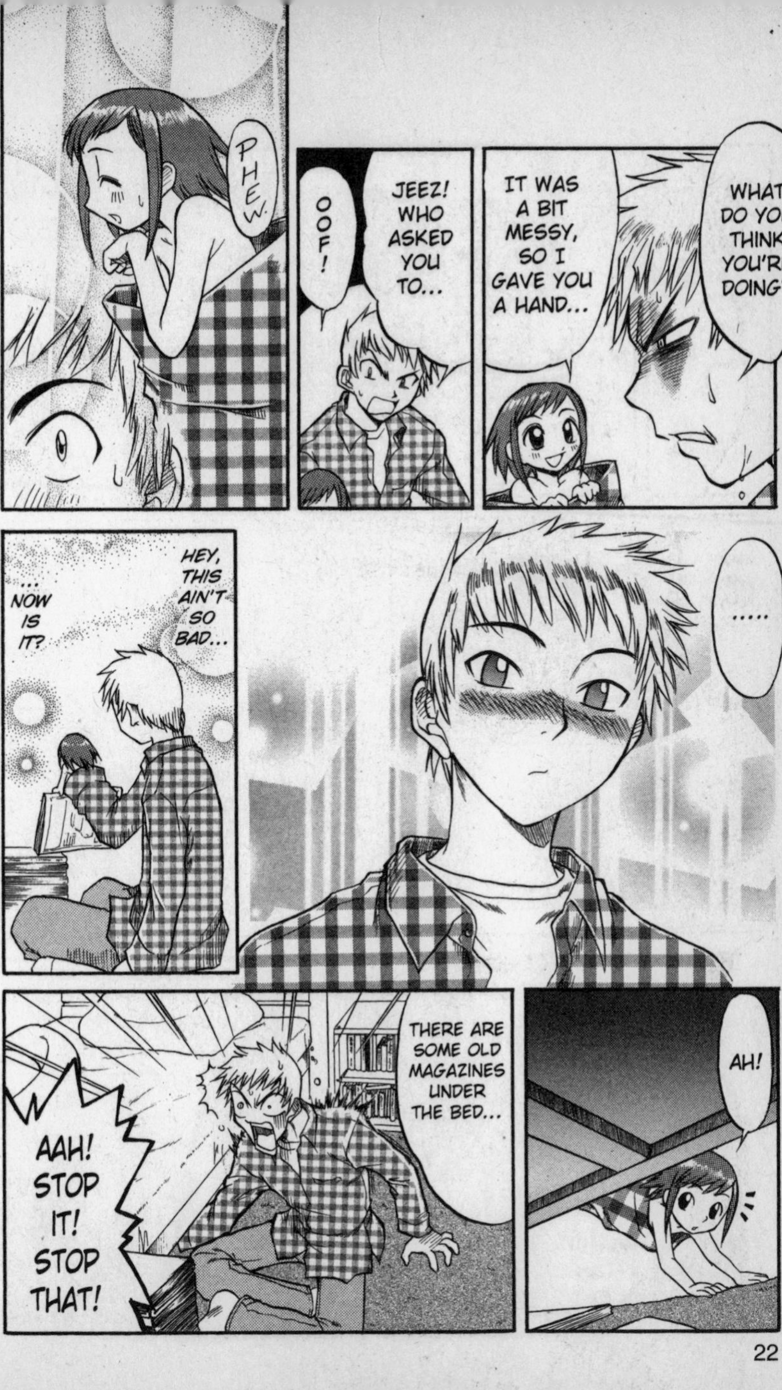
WHAT DO YOU THINK YOU'RE DOING?
IT WAS A BIT MESSY, SO I GAVE YOU A HAND...
JEEZ! WHO ASKED YOU TO...
OOF!
PHEW.
.....
HEY, THIS AIN'T SO BAD...
...NOW IS IT?
AH!
THERE ARE SOME OLD MAGAZINES UNDER THE BED...
AAH! STOP IT! STOP THAT!

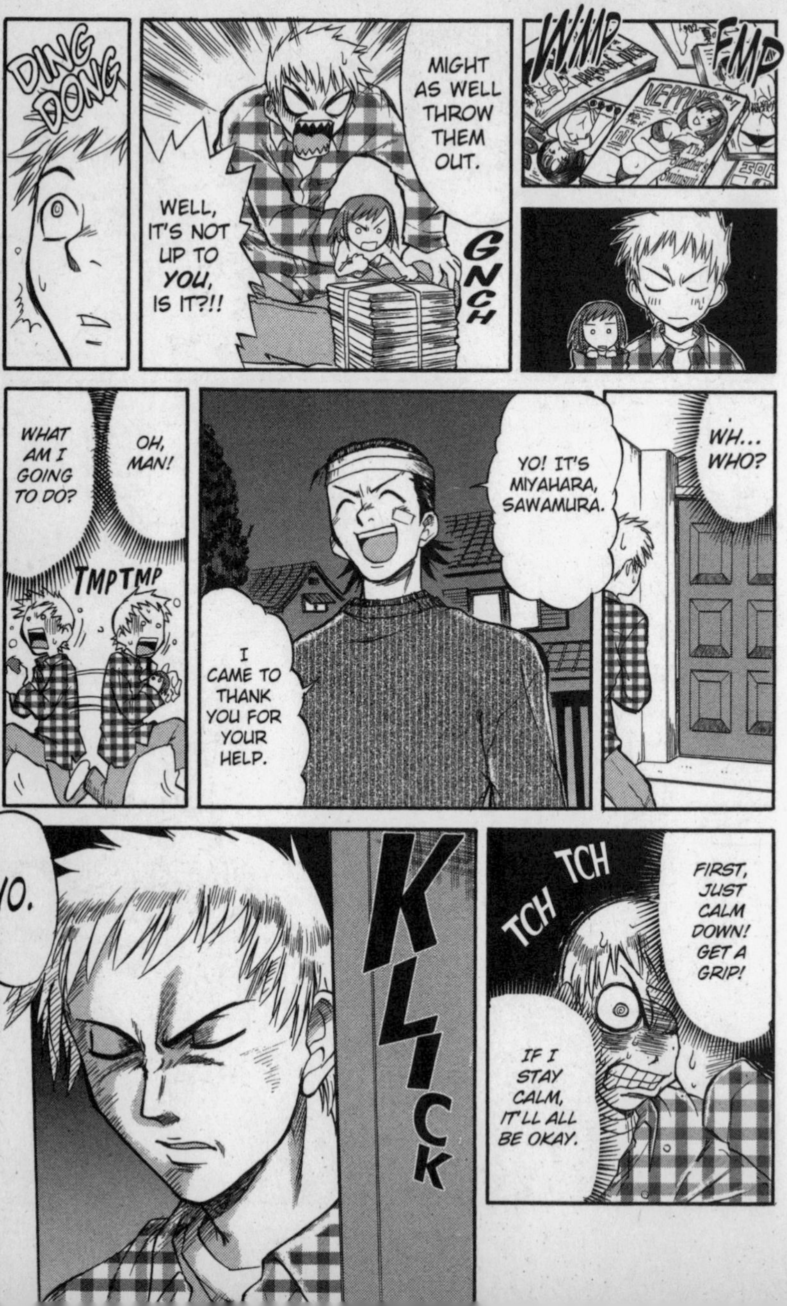
WMP
FMP
VEPPING
MIGHT AS WELL THROW THEM OUT.
GNCH
WELL, IT'S NOT UP TO YOU, IS IT?!!
DING DONG
WH... WHO?
YO! IT'S MIYAHARA, SAWAMURA.
I CAME TO THANK YOU FOR YOUR HELP.
OH, MAN!
WHAT AM I GOING TO DO?
TMPTMP
FIRST, JUST CALM DOWN! GET A GRIP!
TCH TCH
IF I STAY CALM, IT'LL ALL BE OKAY.
KLICK
YO.

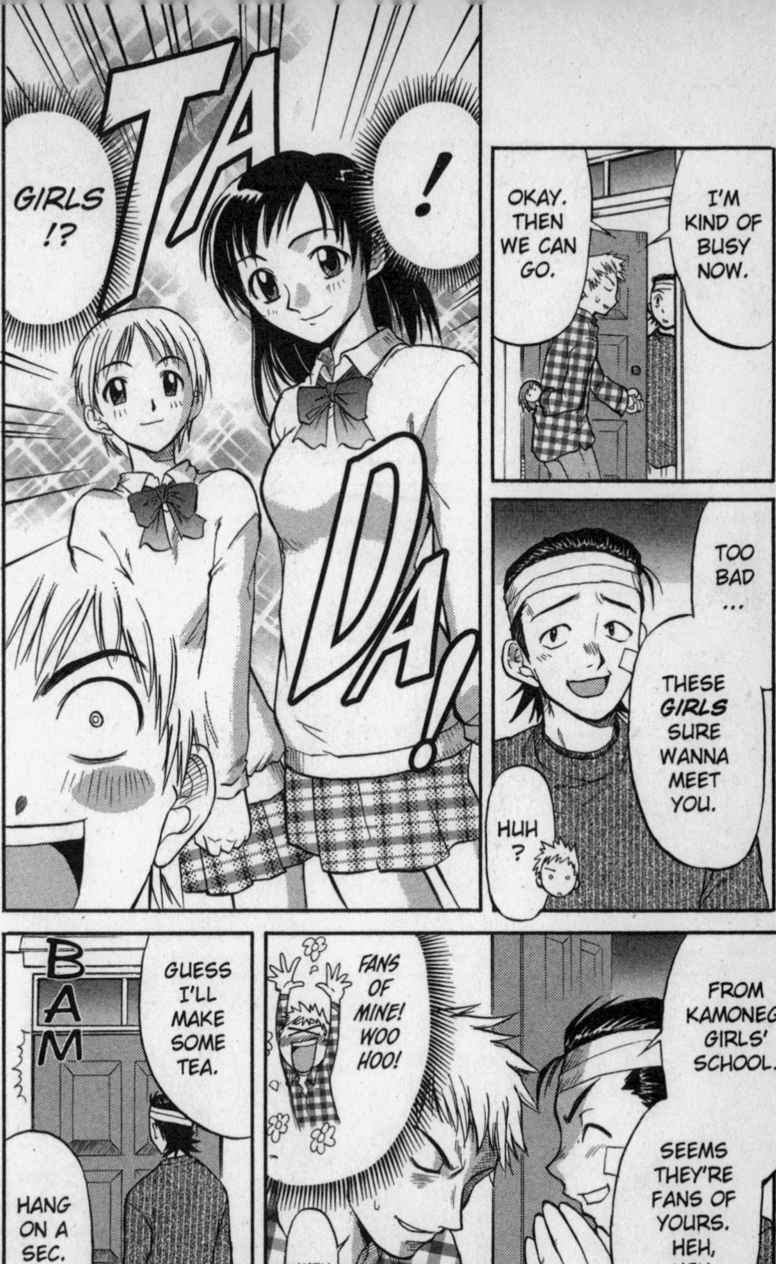
I'M KIND OF BUSY NOW.
OKAY. THEN WE CAN GO.
TOO BAD...
THESE GIRLS SURE WANNA MEET YOU.
HUH?
!
TA
GIRLS!?
DA!
FROM KAMONEGI GIRLS' SCHOOL.
SEEMS THEY'RE FANS OF YOURS. HEH, HEH, HEH!
FANS OF MINE! WOO HOO!
HMPH.
BAM
GUESS I'LL MAKE SOME TEA.
HANG ON A SEC.

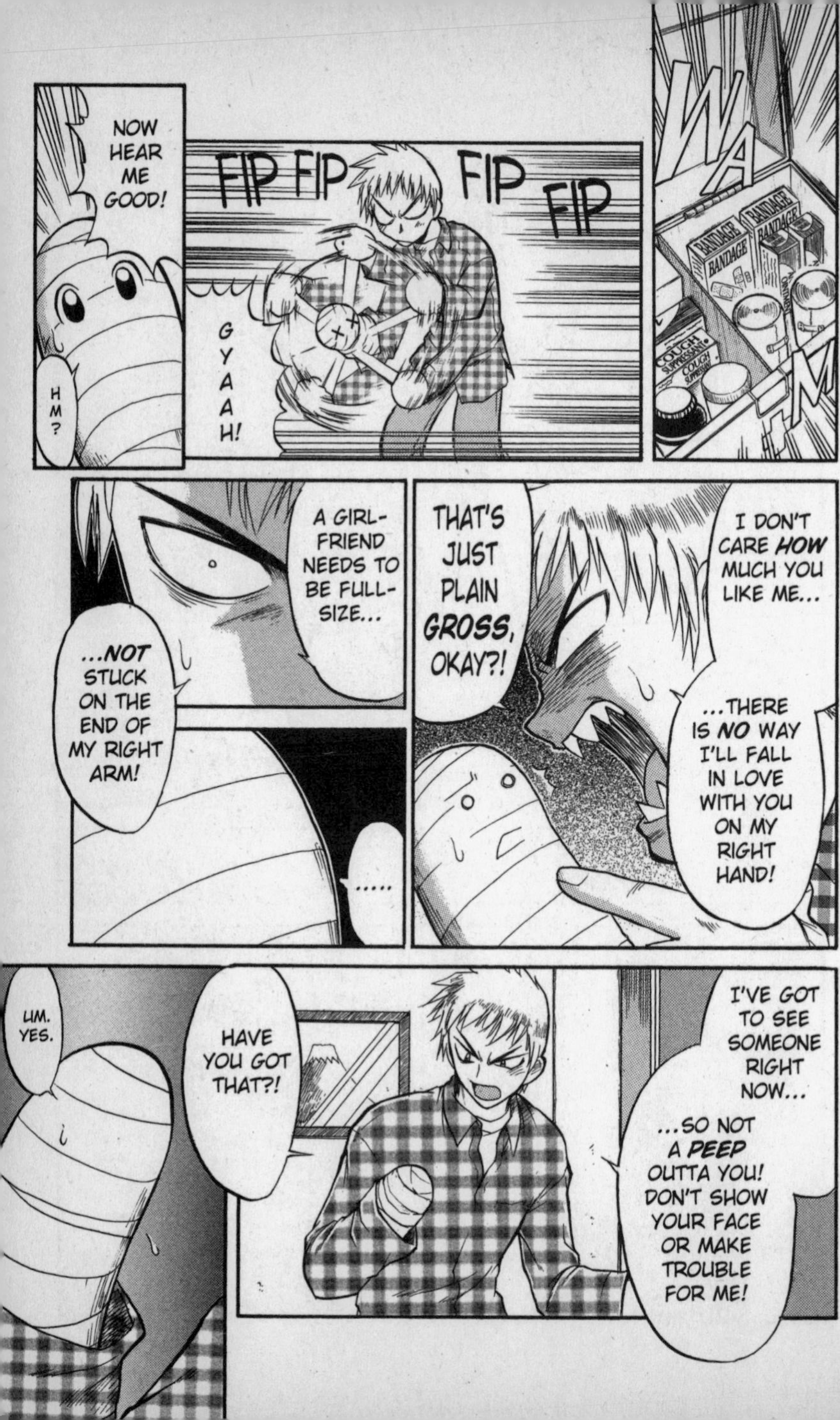
WAM
FIP FIP FIP FIP
GYAAAH!
NOW HEAR ME GOOD!
HM?
I DON'T CARE *HOW* MUCH YOU LIKE ME...
...THERE IS *NO* WAY I'LL FALL IN LOVE WITH YOU ON MY RIGHT HAND!
THAT'S JUST PLAIN *GROSS*, OKAY?!
A GIRLFRIEND NEEDS TO BE FULL-SIZE...
...*NOT* STUCK ON THE END OF MY RIGHT ARM!
.....
I'VE GOT TO SEE SOMEONE RIGHT NOW...
...SO NOT A *PEEP* OUTTA YOU! DON'T SHOW YOUR FACE OR MAKE TROUBLE FOR ME!
HAVE YOU GOT THAT?!
UM. YES.

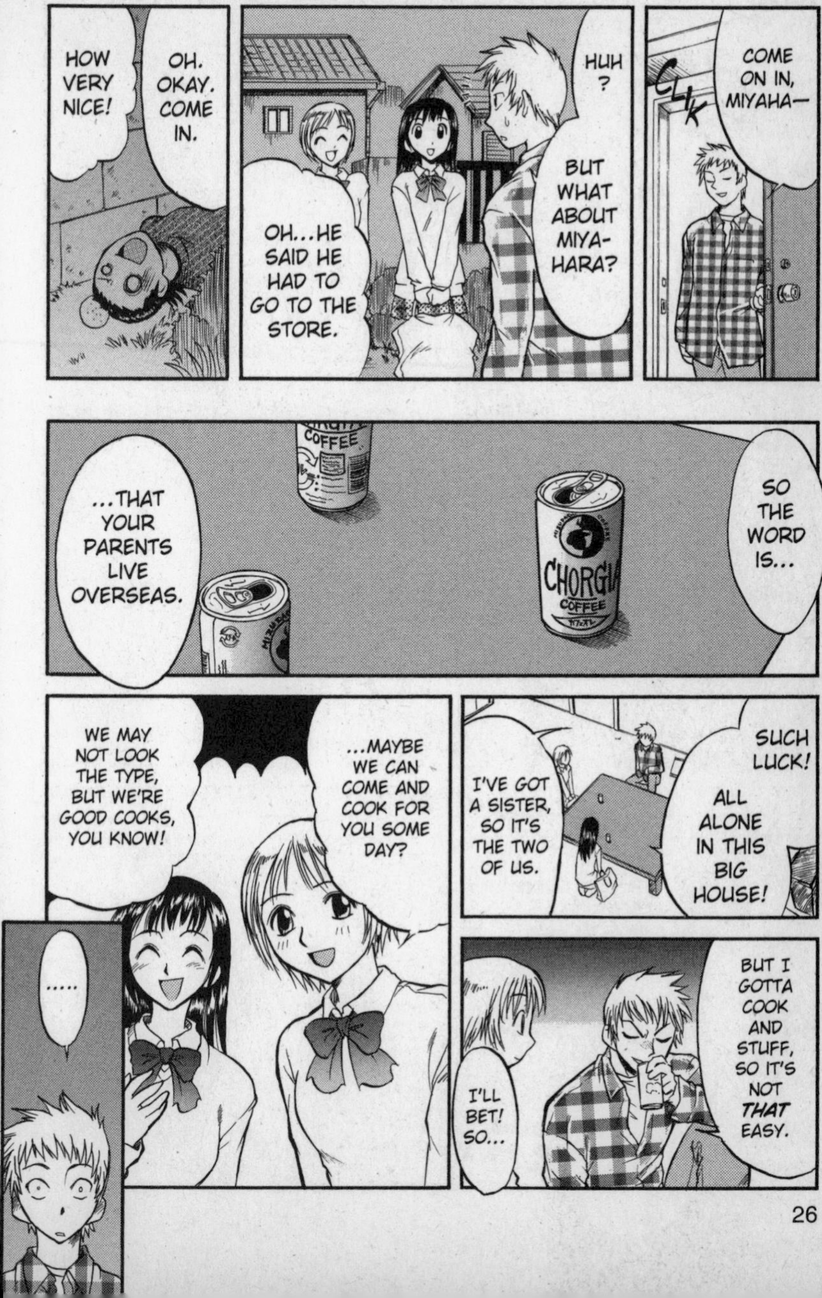
COME ON IN, MIYAHA—
CLIK
HUH?
BUT WHAT ABOUT MIYA-HARA?
OH...HE SAID HE HAD TO GO TO THE STORE.
OH. OKAY. COME IN.
HOW VERY NICE!
SO THE WORD IS...
CHORGIA COFFEE
...THAT YOUR PARENTS LIVE OVERSEAS.
SUCH LUCK!
ALL ALONE IN THIS BIG HOUSE!
I'VE GOT A SISTER, SO IT'S THE TWO OF US.
BUT I GOTTA COOK AND STUFF, SO IT'S NOT *THAT* EASY.
I'LL BET! SO...
...MAYBE WE CAN COME AND COOK FOR YOU SOME DAY?
WE MAY NOT LOOK THE TYPE, BUT WE'RE GOOD COOKS, YOU KNOW!
.....

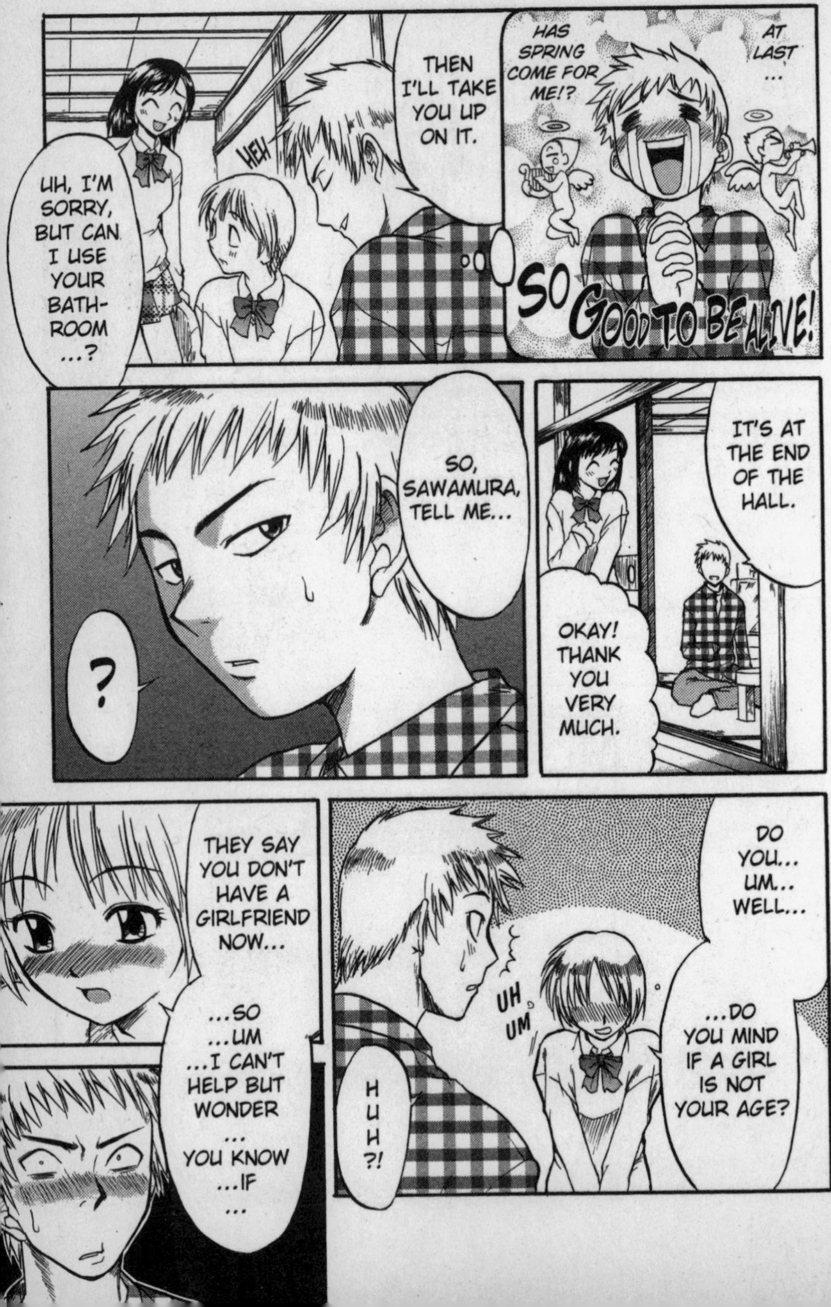
AT LAST ...
HAS SPRING COME FOR ME!?
SO GOOD TO BE ALIVE!
THEN I'LL TAKE YOU UP ON IT.
HEH
UH, I'M SORRY, BUT CAN I USE YOUR BATH-ROOM ...?
IT'S AT THE END OF THE HALL.
OKAY! THANK YOU VERY MUCH.
SO, SAWAMURA, TELL ME...
?
DO YOU... UM... WELL...
...DO YOU MIND IF A GIRL IS NOT YOUR AGE?
UH UM
HUH?!
THEY SAY YOU DON'T HAVE A GIRLFRIEND NOW...
...SO ...UM ...I CAN'T HELP BUT WONDER ... YOU KNOW ...IF ...

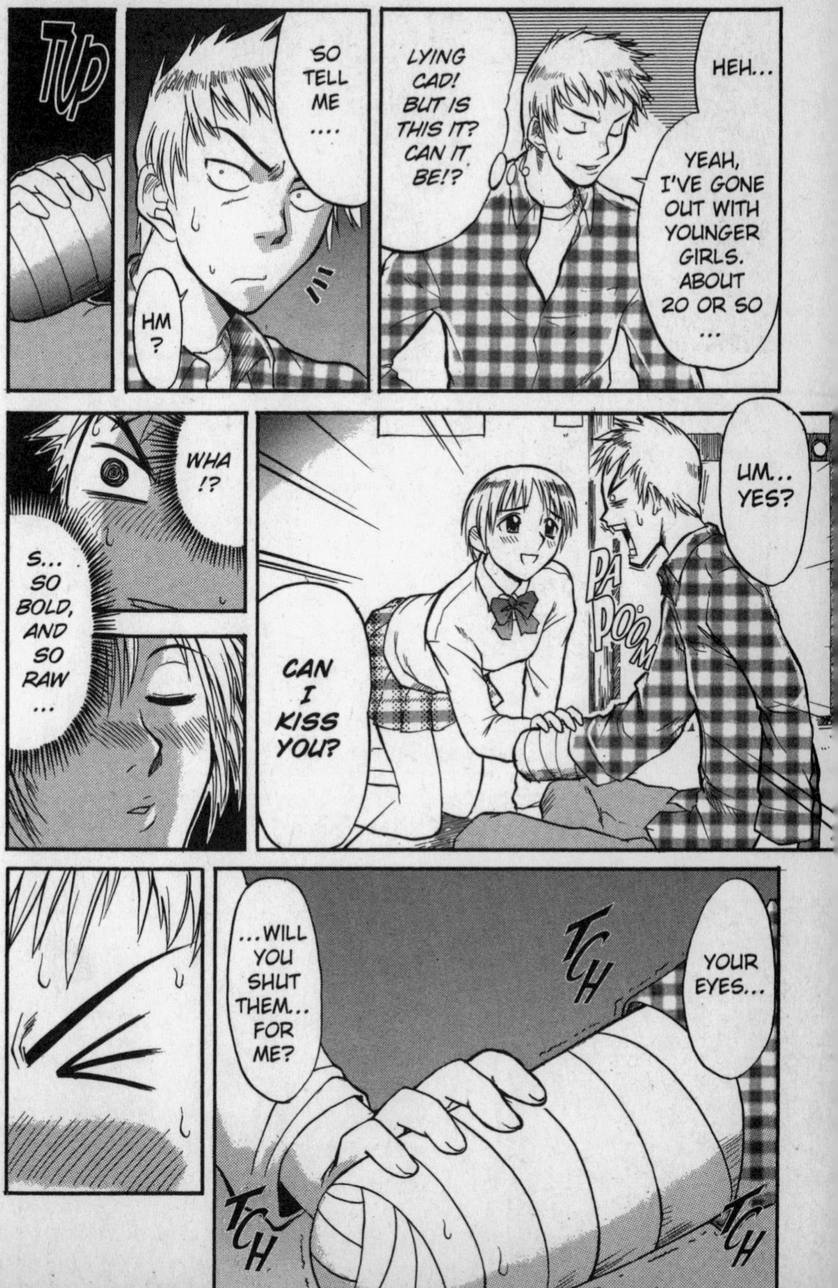
HEH...
YEAH, I'VE GONE OUT WITH YOUNGER GIRLS. ABOUT 20 OR SO ...
LYING CAD! BUT IS THIS IT? CAN IT BE!?
SO TELL ME ....
HM ?
TUP
UM... YES?
PA POOM
CAN I KISS YOU?
WHA !?
S... SO BOLD, AND SO RAW ...
YOUR EYES...
TCH
...WILL YOU SHUT THEM... FOR ME?
TCH
TCH

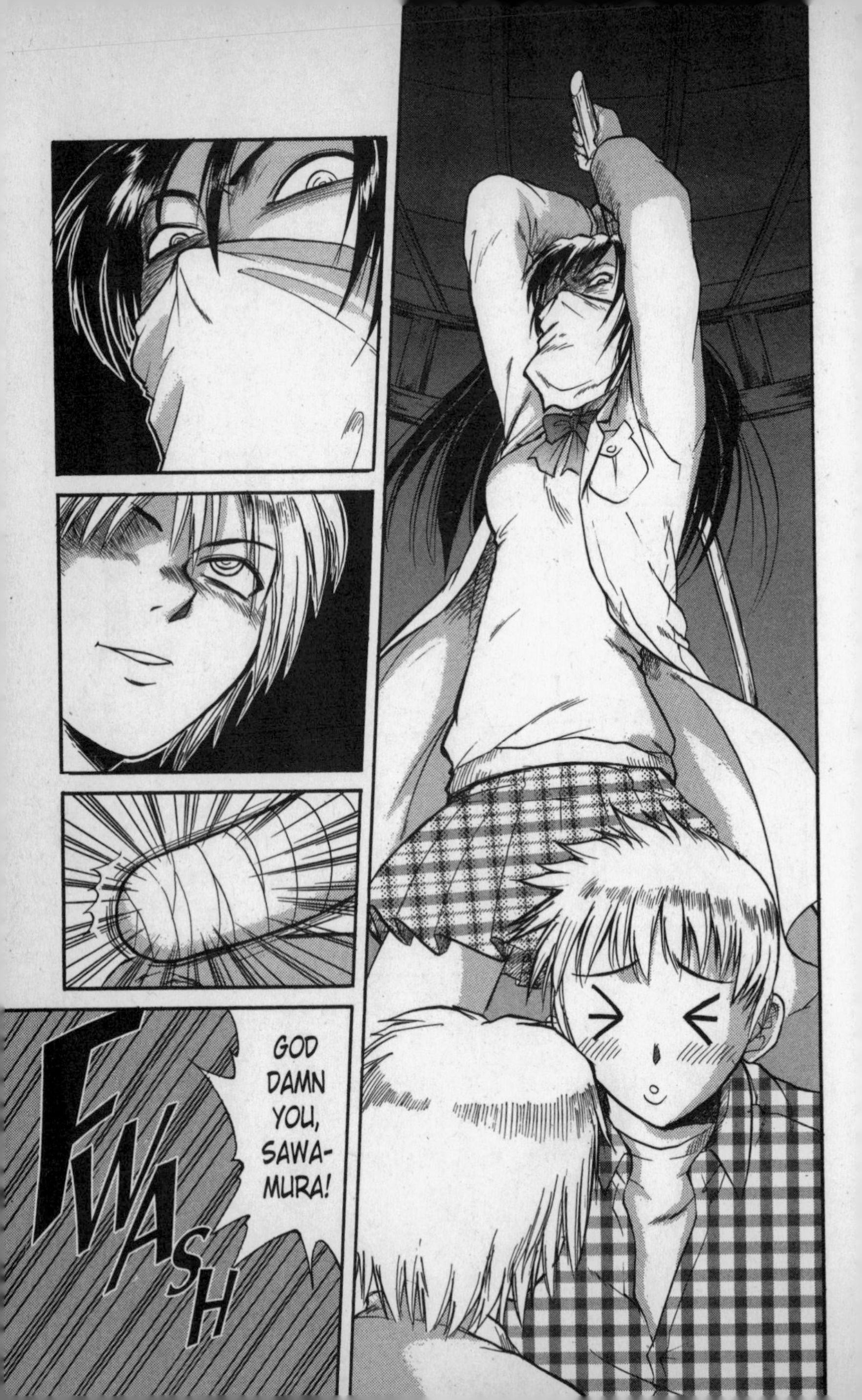
GOD DAMN YOU, SAWA-MURA!
FWASH

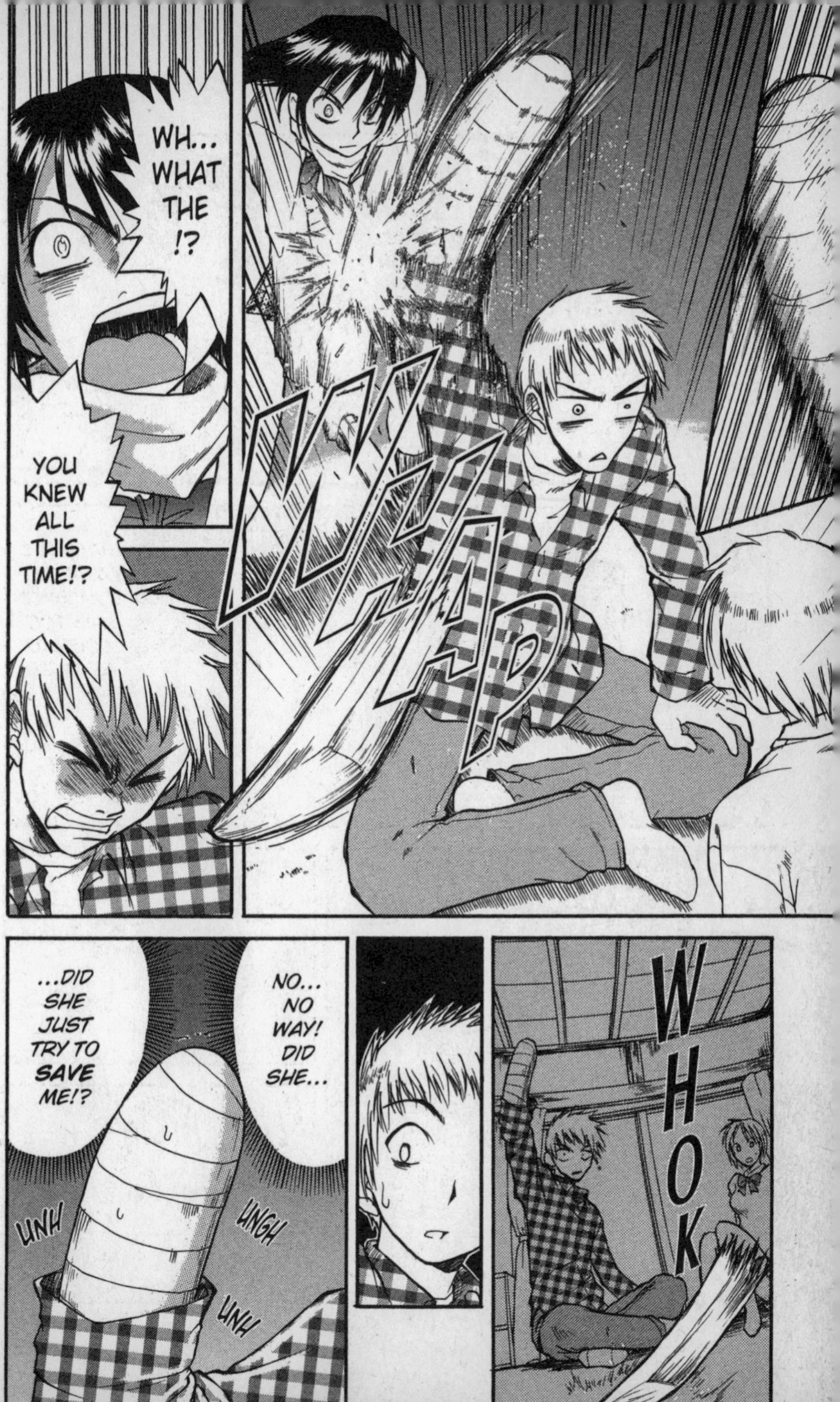
WHAP
WH... WHAT THE!?
YOU KNEW ALL THIS TIME!?
WHOK
NO... NO WAY! DID SHE...
...DID SHE JUST TRY TO SAVE ME!?
UNH
UNGH
UNH

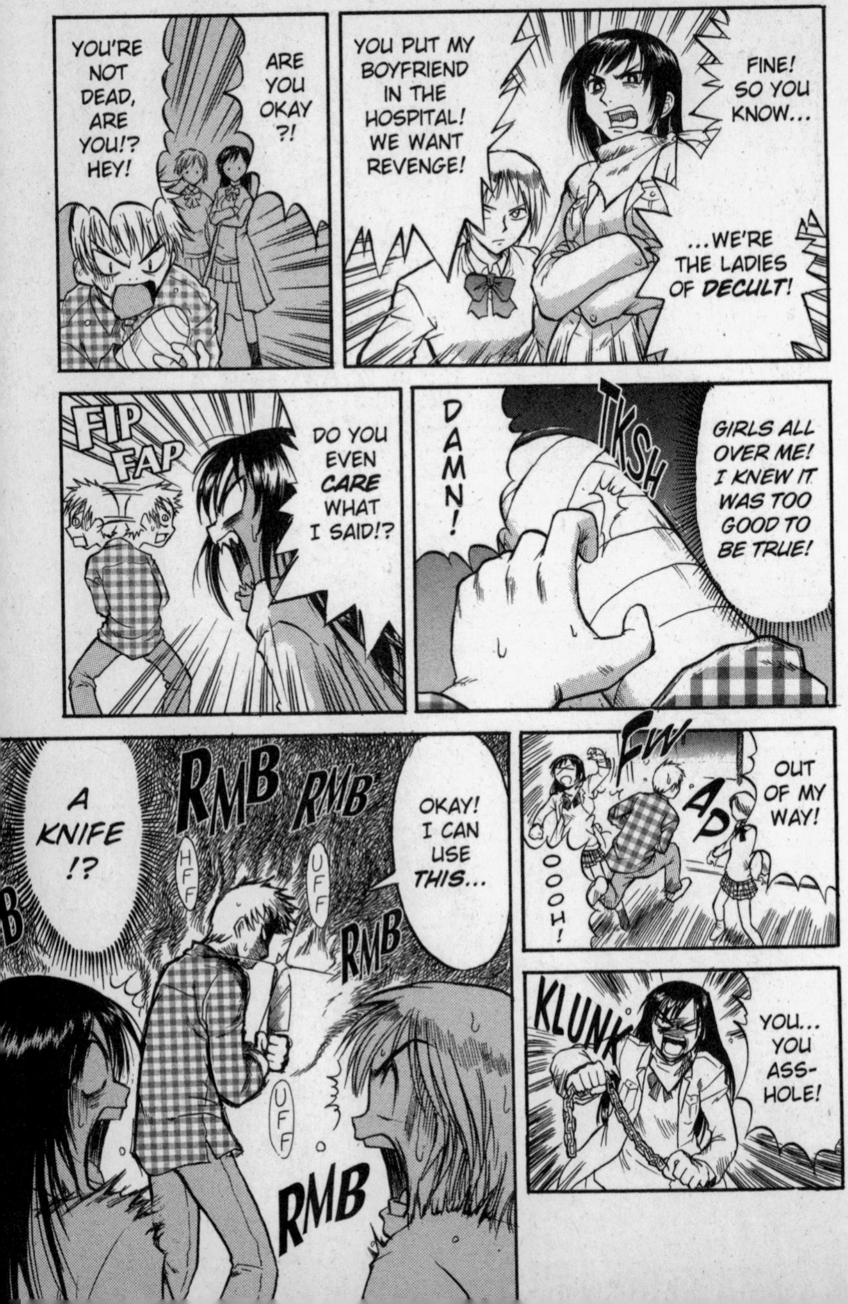
FINE! SO YOU KNOW...
YOU PUT MY BOYFRIEND IN THE HOSPITAL! WE WANT REVENGE!
...WE'RE THE LADIES OF **DECULT**!
ARE YOU OKAY?!
YOU'RE NOT DEAD, ARE YOU!? HEY!
GIRLS ALL OVER ME! I KNEW IT WAS TOO GOOD TO BE TRUE!
TKSH
DAMN!
DO YOU EVEN **CARE** WHAT I SAID!?
FIP FAP
OUT OF MY WAY!
FWAP
OOOOH!
KLUNK
YOU... YOU ASS-HOLE!
OKAY! I CAN USE THIS...
RMB
RMB
A KNIFE!?
UFF
HFF
RMB
UFF
RMB

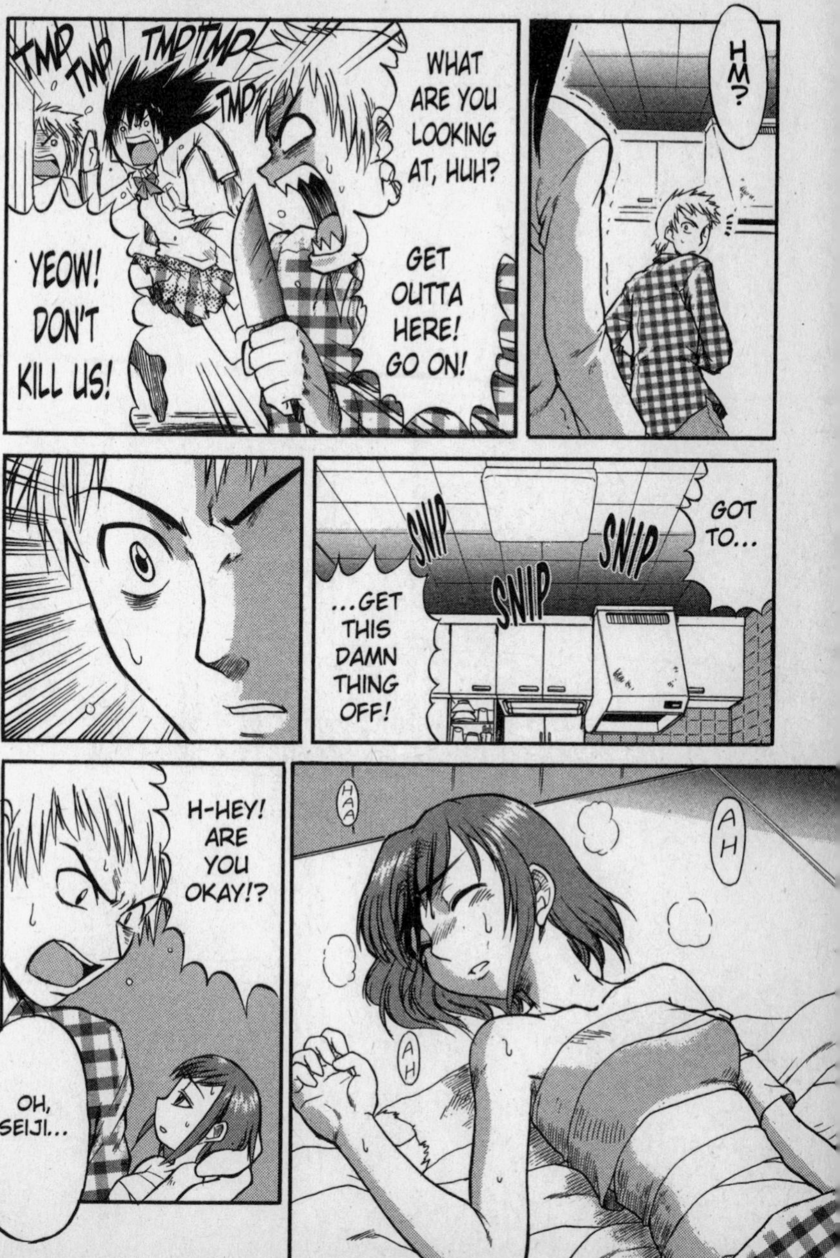
HM?
TMP TMP TMP TMP
TMP
WHAT ARE YOU LOOKING AT, HUH?
GET OUTTA HERE! GO ON!
YEOW! DON'T KILL US!
GOT TO...
SNIP
SNIP
SNIP
...GET THIS DAMN THING OFF!
AH
HAA
AH
H-HEY! ARE YOU OKAY!?
OH, SEIJI...

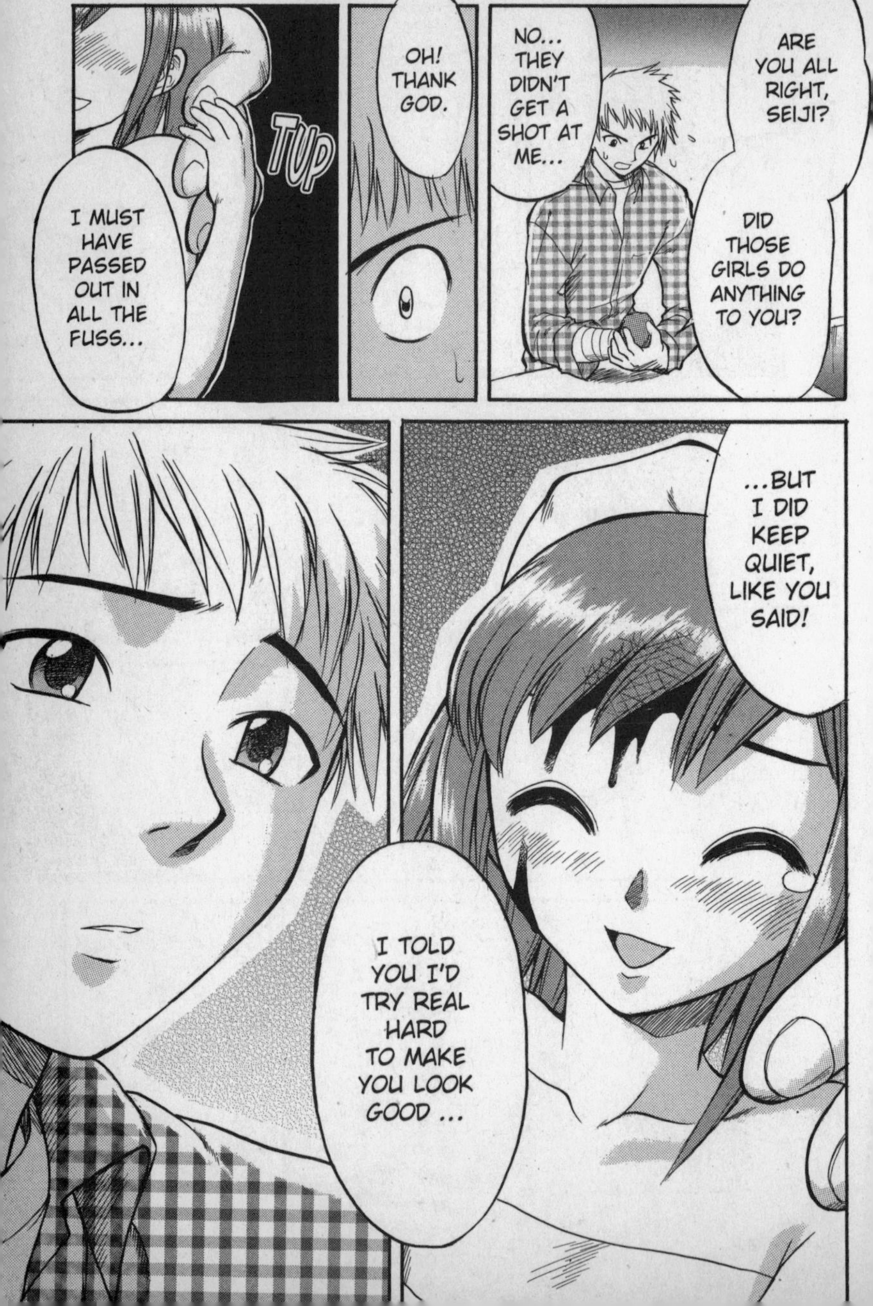
ARE YOU ALL RIGHT, SEIJI?
DID THOSE GIRLS DO ANYTHING TO YOU?
NO... THEY DIDN'T GET A SHOT AT ME...
OH! THANK GOD.
TUP
I MUST HAVE PASSED OUT IN ALL THE FUSS...
...BUT I DID KEEP QUIET, LIKE YOU SAID!
I TOLD YOU I'D TRY REAL HARD TO MAKE YOU LOOK GOOD ...

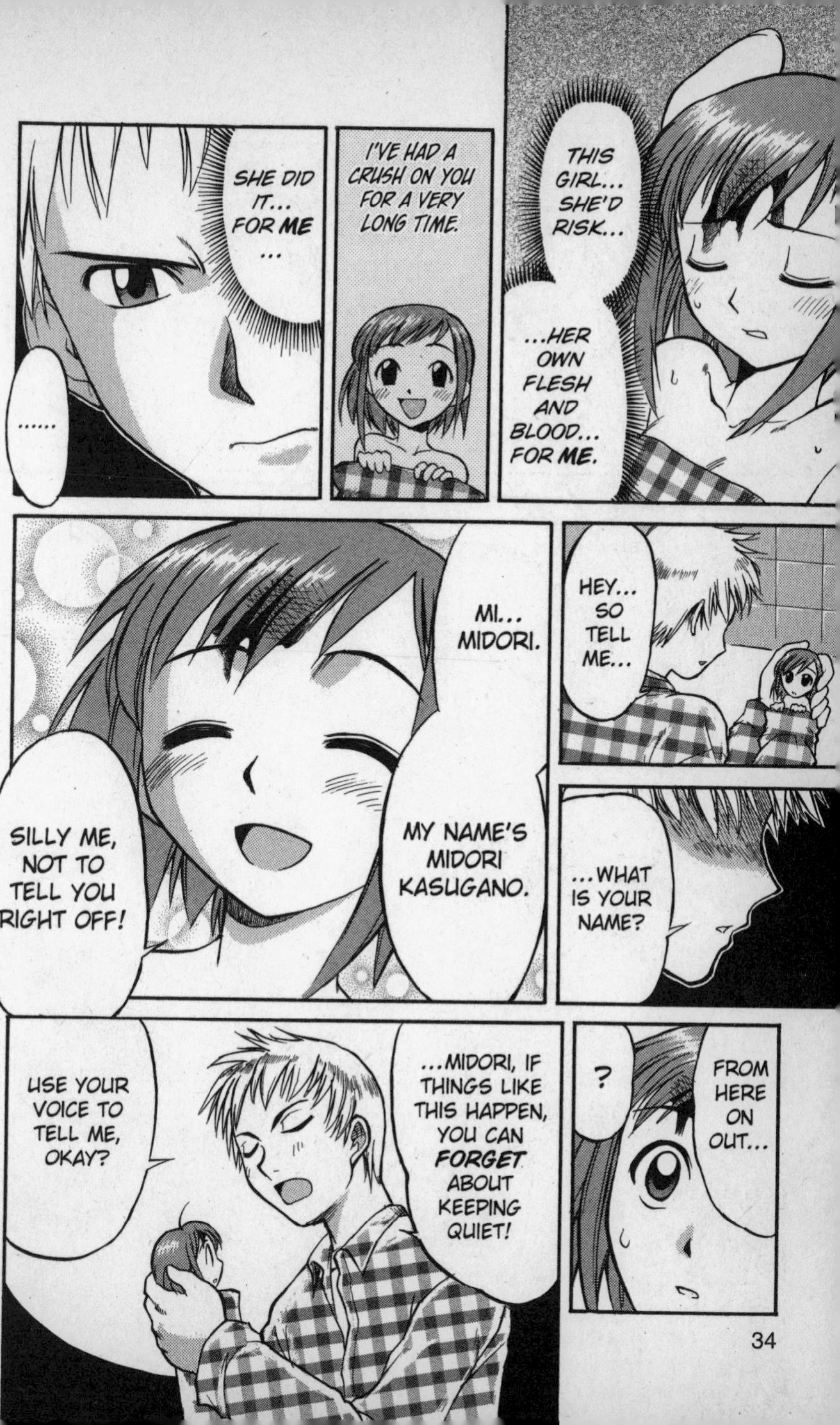
THIS GIRL... SHE'D RISK...
...HER OWN FLESH AND BLOOD... FOR ME.
I'VE HAD A CRUSH ON YOU FOR A VERY LONG TIME.
SHE DID IT... FOR ME ...
......
HEY... SO TELL ME...
...WHAT IS YOUR NAME?
MI... MIDORI.
MY NAME'S MIDORI KASUGANO.
SILLY ME, NOT TO TELL YOU RIGHT OFF!
FROM HERE ON OUT...
?
...MIDORI, IF THINGS LIKE THIS HAPPEN, YOU CAN FORGET ABOUT KEEPING QUIET!
USE YOUR VOICE TO TELL ME, OKAY?

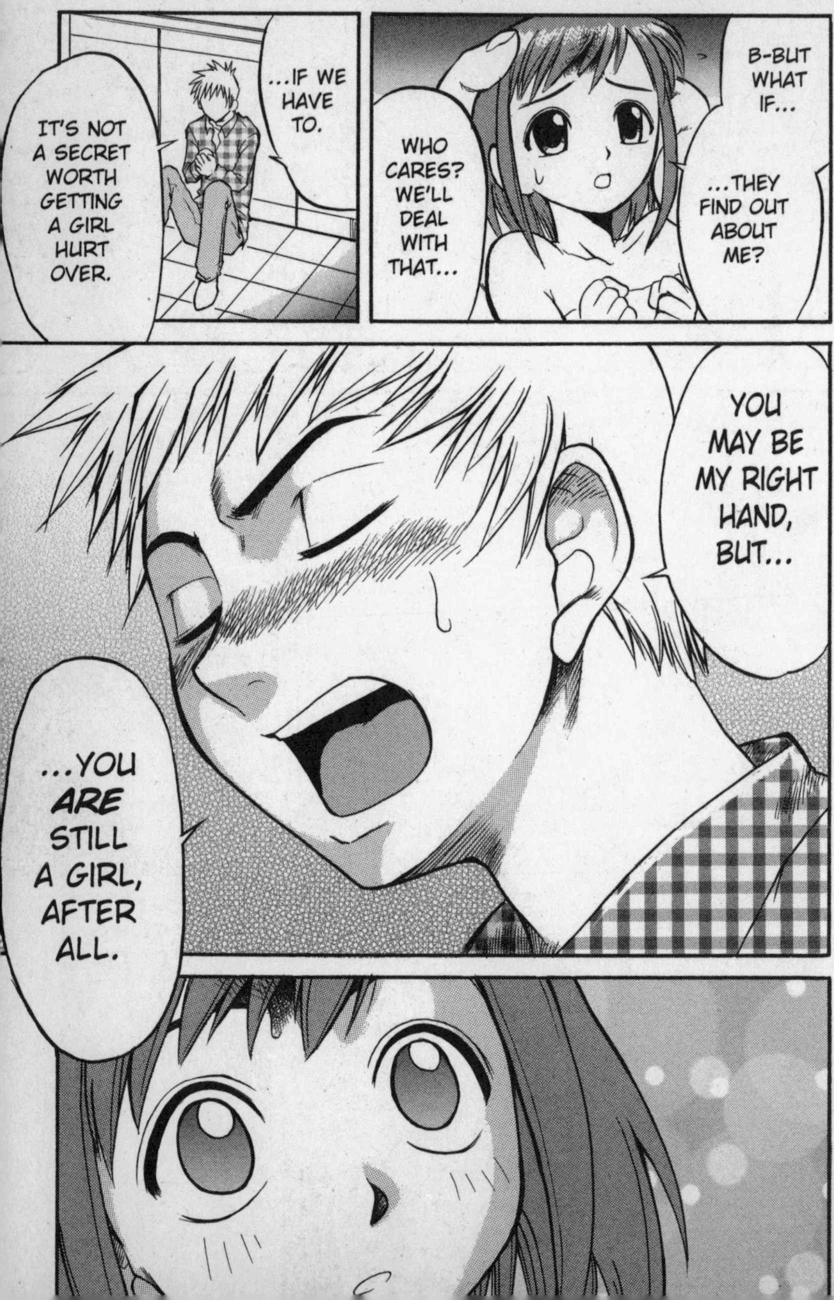
B-BUT WHAT IF...
...THEY FIND OUT ABOUT ME?
WHO CARES? WE'LL DEAL WITH THAT...
...IF WE HAVE TO.
IT'S NOT A SECRET WORTH GETTING A GIRL HURT OVER.
YOU MAY BE MY RIGHT HAND, BUT...
...YOU *ARE* STILL A GIRL, AFTER ALL.

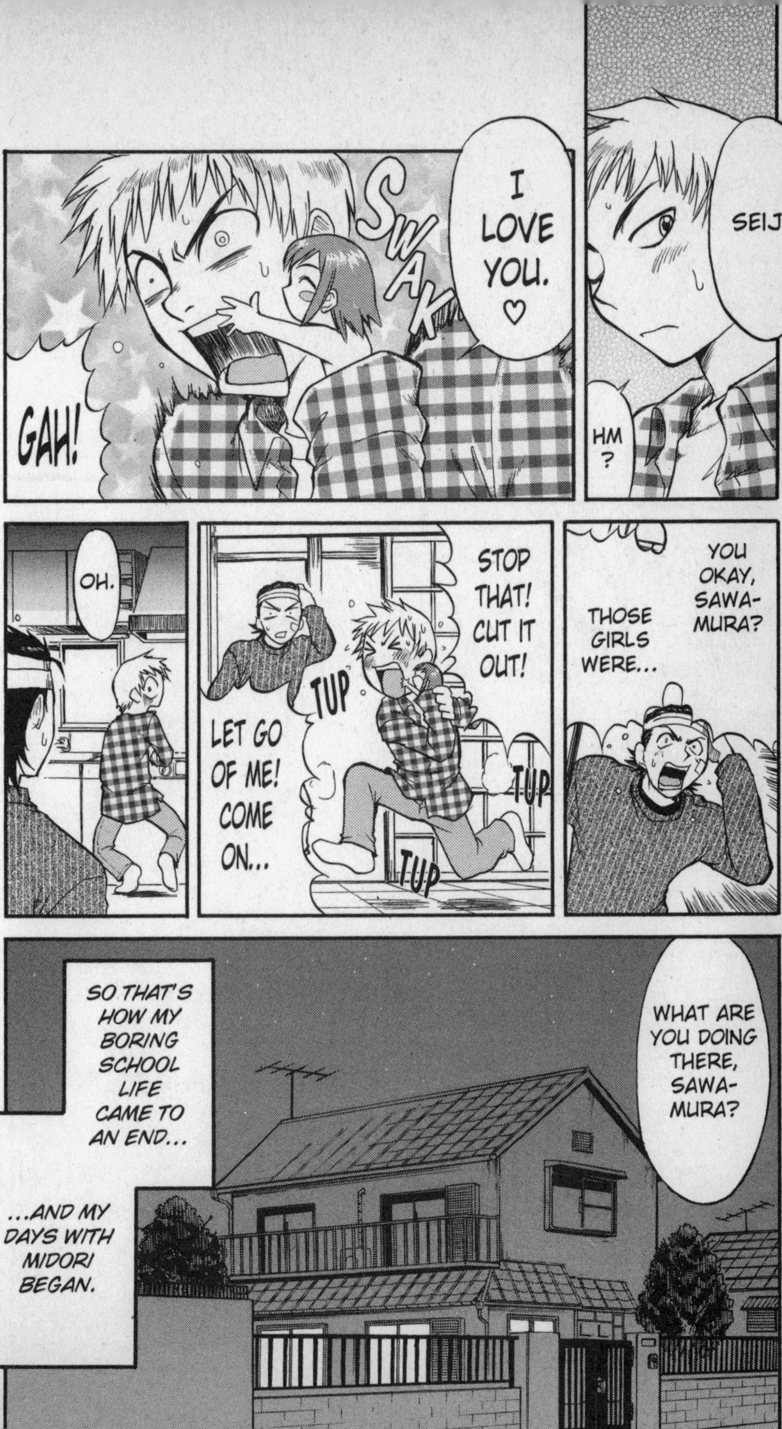
SEIJI.
HM?
I LOVE YOU. ♥
SWAK
GAH!
YOU OKAY, SAWA-MURA?
THOSE GIRLS WERE...
STOP THAT! CUT IT OUT!
TUP
LET GO OF ME! COME ON...
TUP
TUP
OH.
WHAT ARE YOU DOING THERE, SAWA-MURA?
SO THAT'S HOW MY BORING SCHOOL LIFE CAME TO AN END...
...AND MY DAYS WITH MIDORI BEGAN.

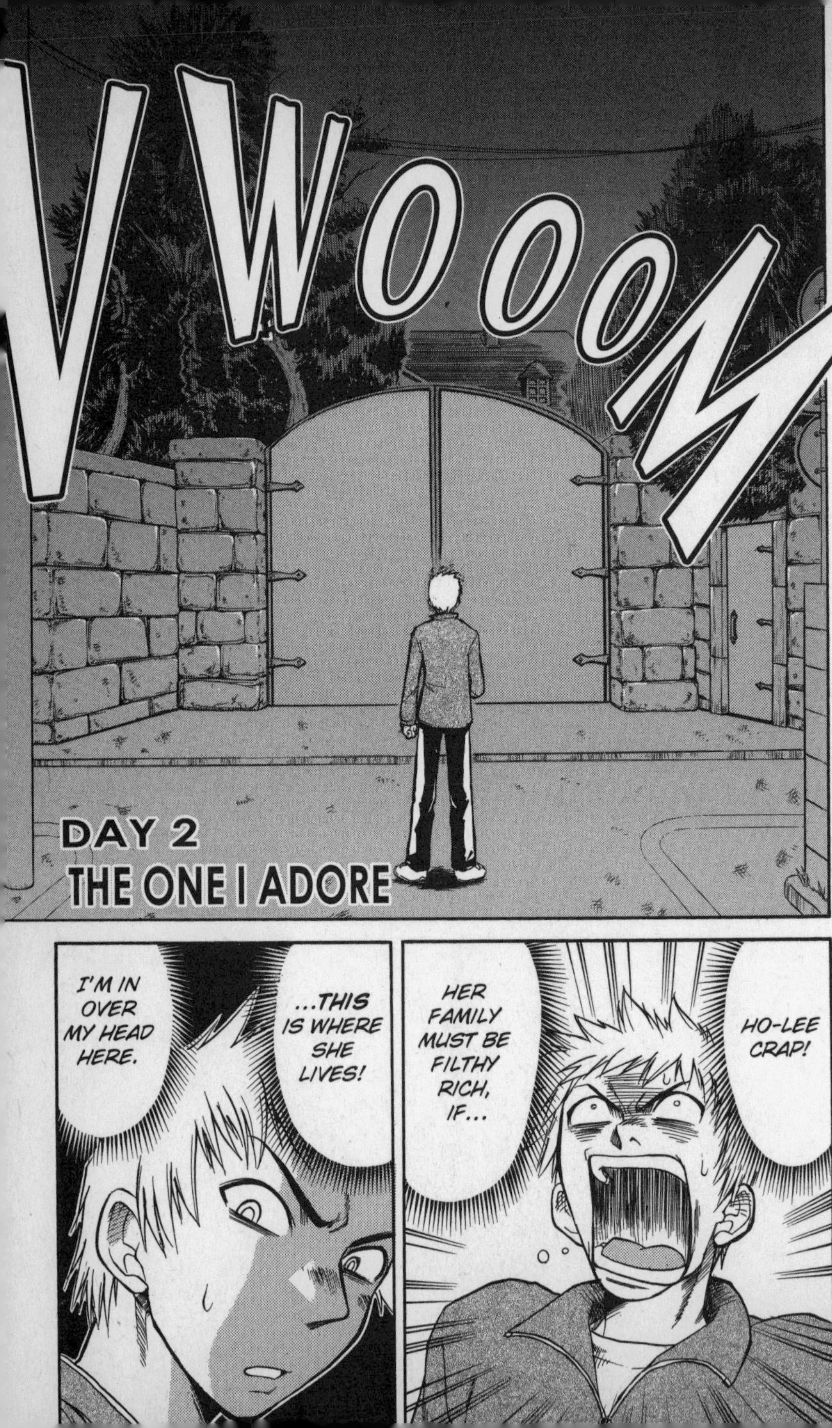
VWOOOM
DAY 2
THE ONE I ADORE
HO-LEE CRAP!
HER FAMILY MUST BE FILTHY RICH, IF...
...THIS IS WHERE SHE LIVES!
I'M IN OVER MY HEAD HERE.

DAY 2
THE ONE I ADORE

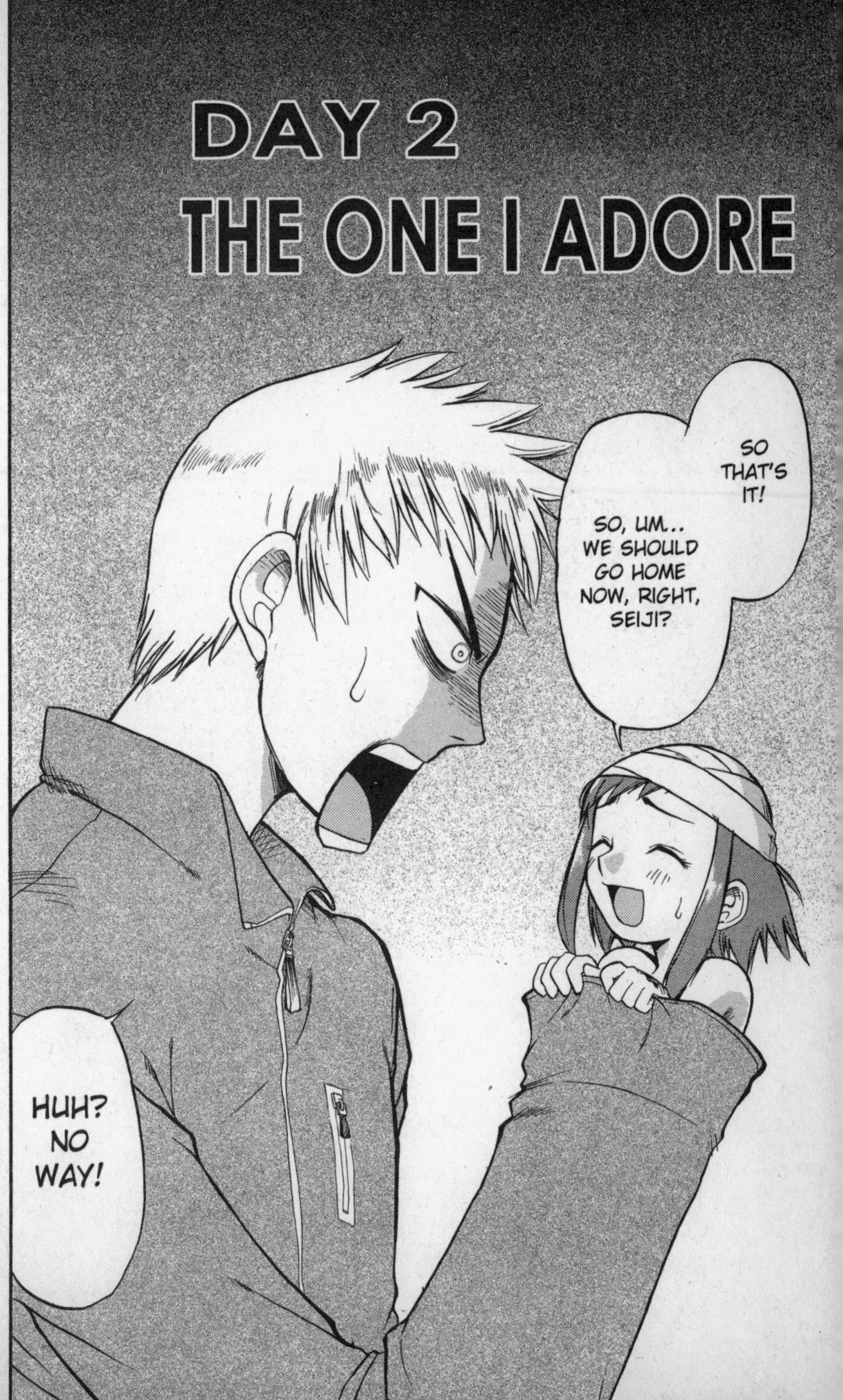
SO THAT'S IT!
SO, UM... WE SHOULD GO HOME NOW, RIGHT, SEIJI?
HUH? NO WAY!

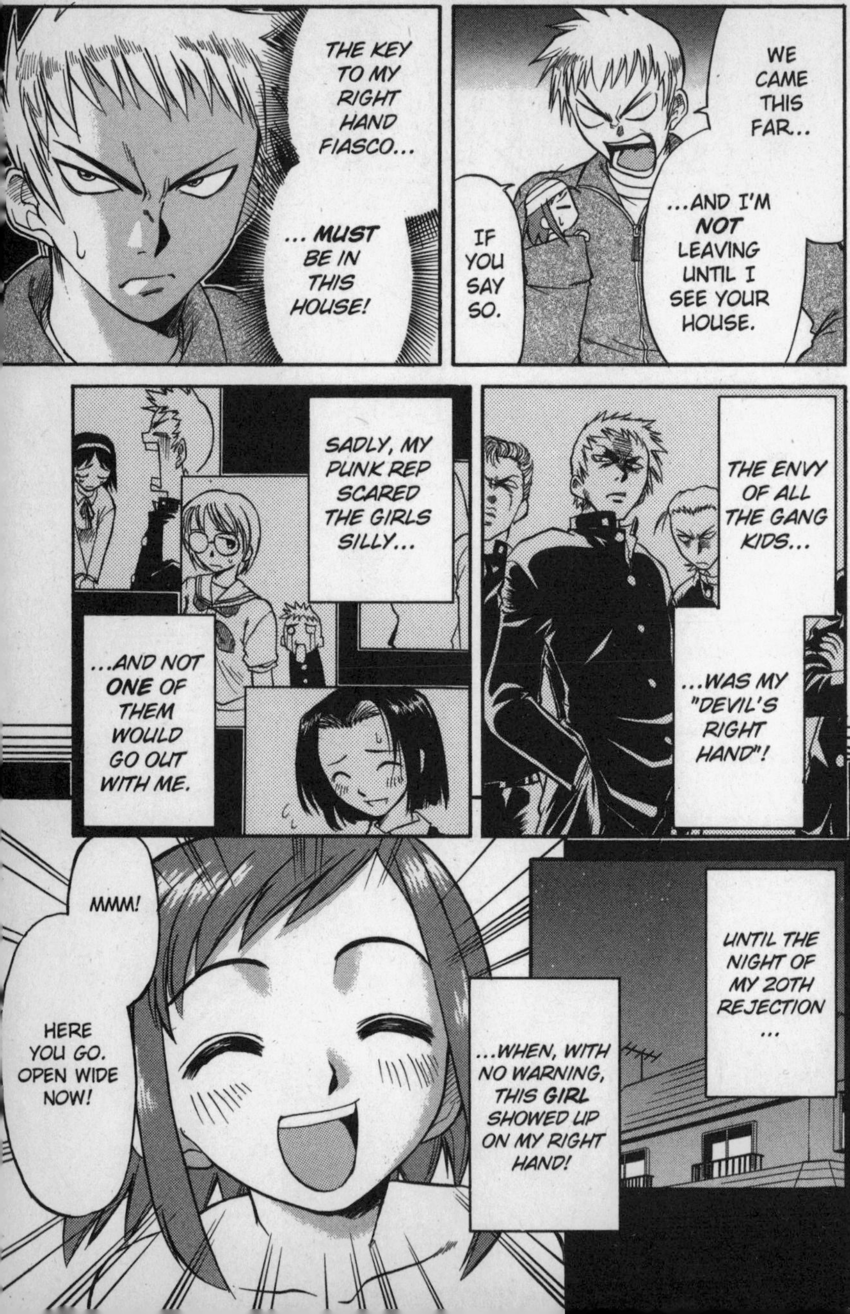
WE CAME THIS FAR...
...AND I'M NOT LEAVING UNTIL I SEE YOUR HOUSE.
IF YOU SAY SO.
THE KEY TO MY RIGHT HAND FIASCO...
...MUST BE IN THIS HOUSE!
THE ENVY OF ALL THE GANG KIDS...
...WAS MY "DEVIL'S RIGHT HAND"!
SADLY, MY PUNK REP SCARED THE GIRLS SILLY...
...AND NOT ONE OF THEM WOULD GO OUT WITH ME.
UNTIL THE NIGHT OF MY 20TH REJECTION...
...WHEN, WITH NO WARNING, THIS GIRL SHOWED UP ON MY RIGHT HAND!
MMM!
HERE YOU GO. OPEN WIDE NOW!

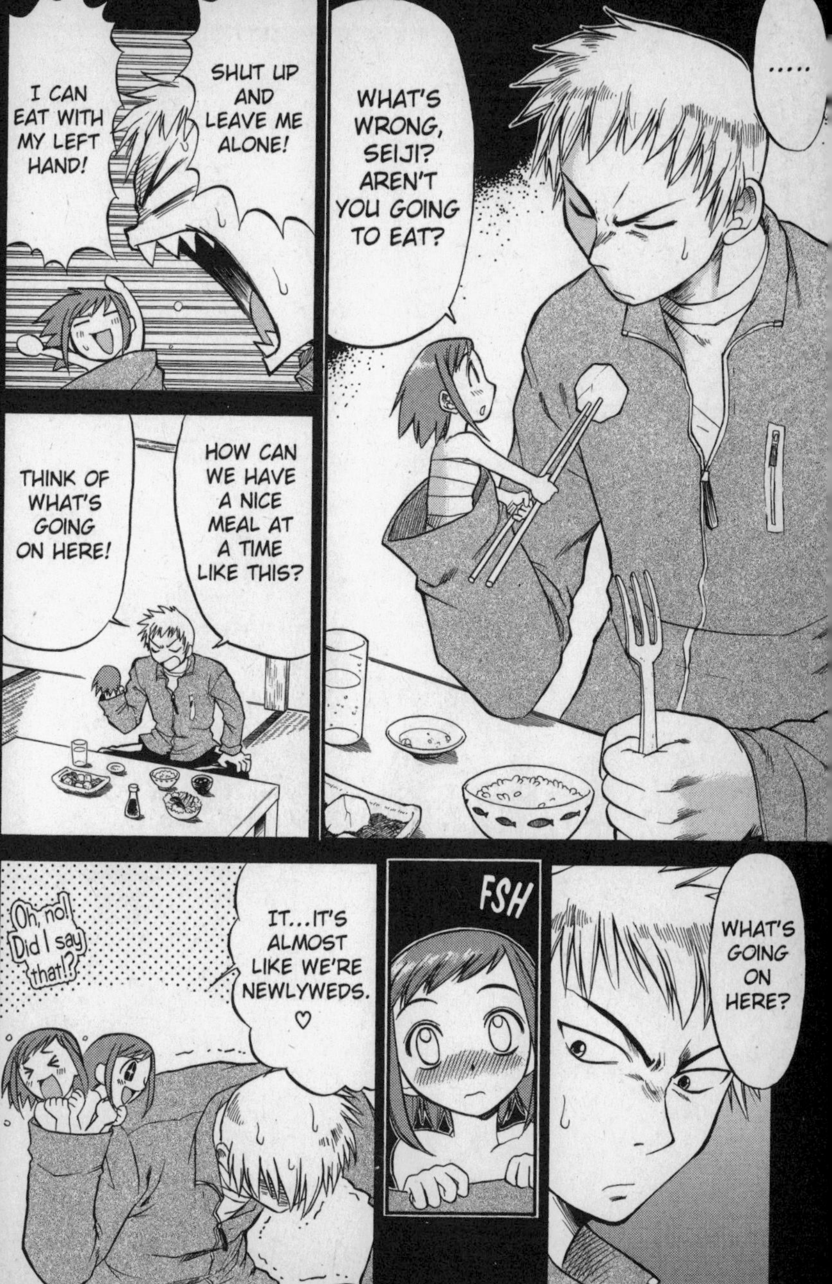

.....
WHAT'S WRONG, SEIJI? AREN'T YOU GOING TO EAT?
SHUT UP AND LEAVE ME ALONE!
I CAN EAT WITH MY LEFT HAND!
HOW CAN WE HAVE A NICE MEAL AT A TIME LIKE THIS?
THINK OF WHAT'S GOING ON HERE!
WHAT'S GOING ON HERE?
FSH
IT...IT'S ALMOST LIKE WE'RE NEWLYWEDS. ♡
Oh, no! Did I say that!?

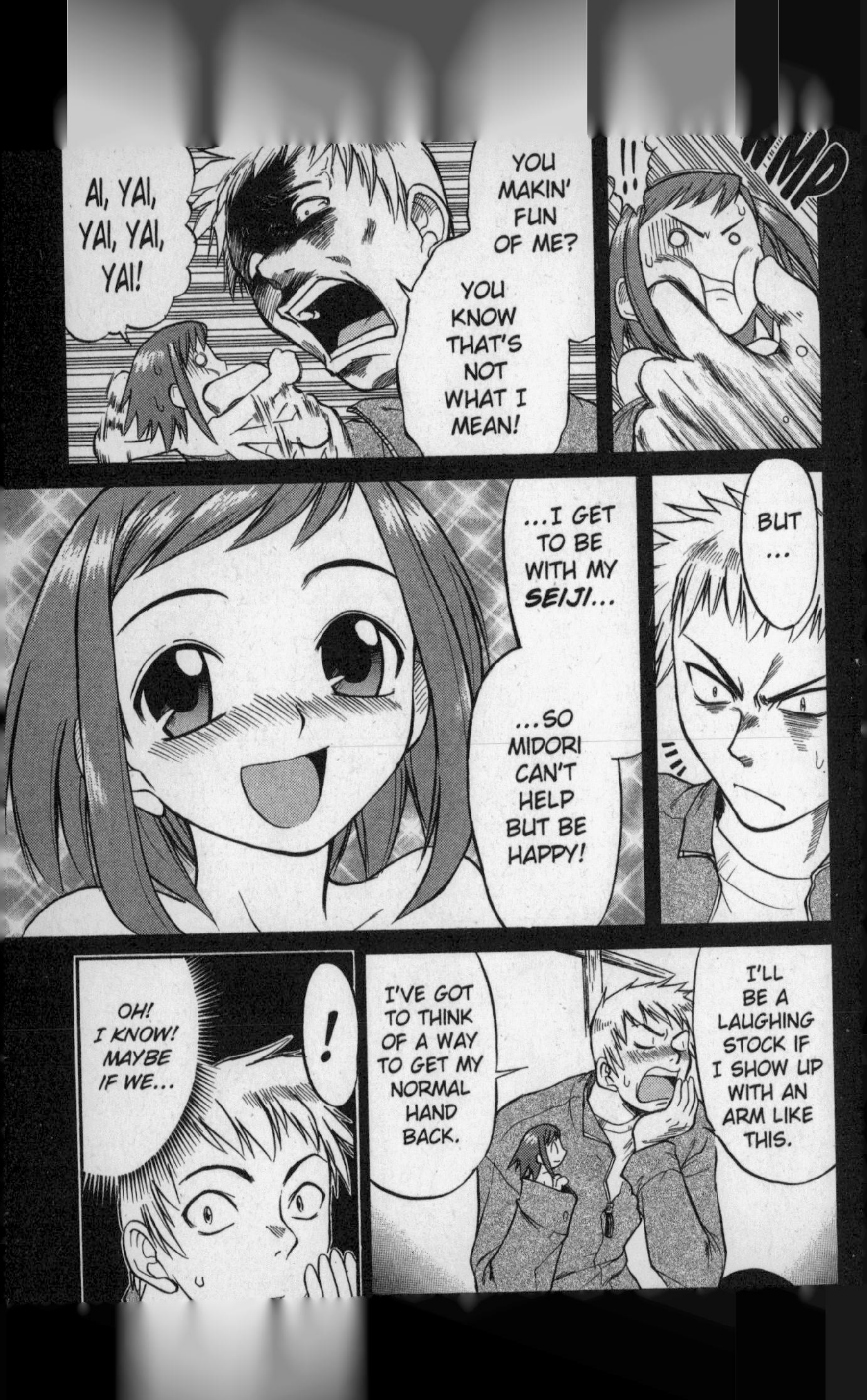
!!
YOU MAKIN' FUN OF ME?
YOU KNOW THAT'S NOT WHAT I MEAN!
AI, YAI, YAI, YAI, YAI!
BUT ...
...I GET TO BE WITH MY *SEIJI*...
...SO MIDORI CAN'T HELP BUT BE HAPPY!
I'LL BE A LAUGHING STOCK IF I SHOW UP WITH AN ARM LIKE THIS.
I'VE GOT TO THINK OF A WAY TO GET MY NORMAL HAND BACK.
!
OH! I KNOW! MAYBE IF WE...

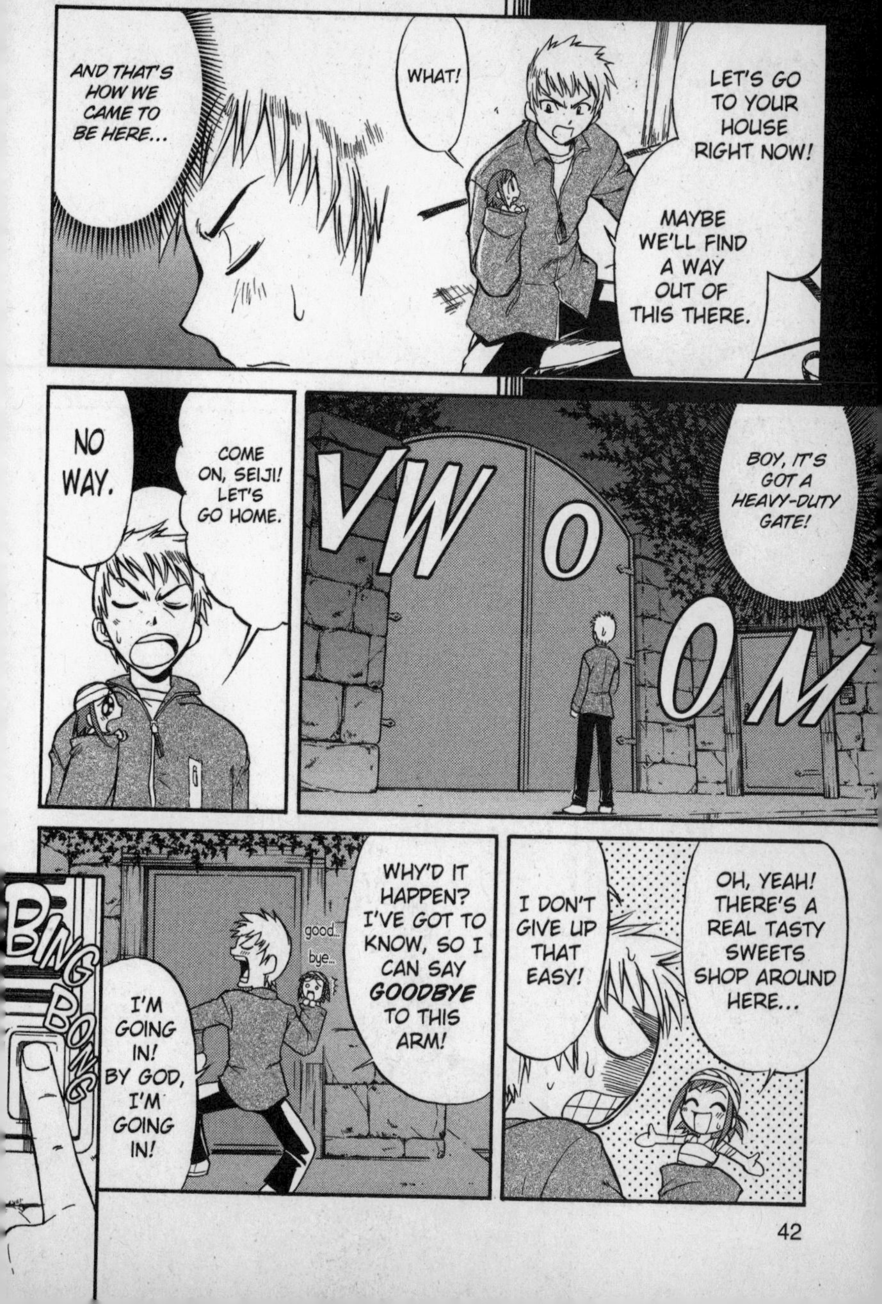
LET'S GO TO YOUR HOUSE RIGHT NOW!
MAYBE WE'LL FIND A WAY OUT OF THIS THERE.
WHAT!
AND THAT'S HOW WE CAME TO BE HERE...
BOY, IT'S GOT A HEAVY-DUTY GATE!
VWOOM
COME ON, SEIJI! LET'S GO HOME.
NO WAY.
OH, YEAH! THERE'S A REAL TASTY SWEETS SHOP AROUND HERE...
I DON'T GIVE UP THAT EASY!
WHY'D IT HAPPEN? I'VE GOT TO KNOW, SO I CAN SAY **GOODBYE** TO THIS ARM!
good... bye...
I'M GOING IN! BY GOD, I'M GOING IN!
BING BONG

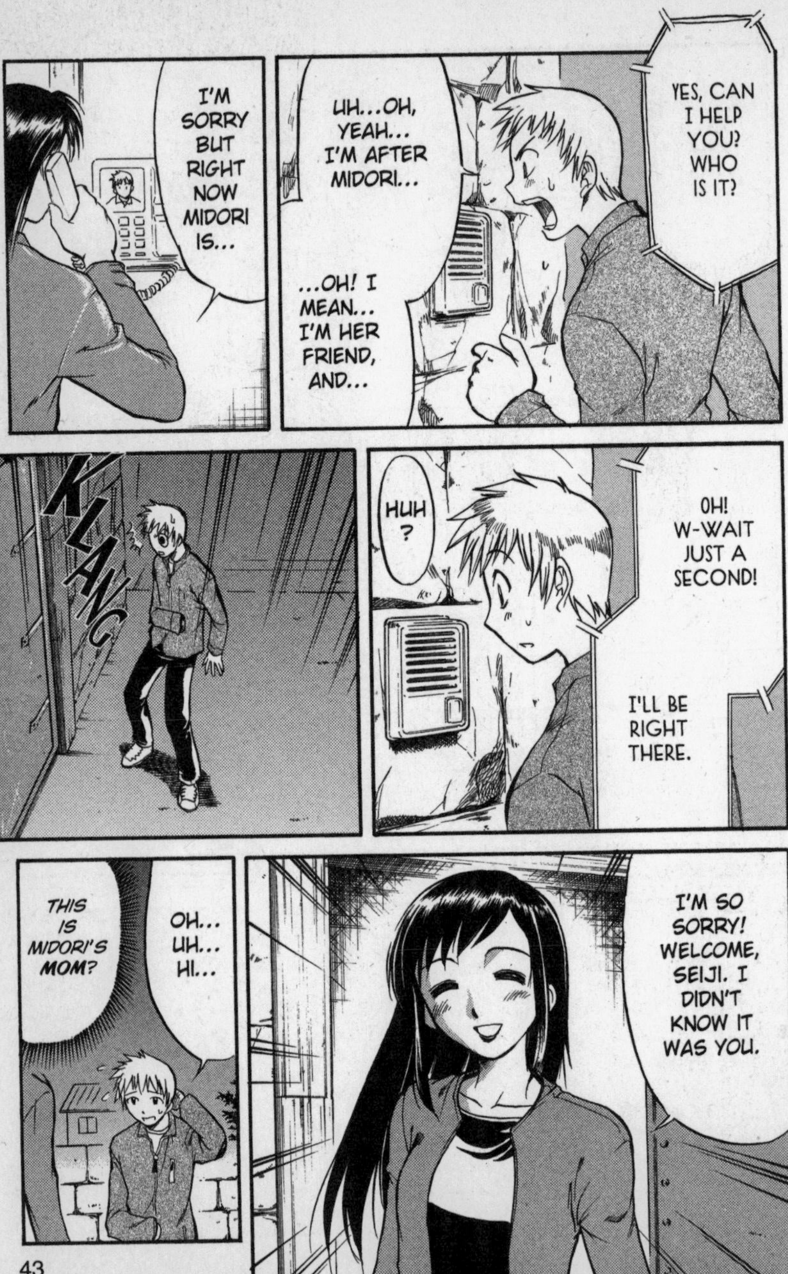

YES, CAN I HELP YOU? WHO IS IT?
UH...OH, YEAH... I'M AFTER MIDORI...
...OH! I MEAN... I'M HER FRIEND, AND...
I'M SORRY BUT RIGHT NOW MIDORI IS...
OH! W-WAIT JUST A SECOND!
HUH?
I'LL BE RIGHT THERE.
KLANG
I'M SO SORRY! WELCOME, SEIJI. I DIDN'T KNOW IT WAS YOU.
OH... UH... HI...
THIS IS MIDORI'S MOM?

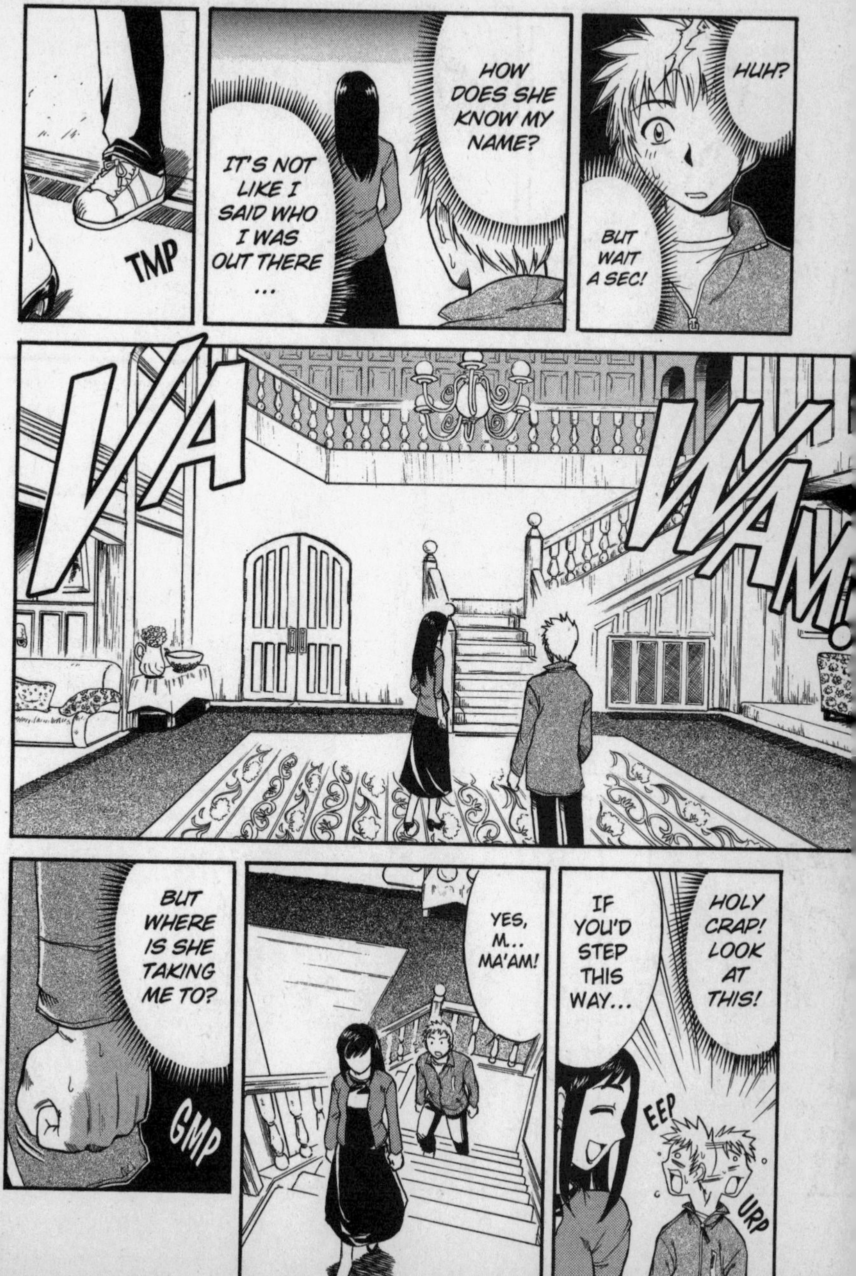
HUH?
BUT WAIT A SEC!
HOW DOES SHE KNOW MY NAME?
IT'S NOT LIKE I SAID WHO I WAS OUT THERE ...
TMP
VA
WAM!
HOLY CRAP! LOOK AT THIS!
IF YOU'D STEP THIS WAY...
EEP
URP
YES, M... MA'AM!
BUT WHERE IS SHE TAKING ME TO?
GMP

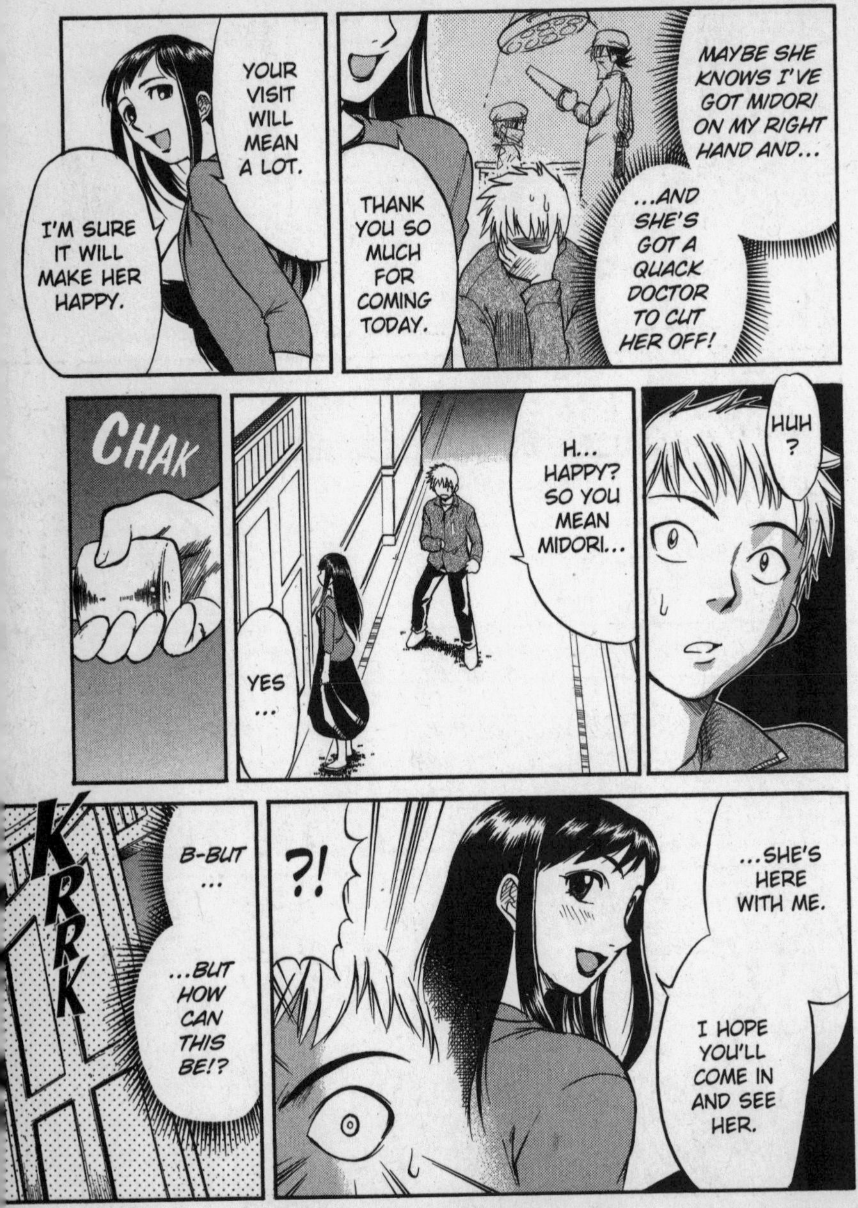
MAYBE SHE KNOWS I'VE GOT MIDORI ON MY RIGHT HAND AND...
...AND SHE'S GOT A QUACK DOCTOR TO CUT HER OFF!
THANK YOU SO MUCH FOR COMING TODAY.
YOUR VISIT WILL MEAN A LOT.
I'M SURE IT WILL MAKE HER HAPPY.
HUH?
H... HAPPY? SO YOU MEAN MIDORI...
YES...
CHAK
...SHE'S HERE WITH ME.
?!
I HOPE YOU'LL COME IN AND SEE HER.
KRRK
B-BUT...
...BUT HOW CAN THIS BE!?

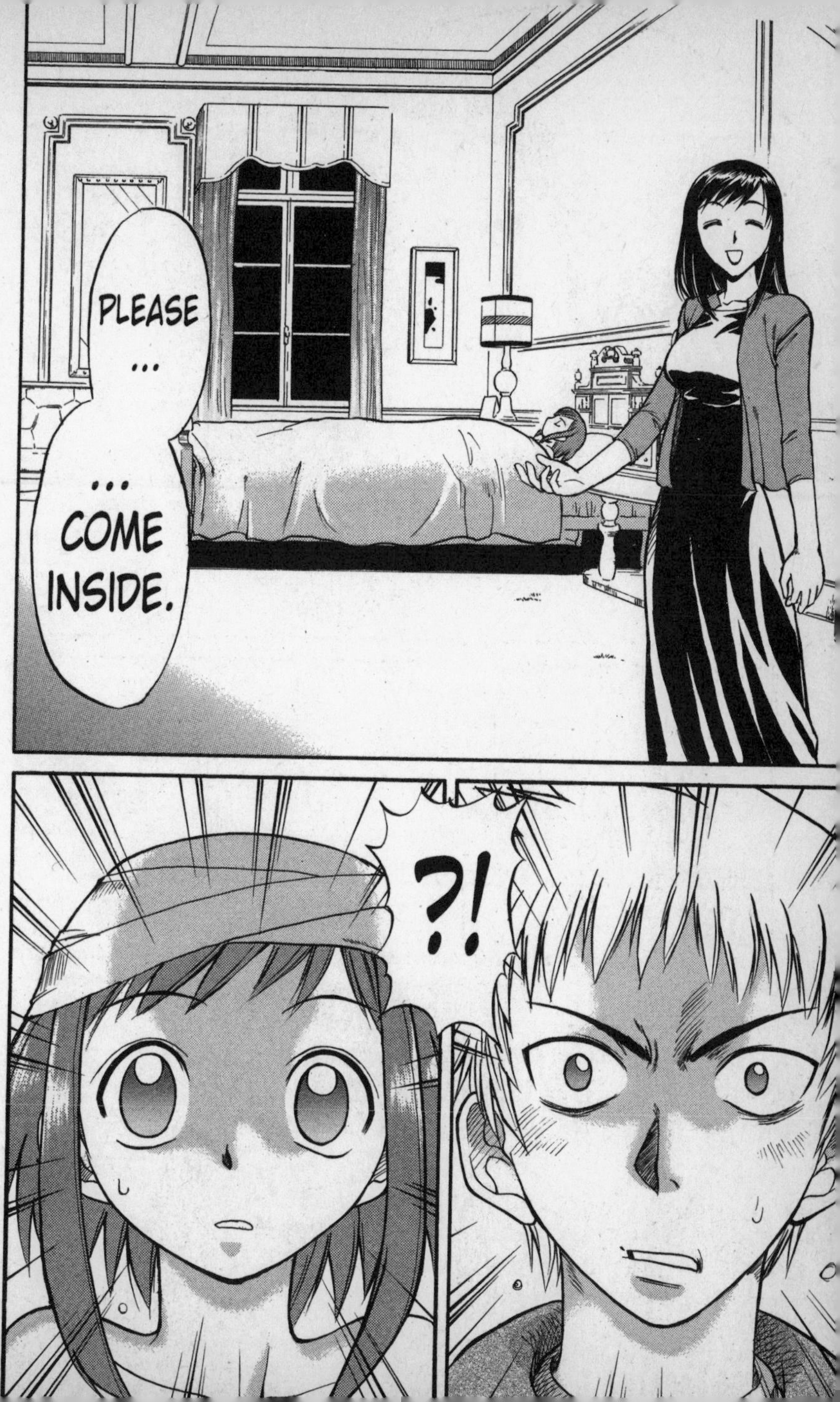
PLEASE ...
... COME INSIDE.
?!

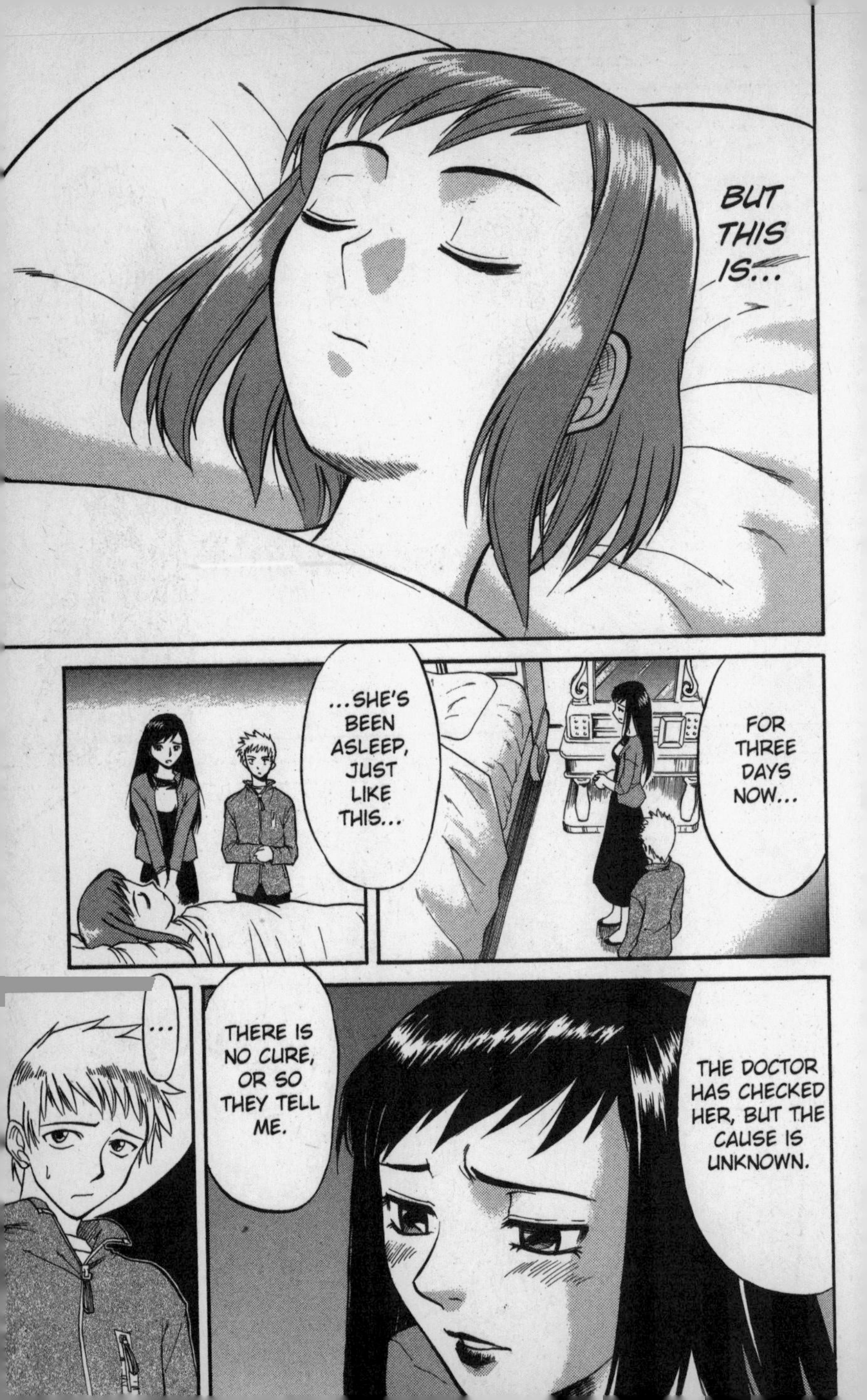
BUT THIS IS...
FOR THREE DAYS NOW...
...SHE'S BEEN ASLEEP, JUST LIKE THIS...
THE DOCTOR HAS CHECKED HER, BUT THE CAUSE IS UNKNOWN.
THERE IS NO CURE, OR SO THEY TELL ME.
...

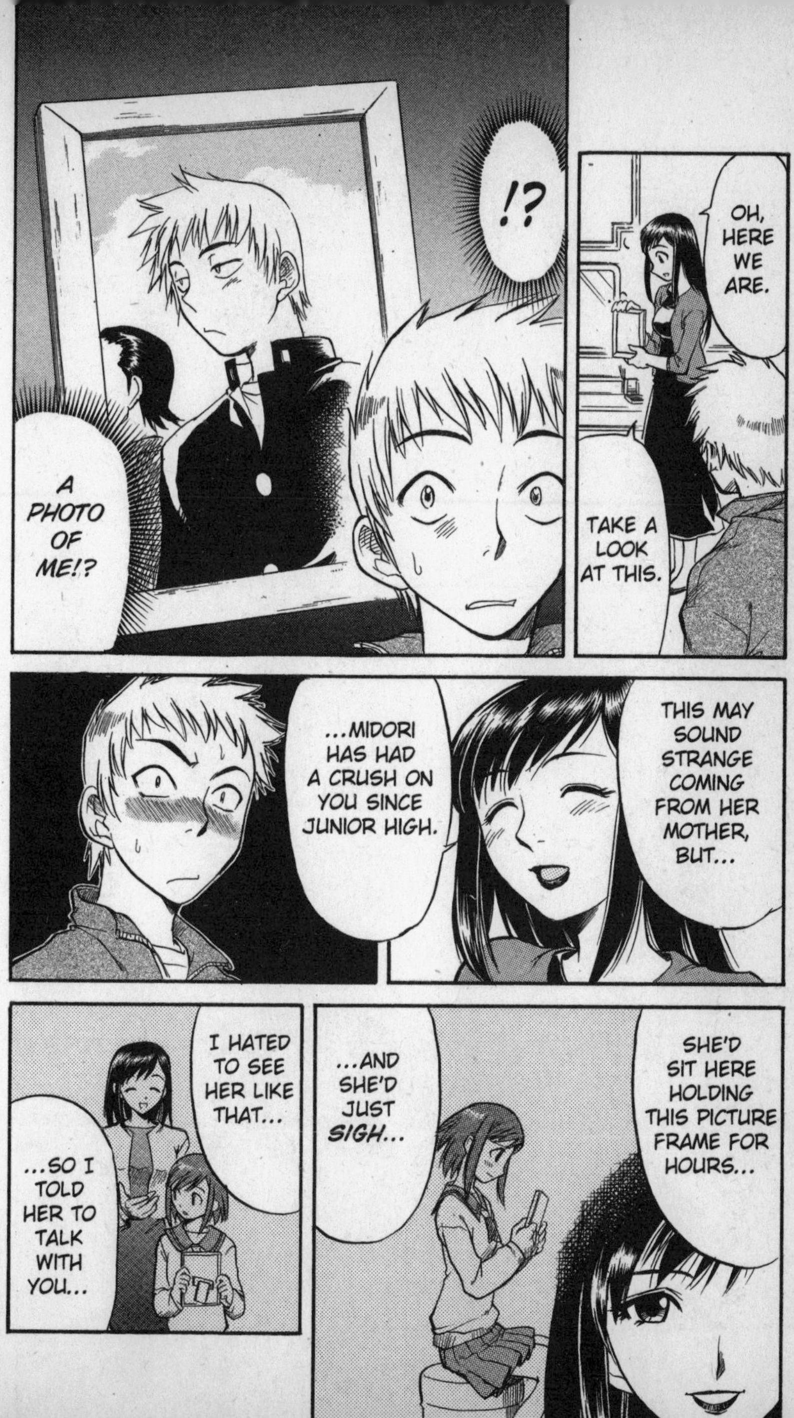
OH, HERE WE ARE.
TAKE A LOOK AT THIS.
!?
A PHOTO OF ME!?
THIS MAY SOUND STRANGE COMING FROM HER MOTHER, BUT...
...MIDORI HAS HAD A CRUSH ON YOU SINCE JUNIOR HIGH.
SHE'D SIT HERE HOLDING THIS PICTURE FRAME FOR HOURS...
...AND SHE'D JUST *SIGH*...
I HATED TO SEE HER LIKE THAT...
...SO I TOLD HER TO TALK WITH YOU...

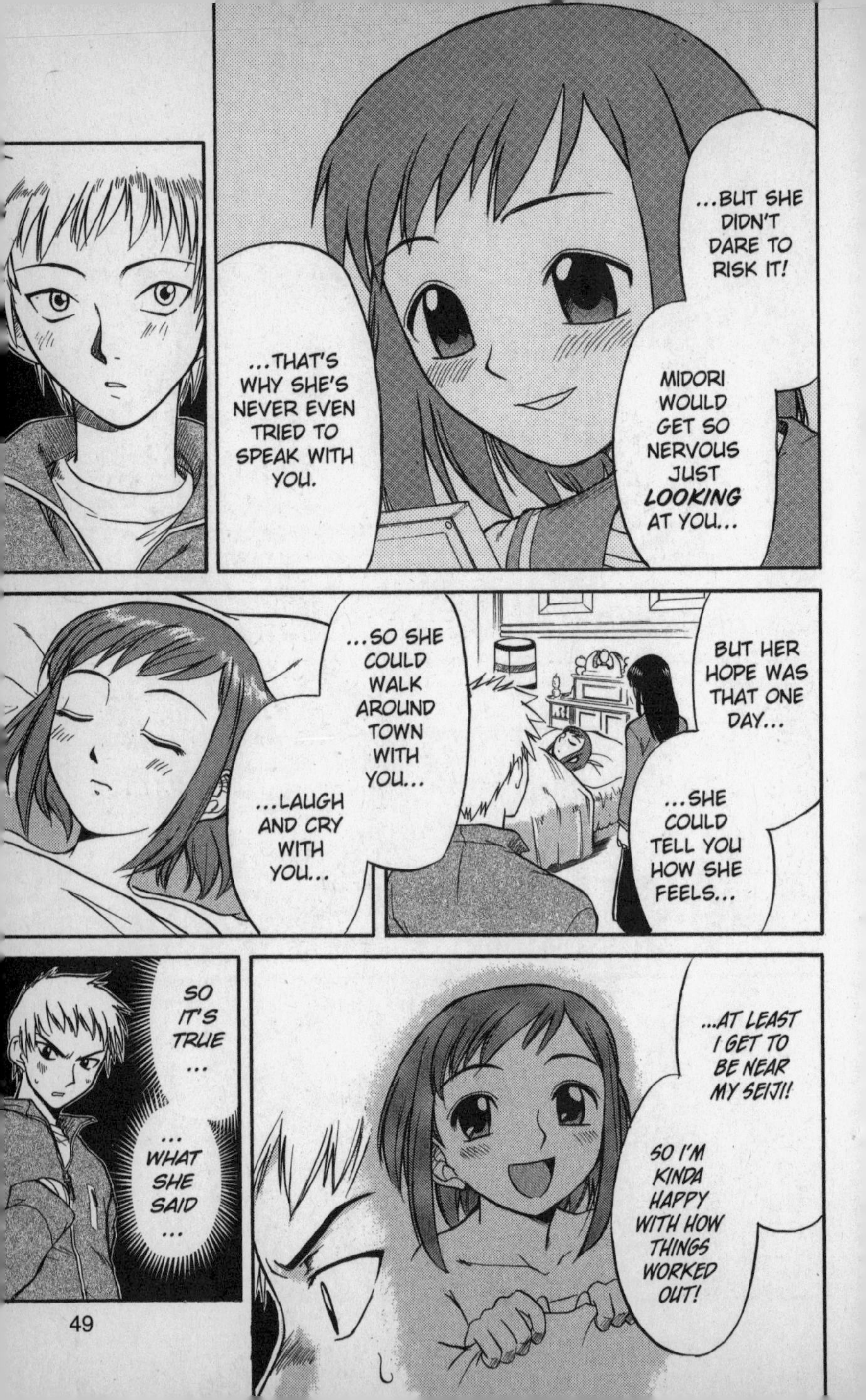
...BUT SHE DIDN'T DARE TO RISK IT!
MIDORI WOULD GET SO NERVOUS JUST **LOOKING** AT YOU...
...THAT'S WHY SHE'S NEVER EVEN TRIED TO SPEAK WITH YOU.
BUT HER HOPE WAS THAT ONE DAY...
...SHE COULD TELL YOU HOW SHE FEELS...
...SO SHE COULD WALK AROUND TOWN WITH YOU...
...LAUGH AND CRY WITH YOU...
...AT LEAST I GET TO BE NEAR MY SEIJI!
SO I'M KINDA HAPPY WITH HOW THINGS WORKED OUT!
SO IT'S TRUE ...
... WHAT SHE SAID ...

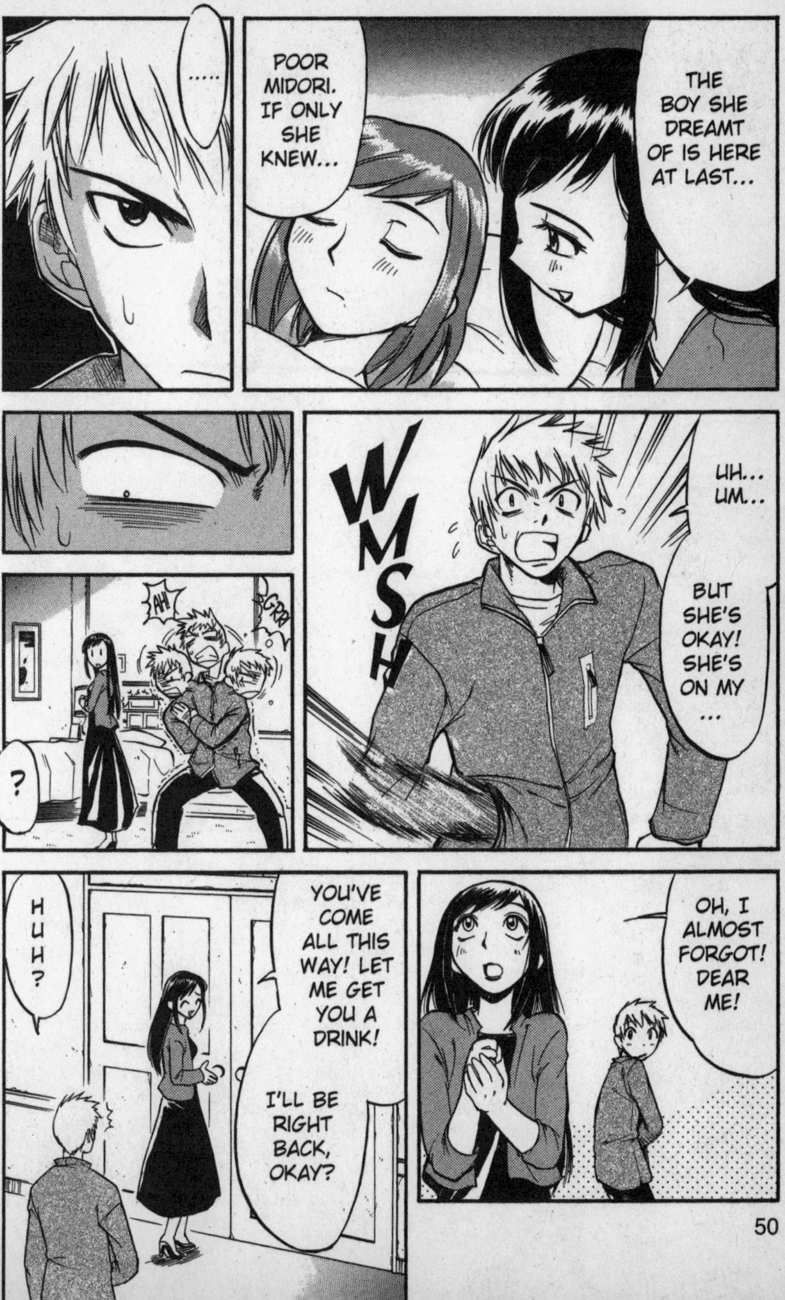
THE BOY SHE DREAMT OF IS HERE AT LAST...
POOR MIDORI. IF ONLY SHE KNEW...
......
UH... UM...
BUT SHE'S OKAY! SHE'S ON MY ...
WMSH
AH!
GRR
?
OH, I ALMOST FORGOT! DEAR ME!
YOU'VE COME ALL THIS WAY! LET ME GET YOU A DRINK!
HUH?
I'LL BE RIGHT BACK, OKAY?

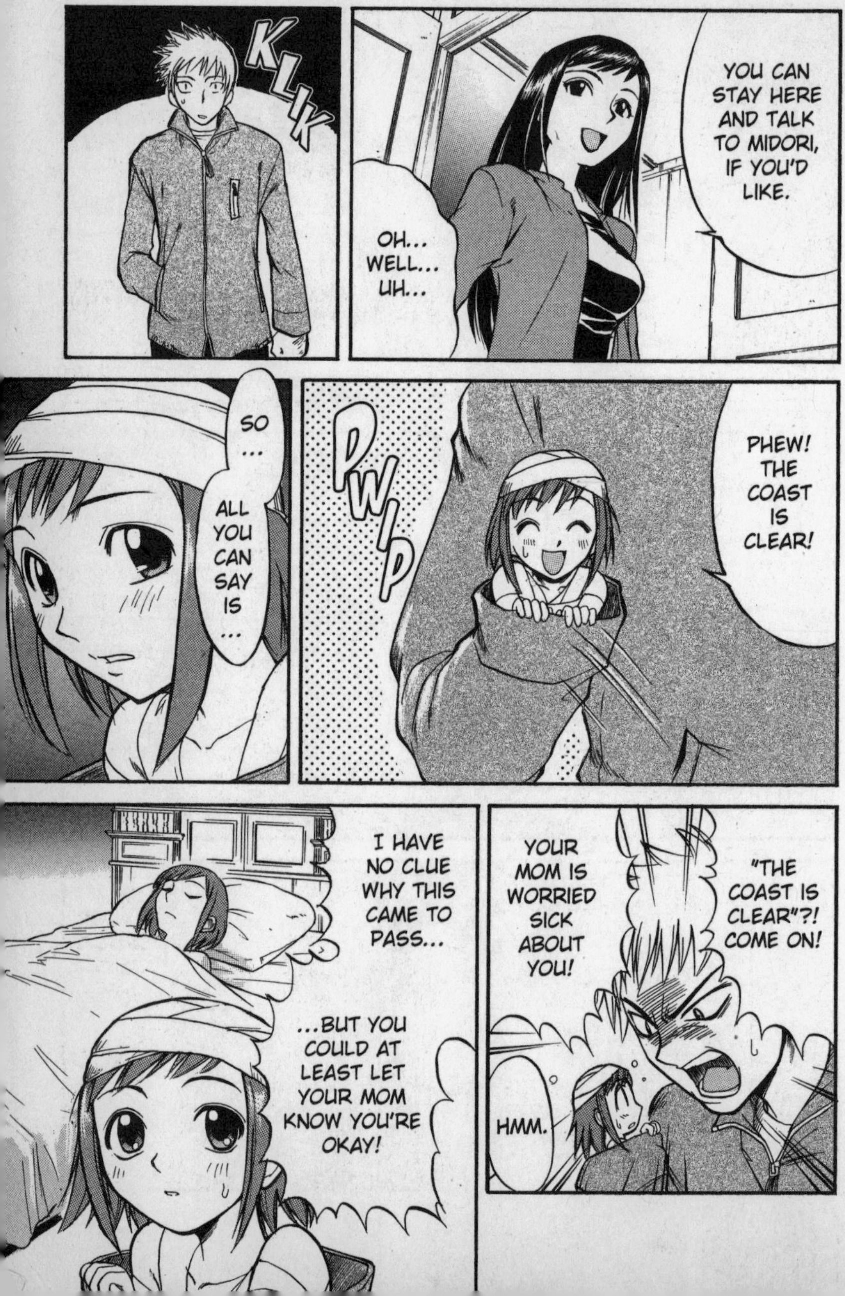
YOU CAN STAY HERE AND TALK TO MIDORI, IF YOU'D LIKE.
OH... WELL... UH...
KLIK
PHEW! THE COAST IS CLEAR!
PWIP
SO ... ALL YOU CAN SAY IS ...
"THE COAST IS CLEAR"?! COME ON!
YOUR MOM IS WORRIED SICK ABOUT YOU!
HMM.
I HAVE NO CLUE WHY THIS CAME TO PASS...
...BUT YOU COULD AT LEAST LET YOUR MOM KNOW YOU'RE OKAY!

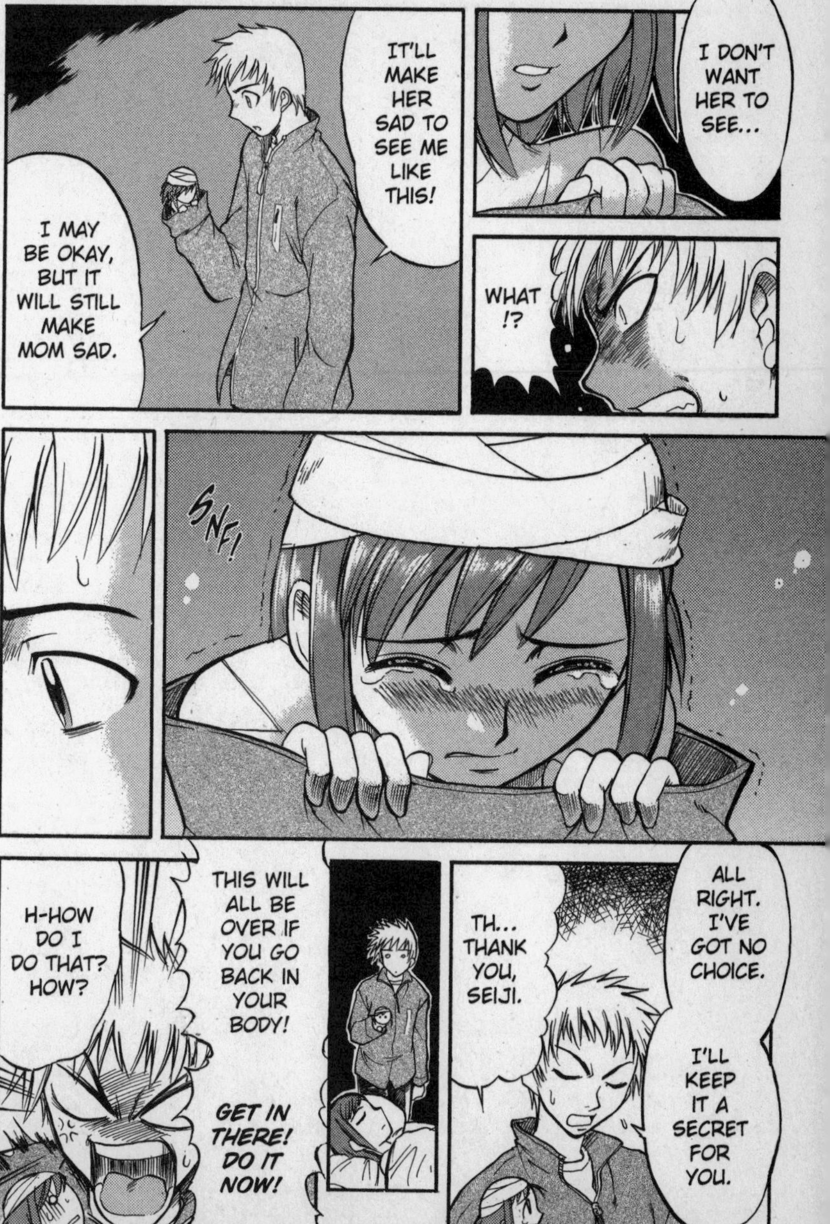
I DON'T WANT HER TO SEE...
WHAT !?
IT'LL MAKE HER SAD TO SEE ME LIKE THIS!
I MAY BE OKAY, BUT IT WILL STILL MAKE MOM SAD.
SNF!
ALL RIGHT. I'VE GOT NO CHOICE.
I'LL KEEP IT A SECRET FOR YOU.
TH... THANK YOU, SEIJI.
THIS WILL ALL BE OVER IF YOU GO BACK IN YOUR BODY!
H-HOW DO I DO THAT? HOW?
GET IN THERE! DO IT NOW!

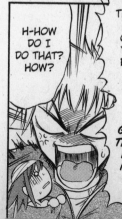

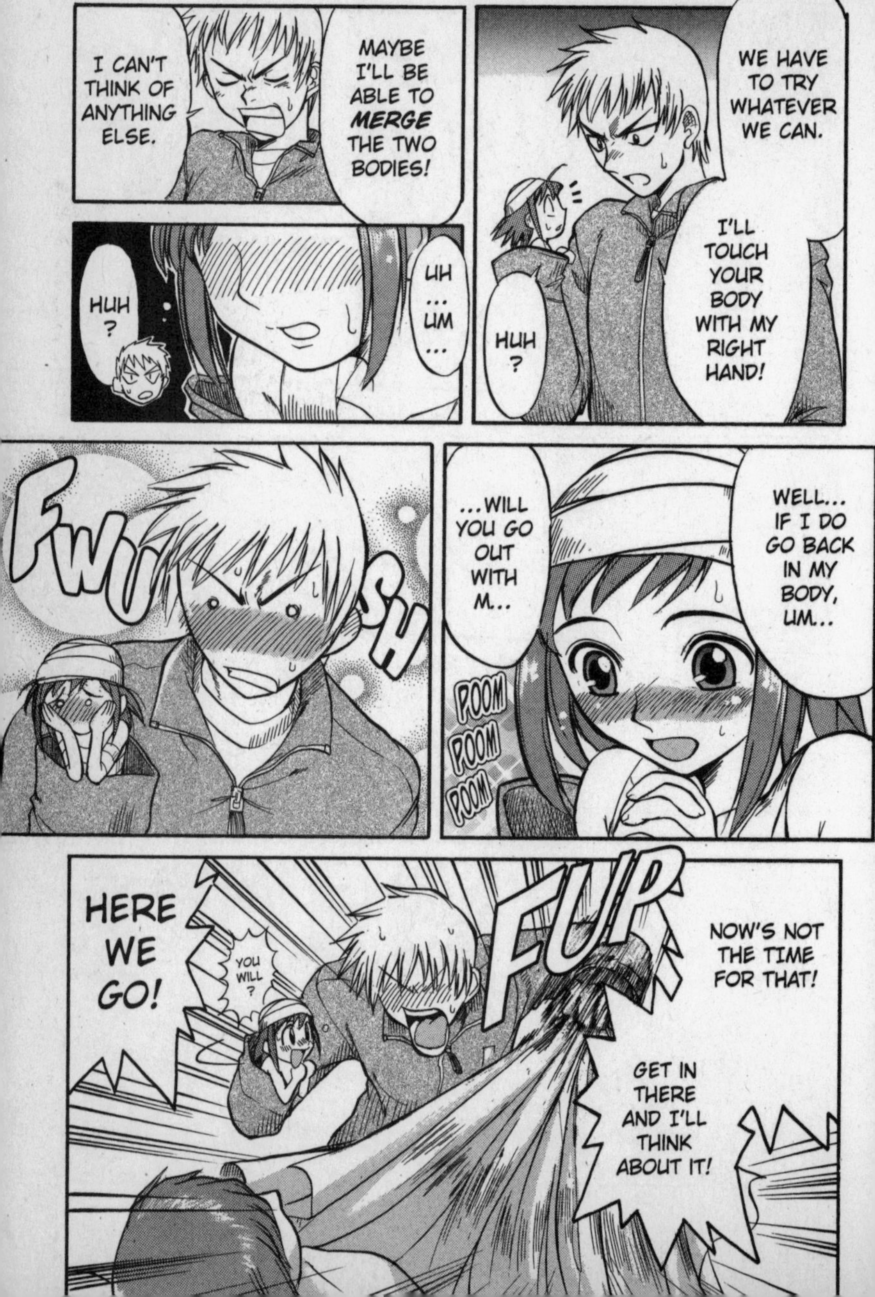
WE HAVE TO TRY WHATEVER WE CAN.
I'LL TOUCH YOUR BODY WITH MY RIGHT HAND!
HUH?
MAYBE I'LL BE ABLE TO **MERGE** THE TWO BODIES!
I CAN'T THINK OF ANYTHING ELSE.
UH... UM...
HUH?
WELL... IF I DO GO BACK IN MY BODY, UM...
...WILL YOU GO OUT WITH M...
POOM POOM POOM
FWUSH
NOW'S NOT THE TIME FOR THAT!
FUP
GET IN THERE AND I'LL THINK ABOUT IT!
YOU WILL?
HERE WE GO!

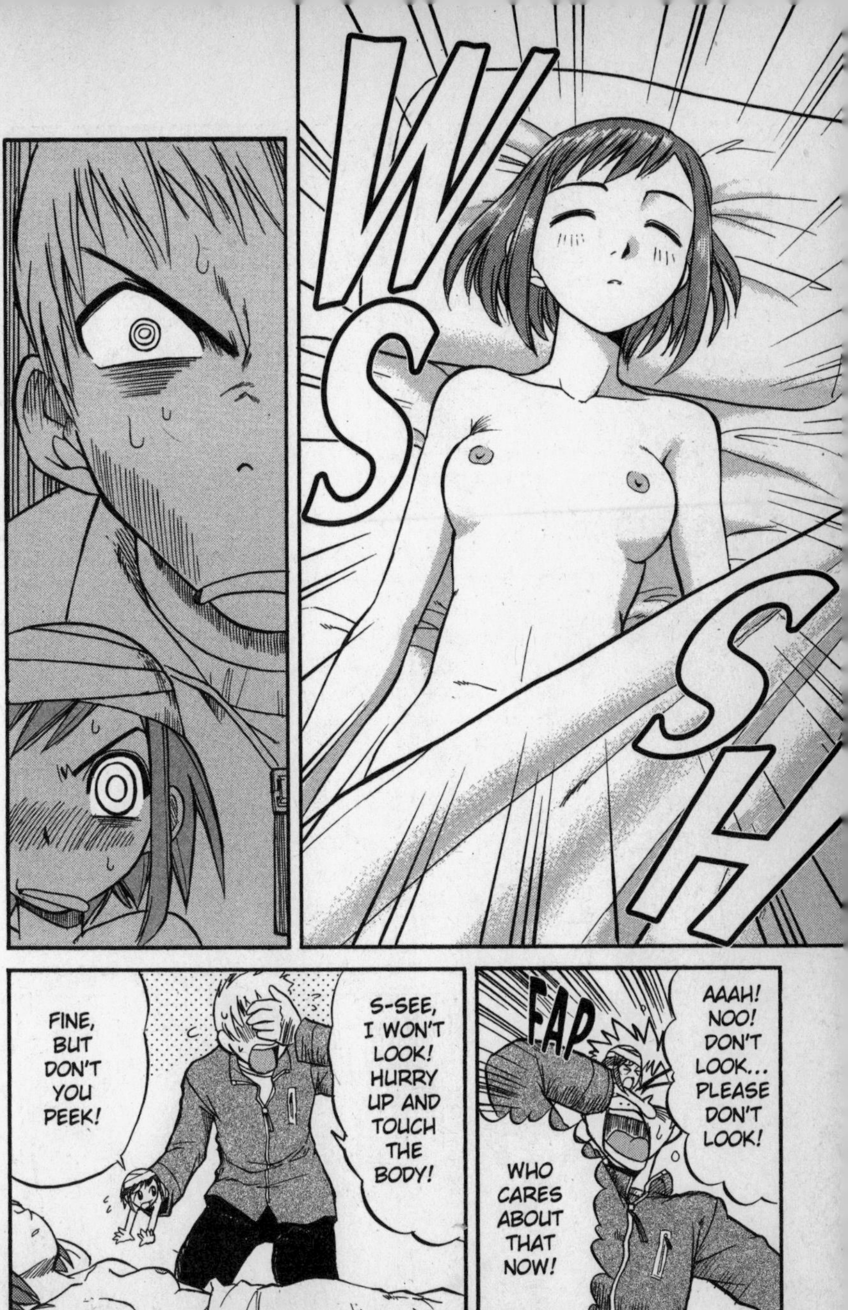

WSSH
AAAH! NOO! DON'T LOOK... PLEASE DON'T LOOK!
FAP
WHO CARES ABOUT THAT NOW!
S-SEE, I WON'T LOOK! HURRY UP AND TOUCH THE BODY!
FINE, BUT DON'T YOU PEEK!

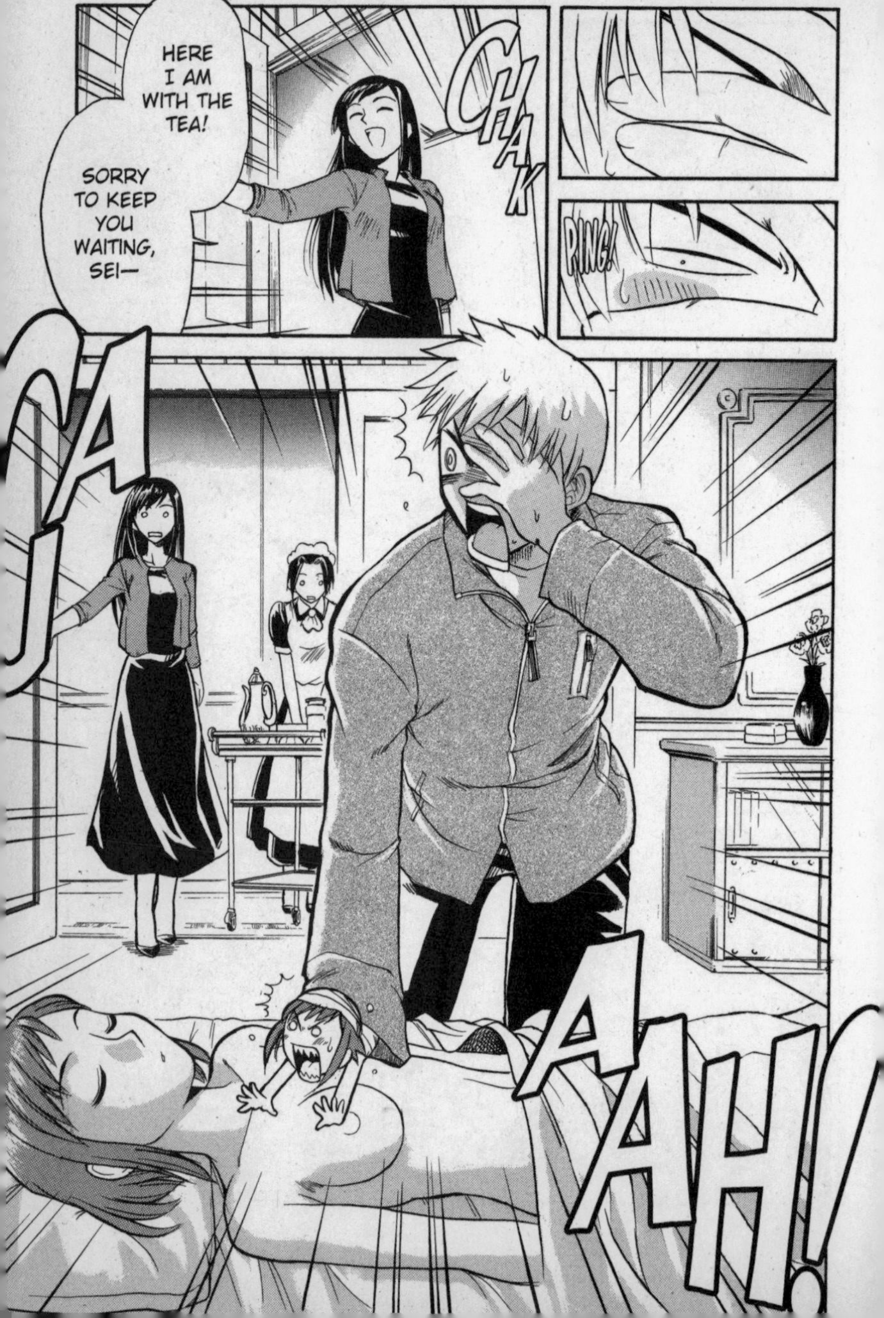
PING!
CHAK
HERE I AM WITH THE TEA!
SORRY TO KEEP YOU WAITING, SEI—
CA
AAH!!

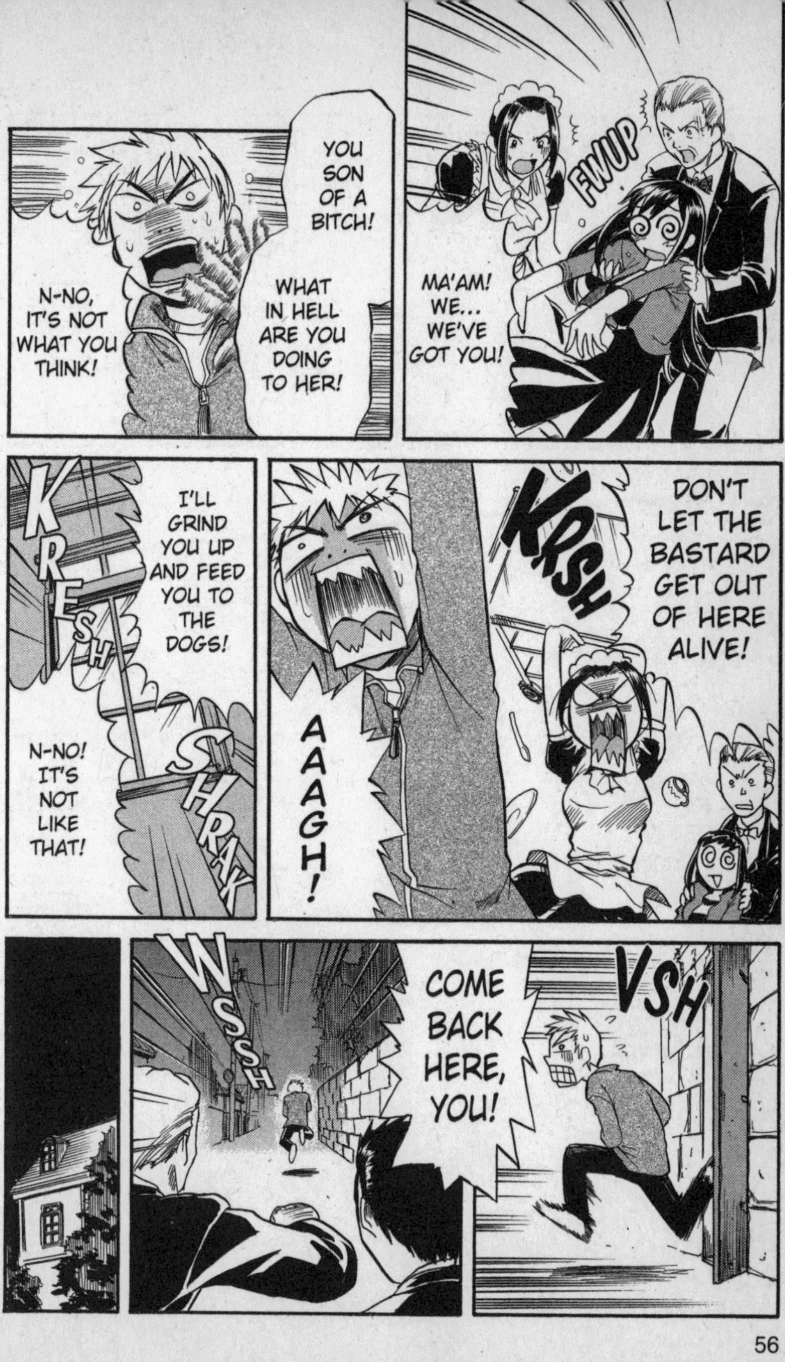
FWUP
MA'AM! WE... WE'VE GOT YOU!
YOU SON OF A BITCH!
WHAT IN HELL ARE YOU DOING TO HER!
N-NO, IT'S NOT WHAT YOU THINK!
KRSH
DON'T LET THE BASTARD GET OUT OF HERE ALIVE!
AAAGH!
KRESH
I'LL GRIND YOU UP AND FEED YOU TO THE DOGS!
SHRAK
N-NO! IT'S NOT LIKE THAT!
VSH
COME BACK HERE, YOU!
WSSSH

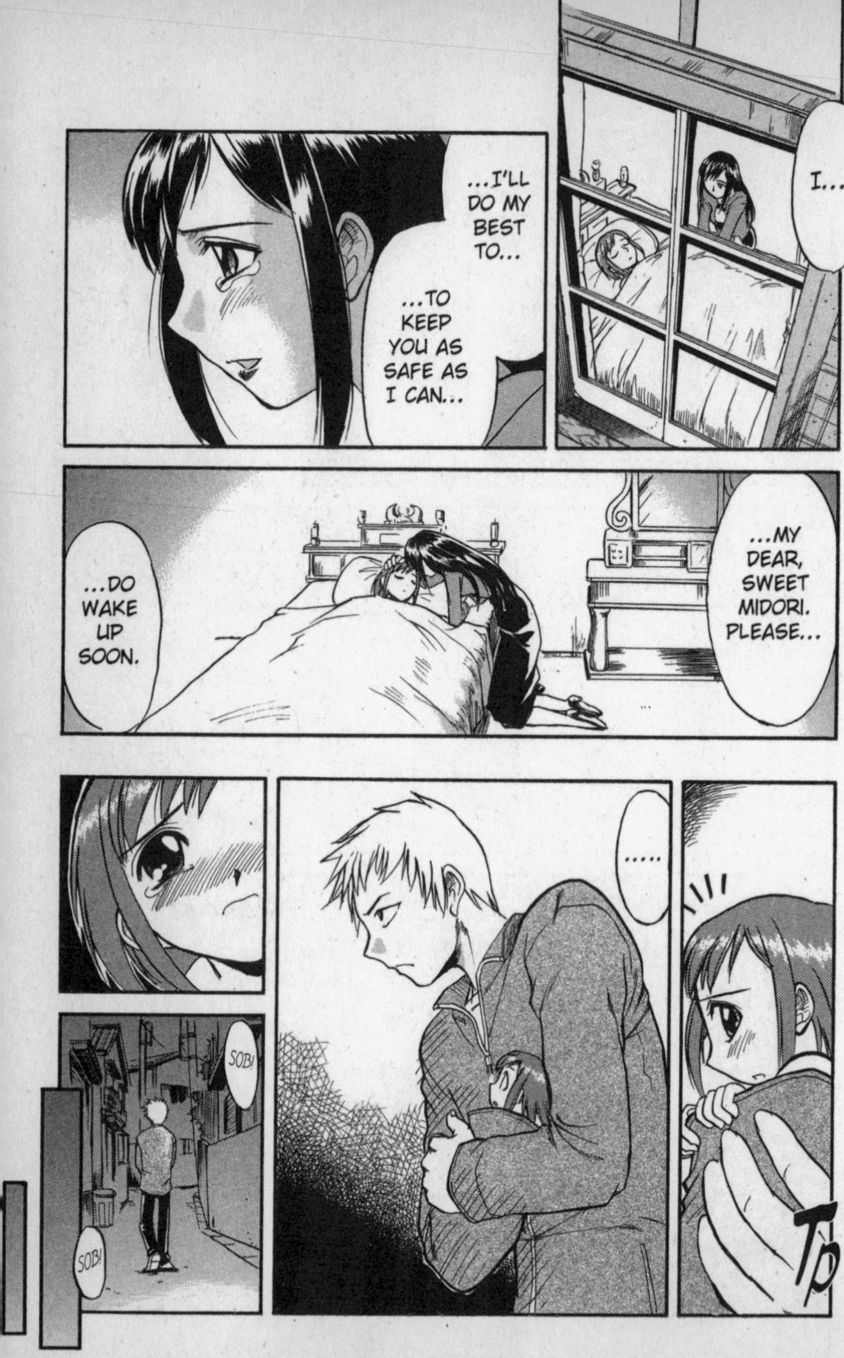

I...
...I'LL DO MY BEST TO...
...TO KEEP YOU AS SAFE AS I CAN...
...MY DEAR, SWEET MIDORI. PLEASE...
...
...DO WAKE UP SOON.
Tp
.....
SOB!
SOB!

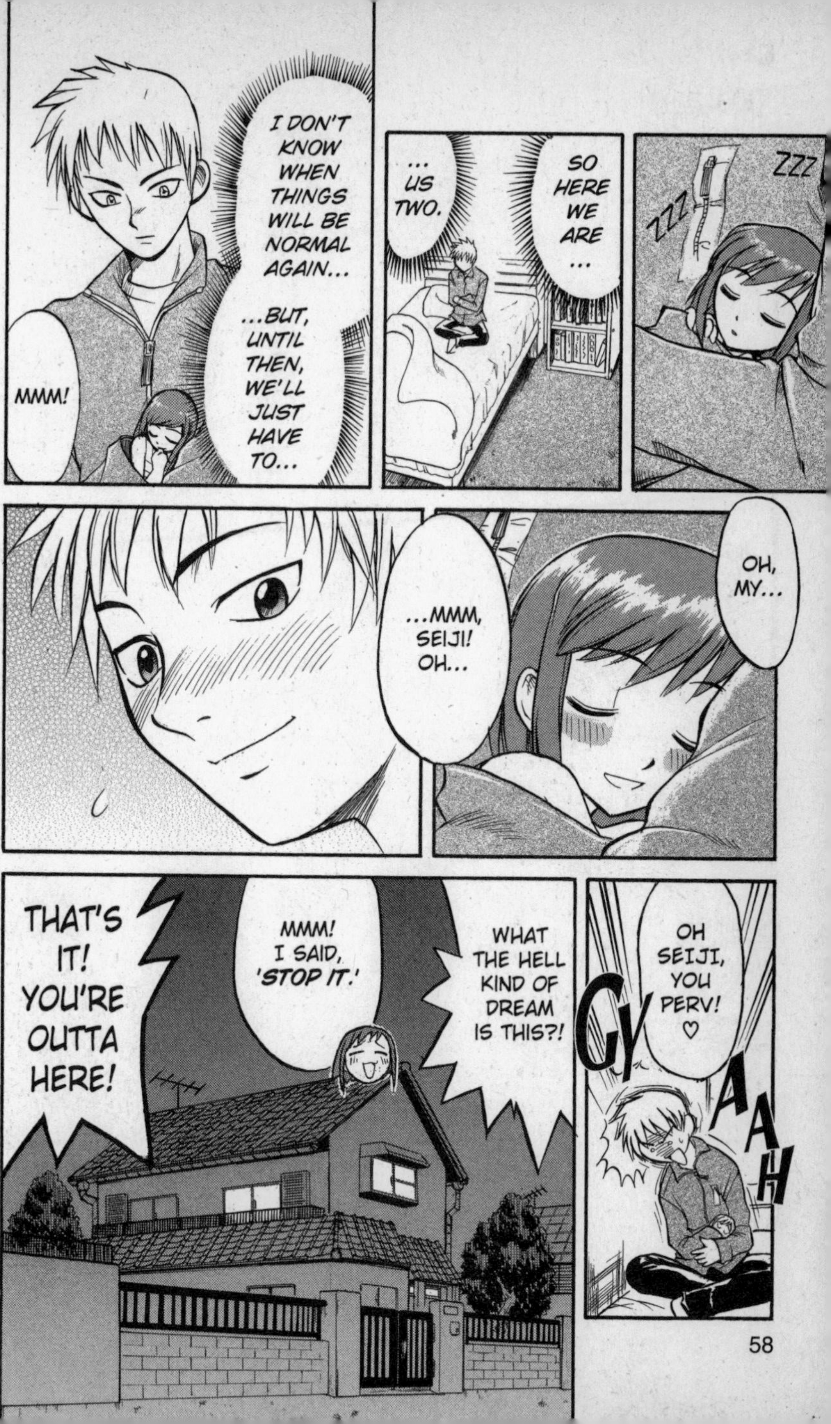
ZZZ
ZZZ
SO HERE WE ARE...
...US TWO.
I DON'T KNOW WHEN THINGS WILL BE NORMAL AGAIN...
...BUT, UNTIL THEN, WE'LL JUST HAVE TO...
MMM!
OH, MY...
...MMM, SEIJI! OH...
OH SEIJI, YOU PERV! ♡
GYAAAH
WHAT THE HELL KIND OF DREAM IS THIS?!
MMM! I SAID, 'STOP IT.'
THAT'S IT! YOU'RE OUTTA HERE!

DAY 3
THE LONELY MAD DOG

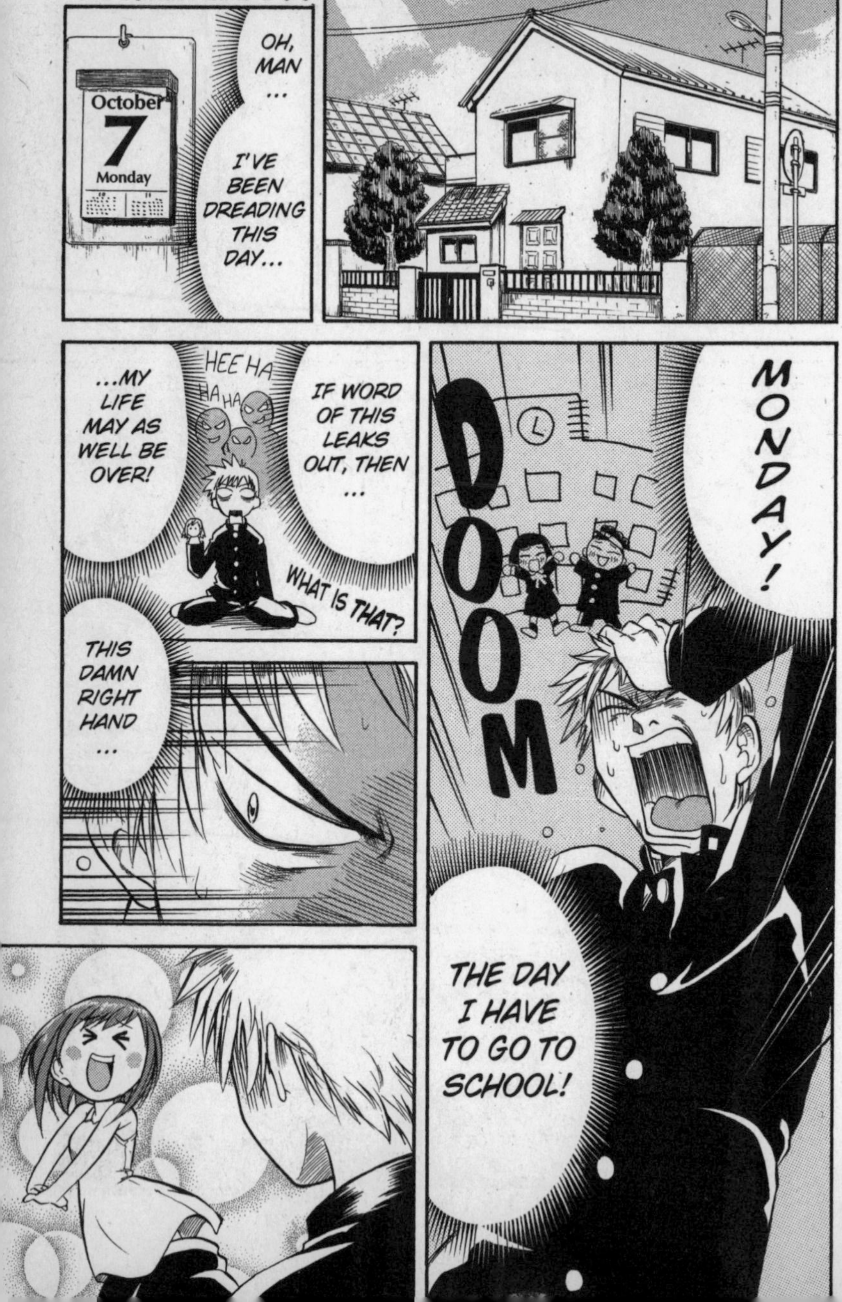
October
7
Monday
OH, MAN ...
I'VE BEEN DREADING THIS DAY...
MONDAY!
DOOM
THE DAY I HAVE TO GO TO SCHOOL!
IF WORD OF THIS LEAKS OUT, THEN ...
HEE HA HA HA
...MY LIFE MAY AS WELL BE OVER!
WHAT IS THAT?
THIS DAMN RIGHT HAND ...

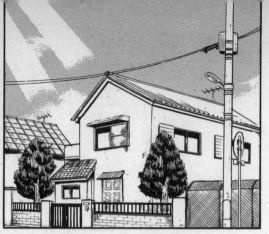

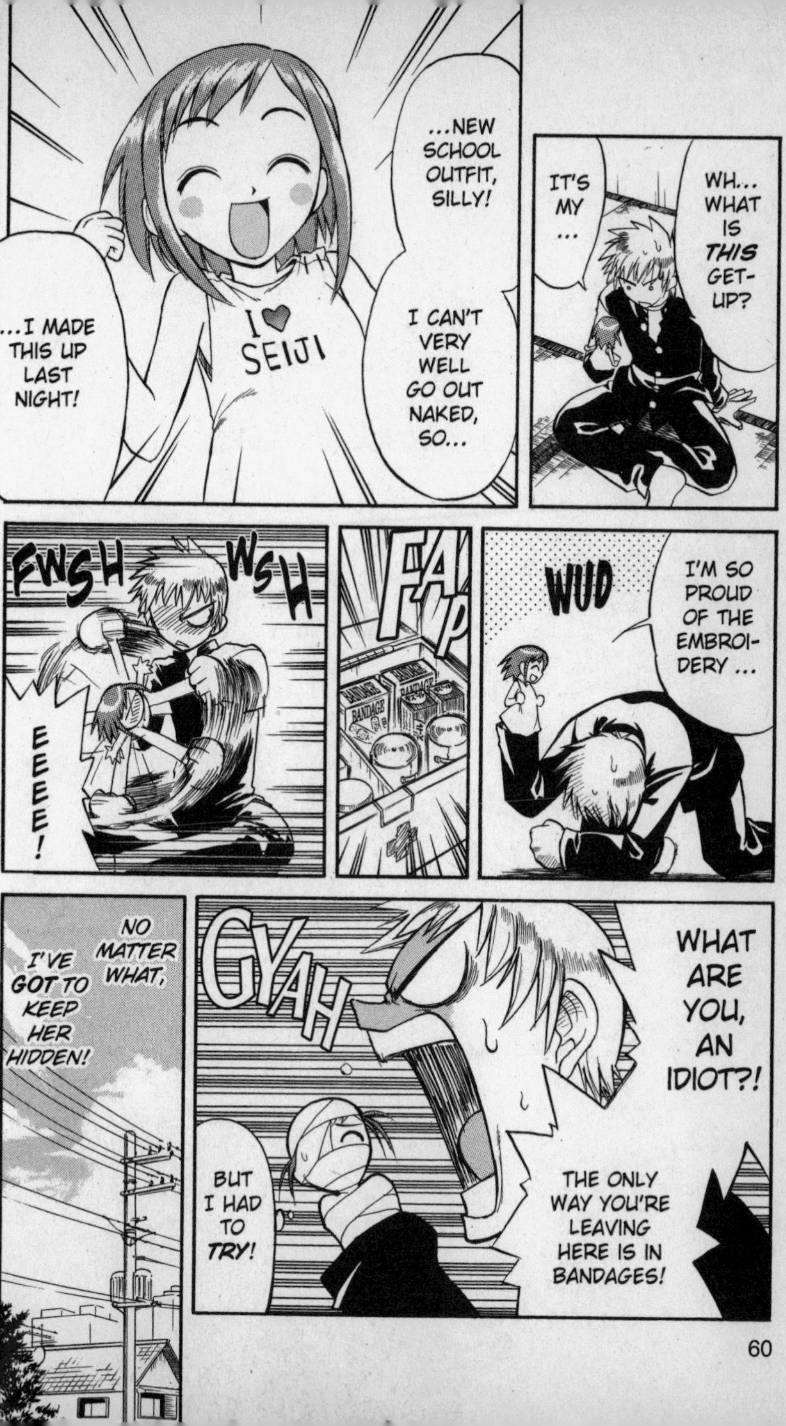
WH... WHAT IS *THIS* GET-UP?
IT'S MY ...
...NEW SCHOOL OUTFIT, SILLY!
I CAN'T VERY WELL GO OUT NAKED, SO...
...I MADE THIS UP LAST NIGHT!
I ♥ SEIJI
WUD
I'M SO PROUD OF THE EMBROIDERY ...
FAP
FWSH
WSH
EEEE!
GYAH
WHAT ARE YOU, AN IDIOT?!
THE ONLY WAY YOU'RE LEAVING HERE IS IN BANDAGES!
BUT I HAD TO *TRY*!
NO MATTER WHAT, I'VE *GOT* TO KEEP HER HIDDEN!

DAY 3
THE LONELY MAD DOG

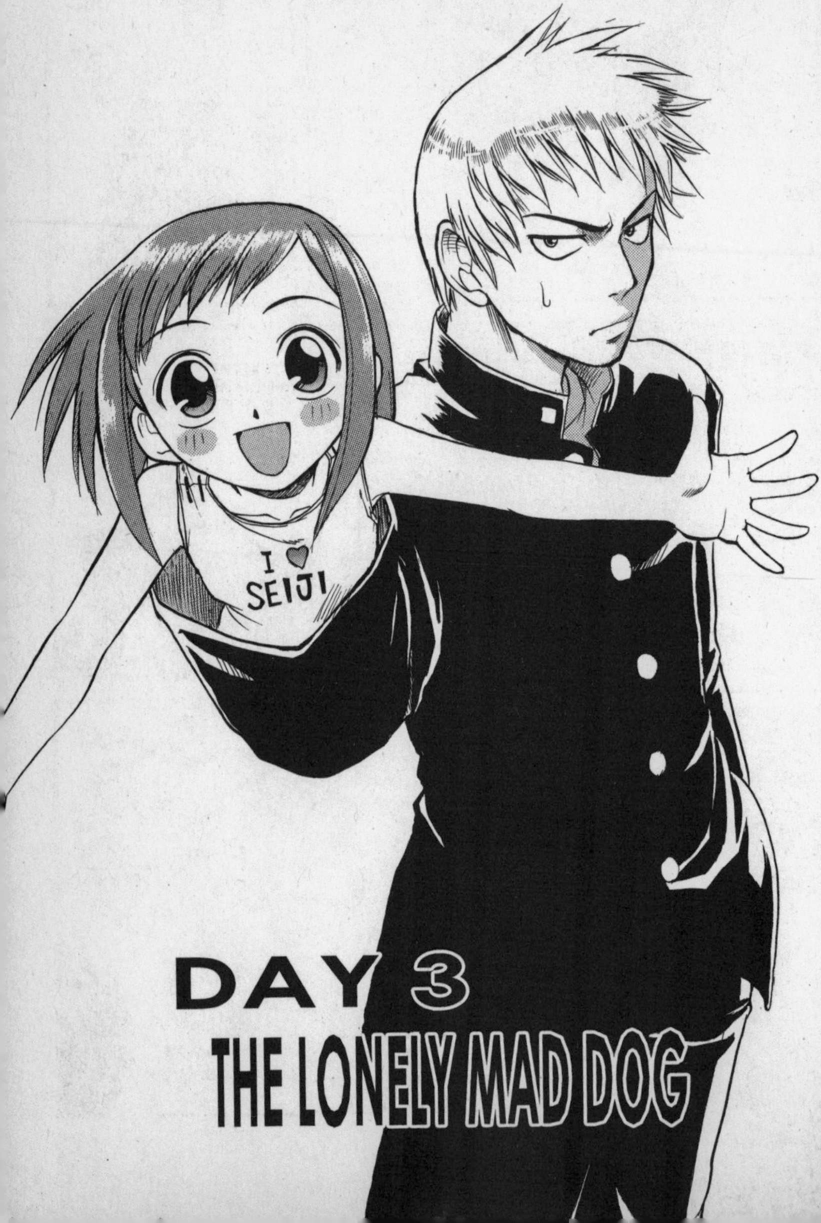
I ♥ SEIJI

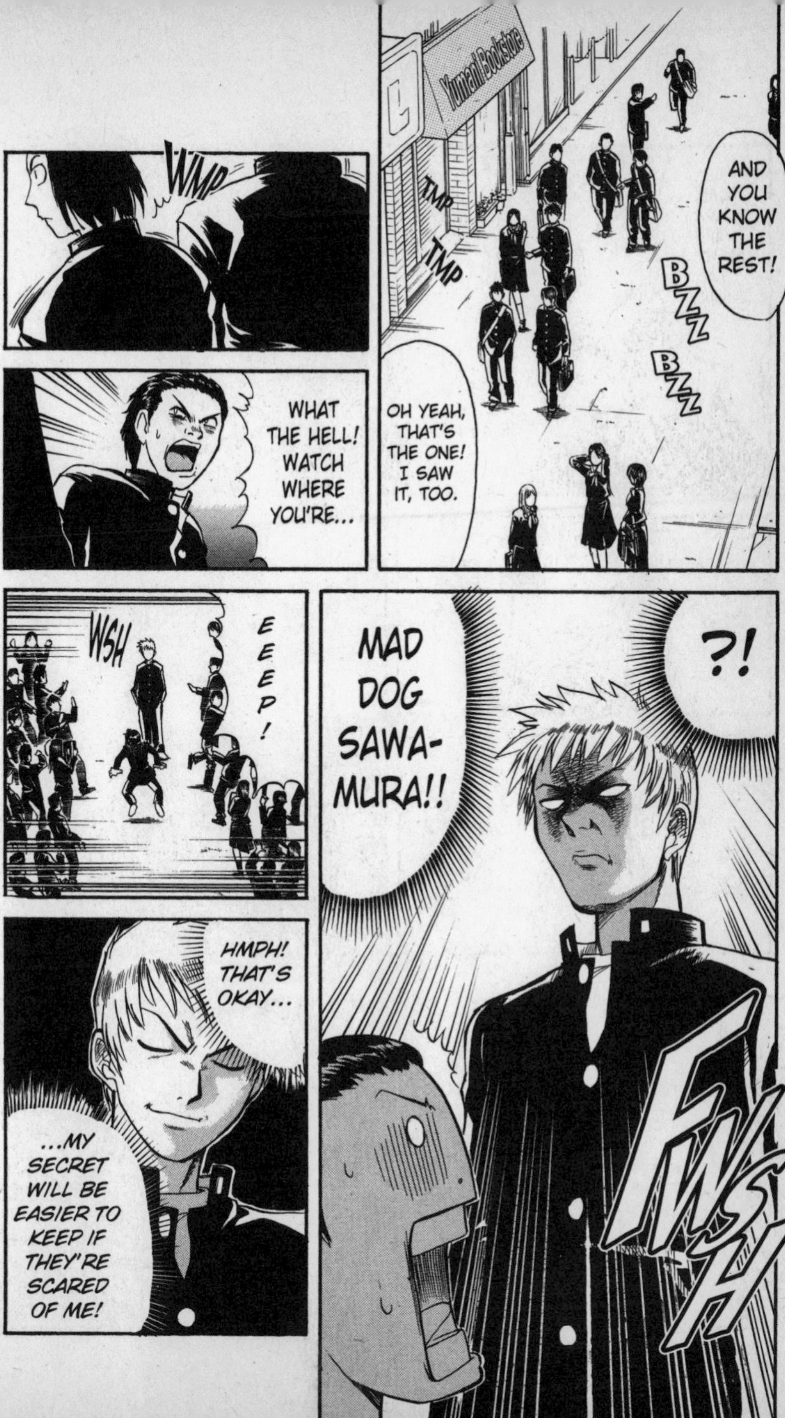
AND YOU KNOW THE REST!
Yumani Bookstore
TMP
TMP
BZZ
BZZ
OH YEAH, THAT'S THE ONE! I SAW IT, TOO.
WMP
WHAT THE HELL! WATCH WHERE YOU'RE...
?!
MAD DOG SAWA-MURA!!
FWSH
WSH
EEEEP!
HMPH! THAT'S OKAY...
...MY SECRET WILL BE EASIER TO KEEP IF THEY'RE SCARED OF ME!

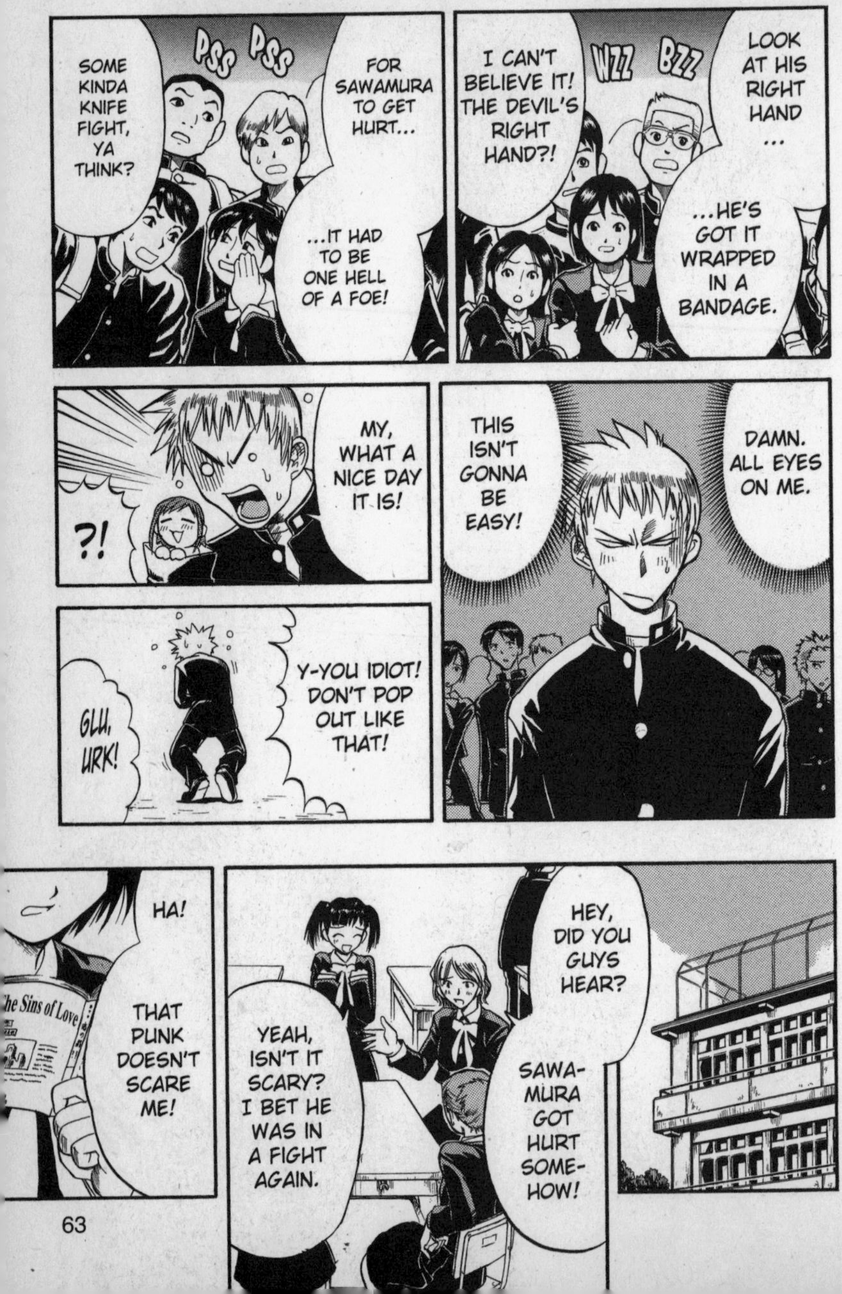
LOOK AT HIS RIGHT HAND ...
WZZ BZZ
I CAN'T BELIEVE IT! THE DEVIL'S RIGHT HAND?!
...HE'S GOT IT WRAPPED IN A BANDAGE.
FOR SAWAMURA TO GET HURT...
PSS PSS
SOME KINDA KNIFE FIGHT, YA THINK?
...IT HAD TO BE ONE HELL OF A FOE!
DAMN. ALL EYES ON ME.
THIS ISN'T GONNA BE EASY!
MY, WHAT A NICE DAY IT IS!
?!
Y-YOU IDIOT! DON'T POP OUT LIKE THAT!
GLU, URK!
HEY, DID YOU GUYS HEAR?
SAWAMURA GOT HURT SOMEHOW!
YEAH, ISN'T IT SCARY? I BET HE WAS IN A FIGHT AGAIN.
HA!
THAT PUNK DOESN'T SCARE ME!
The Sins of Love

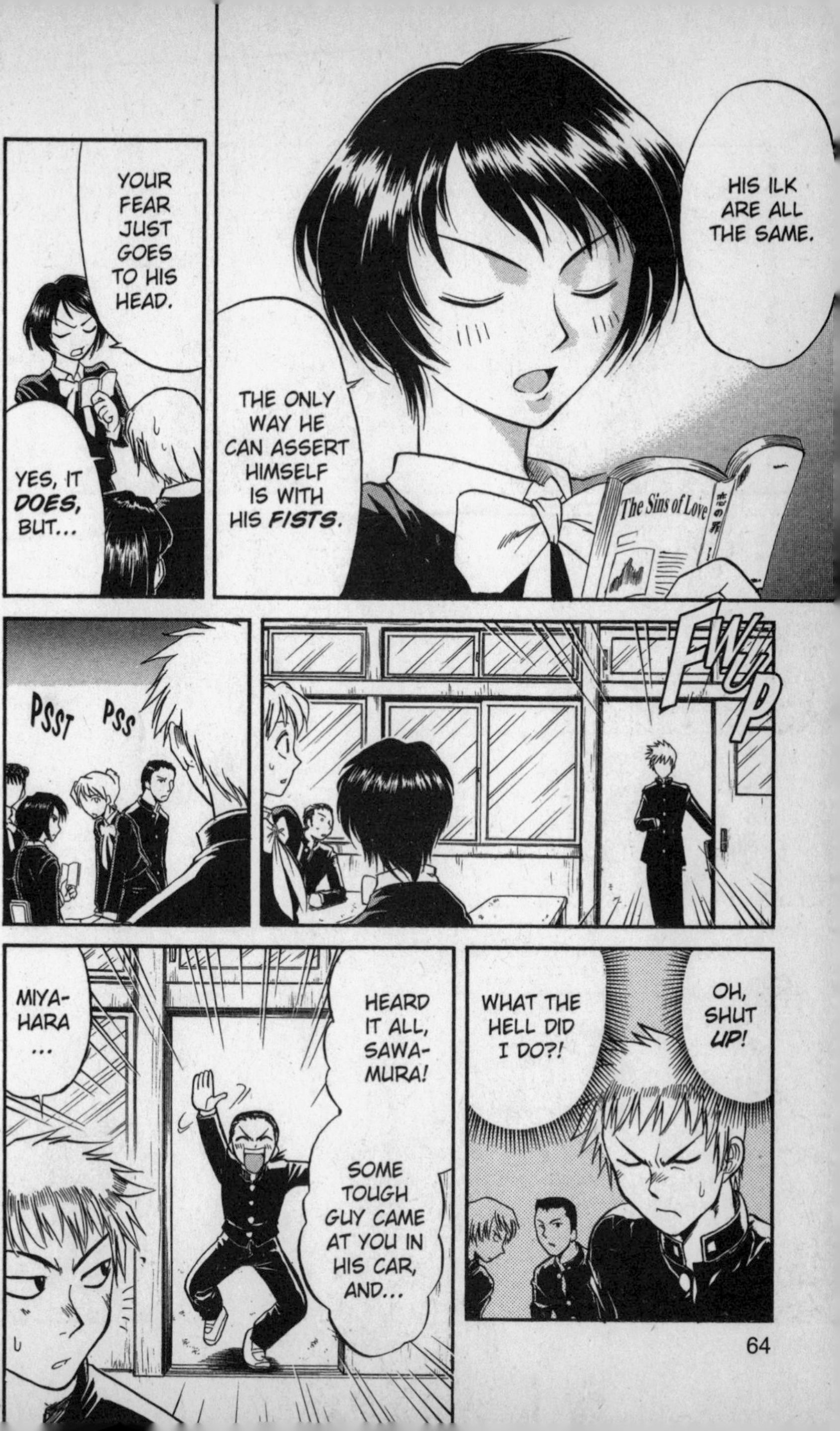
HIS ILK ARE ALL THE SAME.
THE ONLY WAY HE CAN ASSERT HIMSELF IS WITH HIS *FISTS*.
The Sins of Love 恋の罪
YOUR FEAR JUST GOES TO HIS HEAD.
YES, IT *DOES*, BUT...
FWUP
PSST PSS
OH, SHUT *UP*!
WHAT THE HELL DID I DO?!
HEARD IT ALL, SAWAMURA!
SOME TOUGH GUY CAME AT YOU IN HIS CAR, AND...
MIYAHARA ...

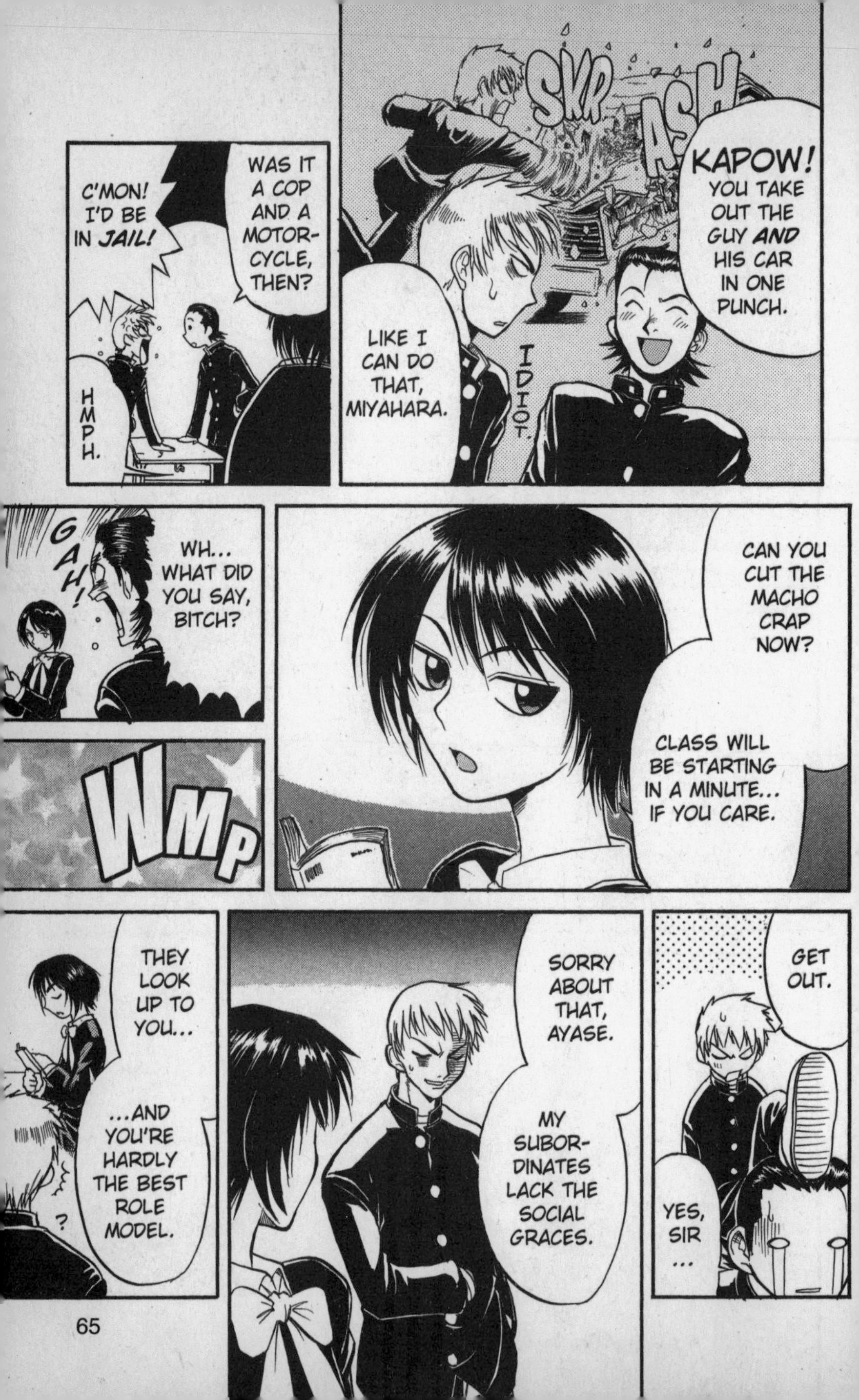
SKRASH
KAPOW! YOU TAKE OUT THE GUY AND HIS CAR IN ONE PUNCH.
LIKE I CAN DO THAT, MIYAHARA.
IDIOT.
WAS IT A COP AND A MOTORCYCLE, THEN?
C'MON! I'D BE IN JAIL!
HMPH.
CAN YOU CUT THE MACHO CRAP NOW?
CLASS WILL BE STARTING IN A MINUTE... IF YOU CARE.
GAH!
WH... WHAT DID YOU SAY, BITCH?
WMP
GET OUT.
YES, SIR...
SORRY ABOUT THAT, AYASE.
MY SUBORDINATES LACK THE SOCIAL GRACES.
THEY LOOK UP TO YOU...
...AND YOU'RE HARDLY THE BEST ROLE MODEL.
?

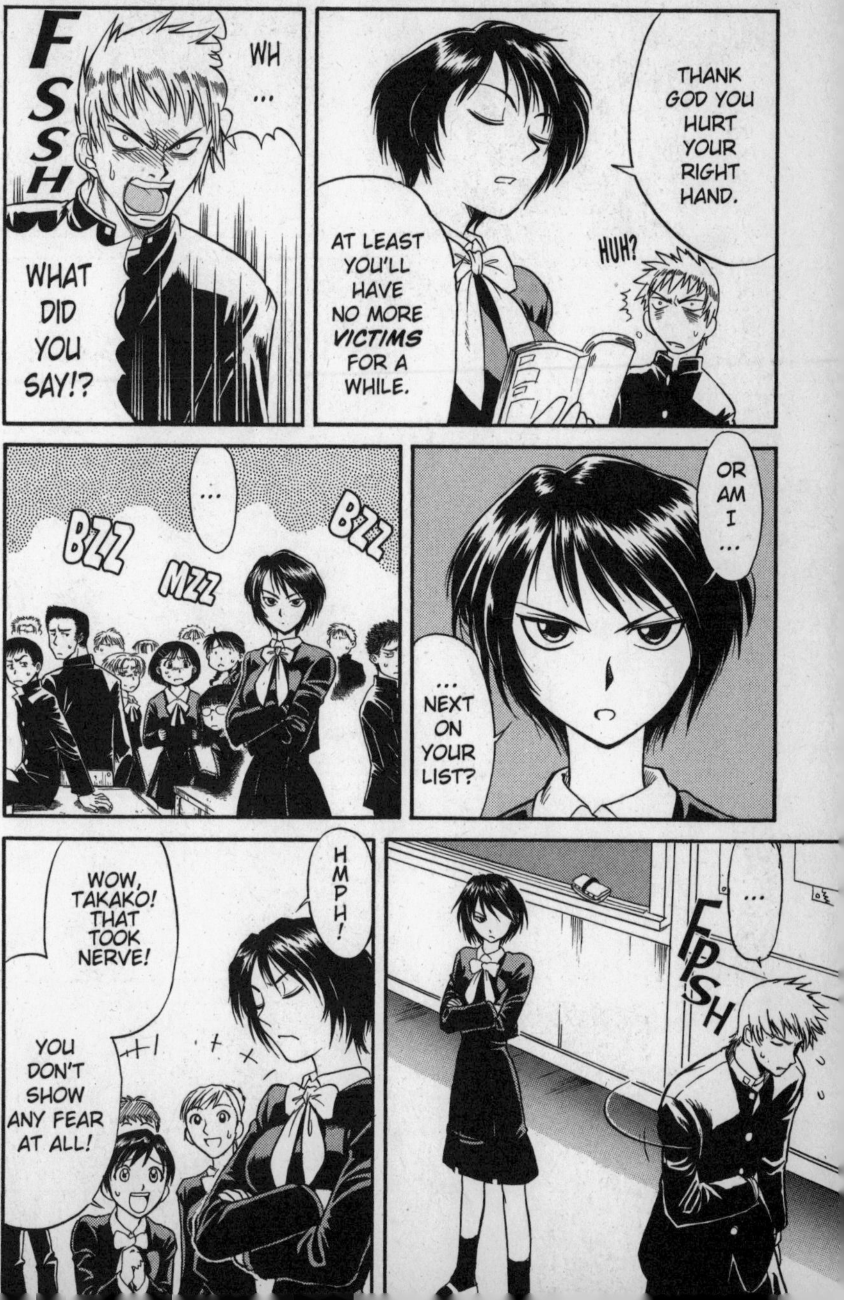
THANK GOD YOU HURT YOUR RIGHT HAND.
HUH?
AT LEAST YOU'LL HAVE NO MORE *VICTIMS* FOR A WHILE.
WH ...
FSSH
WHAT DID YOU SAY!?
OR AM I ...
... NEXT ON YOUR LIST?
...
BZZ
BZZ
MZZ
...
FPSH
HMPH!
WOW, TAKAKO! THAT TOOK NERVE!
YOU DON'T SHOW ANY FEAR AT ALL!

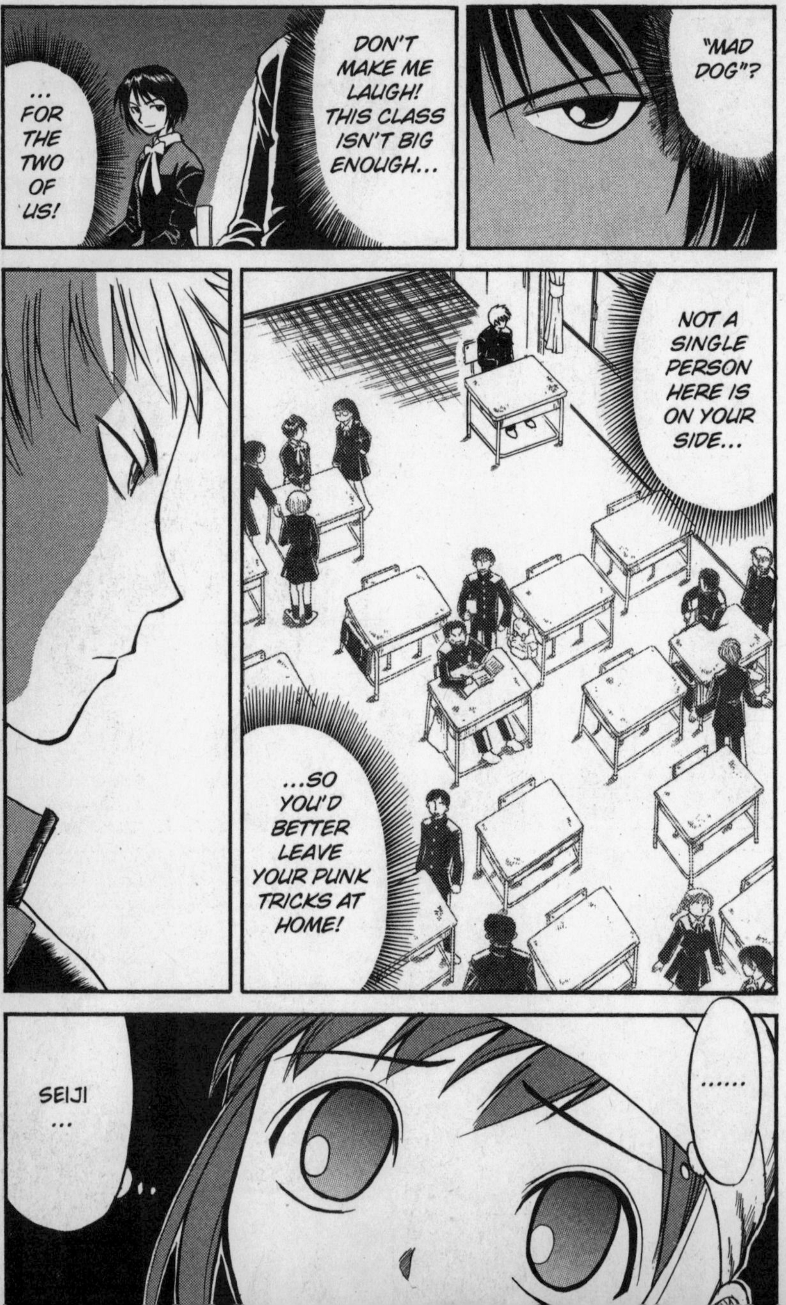
"MAD DOG"?
DON'T MAKE ME LAUGH! THIS CLASS ISN'T BIG ENOUGH...
...FOR THE TWO OF US!
NOT A SINGLE PERSON HERE IS ON YOUR SIDE...
...SO YOU'D BETTER LEAVE YOUR PUNK TRICKS AT HOME!
......
SEIJI ...

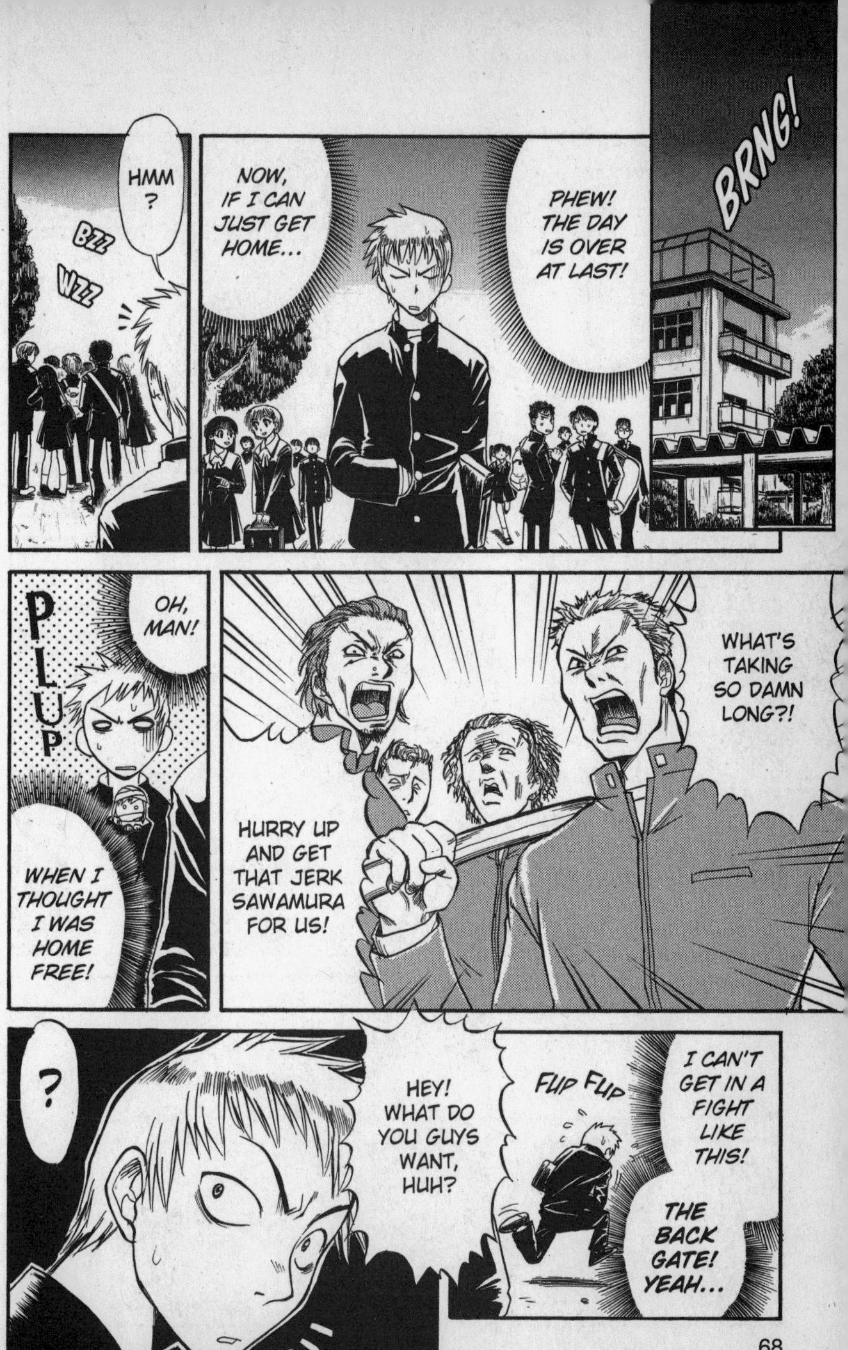
BRNG!
PHEW! THE DAY IS OVER AT LAST!
NOW, IF I CAN JUST GET HOME...
HMM?
BZZ
WZZ
WHAT'S TAKING SO DAMN LONG?!
HURRY UP AND GET THAT JERK SAWAMURA FOR US!
OH, MAN!
PLUP
WHEN I THOUGHT I WAS HOME FREE!
I CAN'T GET IN A FIGHT LIKE THIS!
THE BACK GATE! YEAH...
FUP FUP
HEY! WHAT DO YOU GUYS WANT, HUH?
?

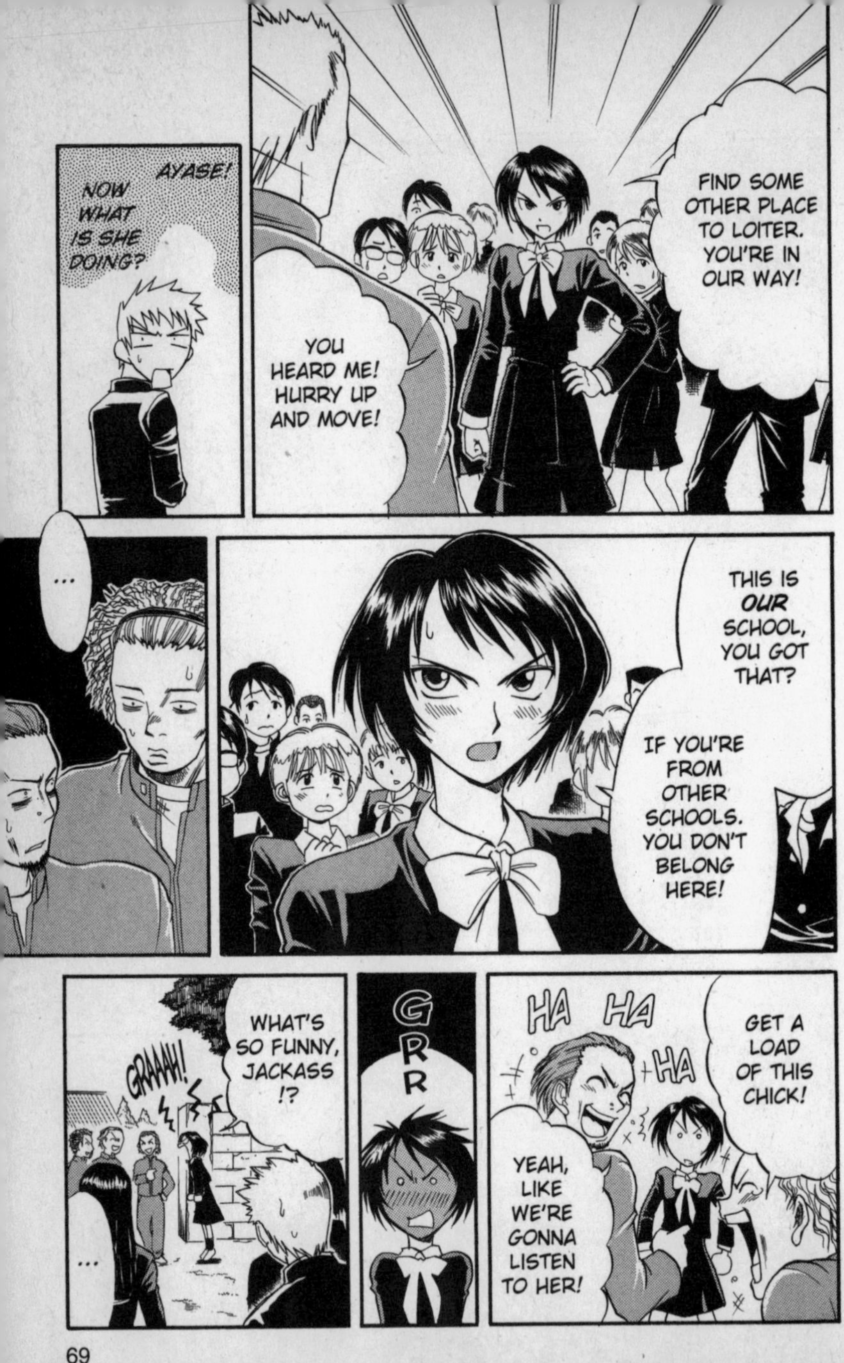
FIND SOME OTHER PLACE TO LOITER. YOU'RE IN OUR WAY!
YOU HEARD ME! HURRY UP AND MOVE!
AYASE!
NOW WHAT IS SHE DOING?
THIS IS **OUR** SCHOOL, YOU GOT THAT?
IF YOU'RE FROM OTHER SCHOOLS. YOU DON'T BELONG HERE!
...
GET A LOAD OF THIS CHICK!
HA HA HA
YEAH, LIKE WE'RE GONNA LISTEN TO HER!
GRR
WHAT'S SO FUNNY, JACKASS!?
GRAAAH!
...

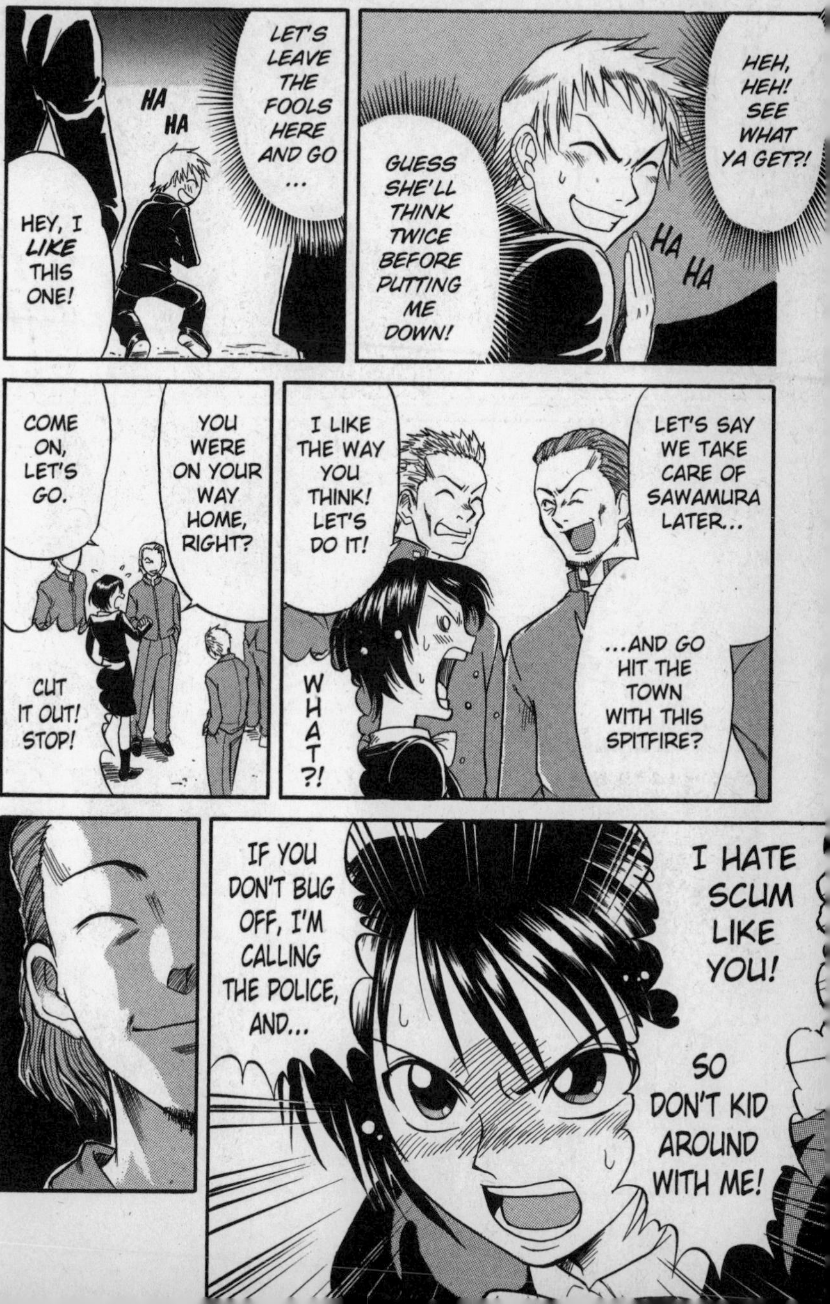
HEH, HEH! SEE WHAT YA GET?!
HA HA
GUESS SHE'LL THINK TWICE BEFORE PUTTING ME DOWN!
LET'S LEAVE THE FOOLS HERE AND GO ...
HA HA
HEY, I *LIKE* THIS ONE!
LET'S SAY WE TAKE CARE OF SAWAMURA LATER...
...AND GO HIT THE TOWN WITH THIS SPITFIRE?
I LIKE THE WAY YOU THINK! LET'S DO IT!
WHAT?!
YOU WERE ON YOUR WAY HOME, RIGHT?
COME ON, LET'S GO.
CUT IT OUT! STOP!
I HATE SCUM LIKE YOU!
IF YOU DON'T BUG OFF, I'M CALLING THE POLICE, AND...
SO DON'T KID AROUND WITH ME!

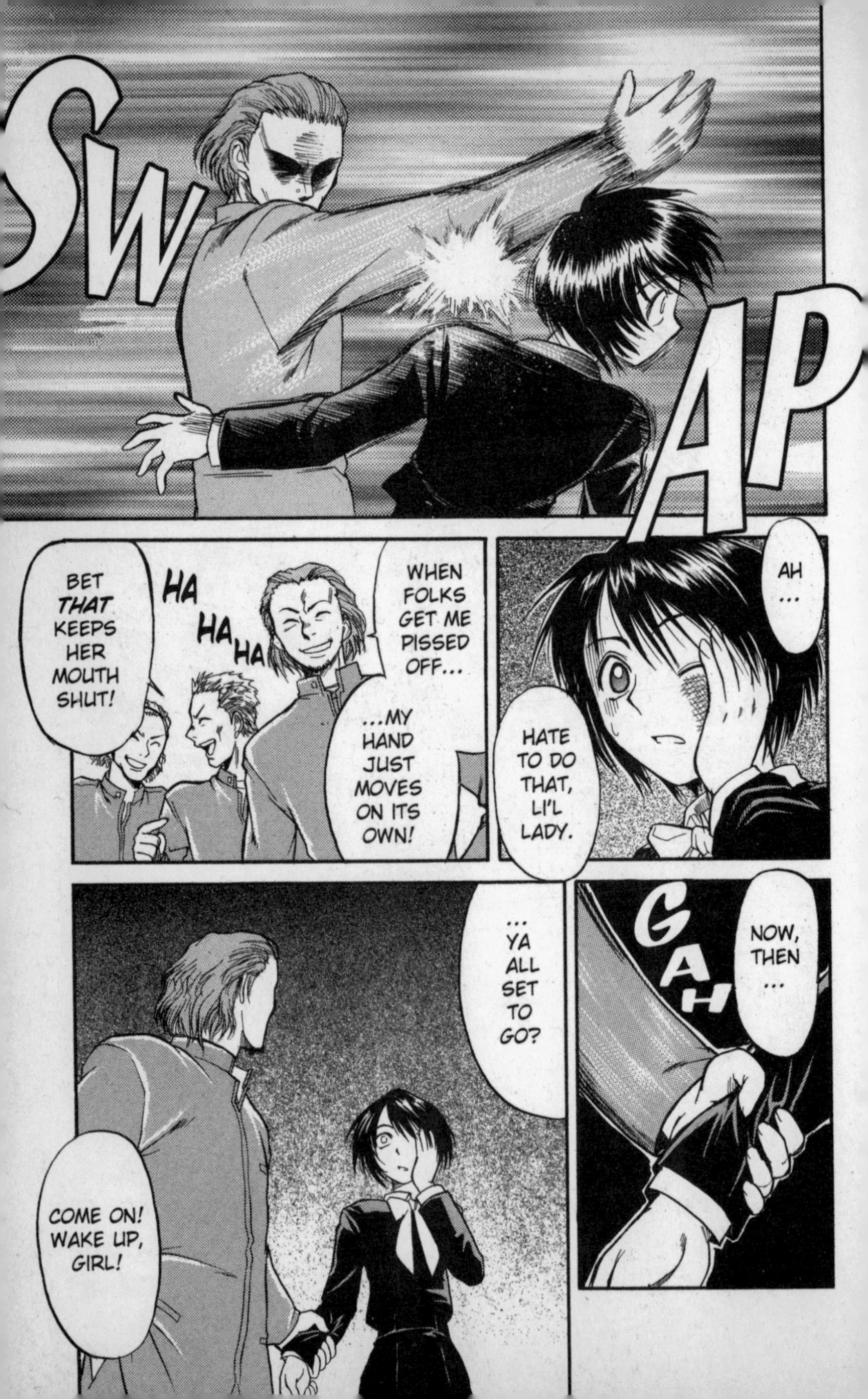
SW
AP
AH ...
HATE TO DO THAT, LI'L LADY.
WHEN FOLKS GET ME PISSED OFF...
...MY HAND JUST MOVES ON ITS OWN!
HA HA HA
BET THAT KEEPS HER MOUTH SHUT!
GAH
NOW, THEN ...
... YA ALL SET TO GO?
COME ON! WAKE UP, GIRL!

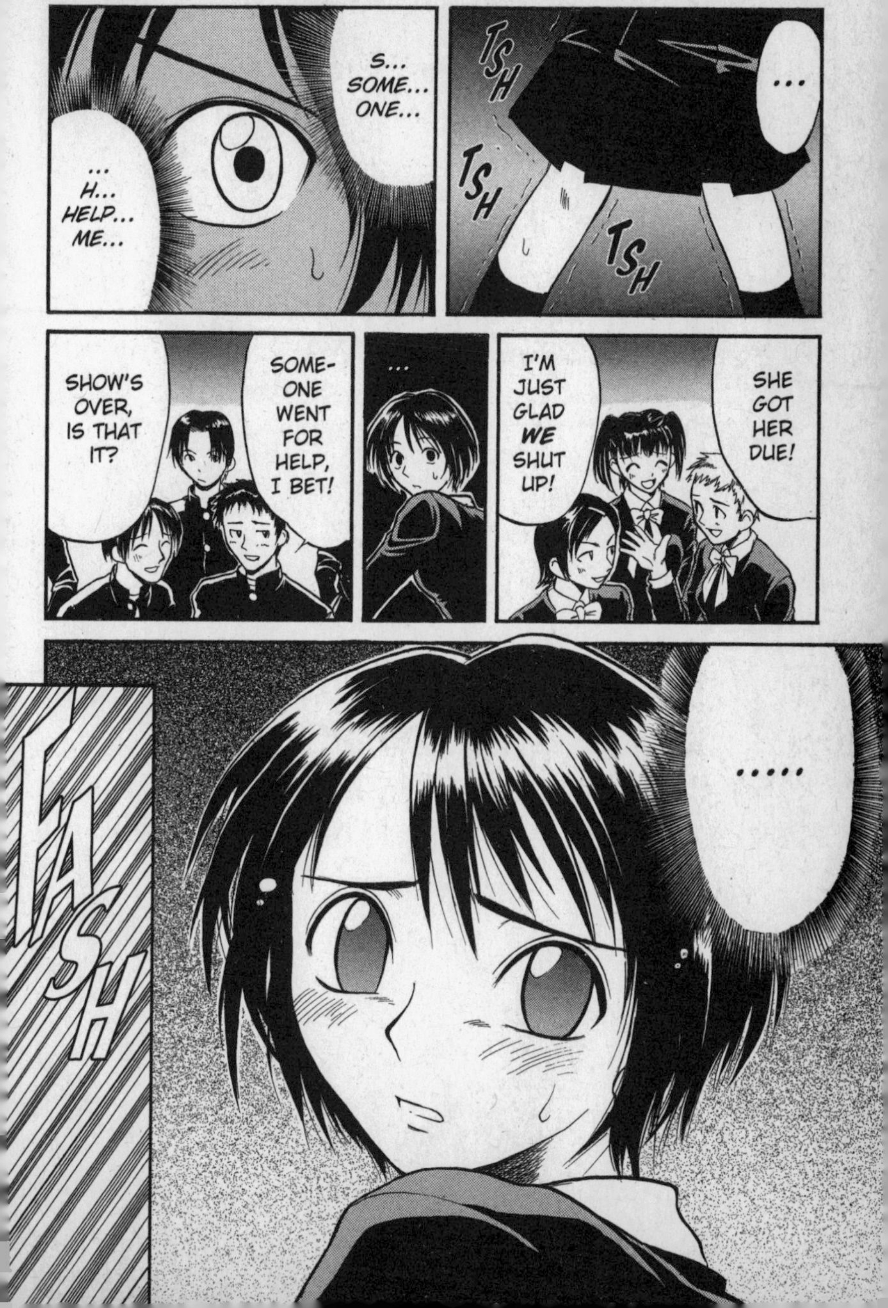
...
TSH
TSH
TSH
S... SOME... ONE...
... H... HELP... ME...
SHE GOT HER DUE!
I'M JUST GLAD **WE** SHUT UP!
...
SOME-ONE WENT FOR HELP, I BET!
SHOW'S OVER, IS THAT IT?
.....
FASH

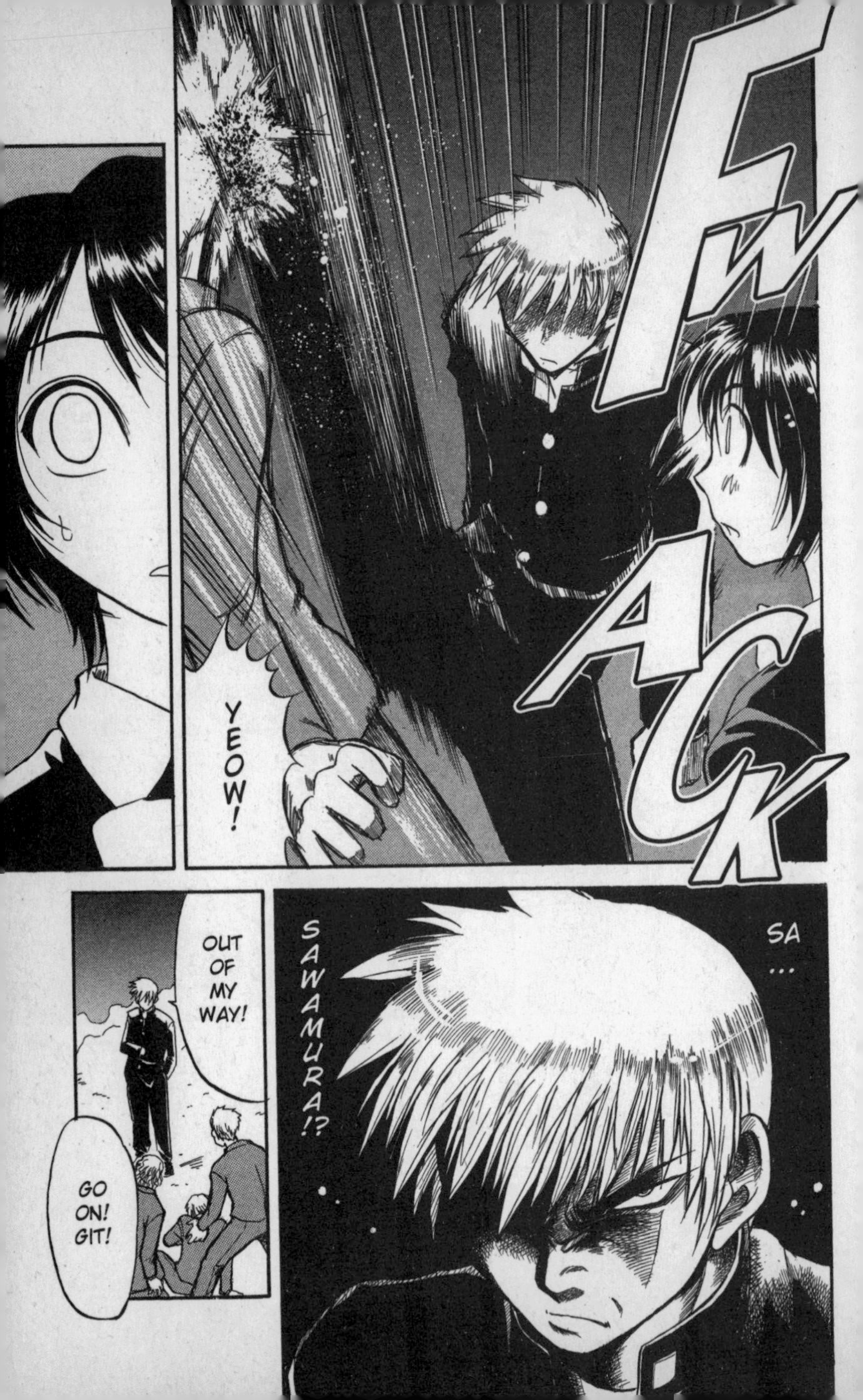
FWACK
YEOW!
SA...
SAWAMURA!?
OUT OF MY WAY!
GO ON! GIT!

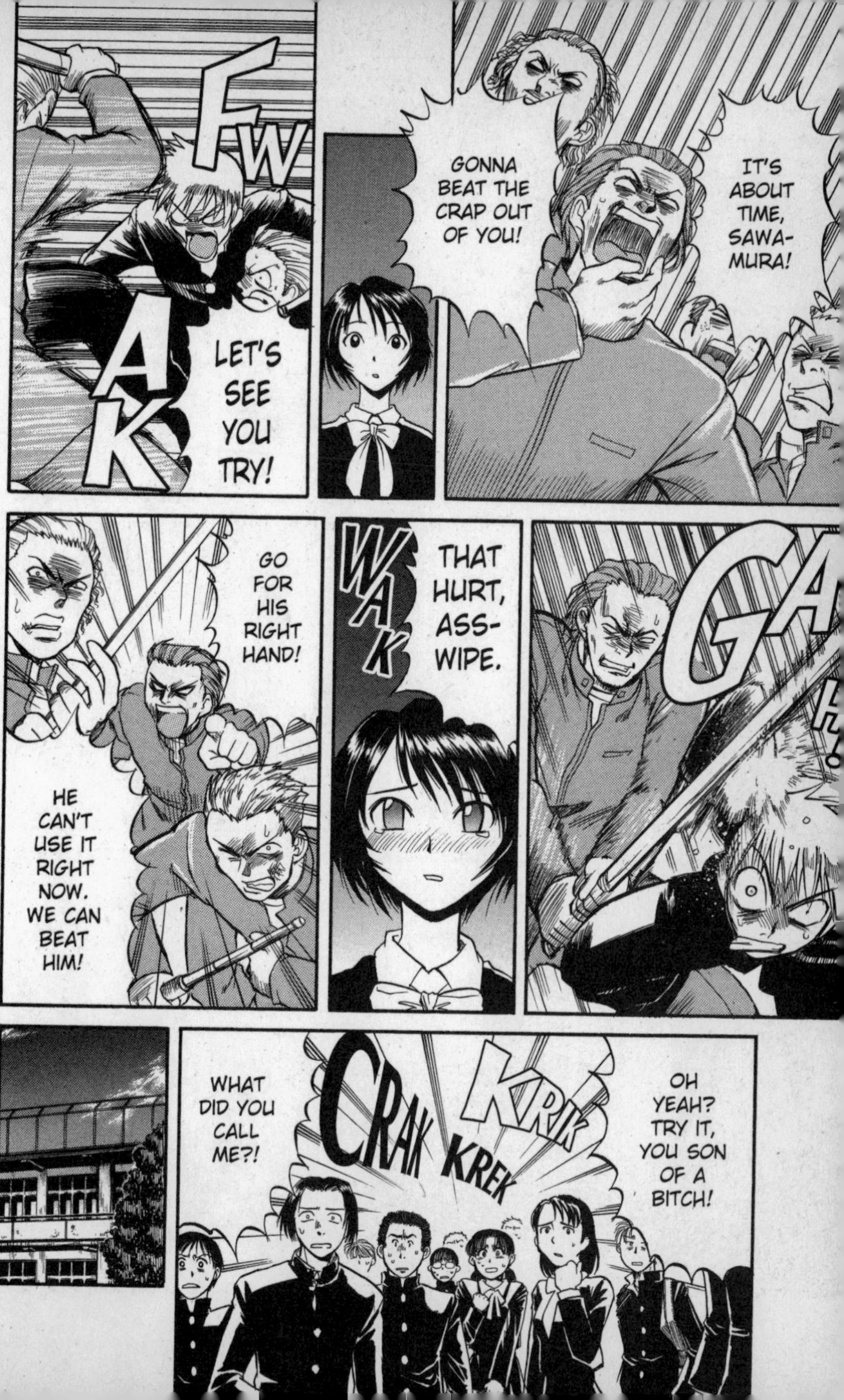
IT'S ABOUT TIME, SAWAMURA!
GONNA BEAT THE CRAP OUT OF YOU!
FWAK
LET'S SEE YOU TRY!
GA
WAK
THAT HURT, ASS-WIPE.
GO FOR HIS RIGHT HAND!
HE CAN'T USE IT RIGHT NOW. WE CAN BEAT HIM!
OH YEAH? TRY IT, YOU SON OF A BITCH!
KRIK
CRAK
KREK
WHAT DID YOU CALL ME?!

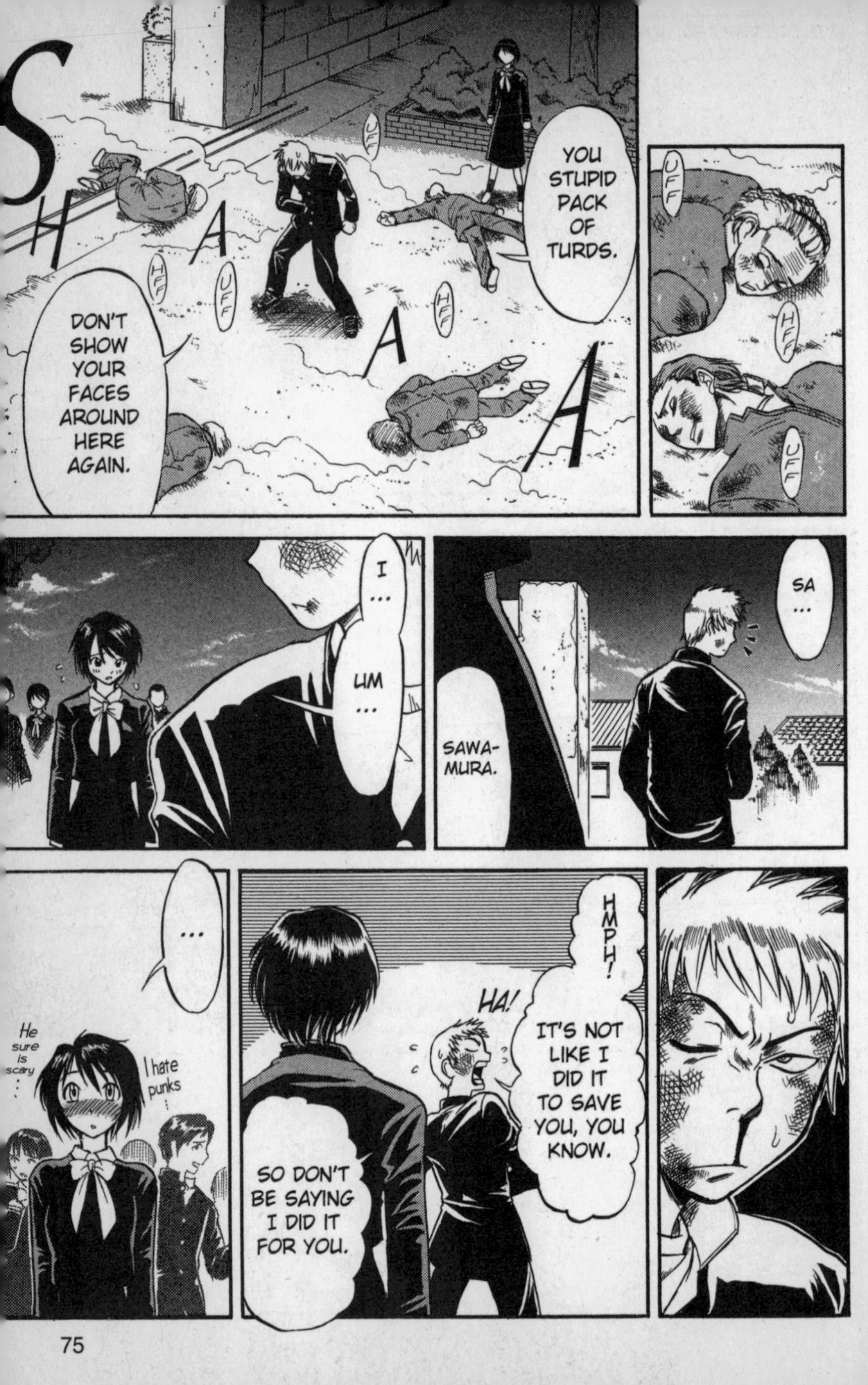
UFF
HFF
UFF
UFF
YOU STUPID PACK OF TURDS.
SHAAAA
HFF
UFF
HFF
DON'T SHOW YOUR FACES AROUND HERE AGAIN.
SA...
SAWAMURA.
I...
UM...
HMPH!
IT'S NOT LIKE I DID IT TO SAVE YOU, YOU KNOW.
HA!
SO DON'T BE SAYING I DID IT FOR YOU.
...
I hate punks...
He sure is scary...

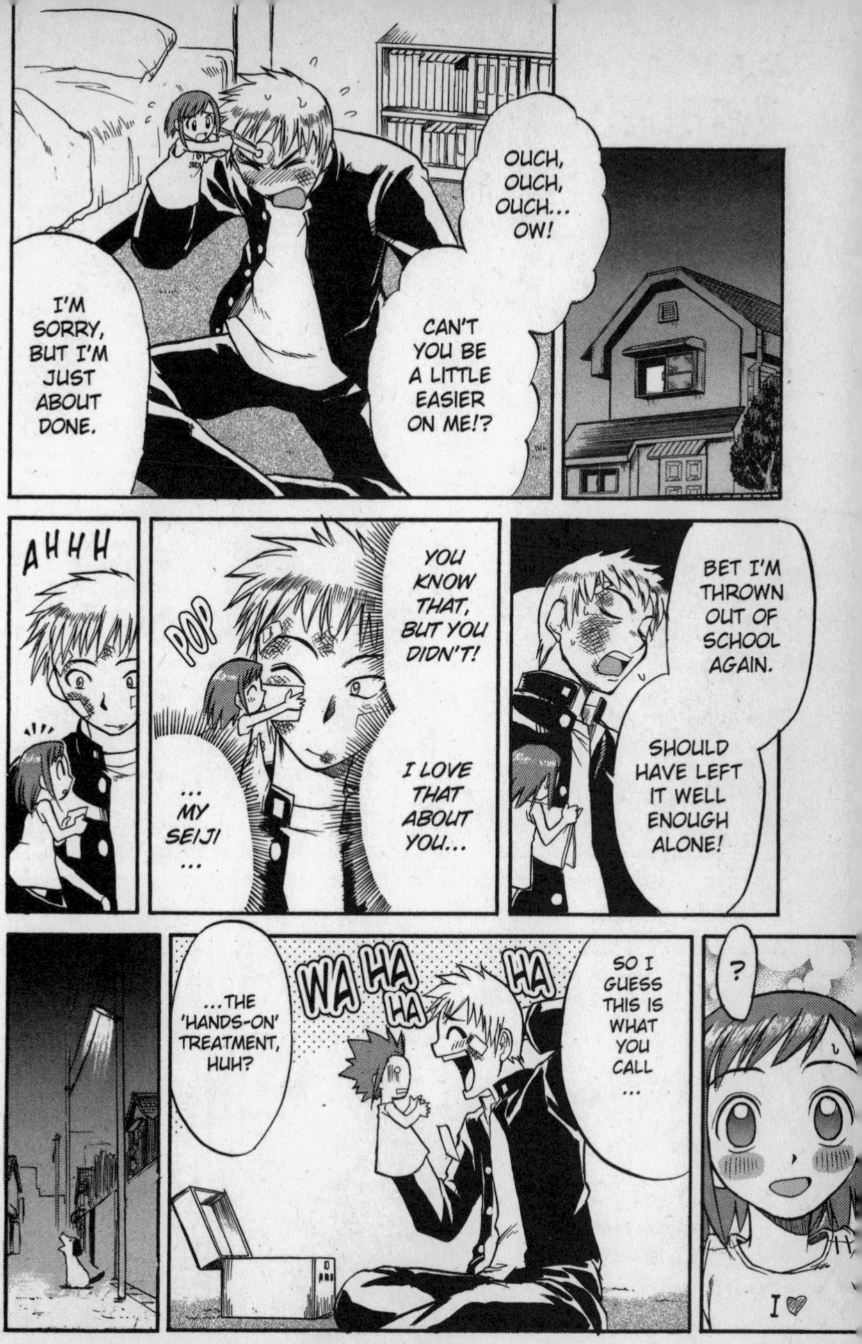
OUCH, OUCH, OUCH... OW!
CAN'T YOU BE A LITTLE EASIER ON ME!?
I'M SORRY, BUT I'M JUST ABOUT DONE.
BET I'M THROWN OUT OF SCHOOL AGAIN.
SHOULD HAVE LEFT IT WELL ENOUGH ALONE!
YOU KNOW THAT, BUT YOU DIDN'T!
POP
I LOVE THAT ABOUT YOU...
...MY SEIJI...
AHHH
?
I ♥
SO I GUESS THIS IS WHAT YOU CALL...
HA
WA HA HA
...THE 'HANDS-ON' TREATMENT, HUH?

DAY 4
THE DISTANCE BETWEEN DESKS

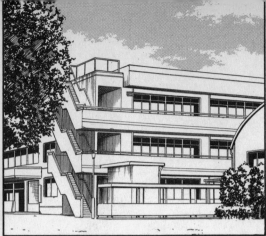

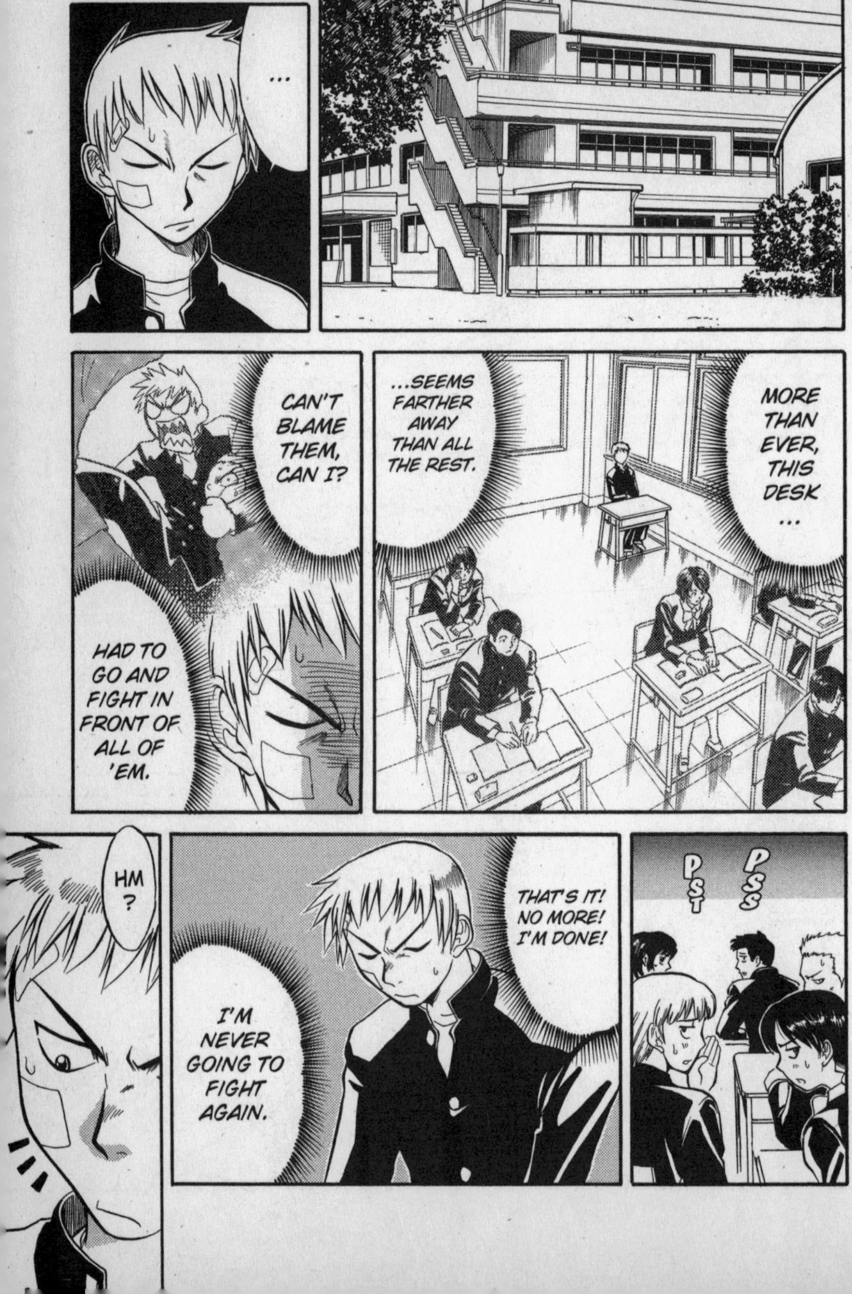
...
MORE THAN EVER, THIS DESK ...
...SEEMS FARTHER AWAY THAN ALL THE REST.
CAN'T BLAME THEM, CAN I?
HAD TO GO AND FIGHT IN FRONT OF ALL OF 'EM.
PSS
PST
THAT'S IT! NO MORE! I'M DONE!
I'M NEVER GOING TO FIGHT AGAIN.
HM?

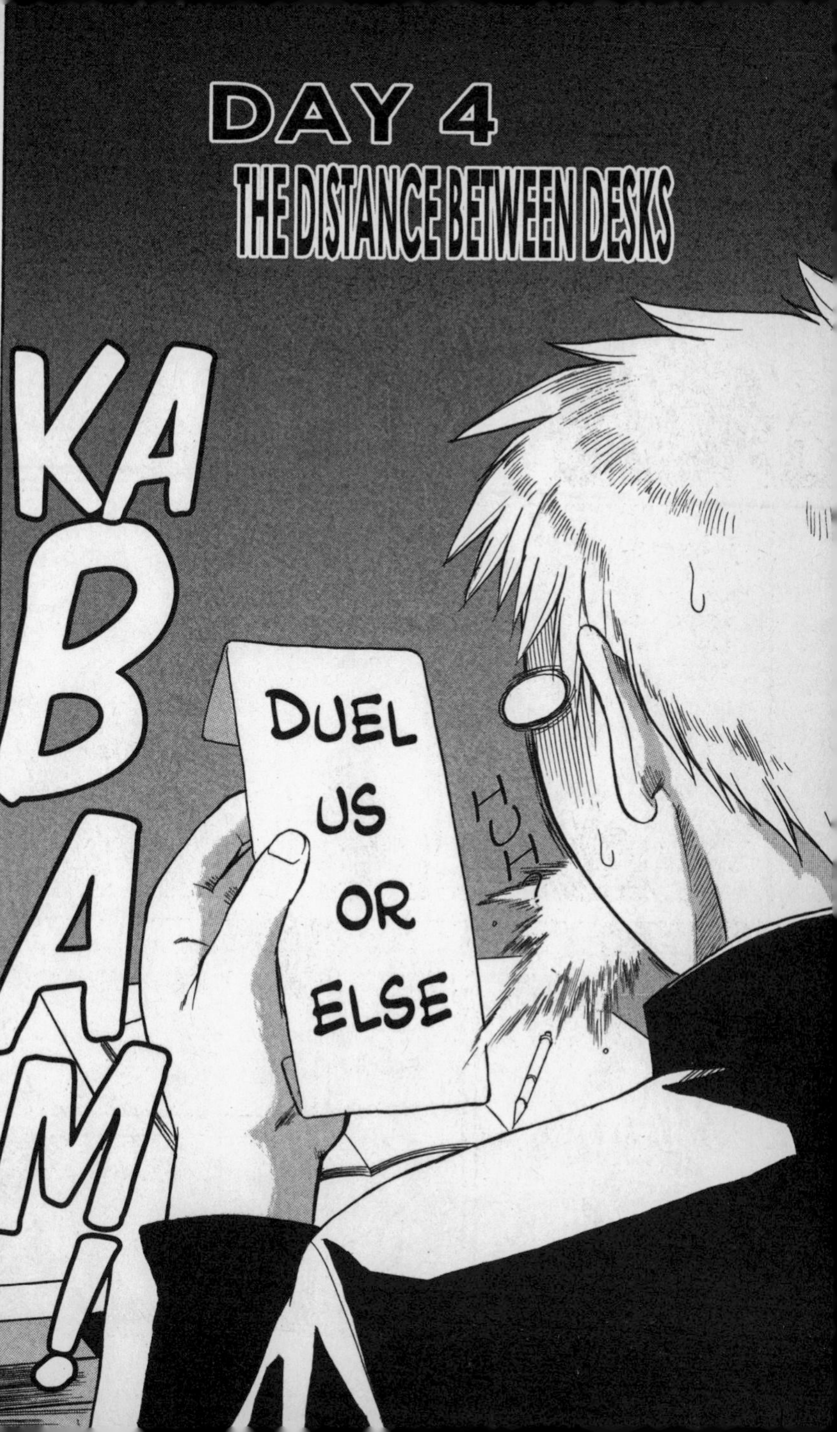
DAY 4
THE DISTANCE BETWEEN DESKS
KABAM!
DUEL US OR ELSE

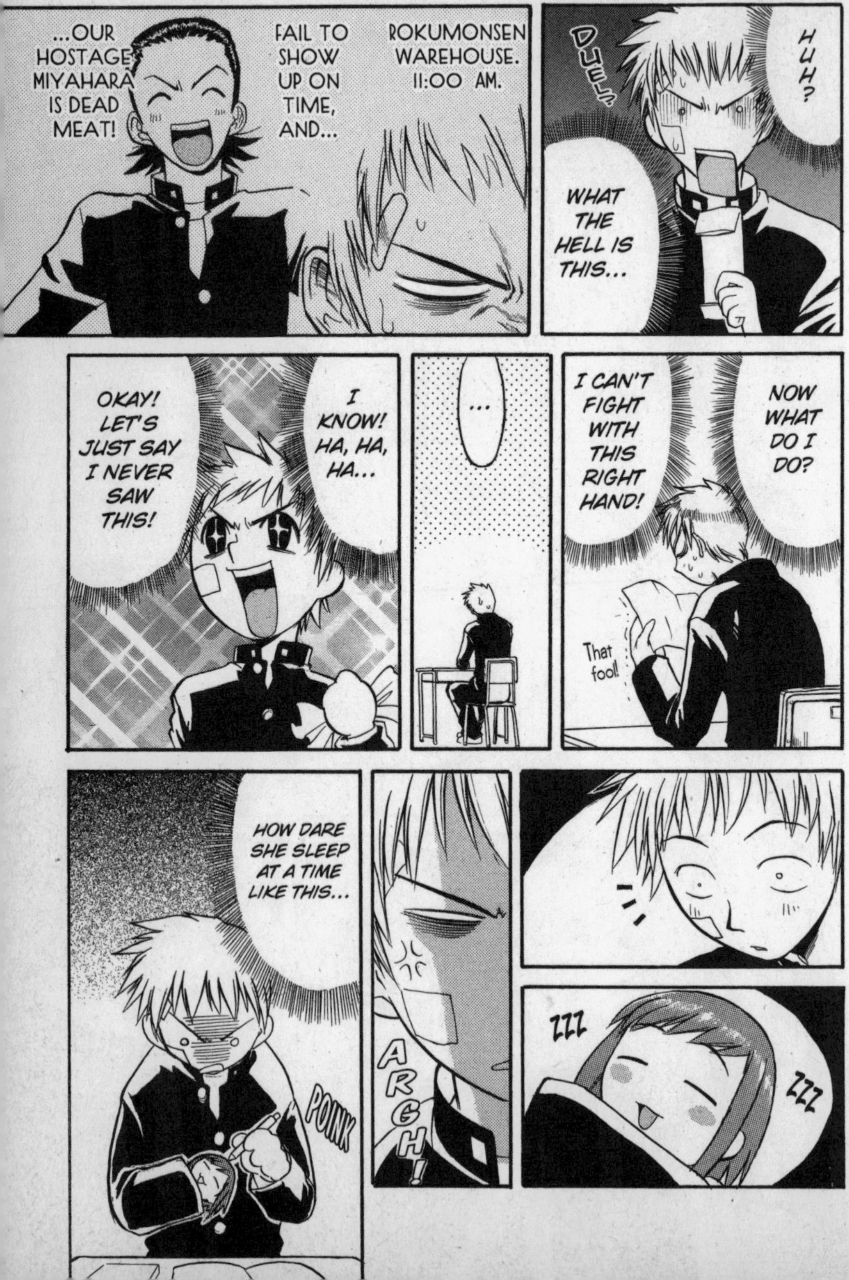
HUH?
DUEL?
WHAT THE HELL IS THIS...
ROKUMONSEN WAREHOUSE. 11:00 AM.
FAIL TO SHOW UP ON TIME, AND...
...OUR HOSTAGE MIYAHARA IS DEAD MEAT!
NOW WHAT DO I DO?
I CAN'T FIGHT WITH THIS RIGHT HAND!
That fool!
...
I KNOW! HA, HA, HA...
OKAY! LET'S JUST SAY I NEVER SAW THIS!
ZZZ
ZZZ
ARGH!
HOW DARE SHE SLEEP AT A TIME LIKE THIS...
POINK

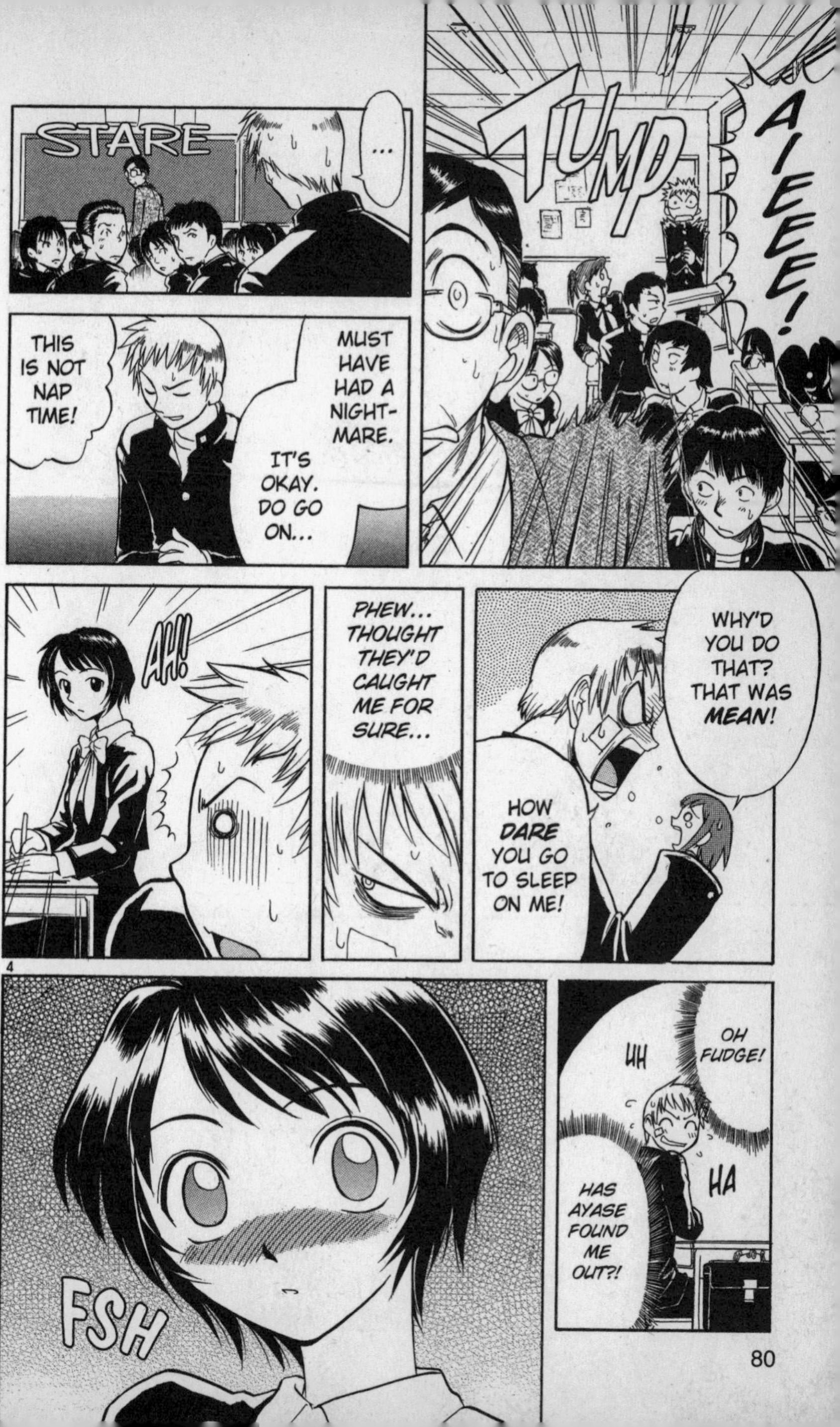
TUMP
AIEEEE!
STARE
...
MUST HAVE HAD A NIGHTMARE.
IT'S OKAY. DO GO ON...
THIS IS NOT NAP TIME!
WHY'D YOU DO THAT? THAT WAS **MEAN!**
HOW **DARE** YOU GO TO SLEEP ON ME!
PHEW... THOUGHT THEY'D CAUGHT ME FOR SURE...
AH!
4
OH FUDGE!
UH
HA
HAS AYASE FOUND ME OUT?!
FSH

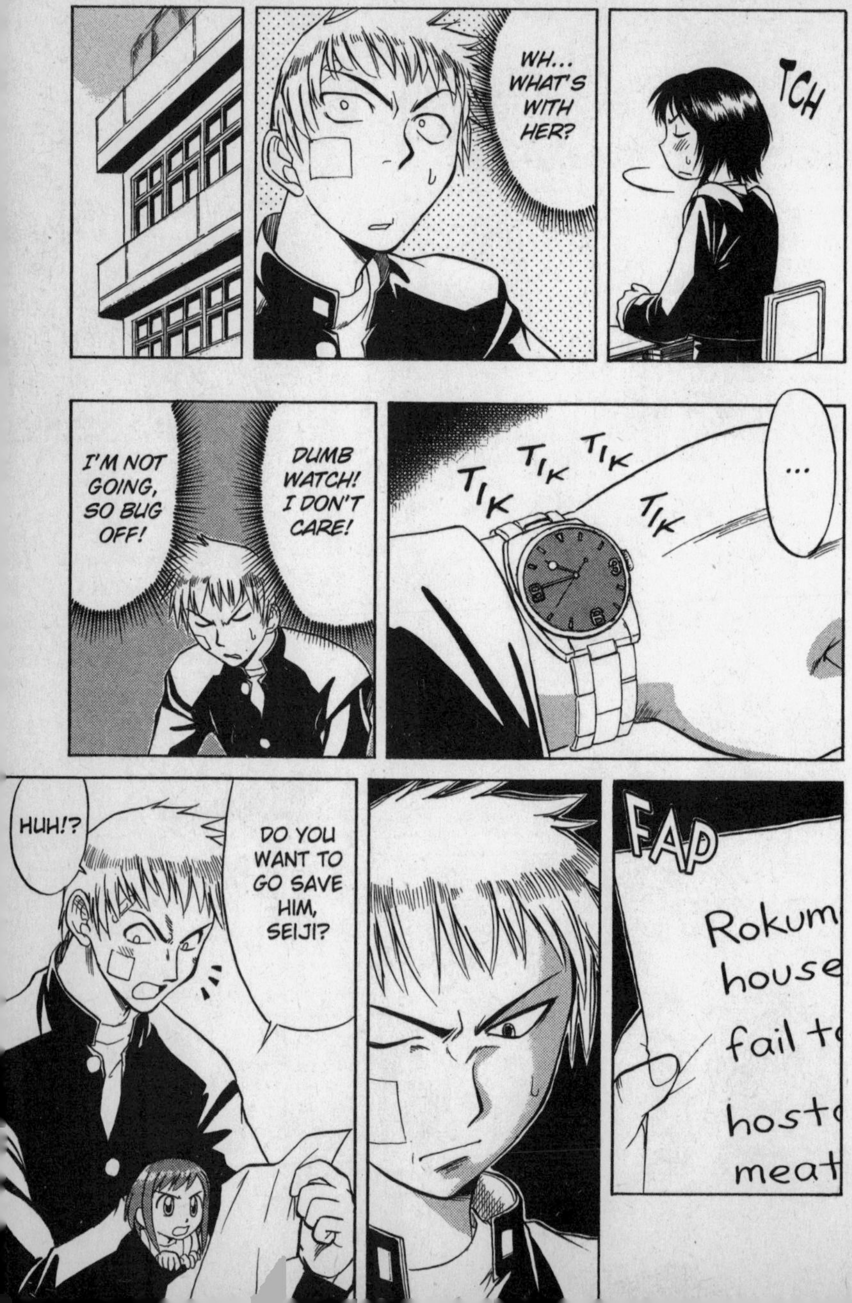
TCH
WH... WHAT'S WITH HER?
...
TIK TIK TIK TIK
DUMB WATCH! I DON'T CARE!
I'M NOT GOING, SO BUG OFF!
FAP
Rokum
house
fail t
host
meat
DO YOU WANT TO GO SAVE HIM, SEIJI?
HUH!?

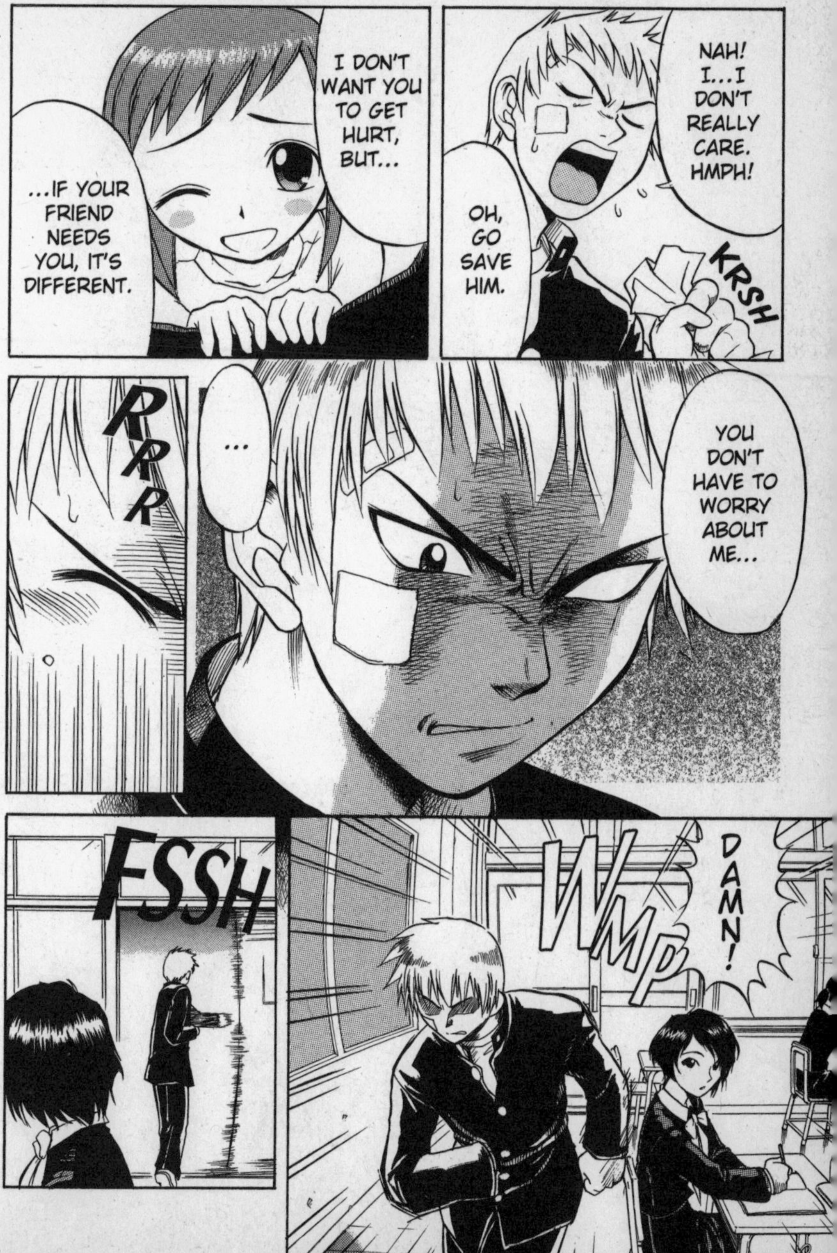
NAH! I...I DON'T REALLY CARE. HMPH!
OH, GO SAVE HIM.
KRSH
I DON'T WANT YOU TO GET HURT, BUT...
...IF YOUR FRIEND NEEDS YOU, IT'S DIFFERENT.
YOU DON'T HAVE TO WORRY ABOUT ME...
...
RRR
DAMN!
WMP
FSSH

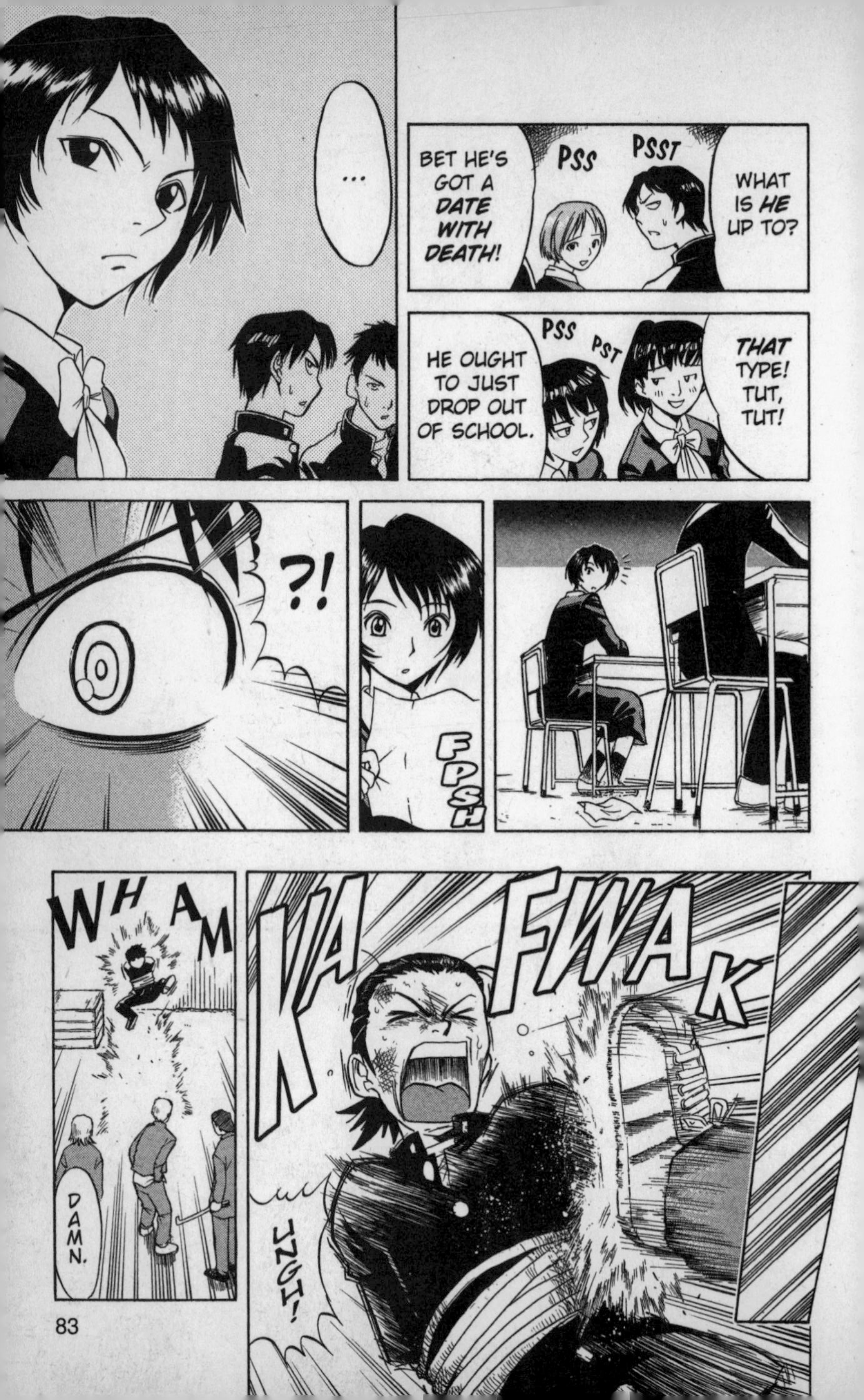
WHAT IS HE UP TO?
PSST
PSS
BET HE'S GOT A DATE WITH DEATH!
THAT TYPE! TUT, TUT!
PST
PSS
HE OUGHT TO JUST DROP OUT OF SCHOOL.
...
FPSH
?!
KA FWAK
UNGH!
WHAM
DAMN.

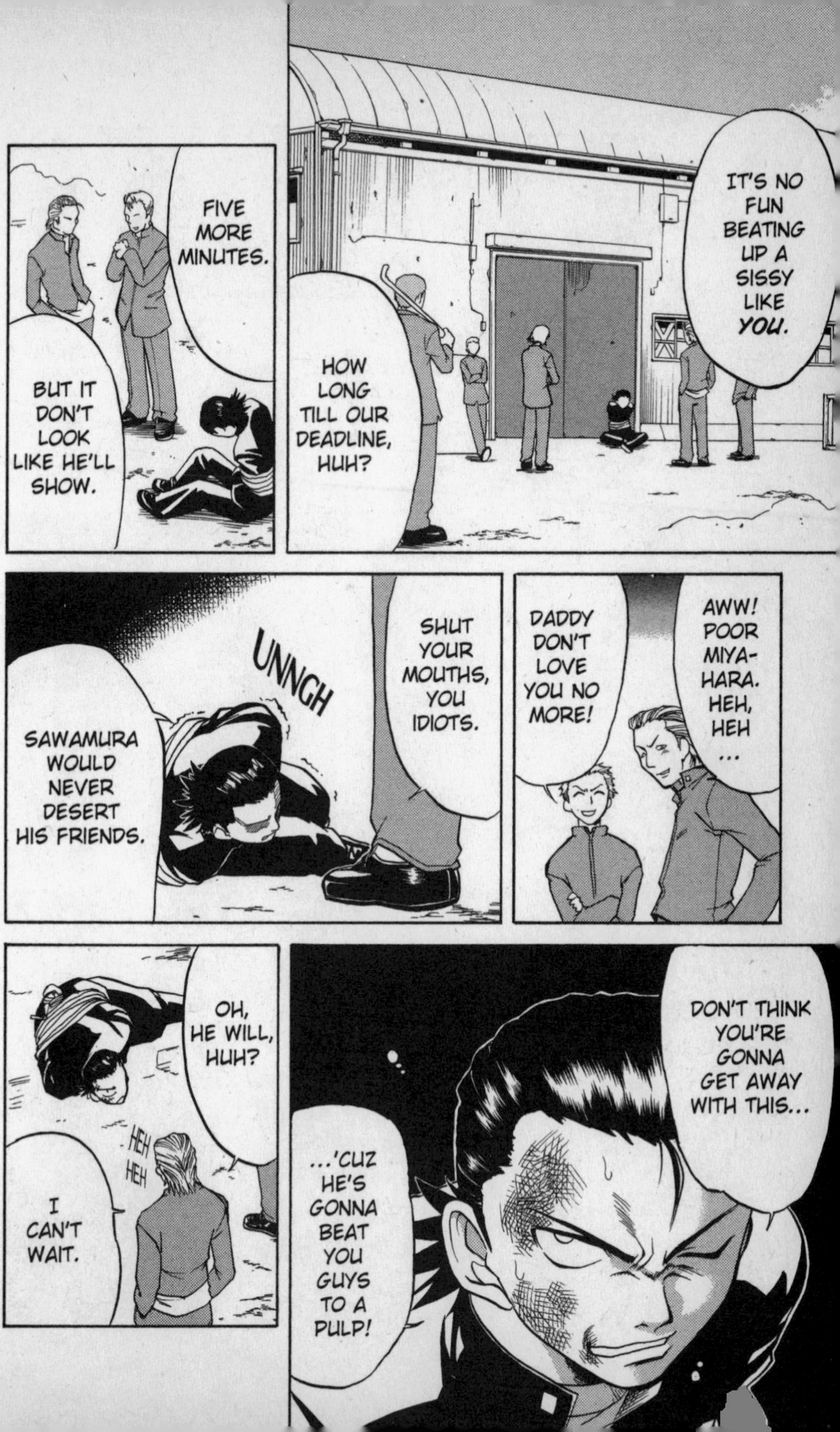
IT'S NO FUN BEATING UP A SISSY LIKE *YOU.*
HOW LONG TILL OUR DEADLINE, HUH?
FIVE MORE MINUTES.
BUT IT DON'T LOOK LIKE HE'LL SHOW.
AWW! POOR MIYA-HARA. HEH, HEH...
DADDY DON'T LOVE YOU NO MORE!
SHUT YOUR MOUTHS, YOU IDIOTS.
UNNGH
SAWAMURA WOULD NEVER DESERT HIS FRIENDS.
DON'T THINK YOU'RE GONNA GET AWAY WITH THIS...
...'CUZ HE'S GONNA BEAT YOU GUYS TO A PULP!
OH, HE WILL, HUH?
HEH HEH
I CAN'T WAIT.

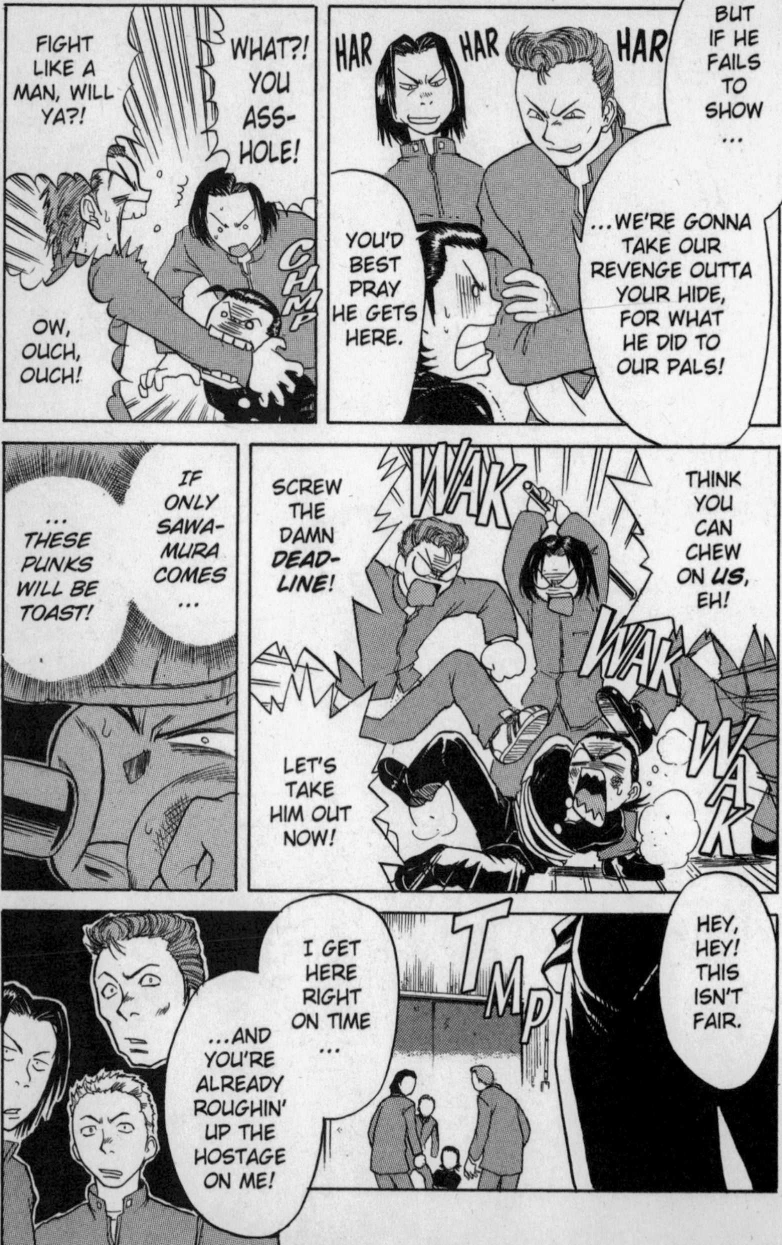

BUT IF HE FAILS TO SHOW ...
HAR HAR HAR
...WE'RE GONNA TAKE OUR REVENGE OUTTA YOUR HIDE, FOR WHAT HE DID TO OUR PALS!
YOU'D BEST PRAY HE GETS HERE.
WHAT?! YOU ASS-HOLE!
FIGHT LIKE A MAN, WILL YA?!
CHMP
OW, OUCH, OUCH!
THINK YOU CAN CHEW ON *US*, EH!
WAK
SCREW THE DAMN *DEAD-LINE*!
WAK
WAK
LET'S TAKE HIM OUT NOW!
IF ONLY SAWA-MURA COMES ...
... THESE PUNKS WILL BE TOAST!
HEY, HEY! THIS ISN'T FAIR.
TMP
I GET HERE RIGHT ON TIME ...
...AND YOU'RE ALREADY ROUGHIN' UP THE HOSTAGE ON ME!

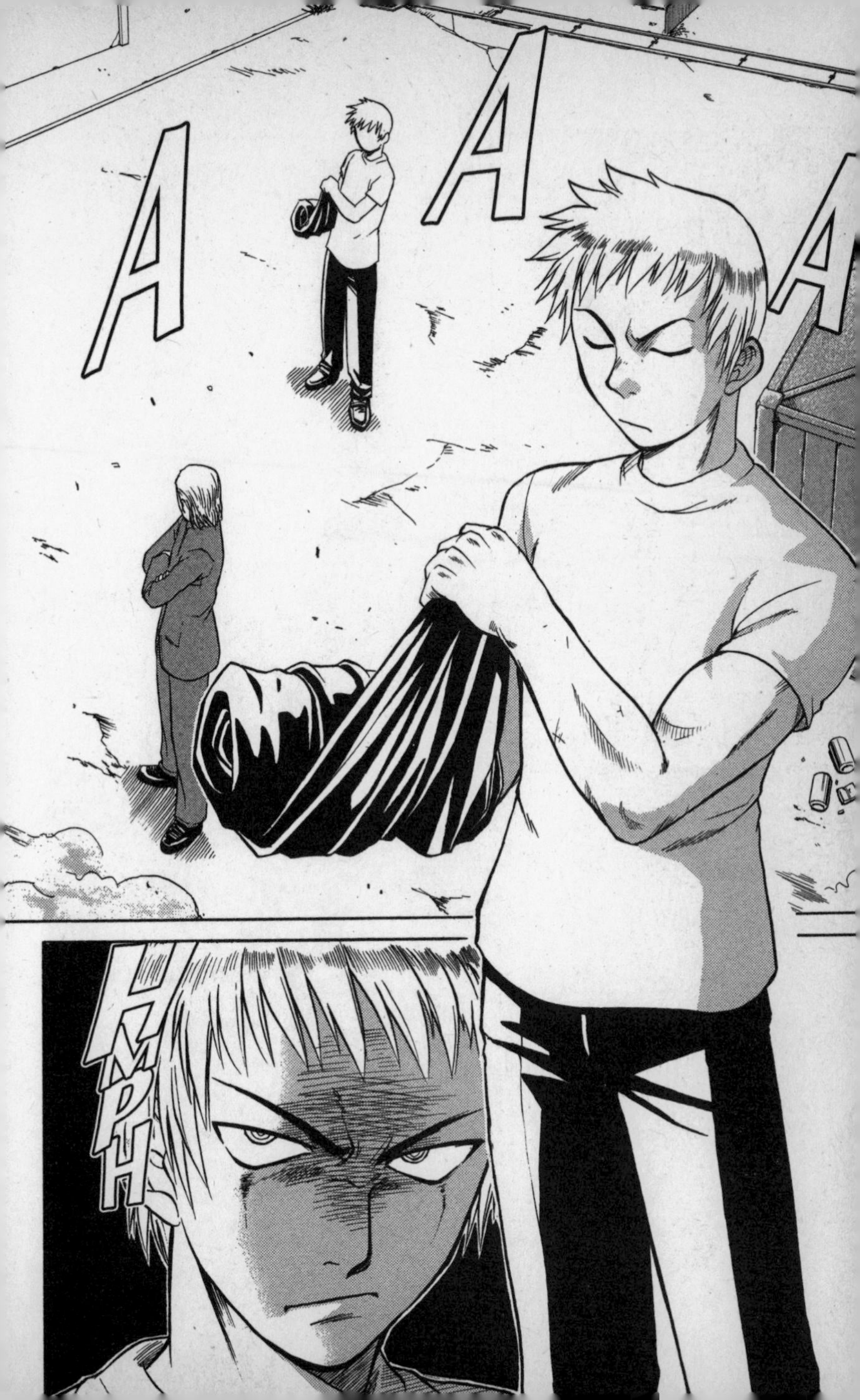
AAAA
HUMPH

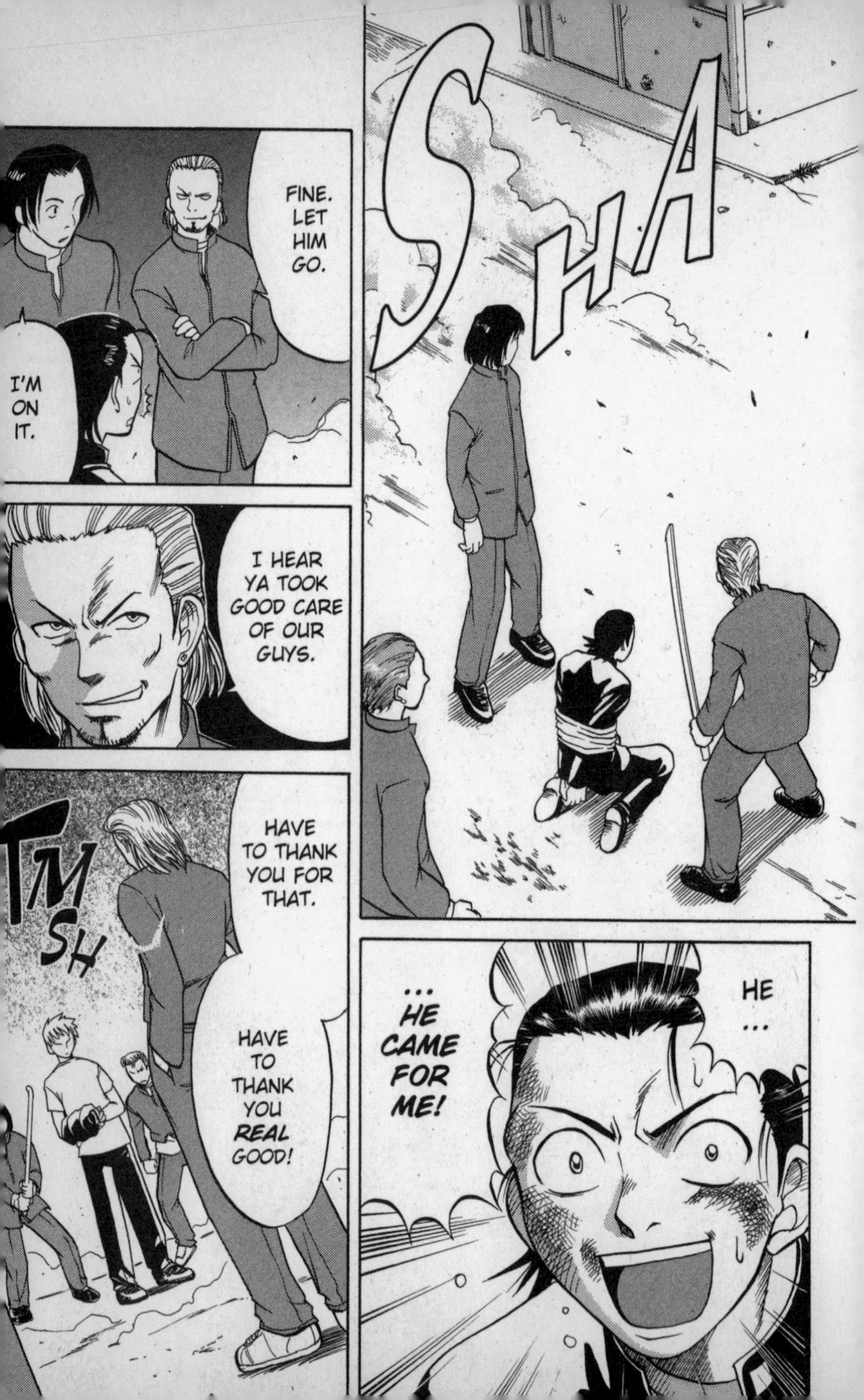
SHA
FINE. LET HIM GO.
I'M ON IT.
I HEAR YA TOOK GOOD CARE OF OUR GUYS.
HAVE TO THANK YOU FOR THAT.
TMSH
HAVE TO THANK YOU REAL GOOD!
HE ...
... HE CAME FOR ME!

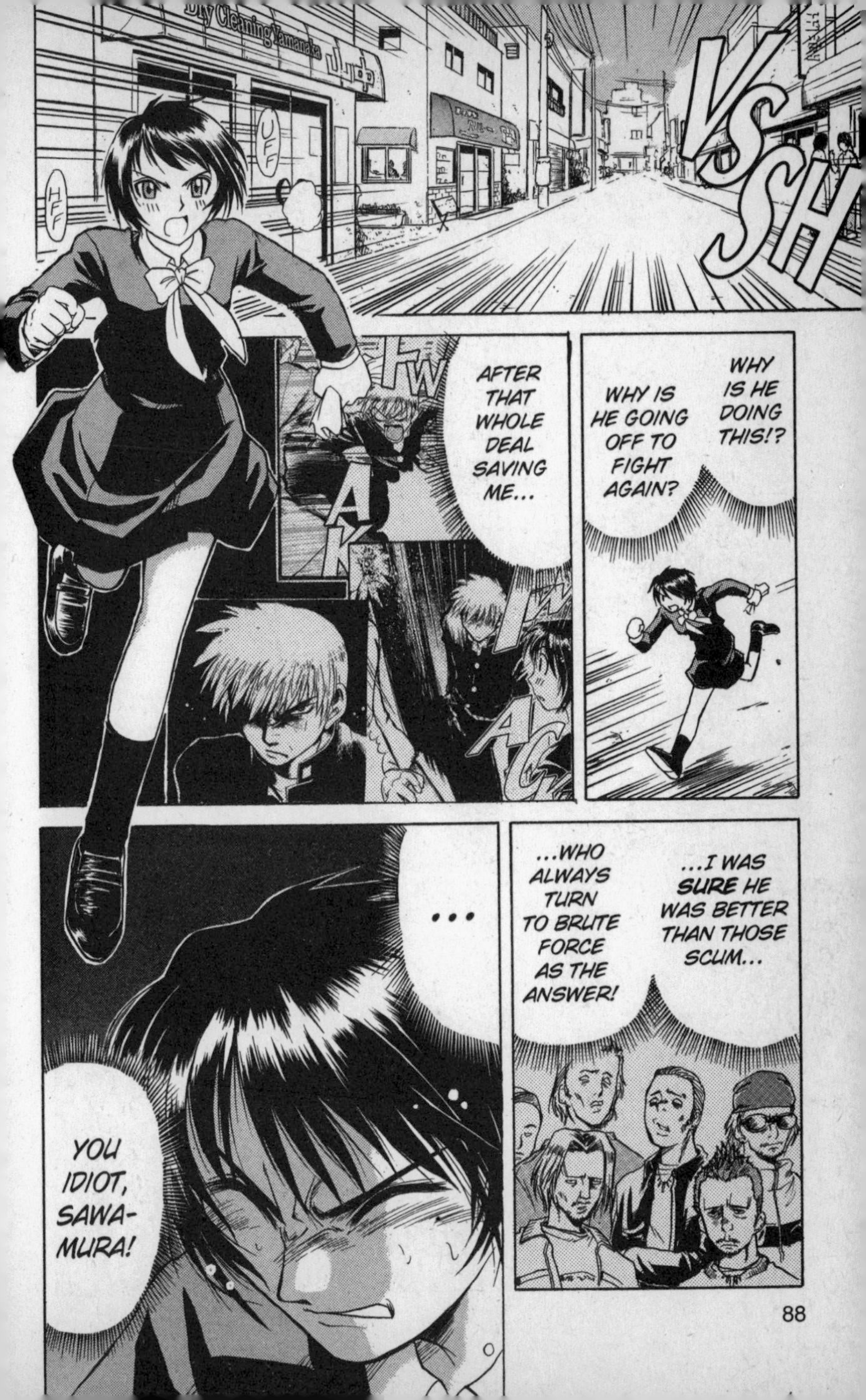
VSSH
Dry Cleaning Yamanaka
UFF
HFF
WHY IS HE DOING THIS!?
WHY IS HE GOING OFF TO FIGHT AGAIN?
AFTER THAT WHOLE DEAL SAVING ME...
...I WAS SURE HE WAS BETTER THAN THOSE SCUM...
...WHO ALWAYS TURN TO BRUTE FORCE AS THE ANSWER!
...
YOU IDIOT, SAWAMURA!

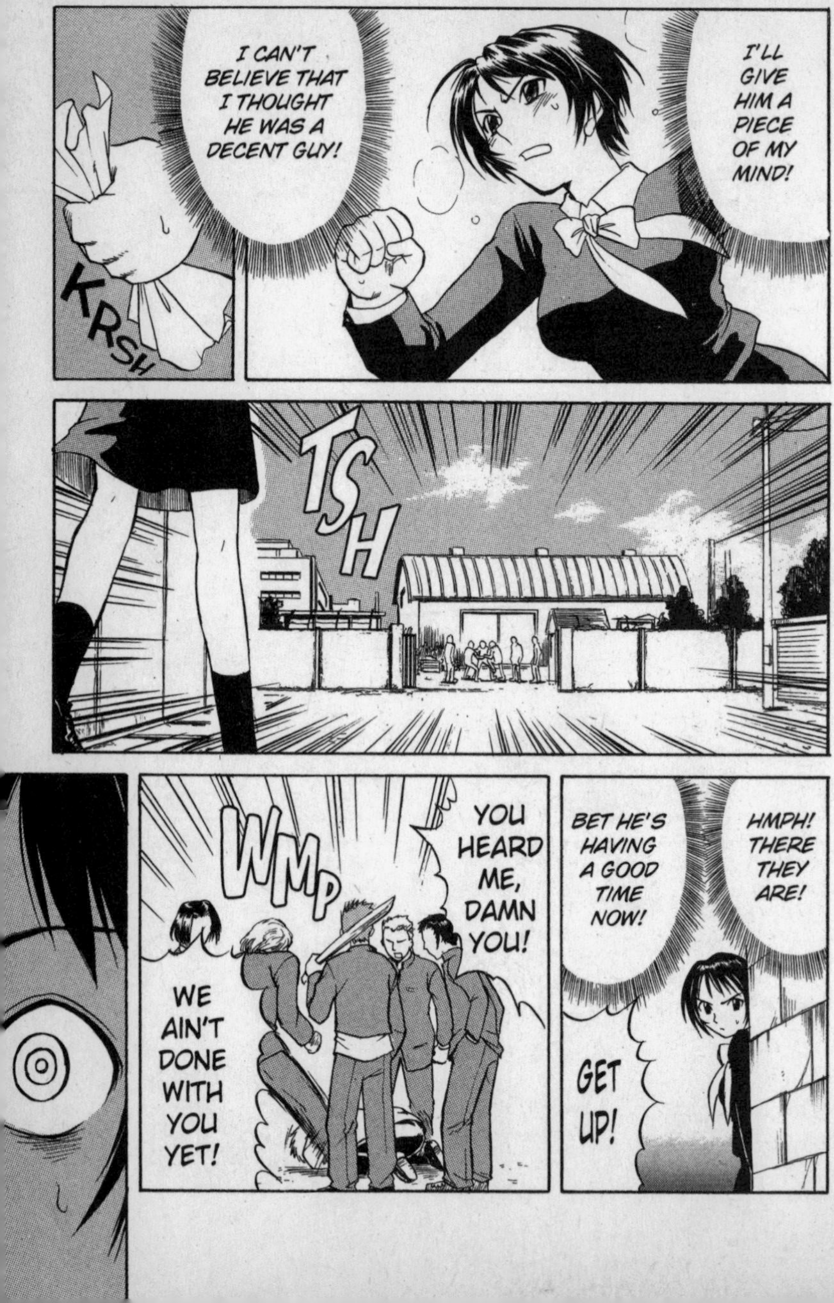
I'LL GIVE HIM A PIECE OF MY MIND!
I CAN'T BELIEVE THAT I THOUGHT HE WAS A DECENT GUY!
KRSH
TSH
HMPH! THERE THEY ARE!
BET HE'S HAVING A GOOD TIME NOW!
GET UP!
YOU HEARD ME, DAMN YOU!
WMP
WE AIN'T DONE WITH YOU YET!

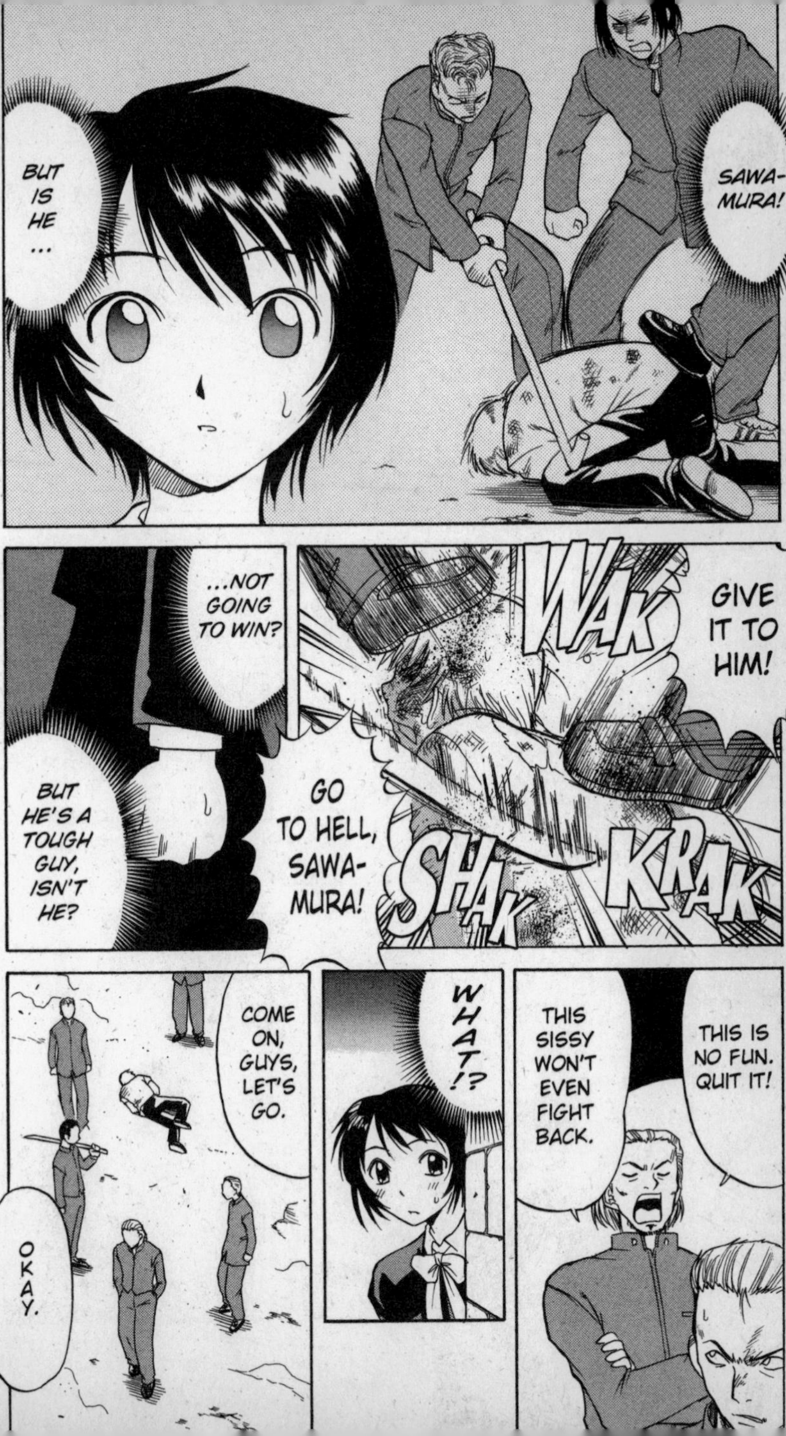

SAWAMURA!
BUT IS HE ...
GIVE IT TO HIM!
WAK
KRAK
GO TO HELL, SAWAMURA!
SHAK
...NOT GOING TO WIN?
BUT HE'S A TOUGH GUY, ISN'T HE?
THIS IS NO FUN. QUIT IT!
THIS SISSY WON'T EVEN FIGHT BACK.
WHAT!?
COME ON, GUYS, LET'S GO.
OKAY.

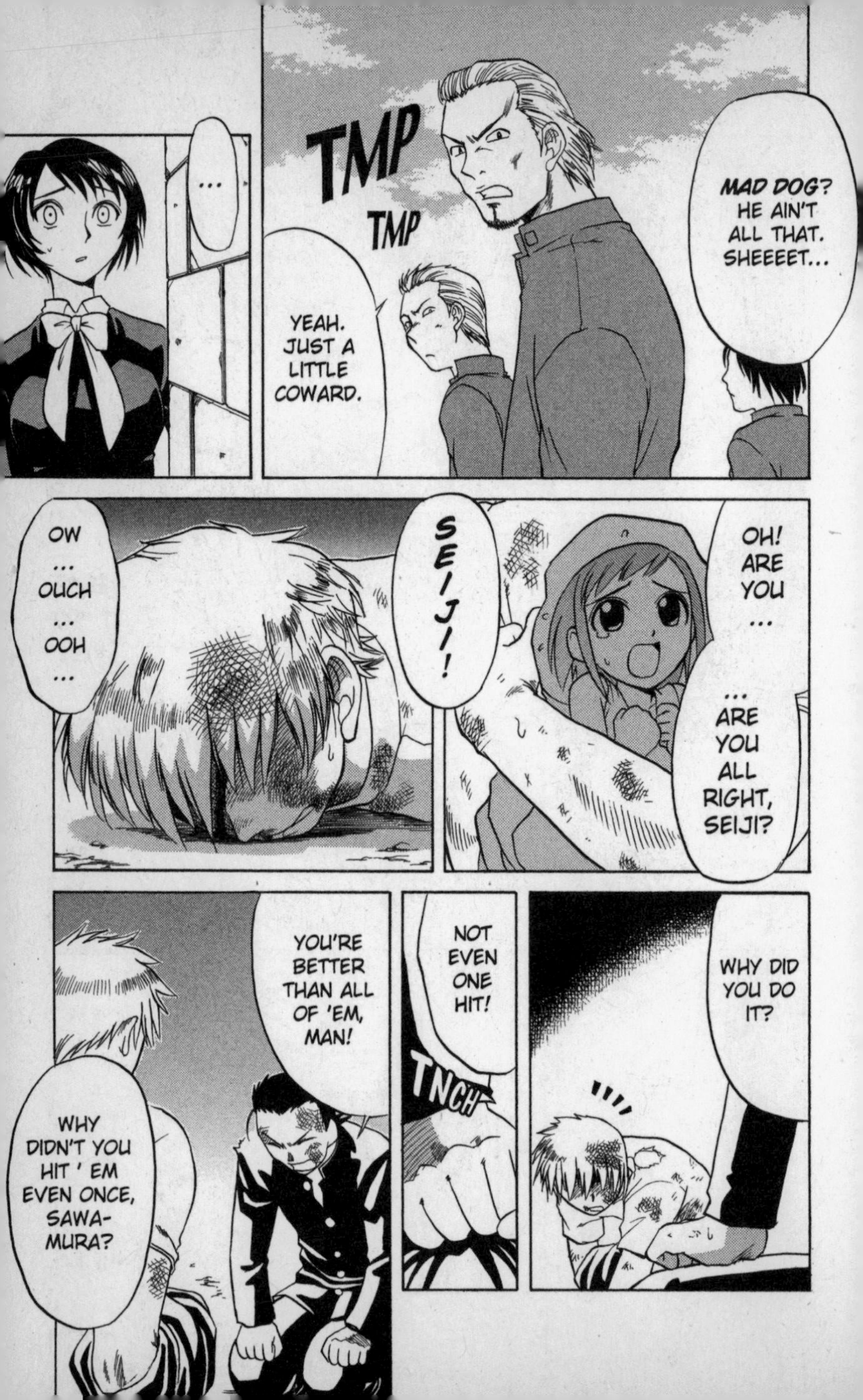
MAD DOG? HE AIN'T ALL THAT. SHEEEET...
TMP
TMP
YEAH. JUST A LITTLE COWARD.
...
OH! ARE YOU ... ... ARE YOU ALL RIGHT, SEIJI?
SEIJI!
OW ... OUCH ... OOH ...
WHY DID YOU DO IT?
NOT EVEN ONE HIT!
TNCH
YOU'RE BETTER THAN ALL OF 'EM, MAN!
WHY DIDN'T YOU HIT 'EM EVEN ONCE, SAWAMURA?

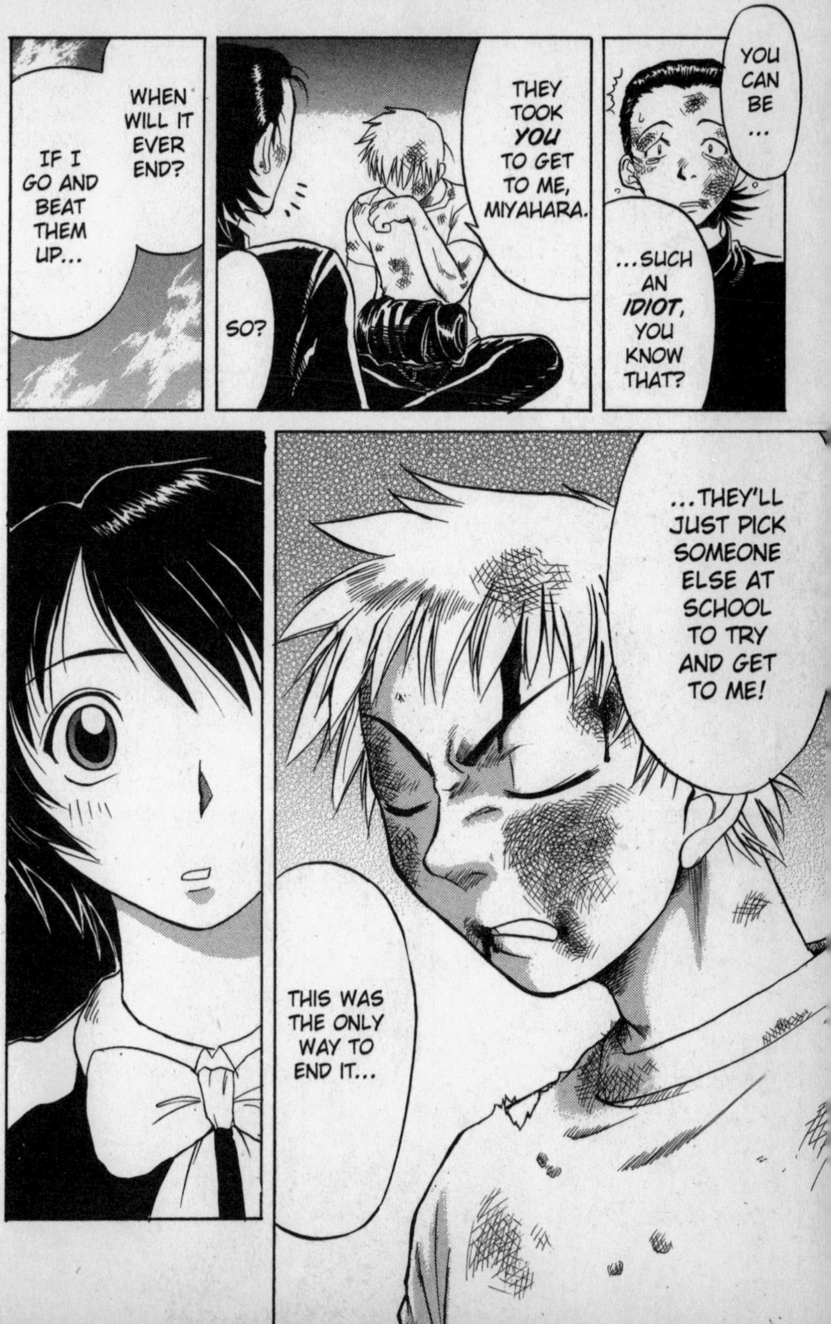

YOU CAN BE ...
...SUCH AN *IDIOT*, YOU KNOW THAT?
THEY TOOK *YOU* TO GET TO ME, MIYAHARA.
SO?
WHEN WILL IT EVER END?
IF I GO AND BEAT THEM UP...
...THEY'LL JUST PICK SOMEONE ELSE AT SCHOOL TO TRY AND GET TO ME!
THIS WAS THE ONLY WAY TO END IT...

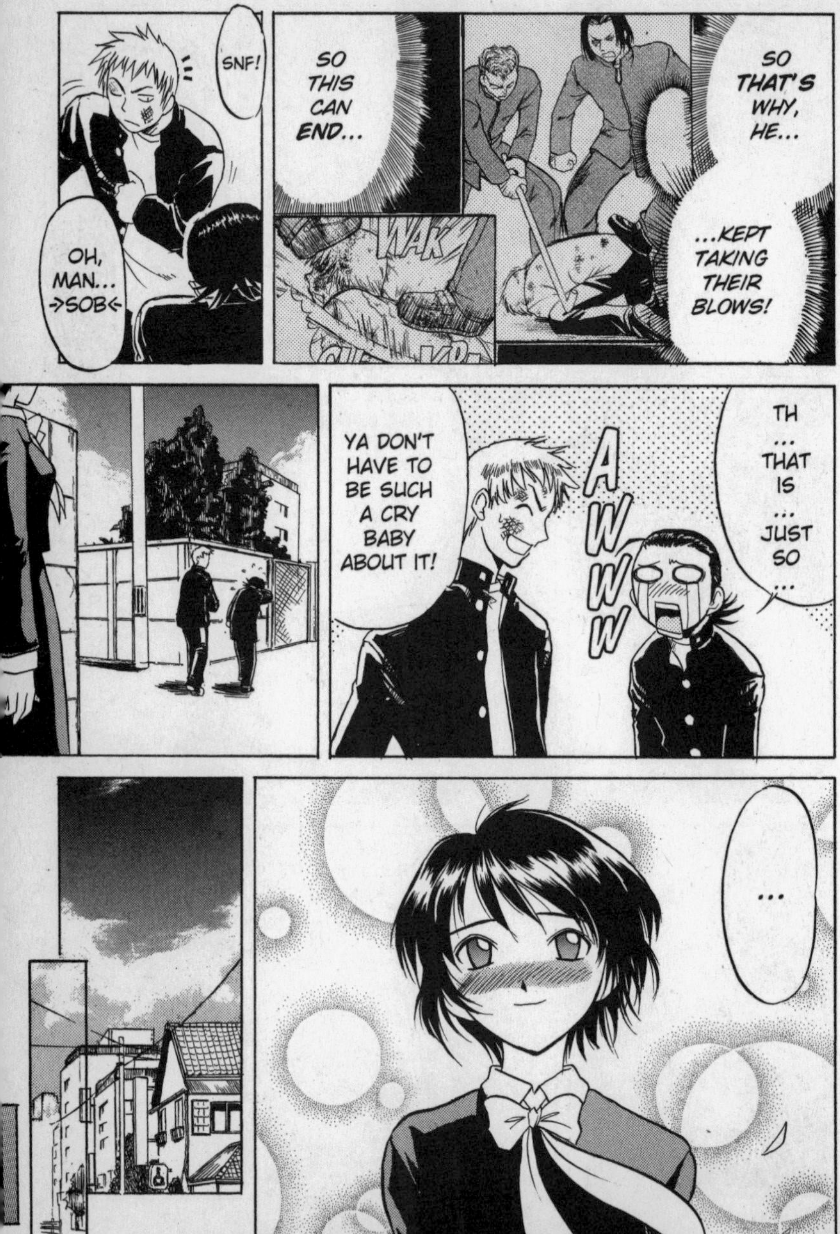
SO THAT'S WHY, HE...
...KEPT TAKING THEIR BLOWS!
SO THIS CAN END...
WAK
SNF!
OH, MAN... ->SOB<-
TH... THAT IS... JUST SO...
AWWW
YA DON'T HAVE TO BE SUCH A CRY BABY ABOUT IT!
...

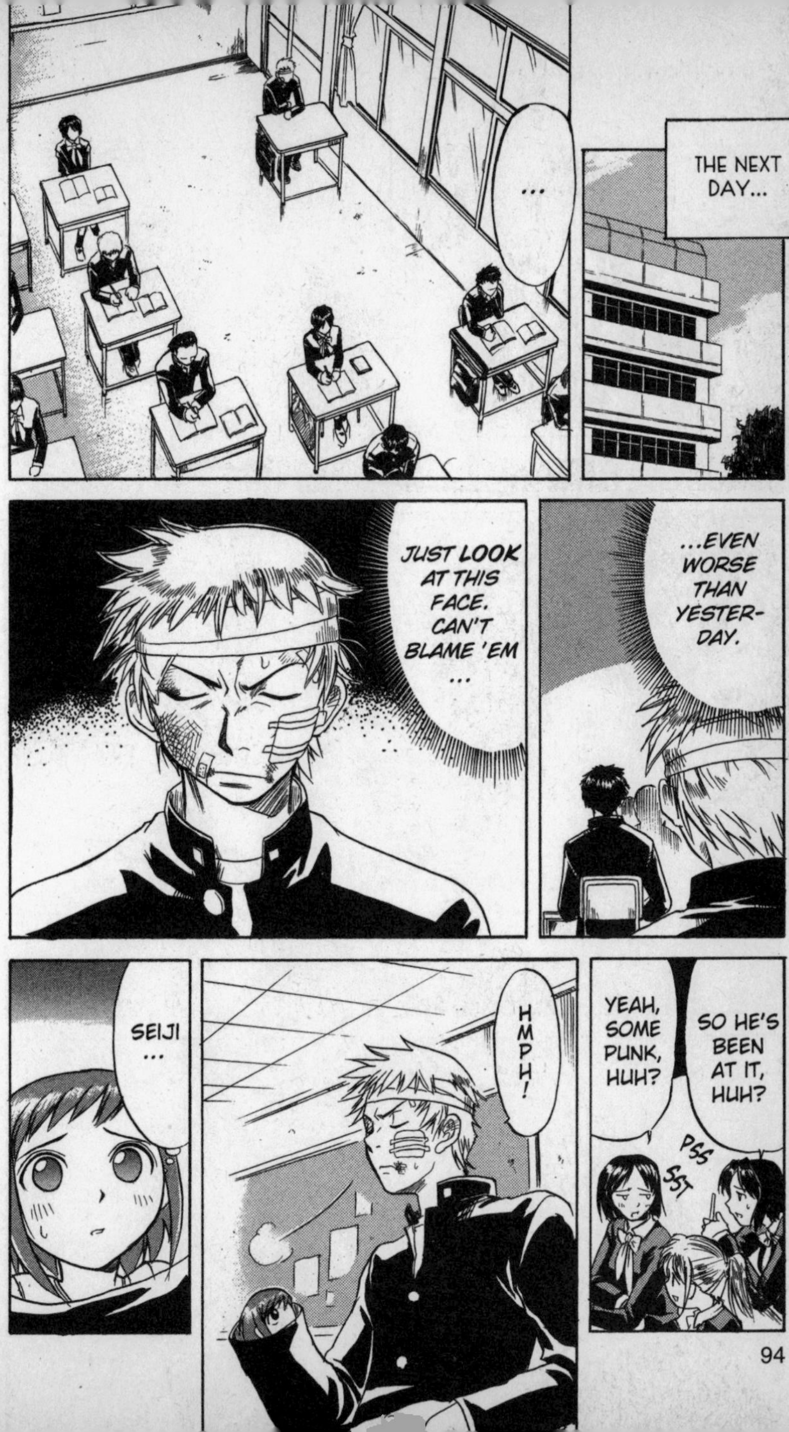
THE NEXT DAY...
...
...EVEN WORSE THAN YESTER-DAY.
JUST LOOK AT THIS FACE. CAN'T BLAME 'EM ...
SO HE'S BEEN AT IT, HUH?
YEAH, SOME PUNK, HUH?
PSS SST
HMPH!
SEIJI ...

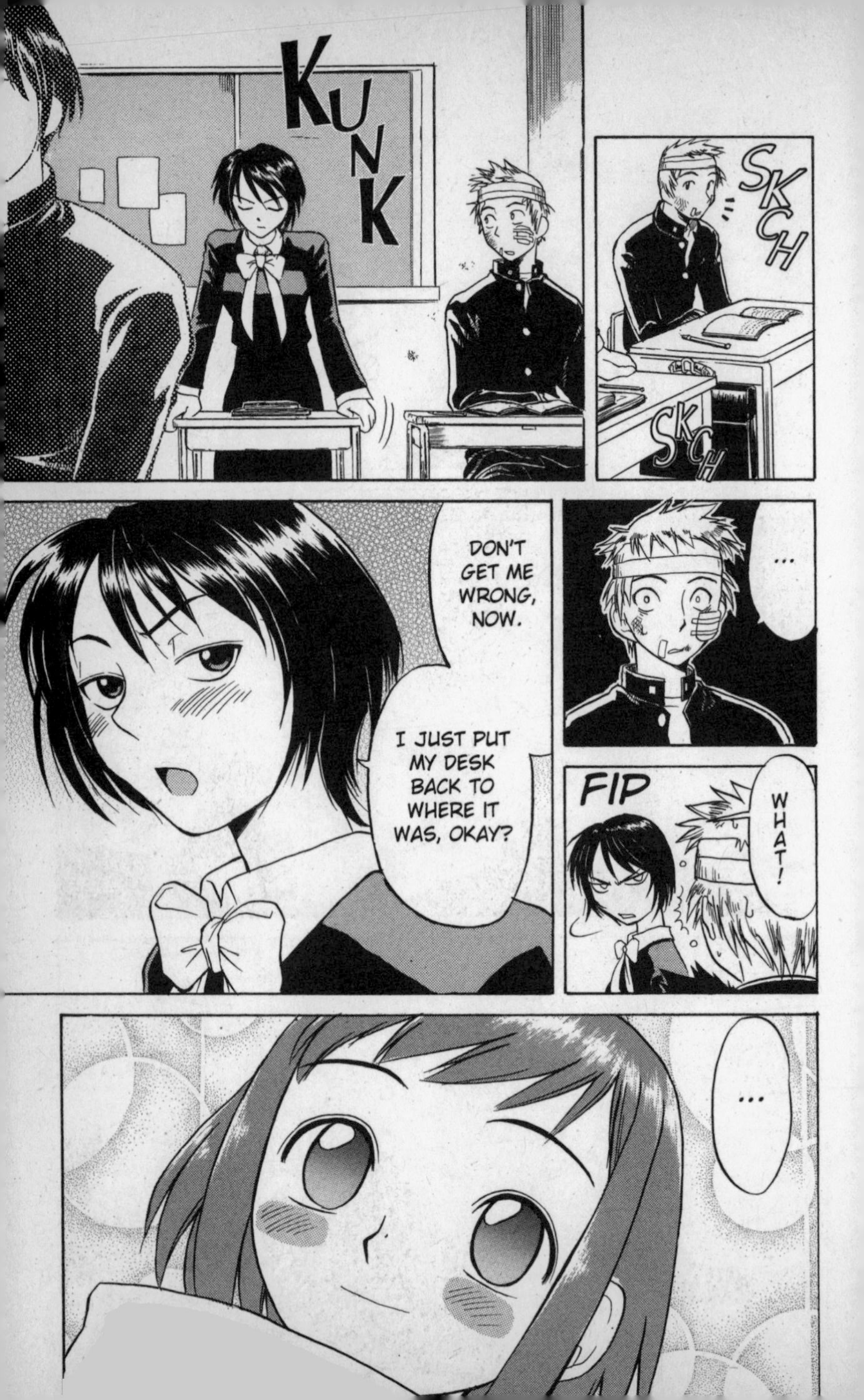
SKCH
SKCH
KUNK
...
FIP
WHAT!
DON'T GET ME WRONG, NOW.
I JUST PUT MY DESK BACK TO WHERE IT WAS, OKAY?
...

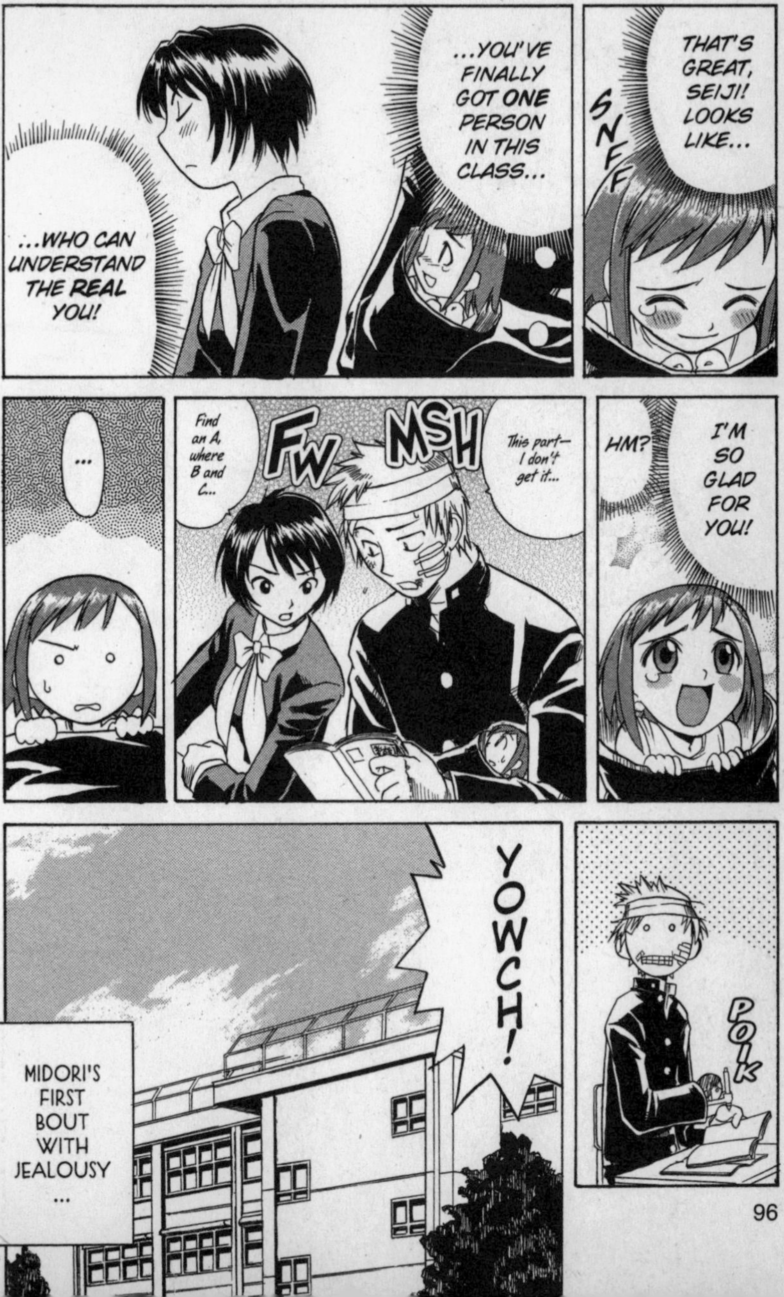
THAT'S GREAT, SEIJI! LOOKS LIKE...
SNFF
...YOU'VE FINALLY GOT ONE PERSON IN THIS CLASS...
...WHO CAN UNDERSTAND THE REAL YOU!
I'M SO GLAD FOR YOU!
HM?
This part— I don't get it...
FWMSH
Find an A, where B and C...
...
POIK
YOWCH!
MIDORI'S FIRST BOUT WITH JEALOUSY ...

DAY 5
SECRET BUDDIES

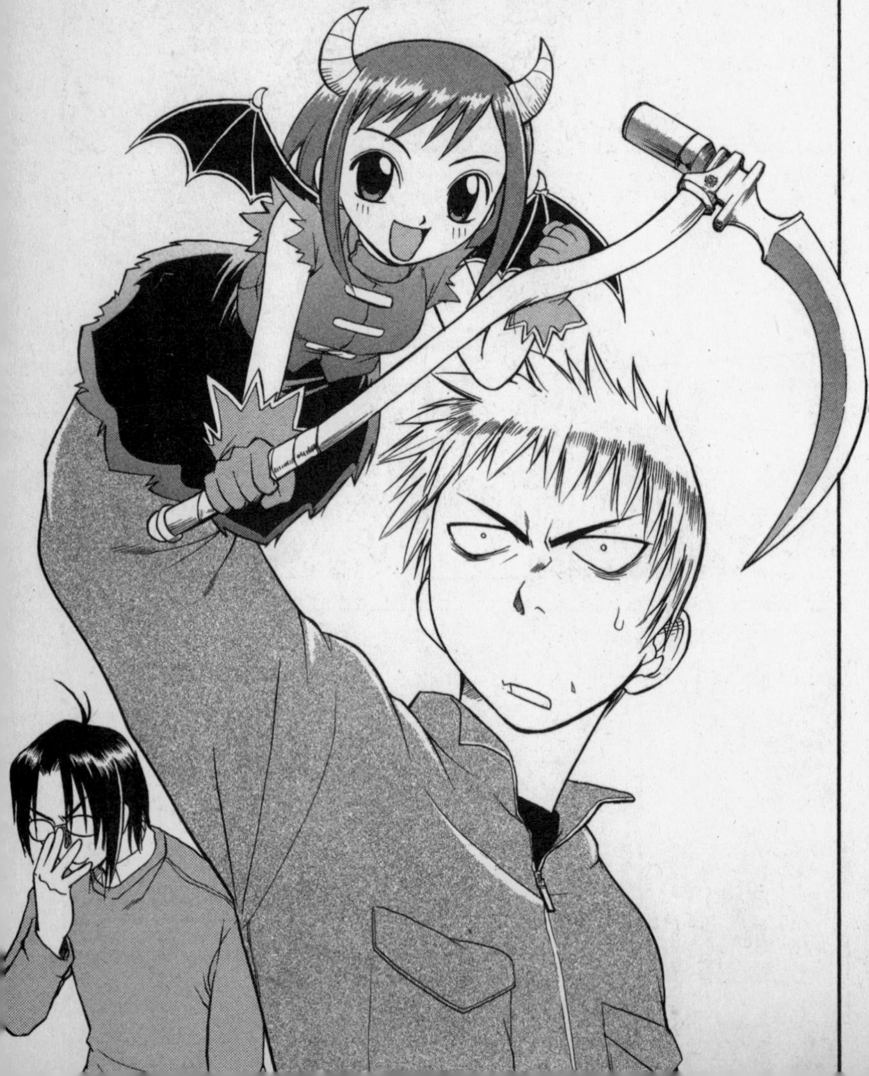

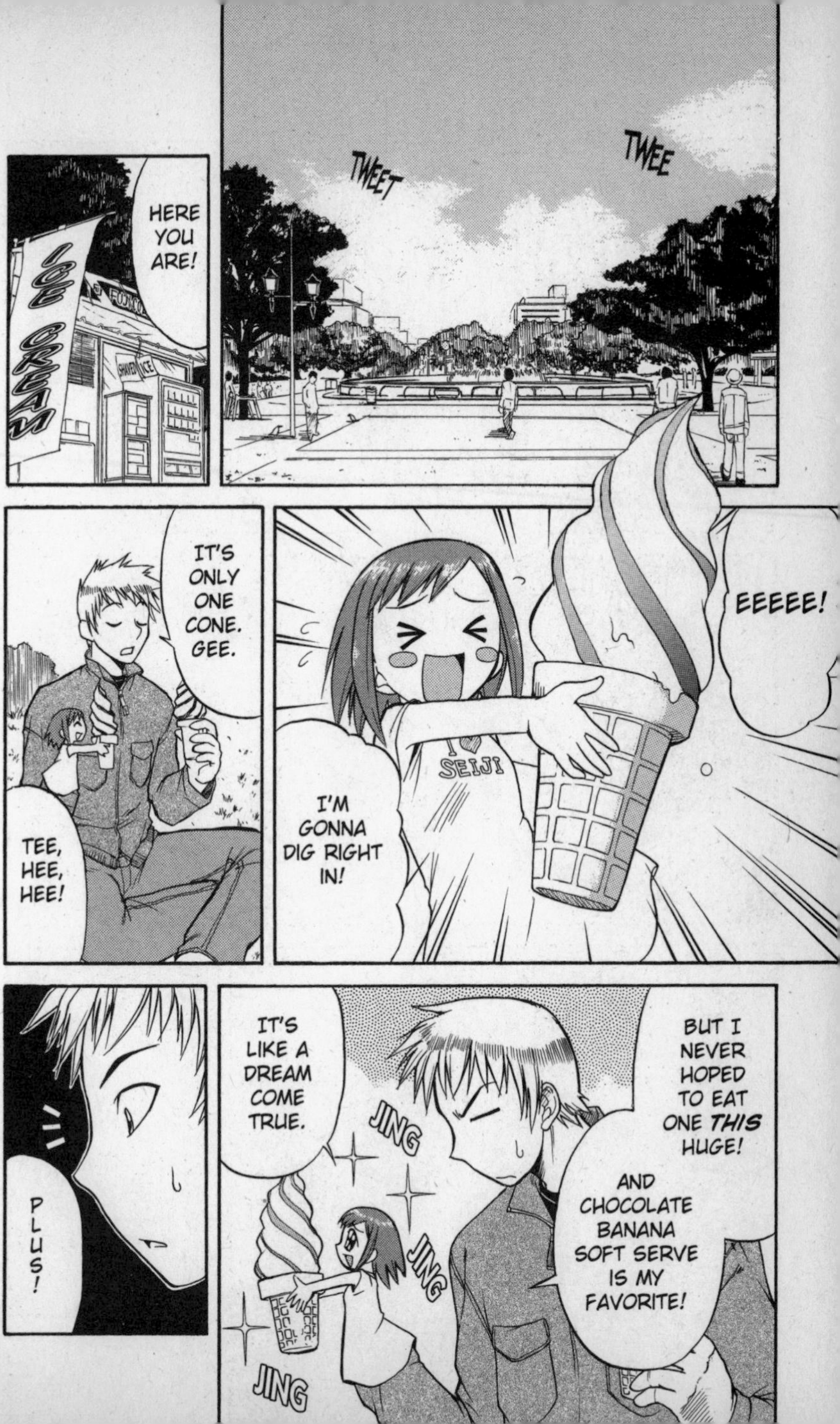
TWEE
TWEET
HERE YOU ARE!
ICE CREAM
SHAVED ICE
EEEEE!
I'M GONNA DIG RIGHT IN!
SEIJI
IT'S ONLY ONE CONE. GEE.
TEE, HEE, HEE!
BUT I NEVER HOPED TO EAT ONE *THIS* HUGE!
AND CHOCOLATE BANANA SOFT SERVE IS MY FAVORITE!
IT'S LIKE A DREAM COME TRUE.
JING
JING
JING
PLUS!

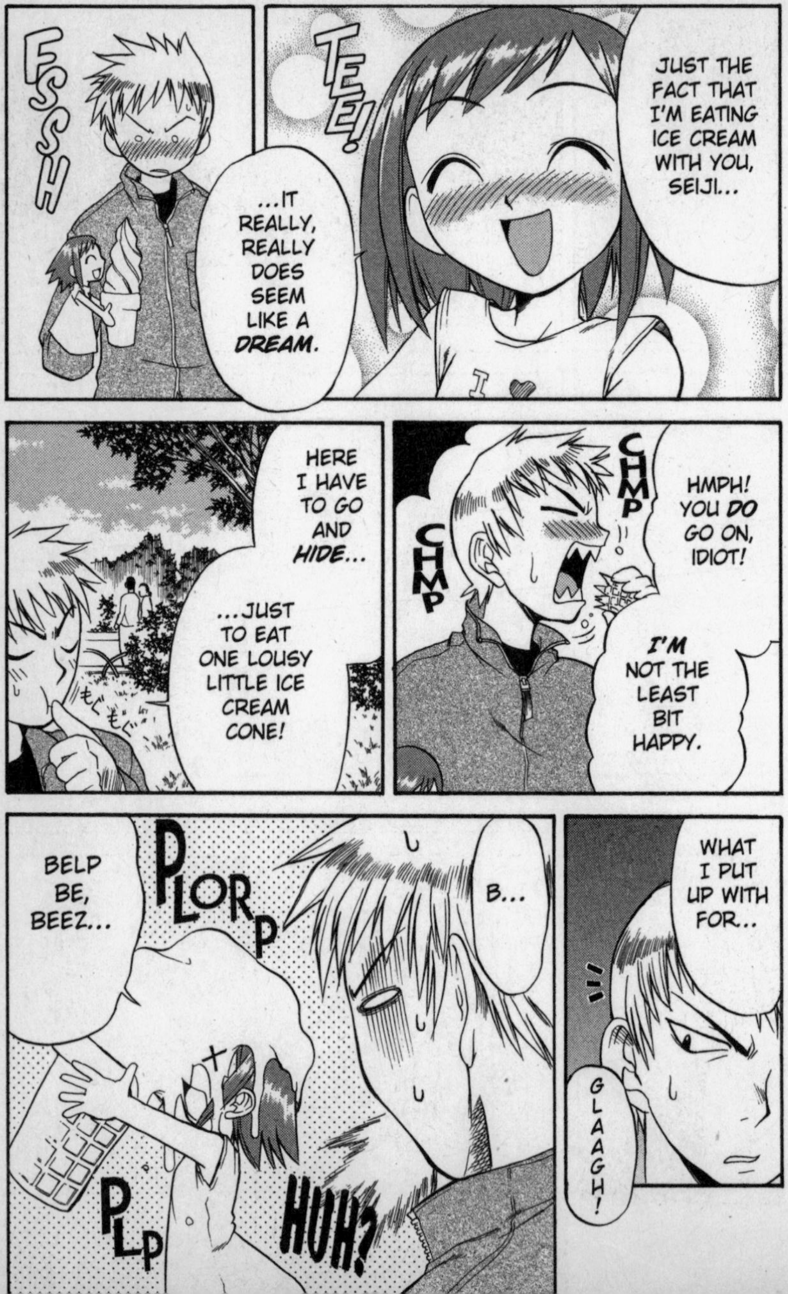
JUST THE FACT THAT I'M EATING ICE CREAM WITH YOU, SEIJI...
TEE!
...IT REALLY, REALLY DOES SEEM LIKE A DREAM.
FSSH
CHMP
CHMP
HMPH! YOU DO GO ON, IDIOT!
I'M NOT THE LEAST BIT HAPPY.
HERE I HAVE TO GO AND HIDE...
...JUST TO EAT ONE LOUSY LITTLE ICE CREAM CONE!
もぐもぐ
WHAT I PUT UP WITH FOR...
GLAAGH!
B...
HUH?
PLORP
BELP BE, BEEZ...
PLP

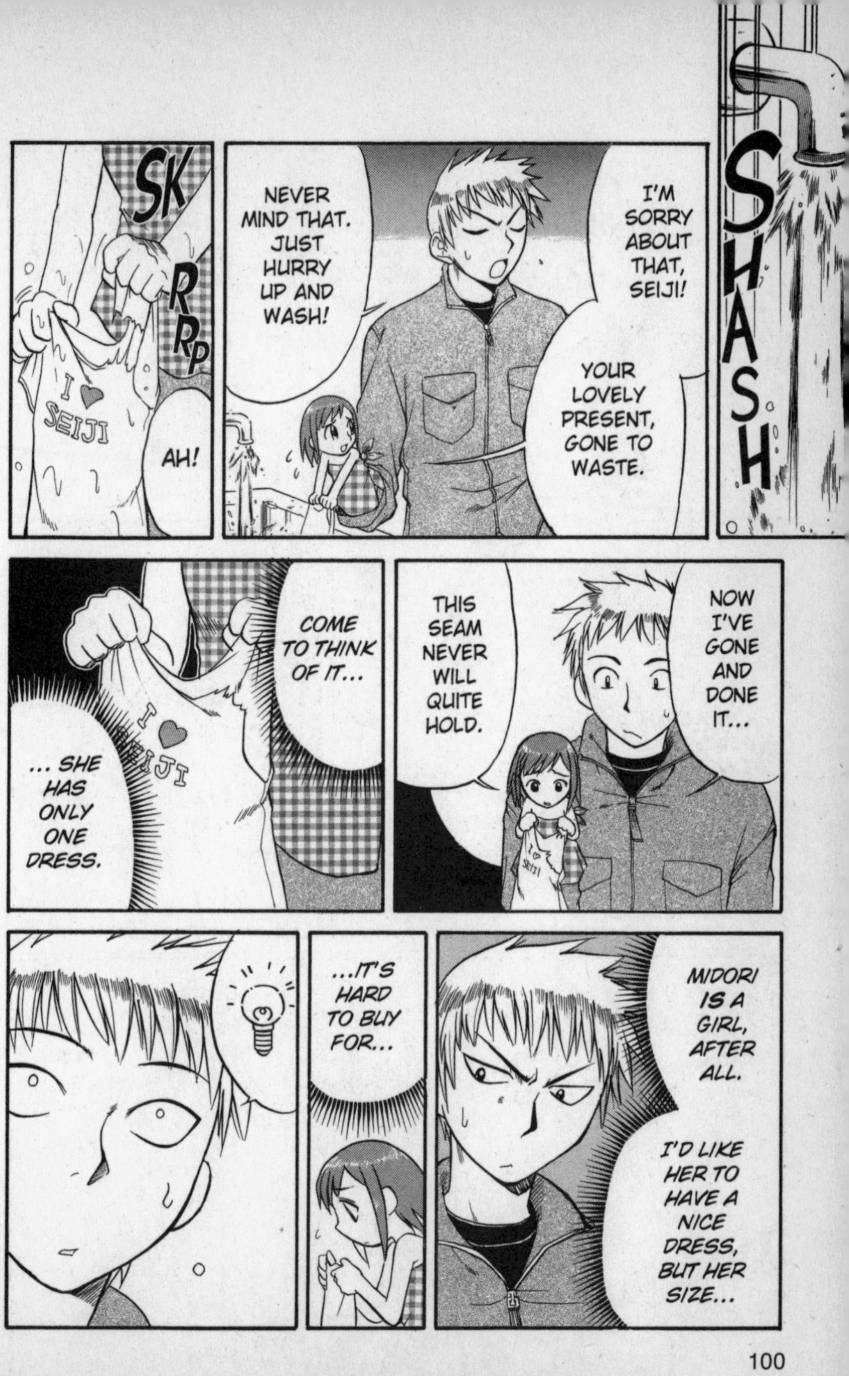
SHASH
I'M SORRY ABOUT THAT, SEIJI!
YOUR LOVELY PRESENT, GONE TO WASTE.
NEVER MIND THAT. JUST HURRY UP AND WASH!
SKRRP
I ♥ SEIJI
AH!
NOW I'VE GONE AND DONE IT...
THIS SEAM NEVER WILL QUITE HOLD.
COME TO THINK OF IT...
I ♥ SEIJI
... SHE HAS ONLY ONE DRESS.
MIDORI IS A GIRL, AFTER ALL.
I'D LIKE HER TO HAVE A NICE DRESS, BUT HER SIZE...
...IT'S HARD TO BUY FOR...

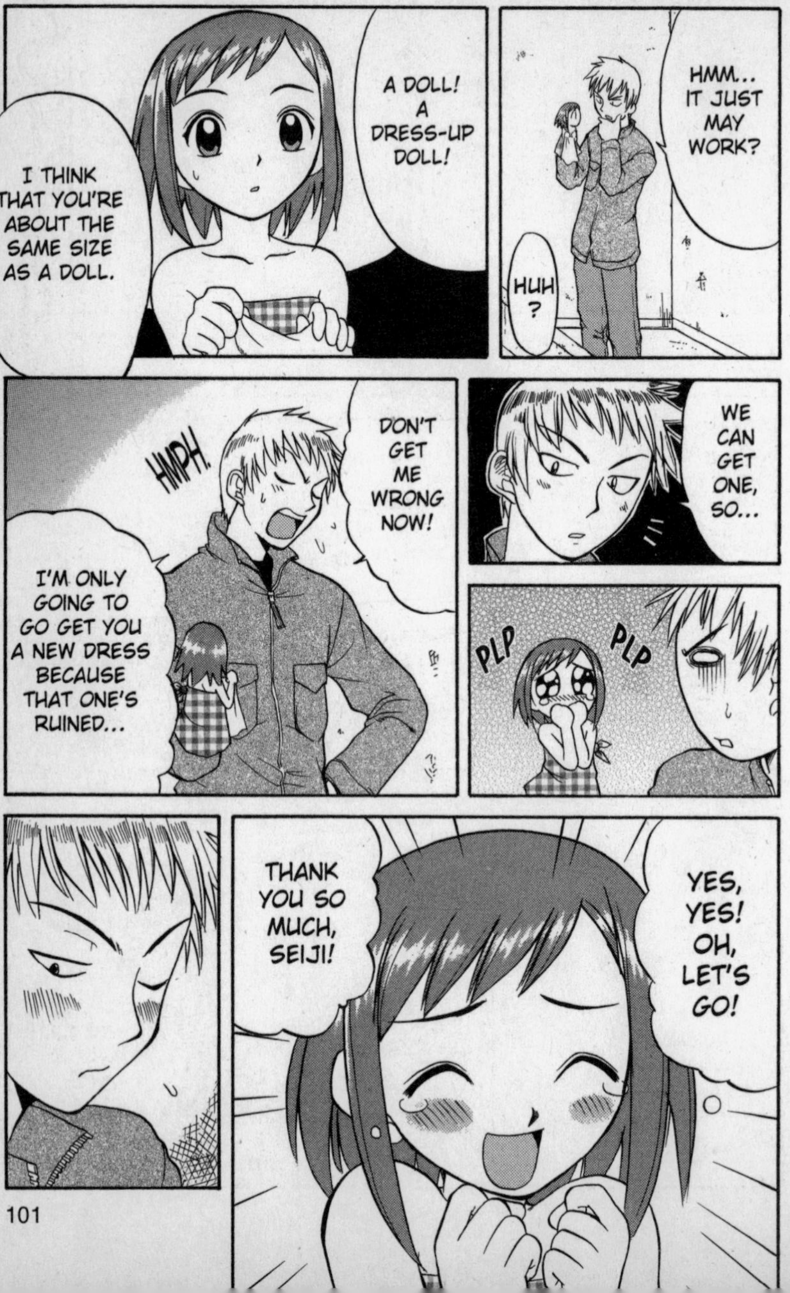
HMM.. IT JUST MAY WORK?
HUH?
A DOLL! A DRESS-UP DOLL!
I THINK THAT YOU'RE ABOUT THE SAME SIZE AS A DOLL.
WE CAN GET ONE, SO...
PLP
PLP
DON'T GET ME WRONG NOW!
HMPH
I'M ONLY GOING TO GO GET YOU A NEW DRESS BECAUSE THAT ONE'S RUINED...
YES, YES! OH, LET'S GO!
THANK YOU SO MUCH, SEIJI!

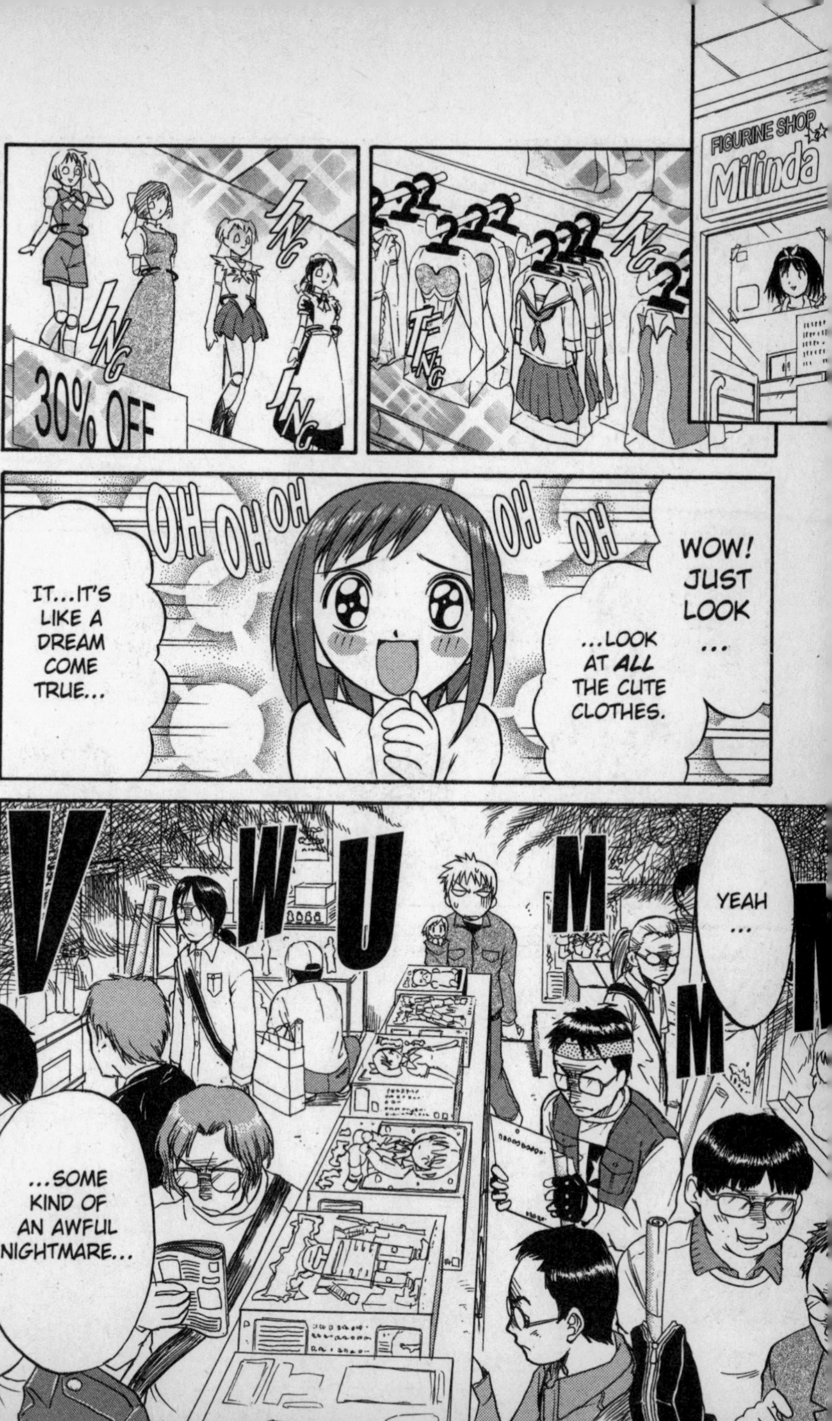
FIGURINE SHOP
Milinda
JING
TING
JING
JING
30% OFF
JING
WOW! JUST LOOK...
...LOOK AT ALL THE CUTE CLOTHES.
OH OH
OH OH OH
IT...IT'S LIKE A DREAM COME TRUE...
YEAH...
M M M
VWUM
...SOME KIND OF AN AWFUL NIGHTMARE...

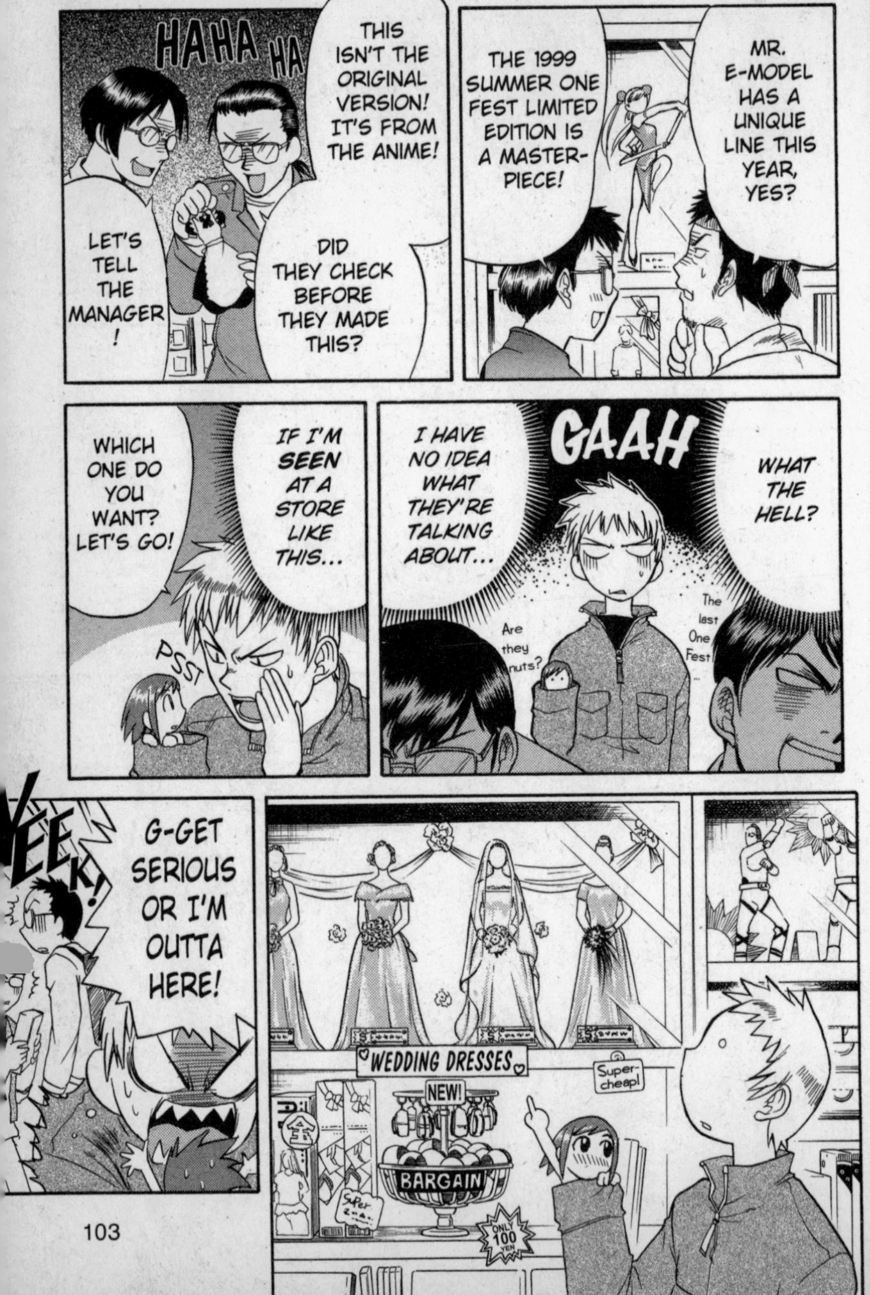
MR. E-MODEL HAS A UNIQUE LINE THIS YEAR, YES?
THE 1999 SUMMER ONE FEST LIMITED EDITION IS A MASTER-PIECE!
THIS ISN'T THE ORIGINAL VERSION! IT'S FROM THE ANIME!
HAHA HA
DID THEY CHECK BEFORE THEY MADE THIS?
LET'S TELL THE MANAGER!
WHAT THE HELL?
GAAH
The last One Fest...
I HAVE NO IDEA WHAT THEY'RE TALKING ABOUT...
Are they nuts?
IF I'M SEEN AT A STORE LIKE THIS...
WHICH ONE DO YOU WANT? LET'S GO!
PSST
WEDDING DRESSES
Super-cheap!
NEW!
BARGAIN
ONLY 100 YEN
G-GET SERIOUS OR I'M OUTTA HERE!
YEEK!

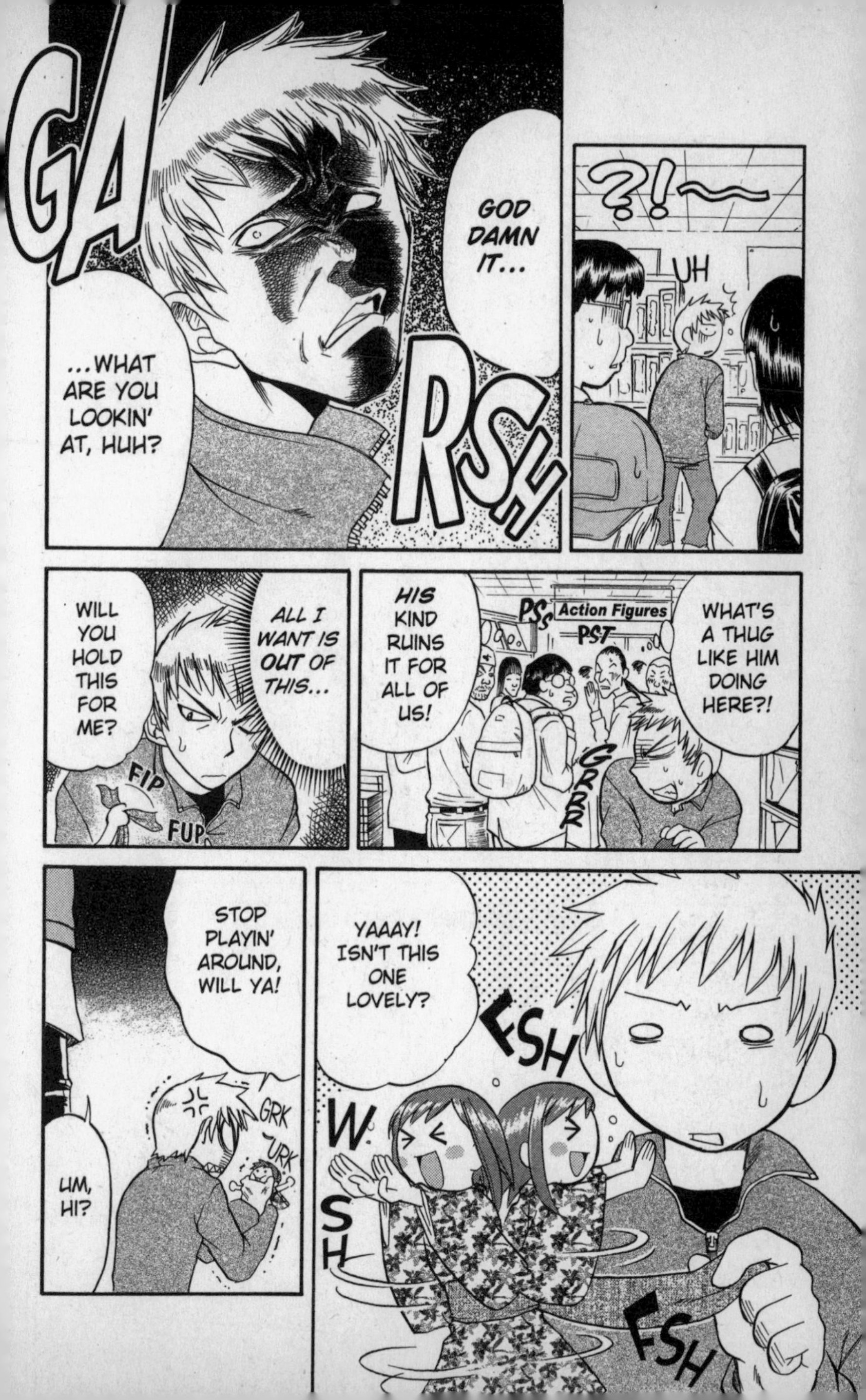
?!~~
UH
GOD DAMN IT...
GA
RSH
...WHAT ARE YOU LOOKIN' AT, HUH?
WHAT'S A THUG LIKE HIM DOING HERE?!
Action Figures
PSS
PST
HIS KIND RUINS IT FOR ALL OF US!
GRRR
ALL I WANT IS OUT OF THIS...
WILL YOU HOLD THIS FOR ME?
FIP
FUP
YAAAY! ISN'T THIS ONE LOVELY?
FSH
WSH
FSH
STOP PLAYIN' AROUND, WILL YA!
GRK
URK
UM, HI?

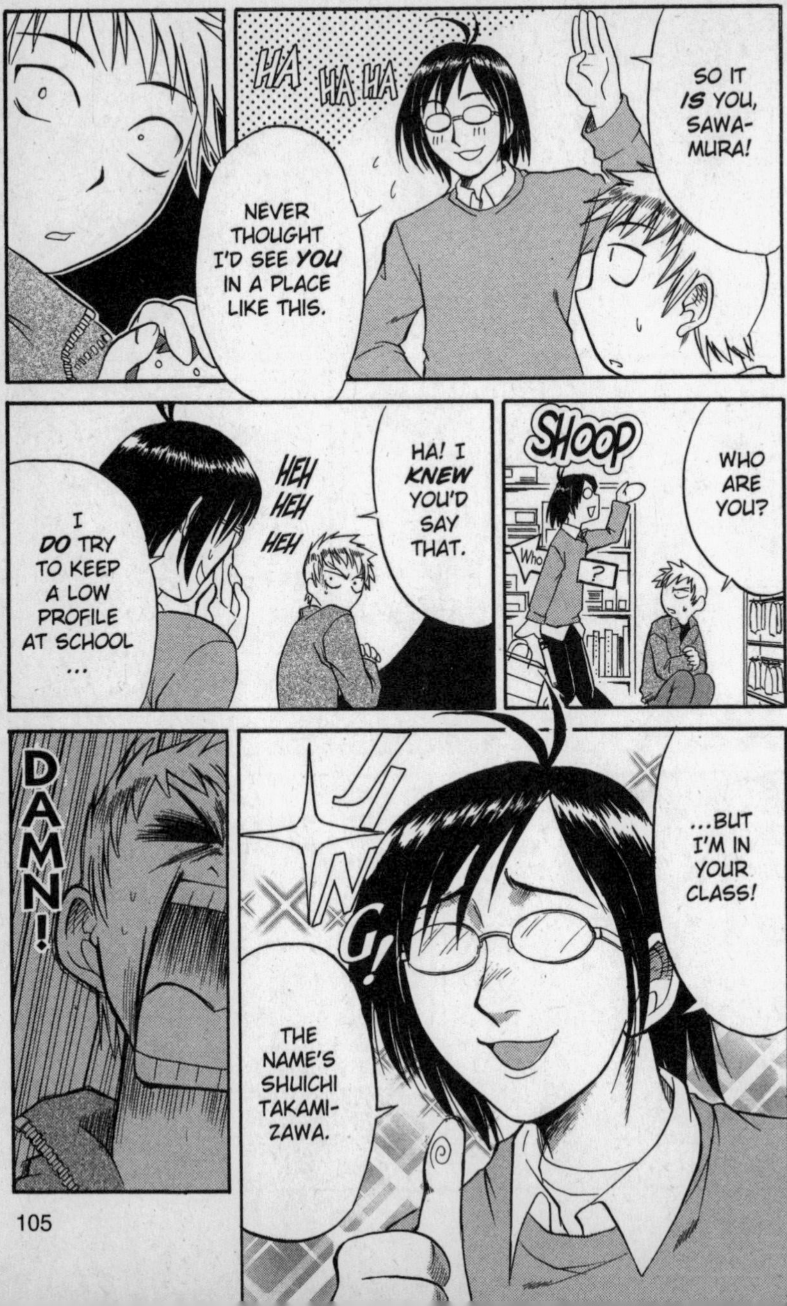
SO IT IS YOU, SAWAMURA!
HA HA HA
NEVER THOUGHT I'D SEE YOU IN A PLACE LIKE THIS.
WHO ARE YOU?
SHOOP
Who
?
HA! I KNEW YOU'D SAY THAT.
HEH HEH HEH
I DO TRY TO KEEP A LOW PROFILE AT SCHOOL ...
...BUT I'M IN YOUR CLASS!
JING!
THE NAME'S SHUICHI TAKAMI-ZAWA.
DAMN!

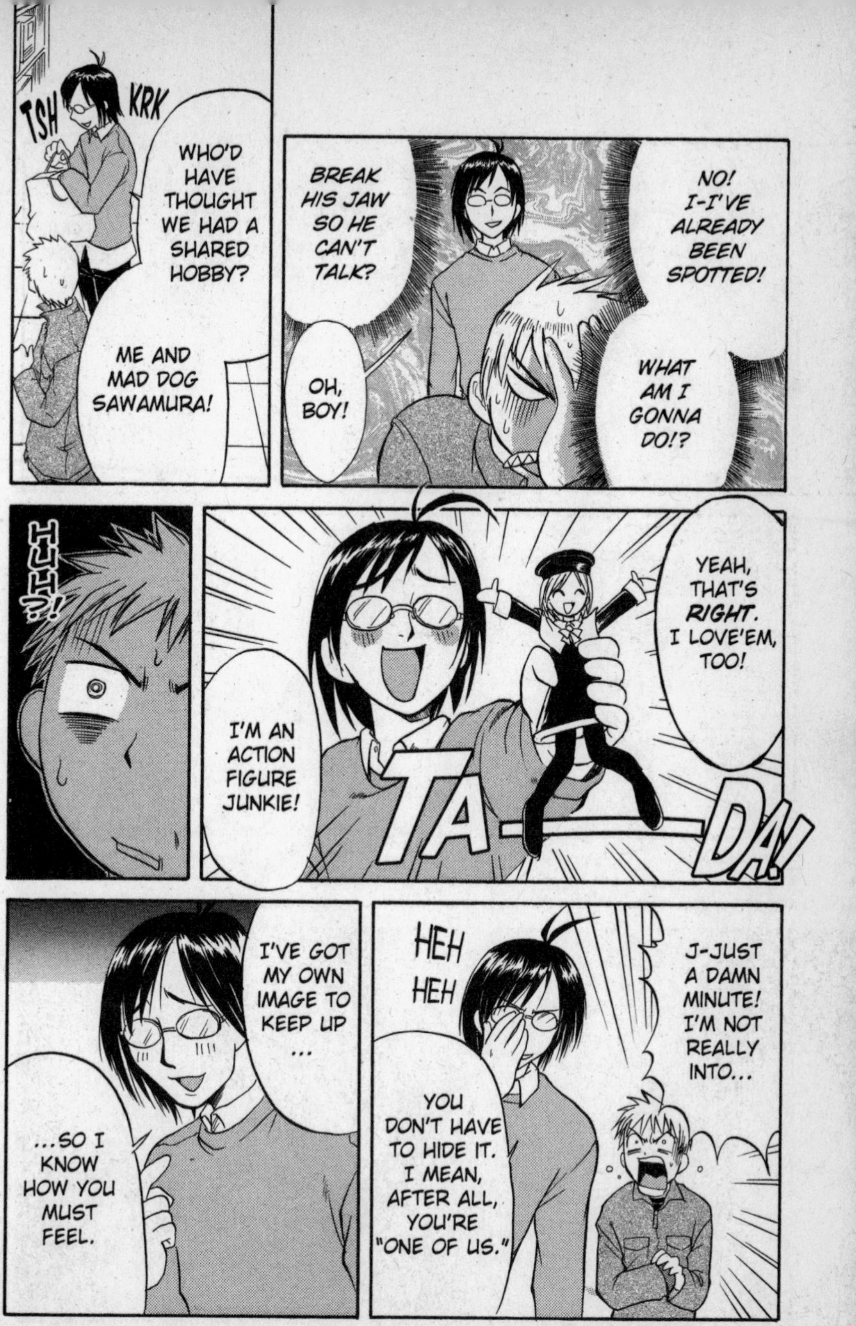
NO! I-I'VE ALREADY BEEN SPOTTED!
BREAK HIS JAW SO HE CAN'T TALK?
WHAT AM I GONNA DO!?
OH, BOY!
TSH KRK
WHO'D HAVE THOUGHT WE HAD A SHARED HOBBY?
ME AND MAD DOG SAWAMURA!
YEAH, THAT'S *RIGHT*. I LOVE'EM, TOO!
I'M AN ACTION FIGURE JUNKIE!
TA-DA!
HUH?!
J-JUST A DAMN MINUTE! I'M NOT REALLY INTO...
HEH HEH
YOU DON'T HAVE TO HIDE IT. I MEAN, AFTER ALL, YOU'RE "ONE OF US."
I'VE GOT MY OWN IMAGE TO KEEP UP ...
...SO I KNOW HOW YOU MUST FEEL.

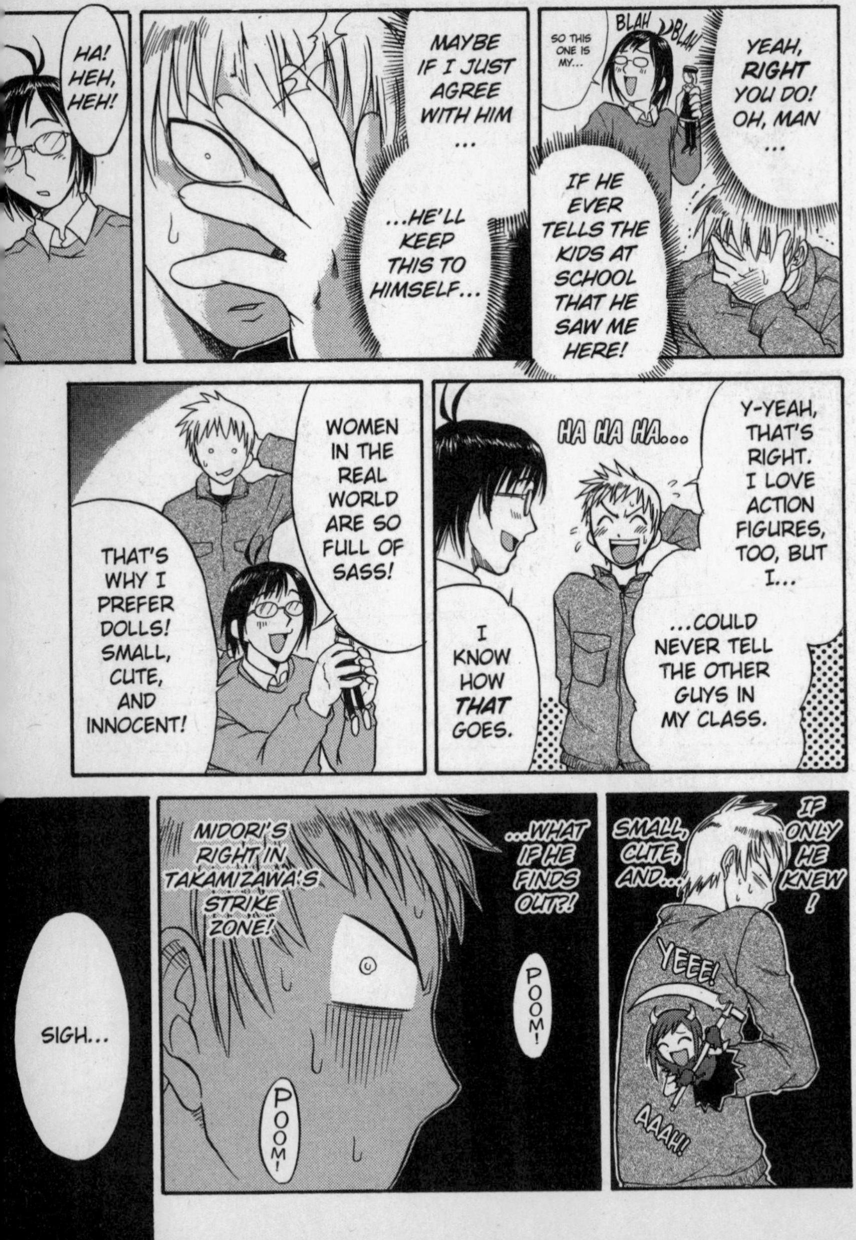
YEAH, RIGHT YOU DO! OH, MAN...
BLAH BLAH
SO THIS ONE IS MY...
IF HE EVER TELLS THE KIDS AT SCHOOL THAT HE SAW ME HERE!
MAYBE IF I JUST AGREE WITH HIM...
...HE'LL KEEP THIS TO HIMSELF...
HA! HEH, HEH!
Y-YEAH, THAT'S RIGHT. I LOVE ACTION FIGURES, TOO, BUT I...
HA HA HA...
...COULD NEVER TELL THE OTHER GUYS IN MY CLASS.
I KNOW HOW THAT GOES.
WOMEN IN THE REAL WORLD ARE SO FULL OF SASS!
THAT'S WHY I PREFER DOLLS! SMALL, CUTE, AND INNOCENT!
IF ONLY HE KNEW!
SMALL, CUTE, AND...
YEEE!
AAAH!
...WHAT IF HE FINDS OUT?!
MIDORI'S RIGHT IN TAKAMIZAWA'S STRIKE ZONE!
POOM!
POOM!
SIGH...

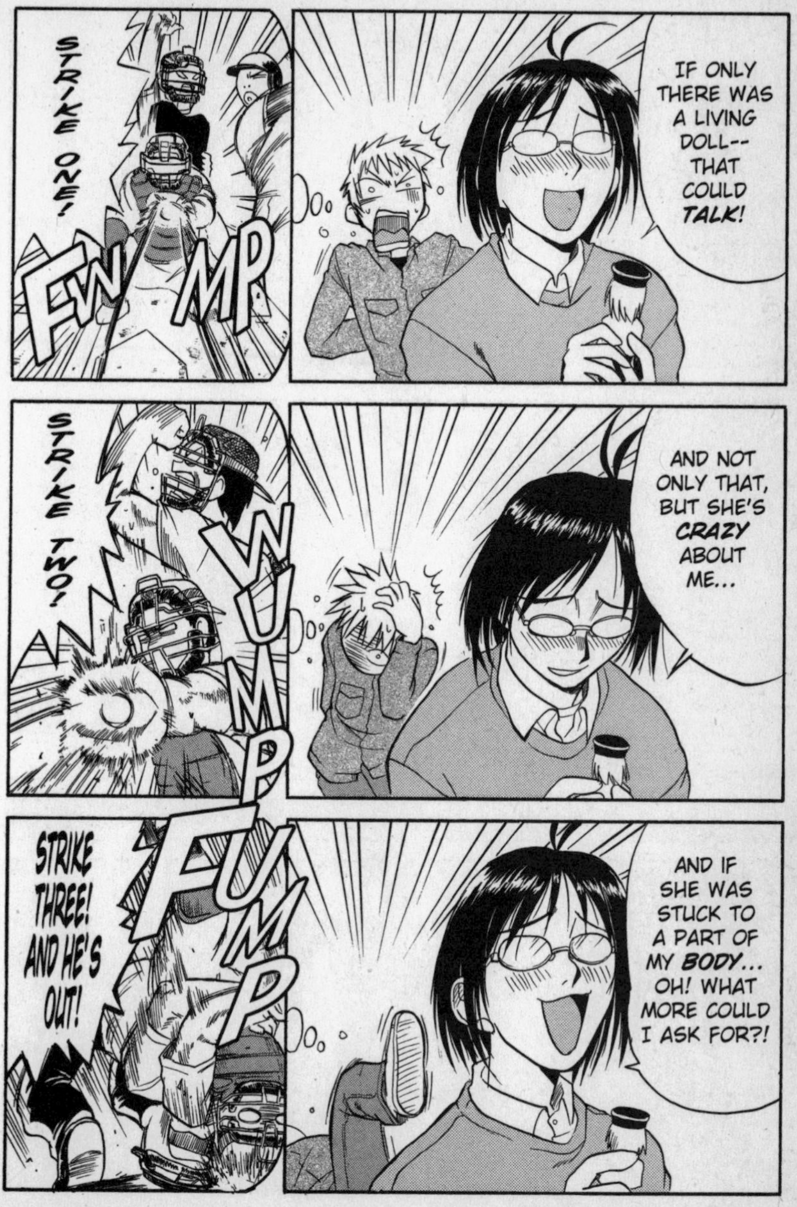
IF ONLY THERE WAS A LIVING DOLL-- THAT COULD *TALK!*
STRIKE ONE!
FWMP
AND NOT ONLY THAT, BUT SHE'S *CRAZY* ABOUT ME...
STRIKE TWO!
WUMP
AND IF SHE WAS STUCK TO A PART OF MY *BODY*... OH! WHAT MORE COULD I ASK FOR?!
STRIKE THREE! AND HE'S OUT!
FUMP

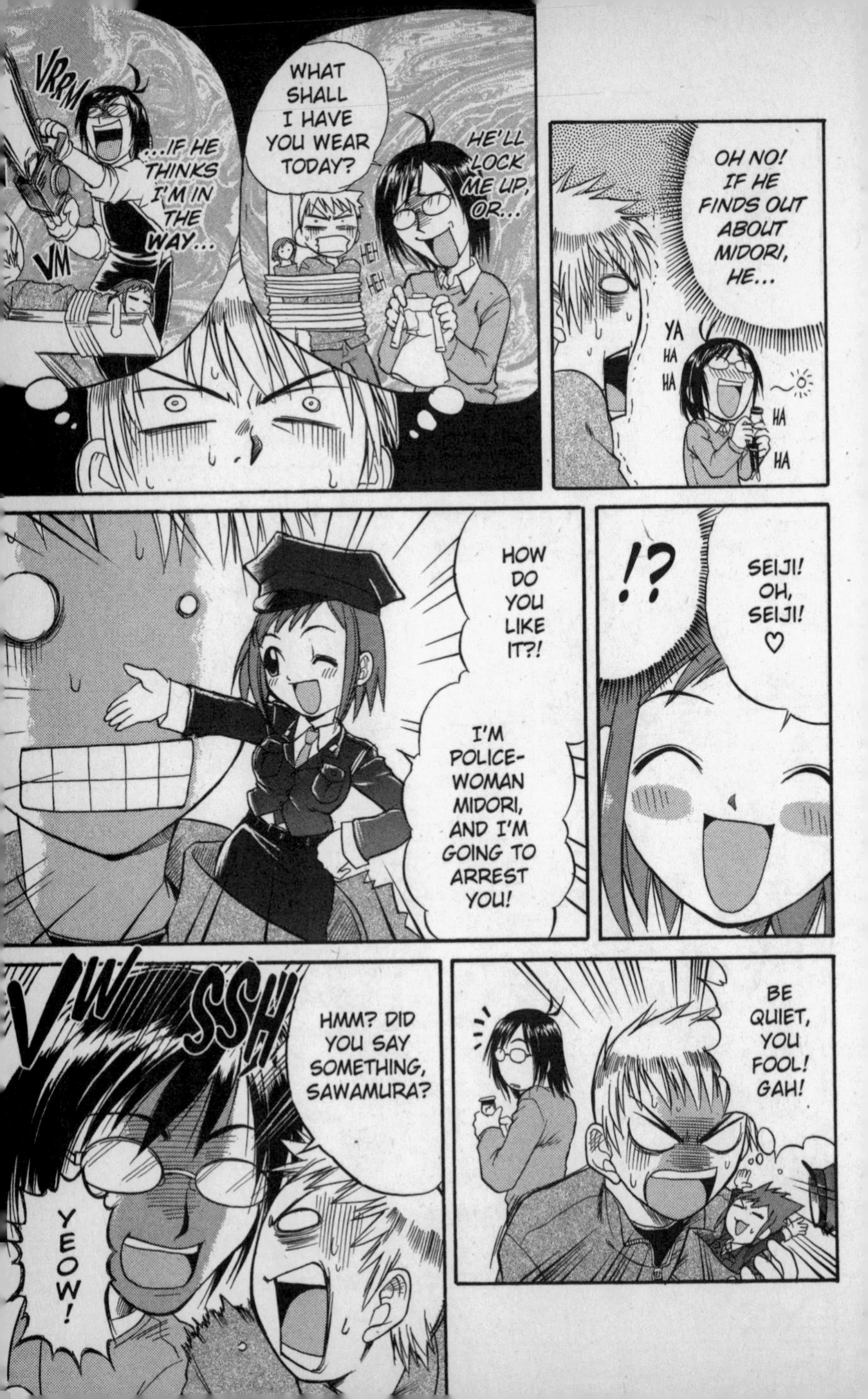
OH NO! IF HE FINDS OUT ABOUT MIDORI, HE...
YA HA HA
HA HA
HE'LL LOCK ME UP, OR...
WHAT SHALL I HAVE YOU WEAR TODAY?
HEH HEH
...IF HE THINKS I'M IN THE WAY...
VRRM
VM
!?
SEIJI! OH, SEIJI! ♡
HOW DO YOU LIKE IT?!
I'M POLICE-WOMAN MIDORI, AND I'M GOING TO ARREST YOU!
BE QUIET, YOU FOOL! GAH!
VWSSH
HMM? DID YOU SAY SOMETHING, SAWAMURA?
YEOW!

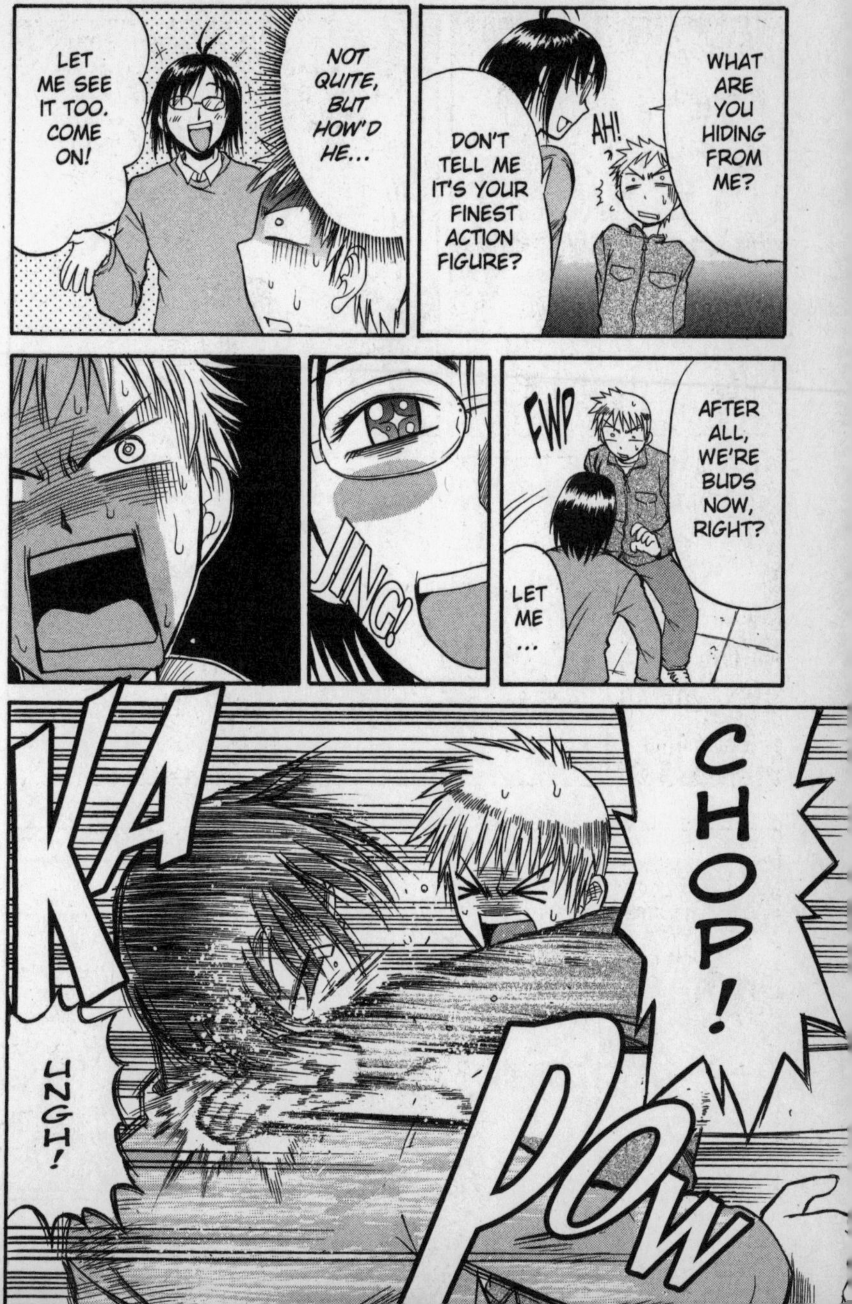
WHAT ARE YOU HIDING FROM ME?
AH!
DON'T TELL ME IT'S YOUR FINEST ACTION FIGURE?
NOT QUITE, BUT HOW'D HE...
LET ME SEE IT TOO. COME ON!
AFTER ALL, WE'RE BUDS NOW, RIGHT?
FWP
LET ME ...
JING!
CHOP!
KA
POW
UNGH!

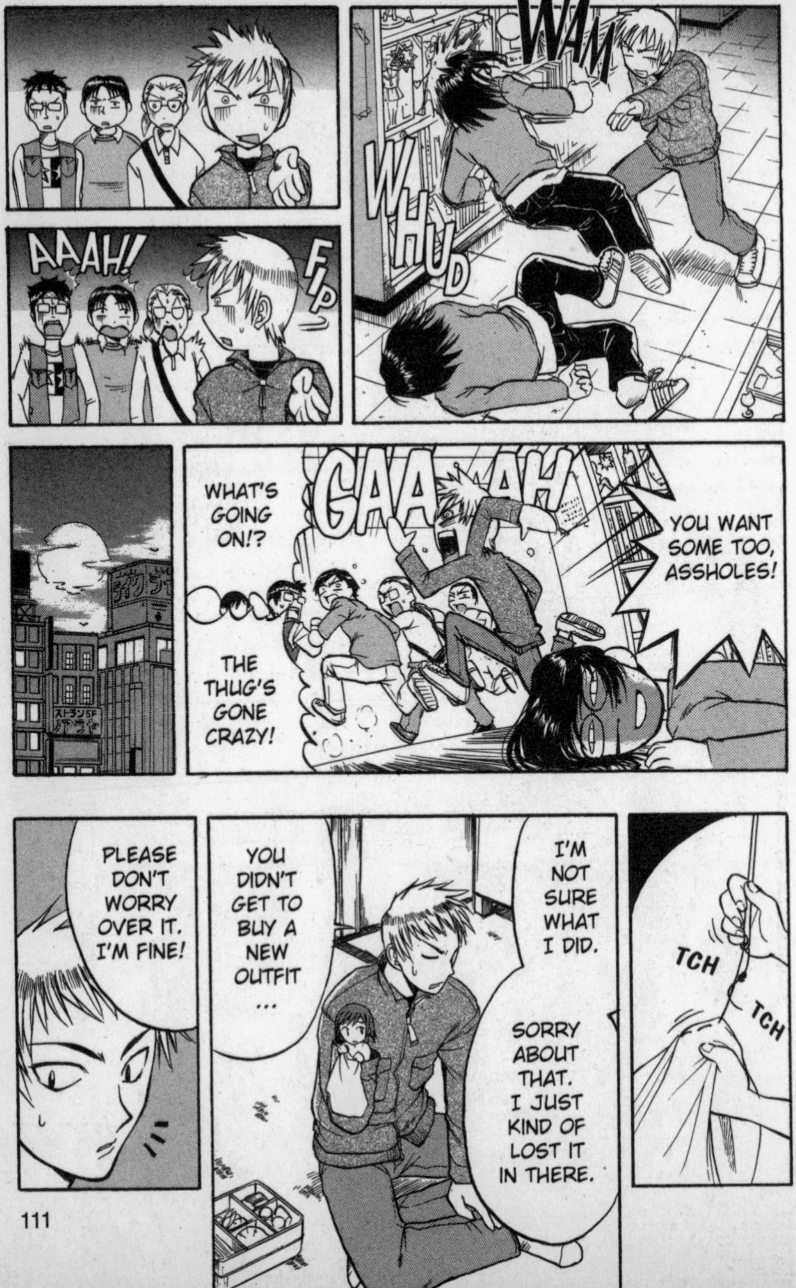
WAM
WHUD
AAAH!
FIP
GAA AH
YOU WANT SOME TOO, ASSHOLES!
WHAT'S GOING ON!?
THE THUG'S GONE CRAZY!
TCH
TCH
I'M NOT SURE WHAT I DID.
SORRY ABOUT THAT. I JUST KIND OF LOST IT IN THERE.
YOU DIDN'T GET TO BUY A NEW OUTFIT...
PLEASE DON'T WORRY OVER IT. I'M FINE!

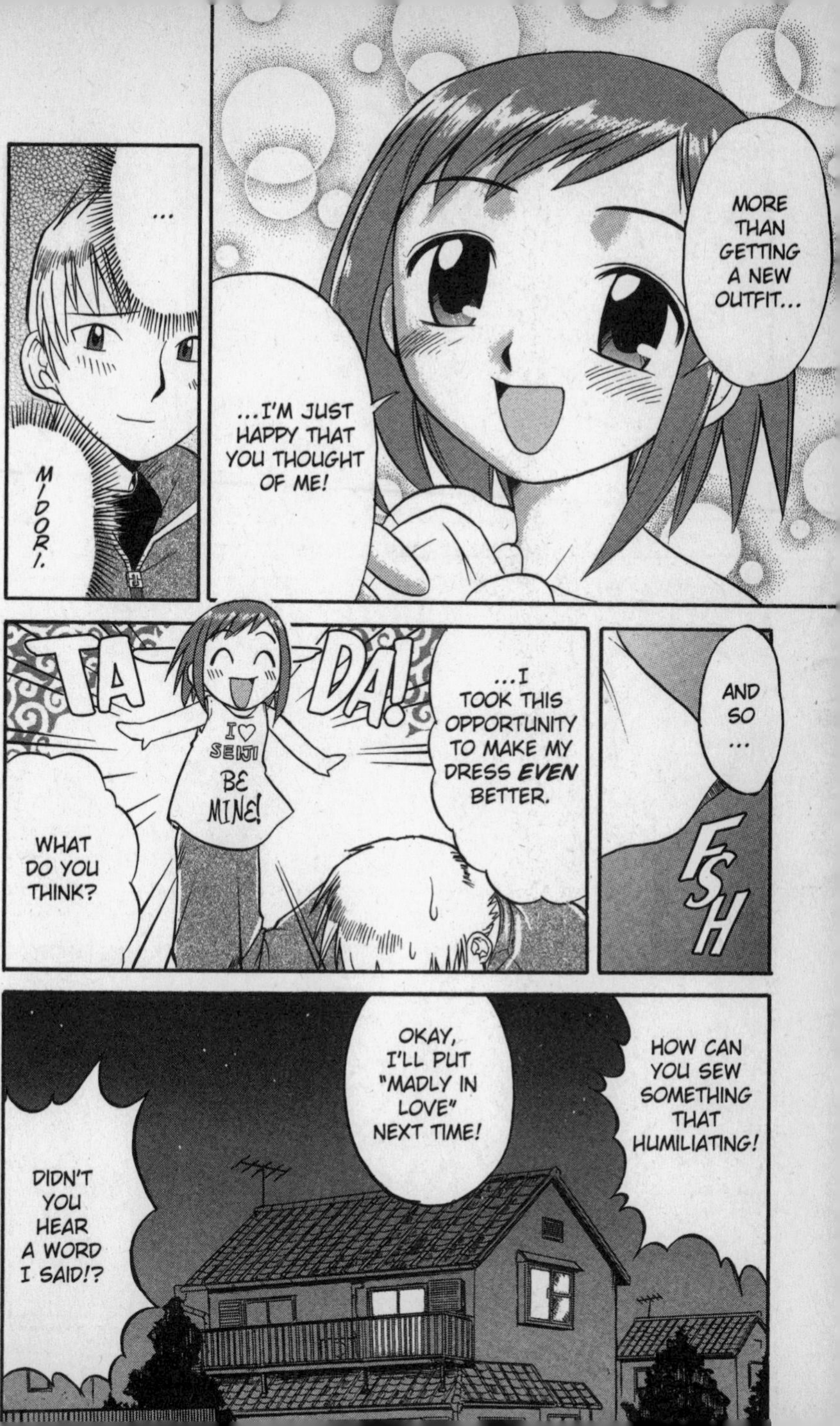
MORE THAN GETTING A NEW OUTFIT...
...I'M JUST HAPPY THAT YOU THOUGHT OF ME!
...
MIDORI.
AND SO...
FSH
...I TOOK THIS OPPORTUNITY TO MAKE MY DRESS *EVEN* BETTER.
TA DA!
I ♥ SEIJI BE MINE!
WHAT DO YOU THINK?
HOW CAN YOU SEW SOMETHING THAT HUMILIATING!
OKAY, I'LL PUT "MADLY IN LOVE" NEXT TIME!
DIDN'T YOU HEAR A WORD I SAID!?

DAY 6 PRECIOUS THING

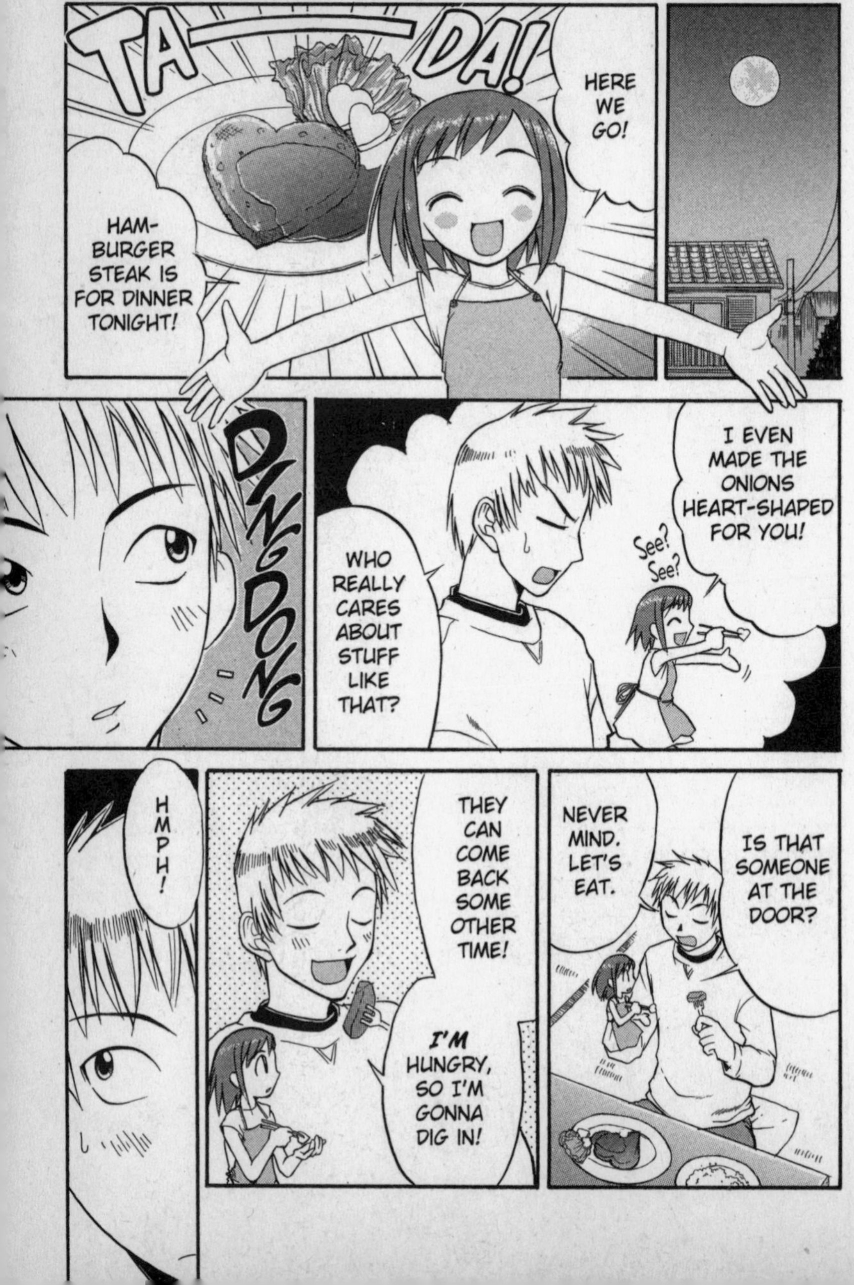
HERE WE GO!
TA—DA!
HAMBURGER STEAK IS FOR DINNER TONIGHT!
I EVEN MADE THE ONIONS HEART-SHAPED FOR YOU!
See? See?
WHO REALLY CARES ABOUT STUFF LIKE THAT?
DING DONG
IS THAT SOMEONE AT THE DOOR?
NEVER MIND. LET'S EAT.
THEY CAN COME BACK SOME OTHER TIME!
I'M HUNGRY, SO I'M GONNA DIG IN!
HMPH!

DAY 6
PRECIOUS THING

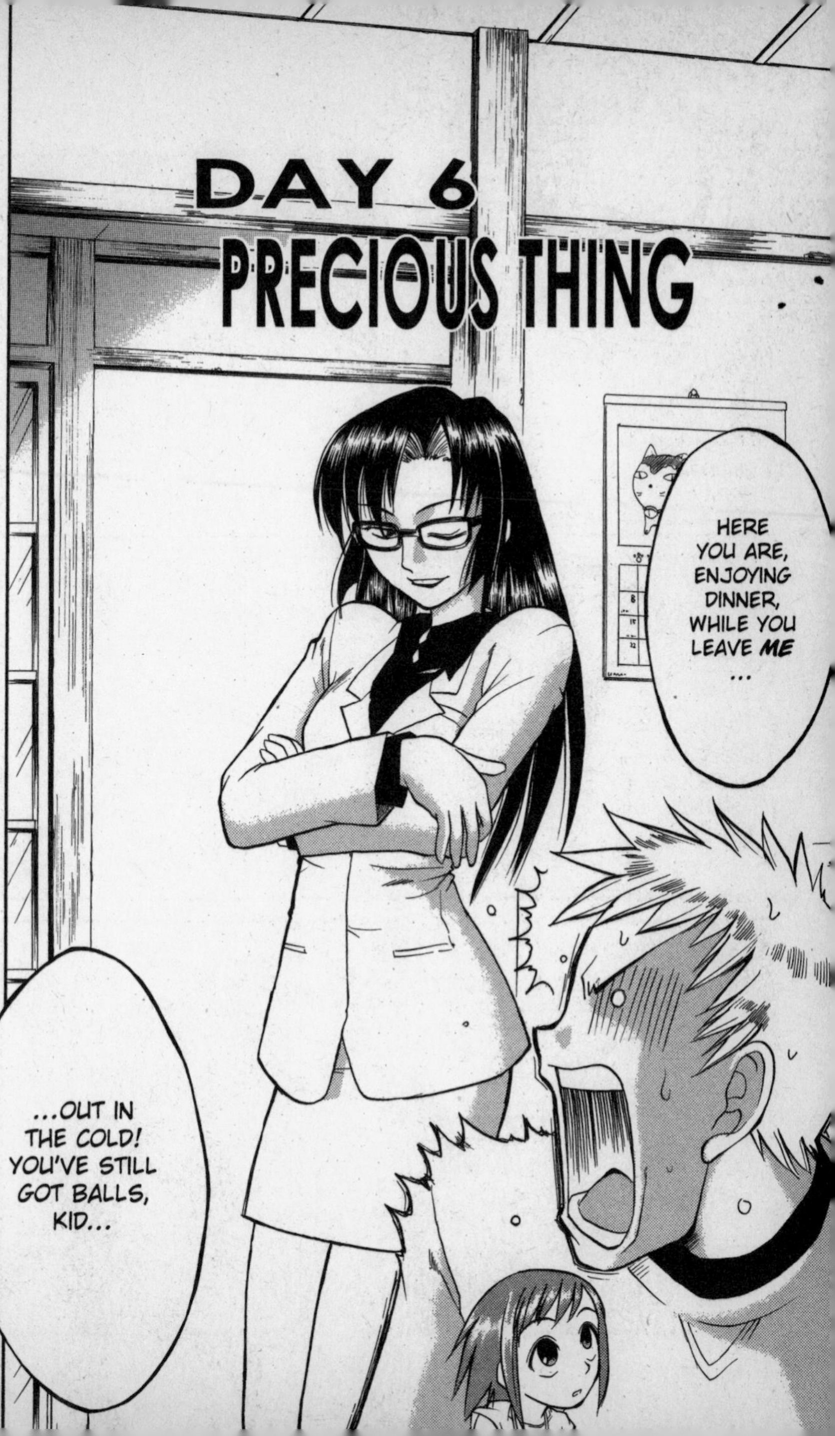
HERE YOU ARE, ENJOYING DINNER, WHILE YOU LEAVE *ME* ...
...OUT IN THE COLD! YOU'VE STILL GOT BALLS, KID...

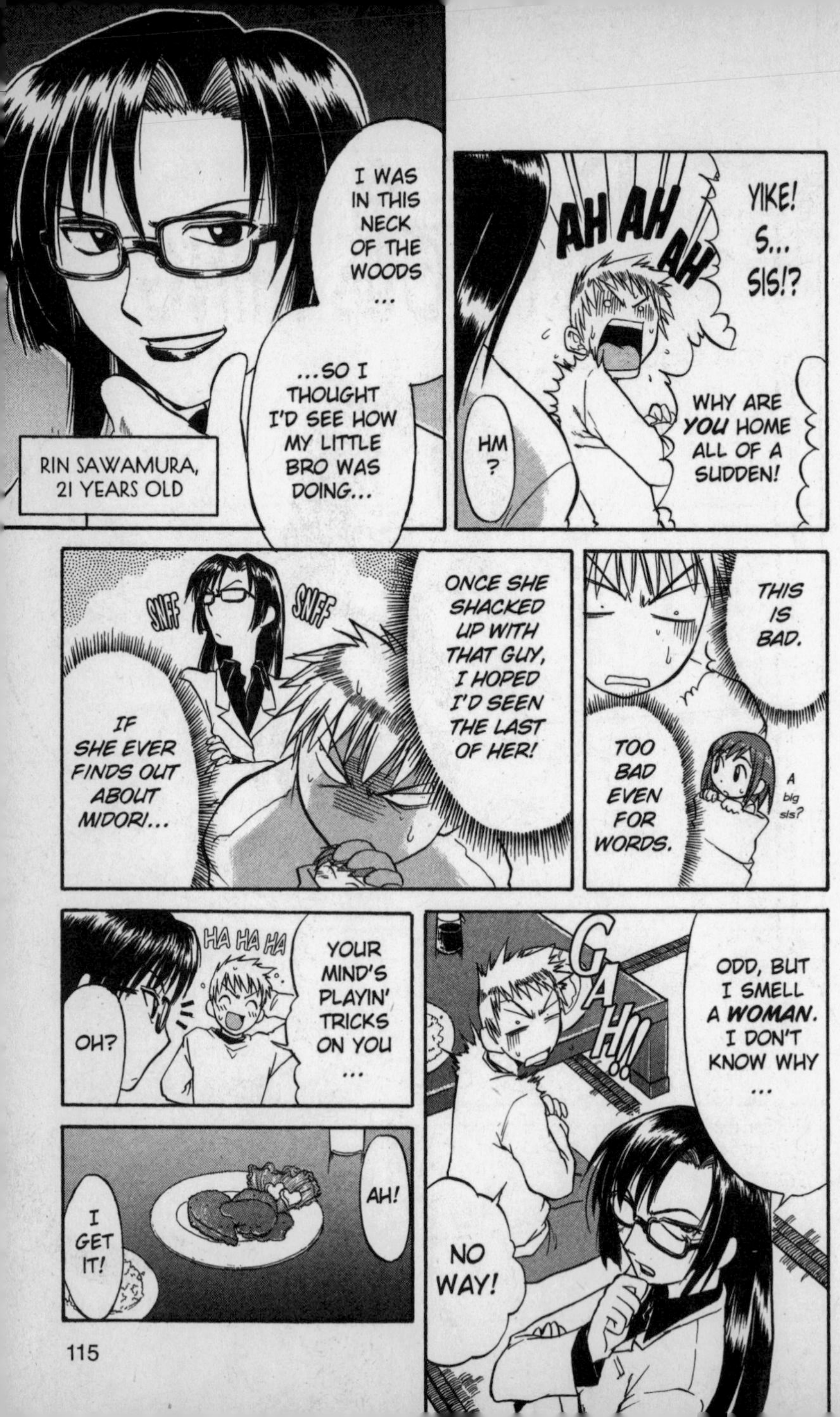
YIKE! S... SIS!?
AH AH AH
WHY ARE **YOU** HOME ALL OF A SUDDEN!
HM?
I WAS IN THIS NECK OF THE WOODS ...
...SO I THOUGHT I'D SEE HOW MY LITTLE BRO WAS DOING...
RIN SAWAMURA, 21 YEARS OLD
THIS IS BAD.
TOO BAD EVEN FOR WORDS.
A big sis?
ONCE SHE SHACKED UP WITH THAT GUY, I HOPED I'D SEEN THE LAST OF HER!
SNIFF
SNIFF
IF SHE EVER FINDS OUT ABOUT MIDORI...
ODD, BUT I SMELL A **WOMAN**. I DON'T KNOW WHY ...
GAH!!
NO WAY!
YOUR MIND'S PLAYIN' TRICKS ON YOU ...
HA HA HA
OH?
AH!
I GET IT!

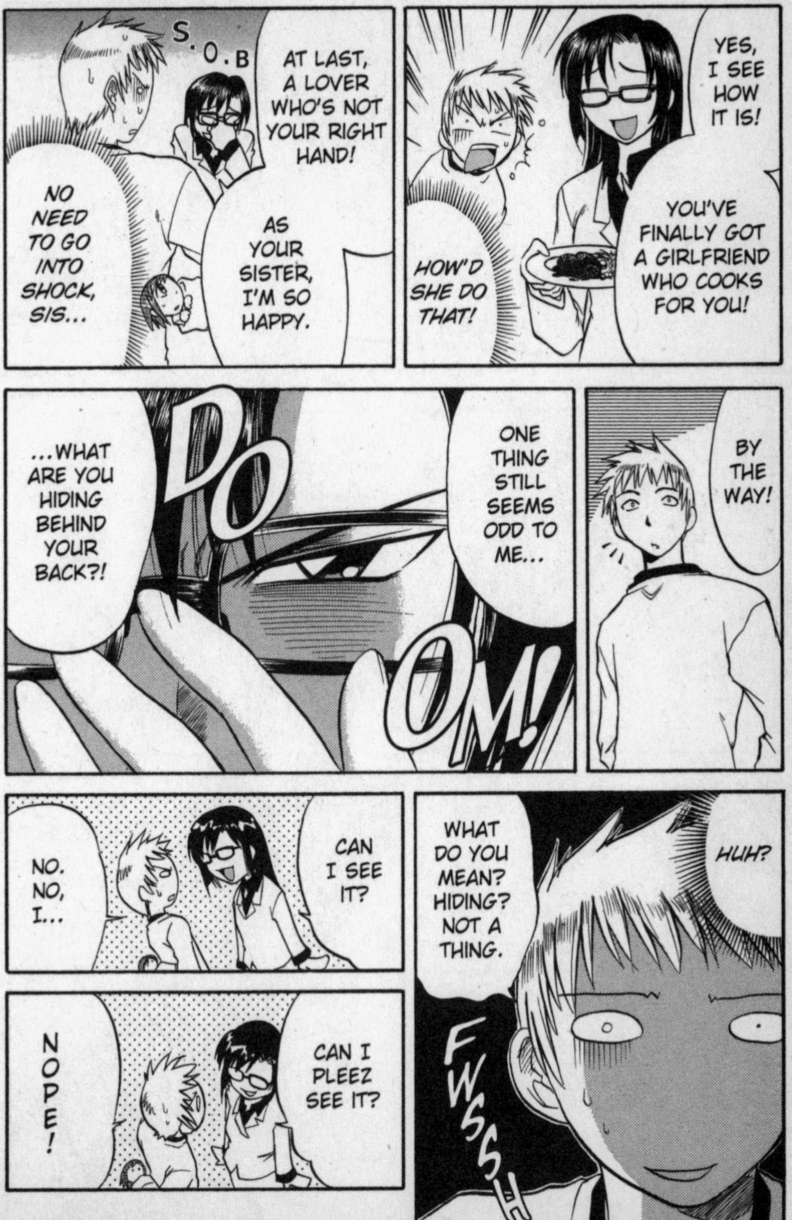
YES, I SEE HOW IT IS!
YOU'VE FINALLY GOT A GIRLFRIEND WHO COOKS FOR YOU!
HOW'D SHE DO THAT!
S.O.B
AT LAST, A LOVER WHO'S NOT YOUR RIGHT HAND!
AS YOUR SISTER, I'M SO HAPPY.
NO NEED TO GO INTO SHOCK, SIS...
BY THE WAY!
ONE THING STILL SEEMS ODD TO ME...
DOOM!
...WHAT ARE YOU HIDING BEHIND YOUR BACK?!
HUH?
WHAT DO YOU MEAN? HIDING? NOT A THING.
FWSSH
CAN I SEE IT?
NO. NO, I...
CAN I PLEEZ SEE IT?
NOPE!

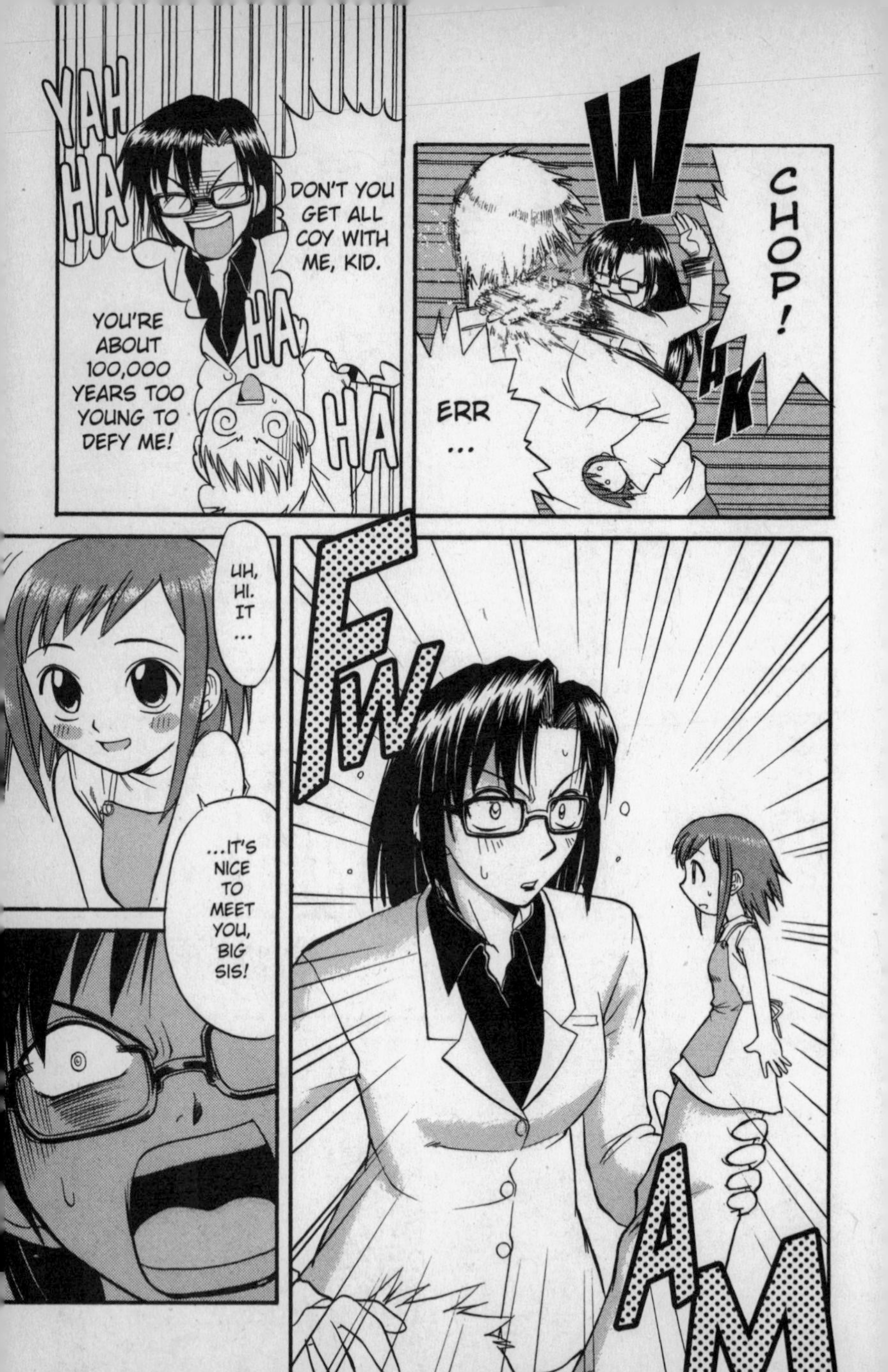
WHAK
CHOP!
ERR...
YAH HA HA HA HA
DON'T YOU GET ALL COY WITH ME, KID.
YOU'RE ABOUT 100,000 YEARS TOO YOUNG TO DEFY ME!
FWAM
UH, HI. IT...
...IT'S NICE TO MEET YOU, BIG SIS!

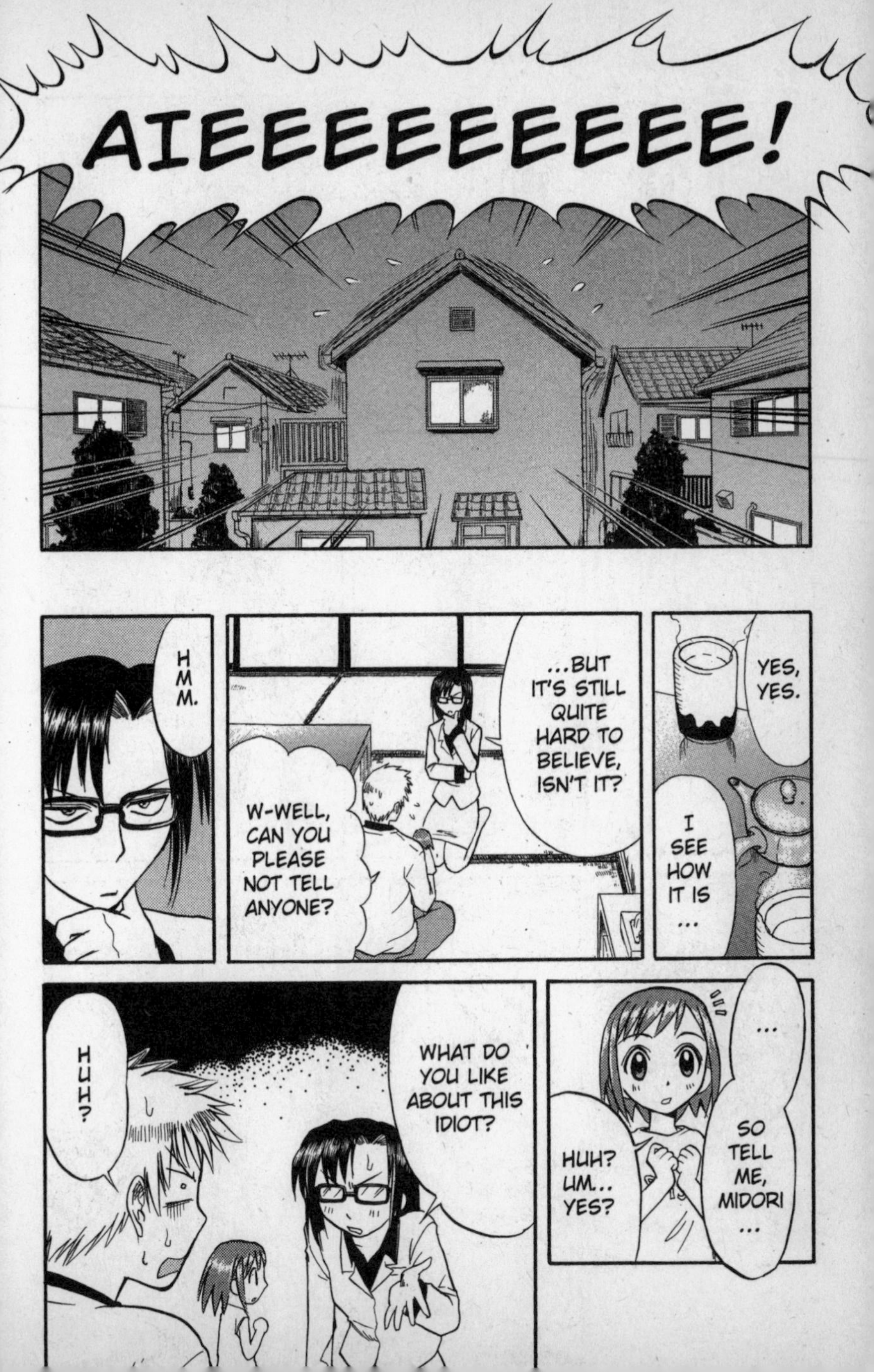
AIEEEEEEEEEE!
YES, YES.
I SEE HOW IT IS...
...BUT IT'S STILL QUITE HARD TO BELIEVE, ISN'T IT?
W-WELL, CAN YOU PLEASE NOT TELL ANYONE?
HMM.
...
SO TELL ME, MIDORI...
HUH? UM... YES?
WHAT DO YOU LIKE ABOUT THIS IDIOT?
HUH?

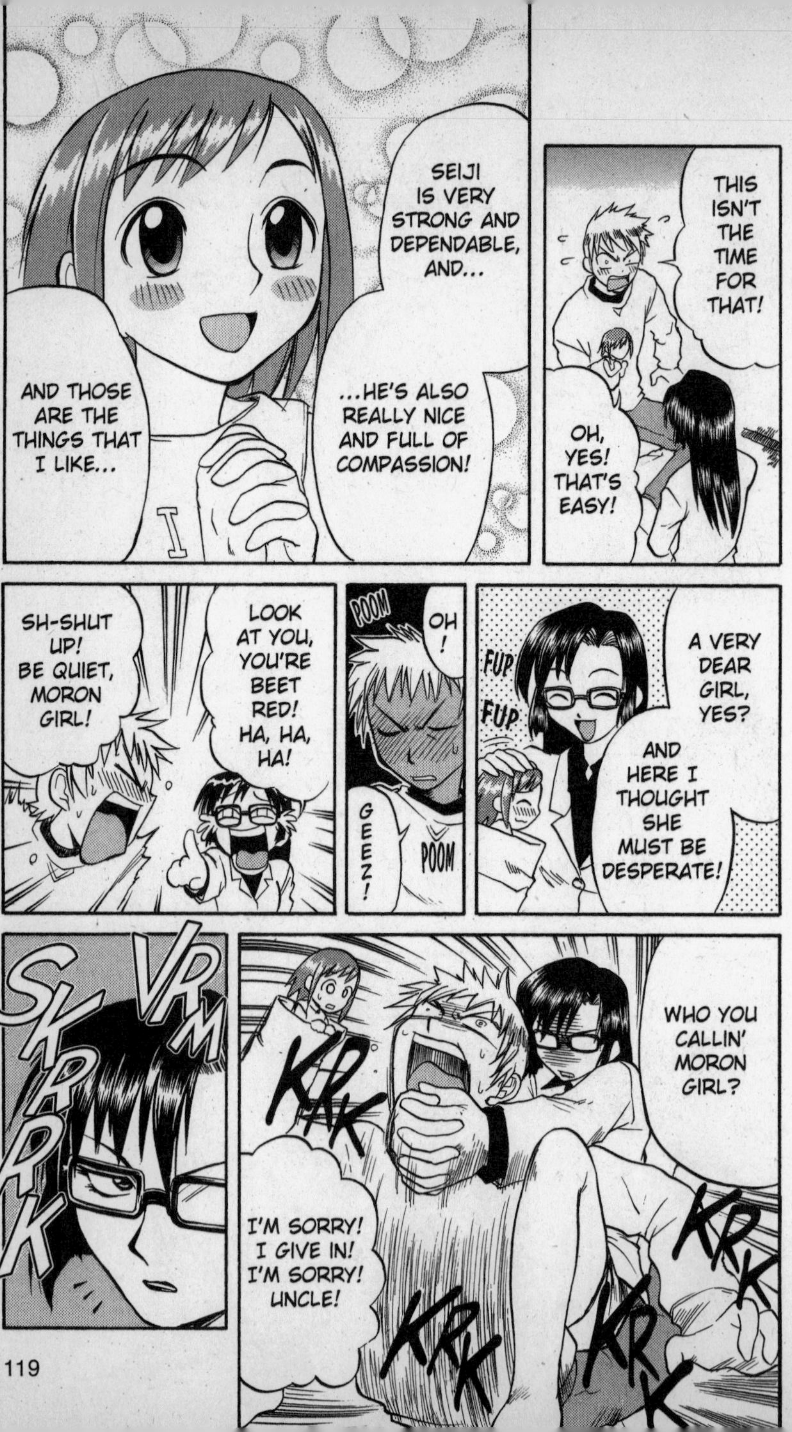
THIS ISN'T THE TIME FOR THAT!
OH, YES! THAT'S EASY!
SEIJI IS VERY STRONG AND DEPENDABLE, AND...
...HE'S ALSO REALLY NICE AND FULL OF COMPASSION!
AND THOSE ARE THE THINGS THAT I LIKE...
A VERY DEAR GIRL, YES?
FUP
FUP
AND HERE I THOUGHT SHE MUST BE DESPERATE!
POOM
OH!
GEEZ!
POOM
LOOK AT YOU, YOU'RE BEET RED! HA, HA, HA!
SH-SHUT UP! BE QUIET, MORON GIRL!
WHO YOU CALLIN' MORON GIRL?
KRK
I'M SORRY! I GIVE IN! I'M SORRY! UNCLE!
KRK
KRK
KRK
VRM
SKRRK

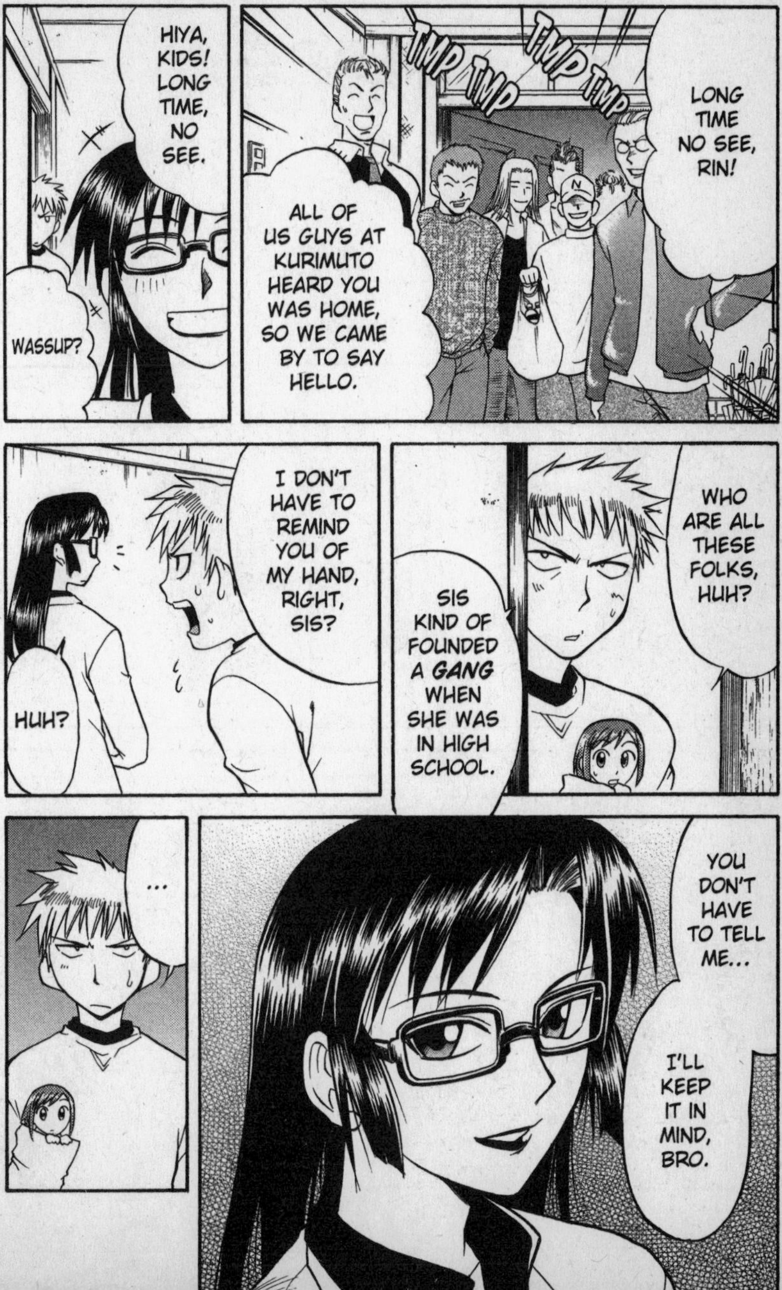
TMP TMP TMP TMP
LONG TIME NO SEE, RIN!
ALL OF US GUYS AT KURIMUTO HEARD YOU WAS HOME, SO WE CAME BY TO SAY HELLO.
HIYA, KIDS! LONG TIME, NO SEE.
WASSUP?
WHO ARE ALL THESE FOLKS, HUH?
SIS KIND OF FOUNDED A GANG WHEN SHE WAS IN HIGH SCHOOL.
I DON'T HAVE TO REMIND YOU OF MY HAND, RIGHT, SIS?
HUH?
YOU DON'T HAVE TO TELL ME...
I'LL KEEP IT IN MIND, BRO.
...

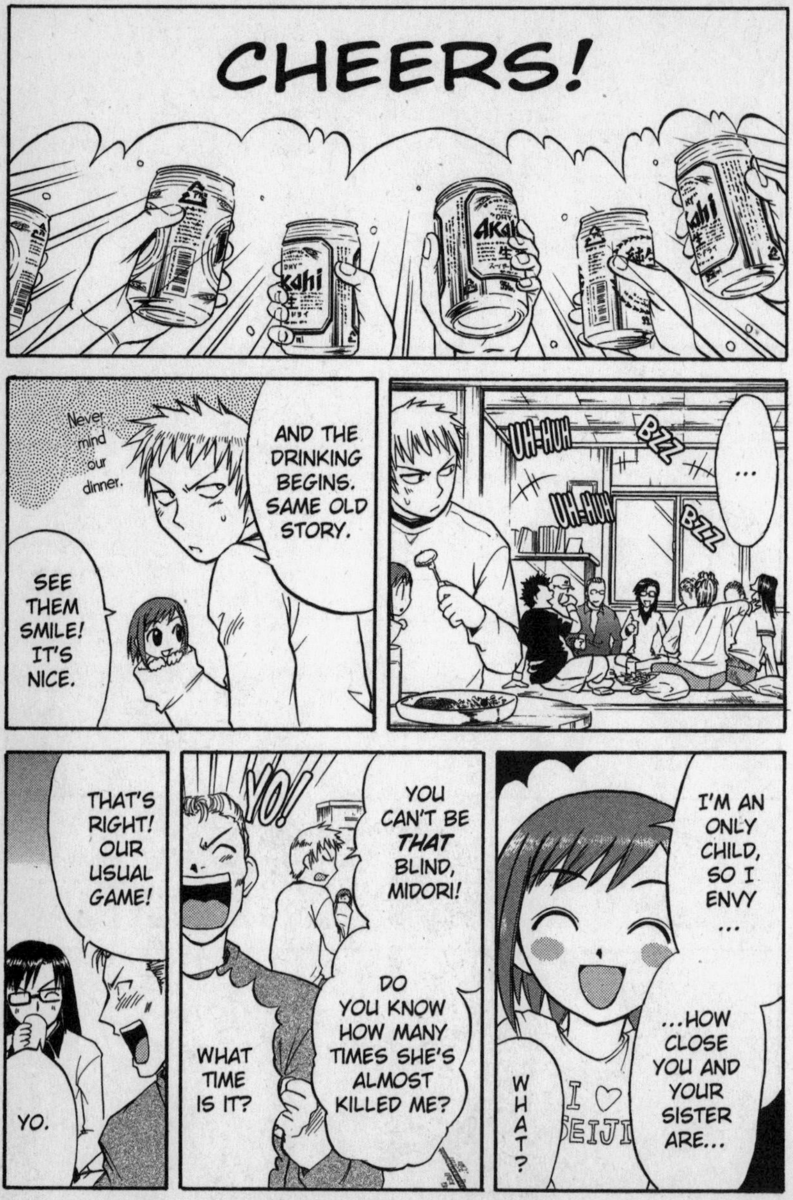
CHEERS!
...
UH-HUH
BZZ
UH-HUH
BZZ
AND THE DRINKING BEGINS. SAME OLD STORY.
Never mind our dinner.
SEE THEM SMILE! IT'S NICE.
I'M AN ONLY CHILD, SO I ENVY ...
...HOW CLOSE YOU AND YOUR SISTER ARE...
WHAT?
I ♡ SEIJI
YOU CAN'T BE *THAT* BLIND, MIDORI!
YO!
DO YOU KNOW HOW MANY TIMES SHE'S ALMOST KILLED ME?
WHAT TIME IS IT?
THAT'S RIGHT! OUR USUAL GAME!
YO.

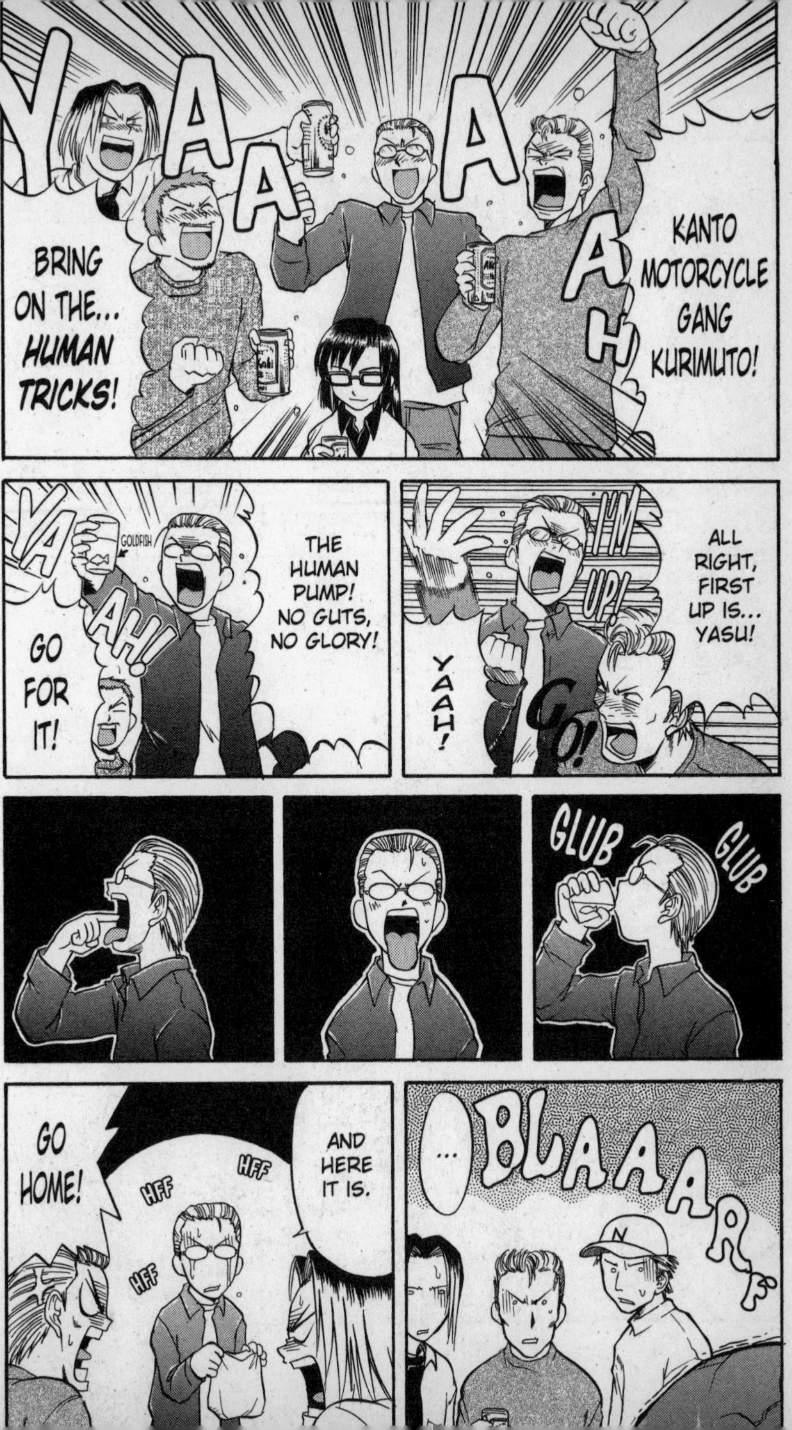
YAAAAAH
KANTO MOTORCYCLE GANG KURIMUTO!
BRING ON THE... HUMAN TRICKS!
ALL RIGHT, FIRST UP IS... YASU!
I'M UP!
GO!
YAAH!
THE HUMAN PUMP! NO GUTS, NO GLORY!
YAAH!
GOLDFISH
GO FOR IT!
GLUB
GLUB
BLAAARF
...
AND HERE IT IS.
HFF
HFF
HFF
GO HOME!

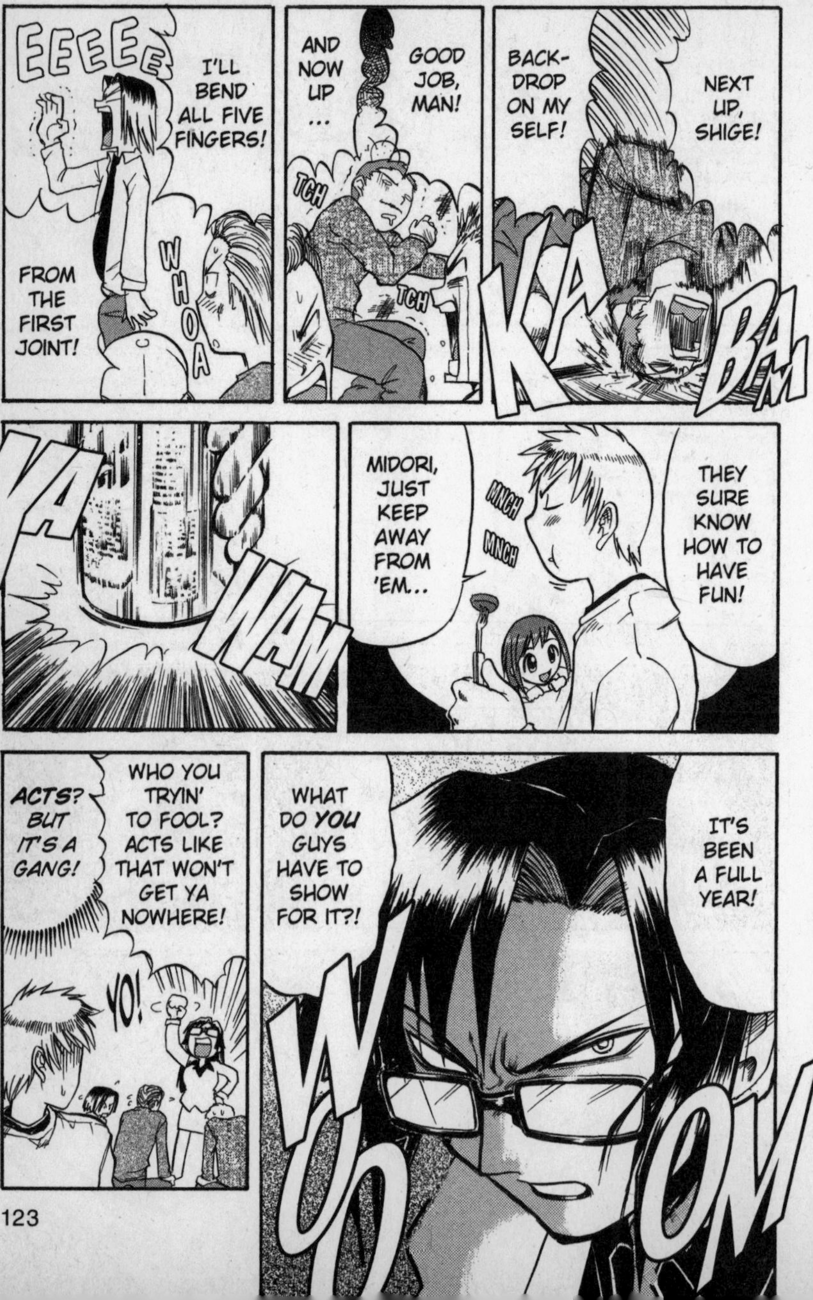
NEXT UP, SHIGE!
BACK-DROP ON MY SELF!
KA BAM
GOOD JOB, MAN!
AND NOW UP …
TCH
TCH
EEEEE
I'LL BEND ALL FIVE FINGERS!
FROM THE FIRST JOINT!
WHOA
THEY SURE KNOW HOW TO HAVE FUN!
MIDORI, JUST KEEP AWAY FROM 'EM…
MNCH
MNCH
KA WAM
IT'S BEEN A FULL YEAR!
WHAT DO YOU GUYS HAVE TO SHOW FOR IT?!
WOOOM
WHO YOU TRYIN' TO FOOL? ACTS LIKE THAT WON'T GET YA NOWHERE!
ACTS? BUT IT'S A GANG!
YO!

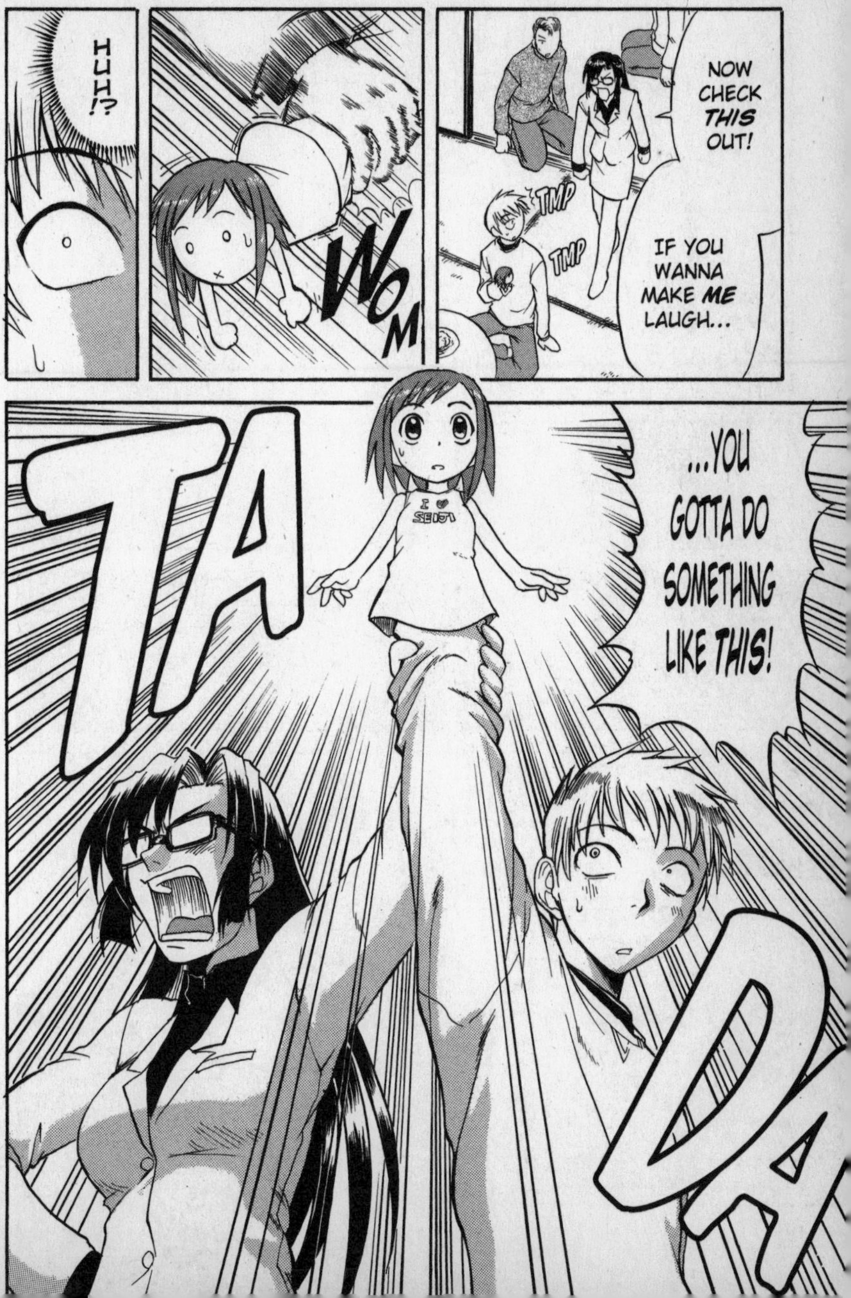
NOW CHECK THIS OUT!
TMP
TMP
IF YOU WANNA MAKE ME LAUGH...
WOM
HUH!?
...YOU GOTTA DO SOMETHING LIKE THIS!
TA
DA

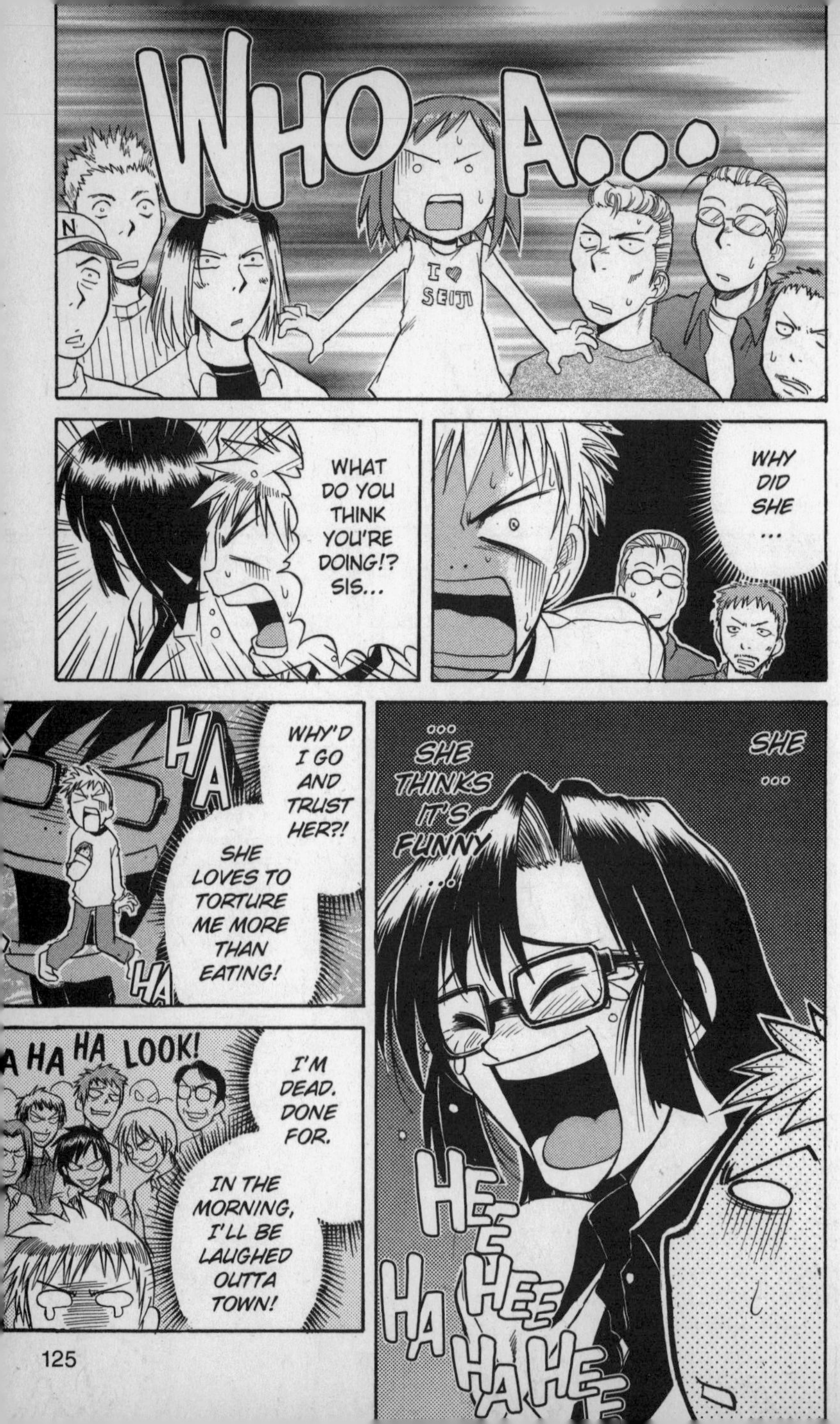
WHOA...
WHY DID SHE ...
WHAT DO YOU THINK YOU'RE DOING!? SIS...
SHE ...
...SHE THINKS IT'S FUNNY...
HEE HEE HA HA HEE HA HEE
HA HA
WHY'D I GO AND TRUST HER?!
SHE LOVES TO TORTURE ME MORE THAN EATING!
HA HA HA LOOK!
I'M DEAD. DONE FOR.
IN THE MORNING, I'LL BE LAUGHED OUTTA TOWN!

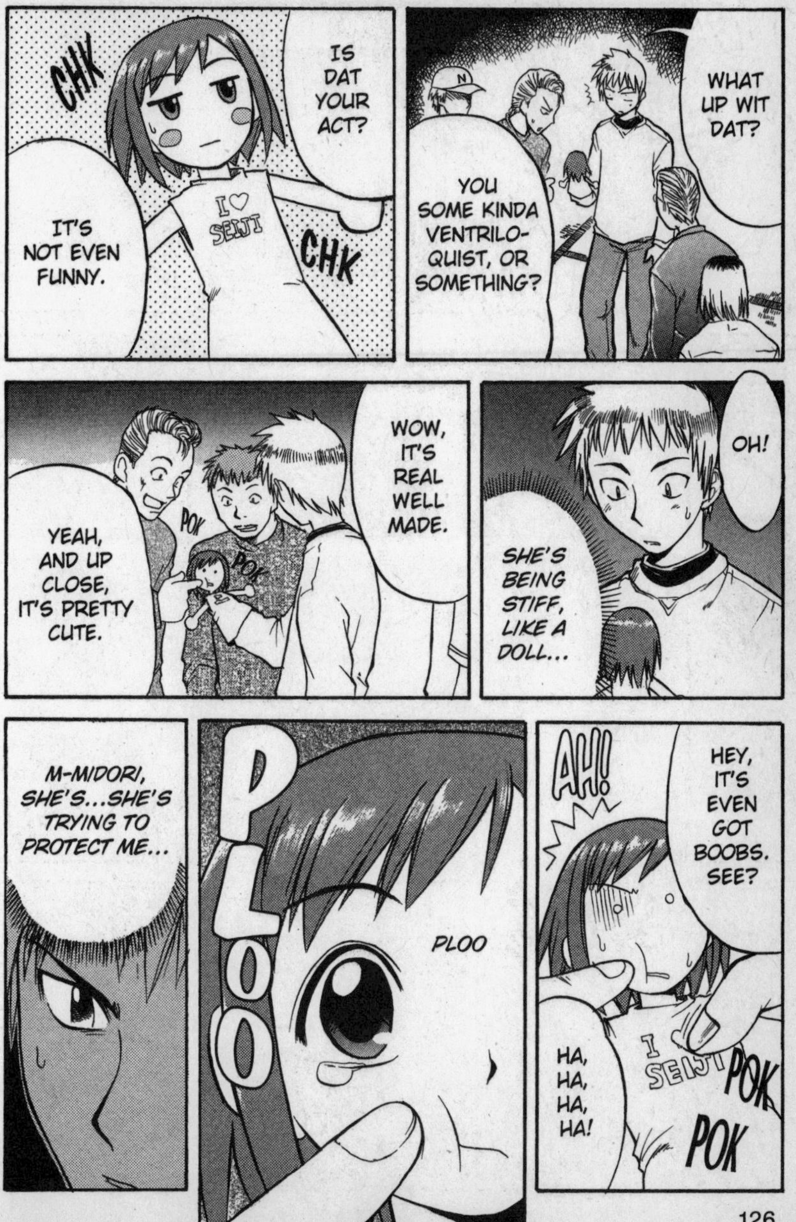
WHAT UP WIT DAT?
YOU SOME KINDA VENTRILO-QUIST, OR SOMETHING?
IS DAT YOUR ACT?
CHK
CHK
IT'S NOT EVEN FUNNY.
I ♡ SEIJI
OH!
SHE'S BEING STIFF, LIKE A DOLL...
WOW, IT'S REAL WELL MADE.
POK
POK
YEAH, AND UP CLOSE, IT'S PRETTY CUTE.
HEY, IT'S EVEN GOT BOOBS. SEE?
AH!
I SEIJI
POK
POK
HA, HA, HA, HA!
PLOO
PLOO
M-MIDORI, SHE'S...SHE'S TRYING TO PROTECT ME...

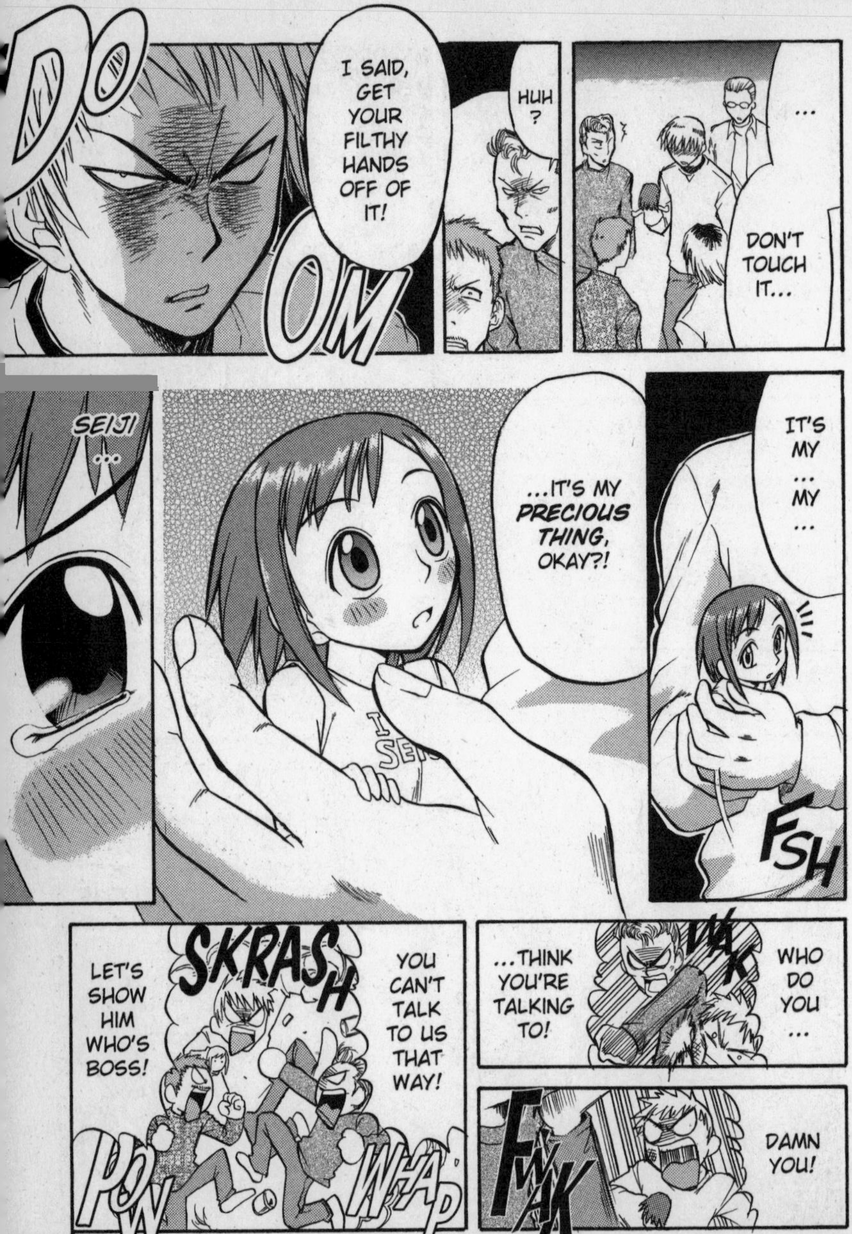
...
DON'T TOUCH IT...
HUH ?
I SAID, GET YOUR FILTHY HANDS OFF OF IT!
DOOM
IT'S MY ... MY ...
FSH
...IT'S MY *PRECIOUS THING*, OKAY?!
SEIJI ...
WHO DO YOU ...
WAK
...THINK YOU'RE TALKING TO!
DAMN YOU!
FWAK
YOU CAN'T TALK TO US THAT WAY!
SKRASH
LET'S SHOW HIM WHO'S BOSS!
POW
WHAP

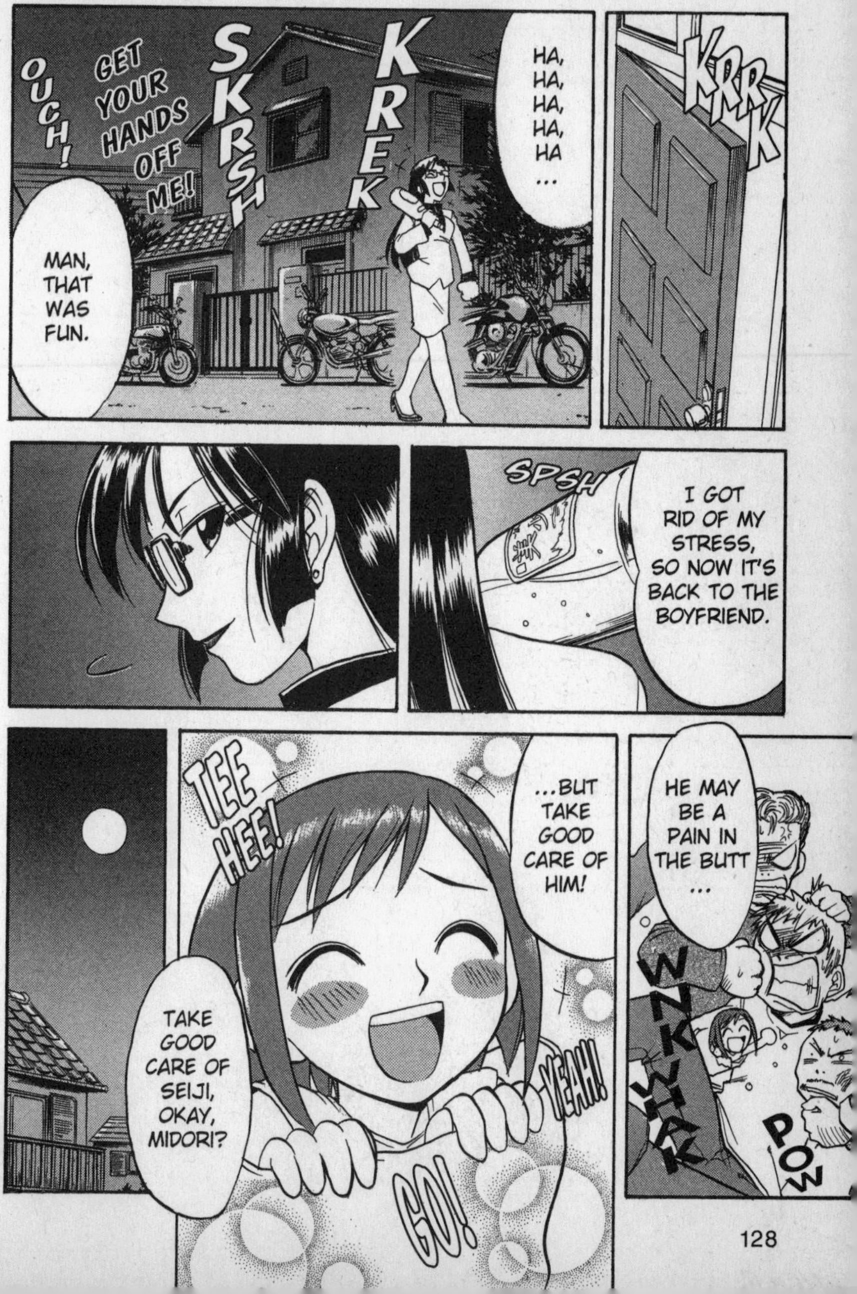
KRRRK
HA, HA, HA, HA, HA...
KREK
SKRSH
GET YOUR HANDS OFF ME!
OUCH!
MAN, THAT WAS FUN.
SPSH
I GOT RID OF MY STRESS, SO NOW IT'S BACK TO THE BOYFRIEND.
HE MAY BE A PAIN IN THE BUTT...
WNK
WHRK
POW
...BUT TAKE GOOD CARE OF HIM!
TEE HEE!
TAKE GOOD CARE OF SEIJI, OKAY, MIDORI?
YEAH!!
GO!

DAY 7
DOING CHIN-UPS TOGETHER

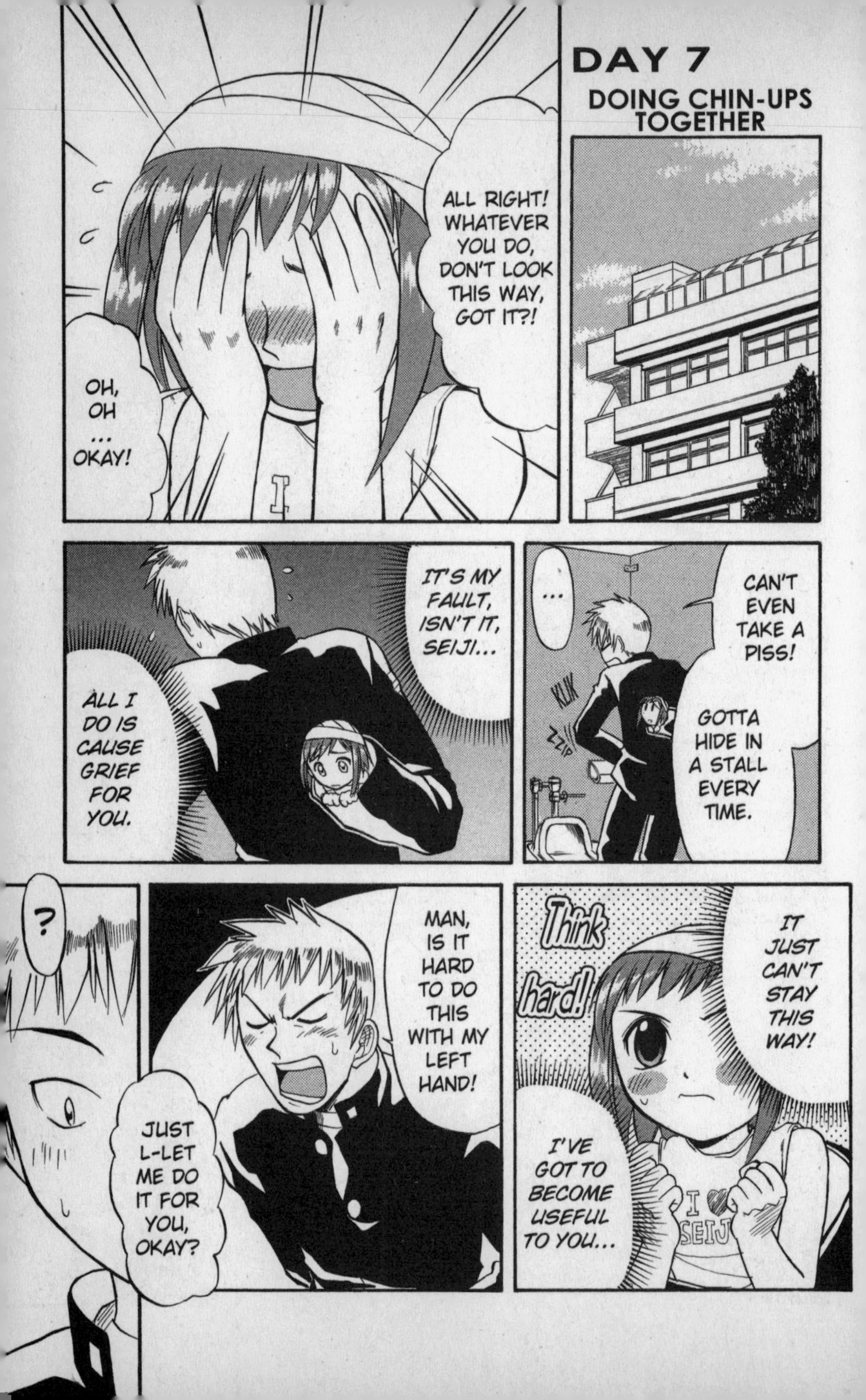
ALL RIGHT! WHATEVER YOU DO, DON'T LOOK THIS WAY, GOT IT?!
OH, OH ... OKAY!
...
CAN'T EVEN TAKE A PISS!
KLIK
ZZIP
GOTTA HIDE IN A STALL EVERY TIME.
IT'S MY FAULT, ISN'T IT, SEIJI...
ALL I DO IS CAUSE GRIEF FOR YOU.
IT JUST CAN'T STAY THIS WAY!
Think hard!
I'VE GOT TO BECOME USEFUL TO YOU...
MAN, IS IT HARD TO DO THIS WITH MY LEFT HAND!
JUST L-LET ME DO IT FOR YOU, OKAY?
?

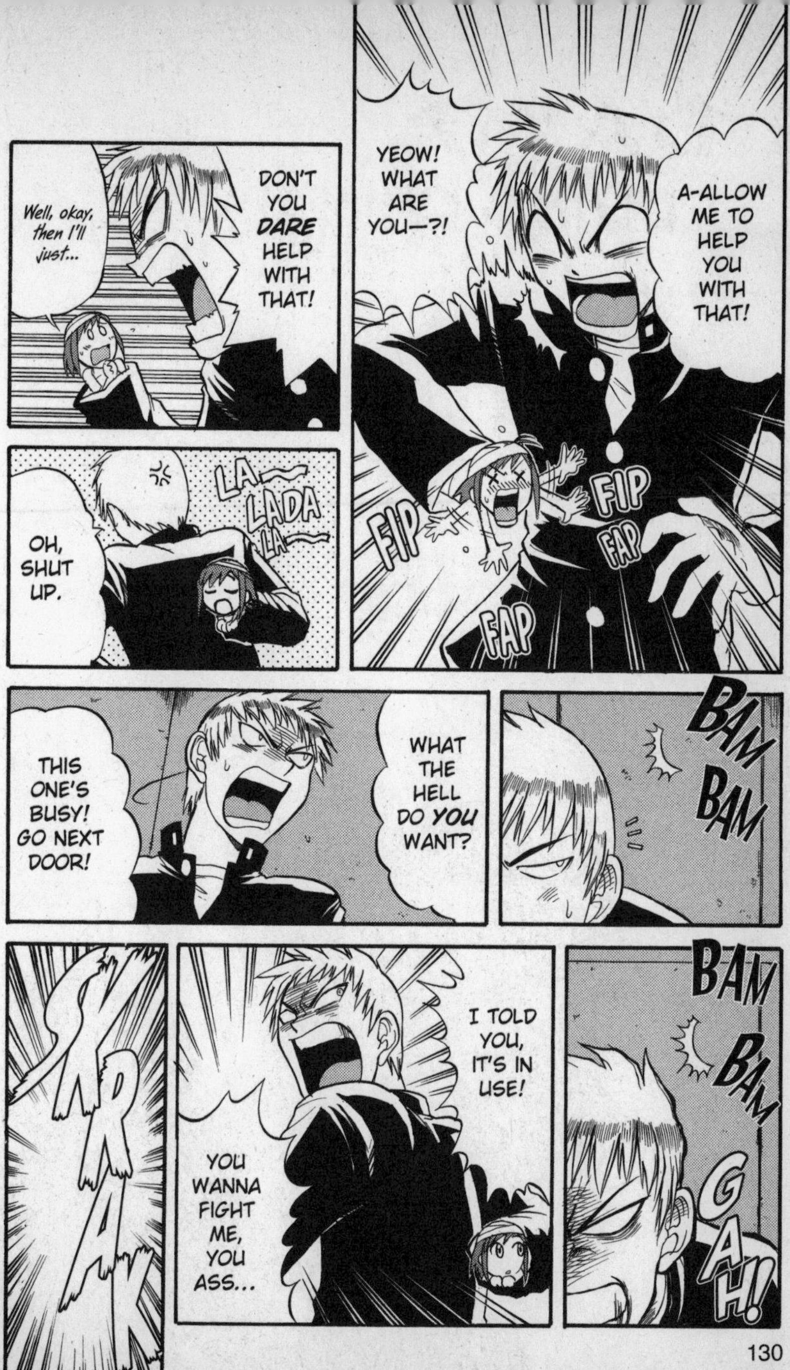
A-ALLOW ME TO HELP YOU WITH THAT!
YEOW! WHAT ARE YOU—?!
FIP
FIP
FAP
FAP
DON'T YOU DARE HELP WITH THAT!
Well, okay, then I'll just...
LA~ LADA LA~
OH, SHUT UP.
BAM BAM
WHAT THE HELL DO YOU WANT?
THIS ONE'S BUSY! GO NEXT DOOR!
BAM BAM
GAH!
I TOLD YOU, IT'S IN USE!
YOU WANNA FIGHT ME, YOU ASS...
KRAK

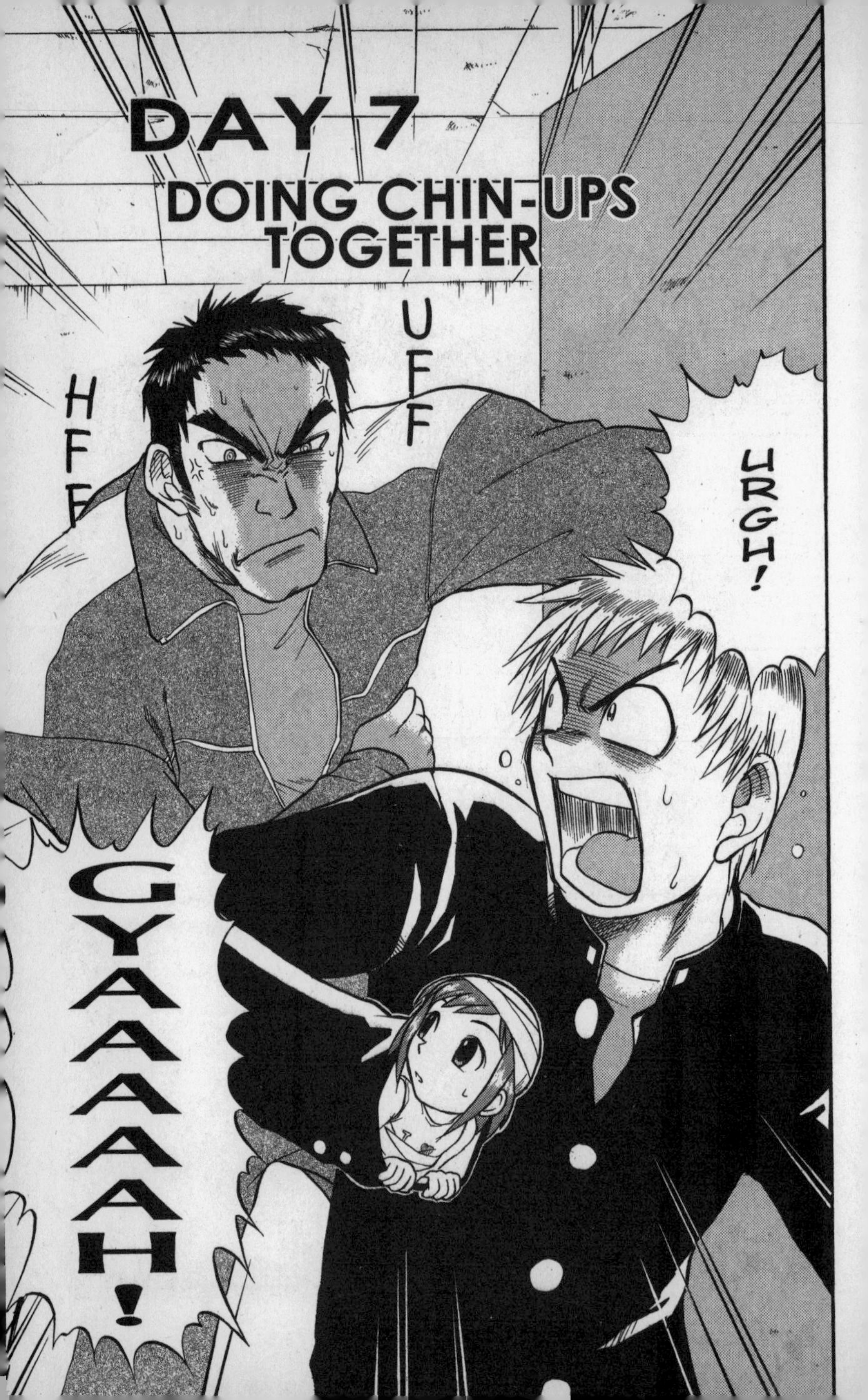
DAY 7
DOING CHIN-UPS TOGETHER
URGH!
UFF
HFF
GYAAAAAH!

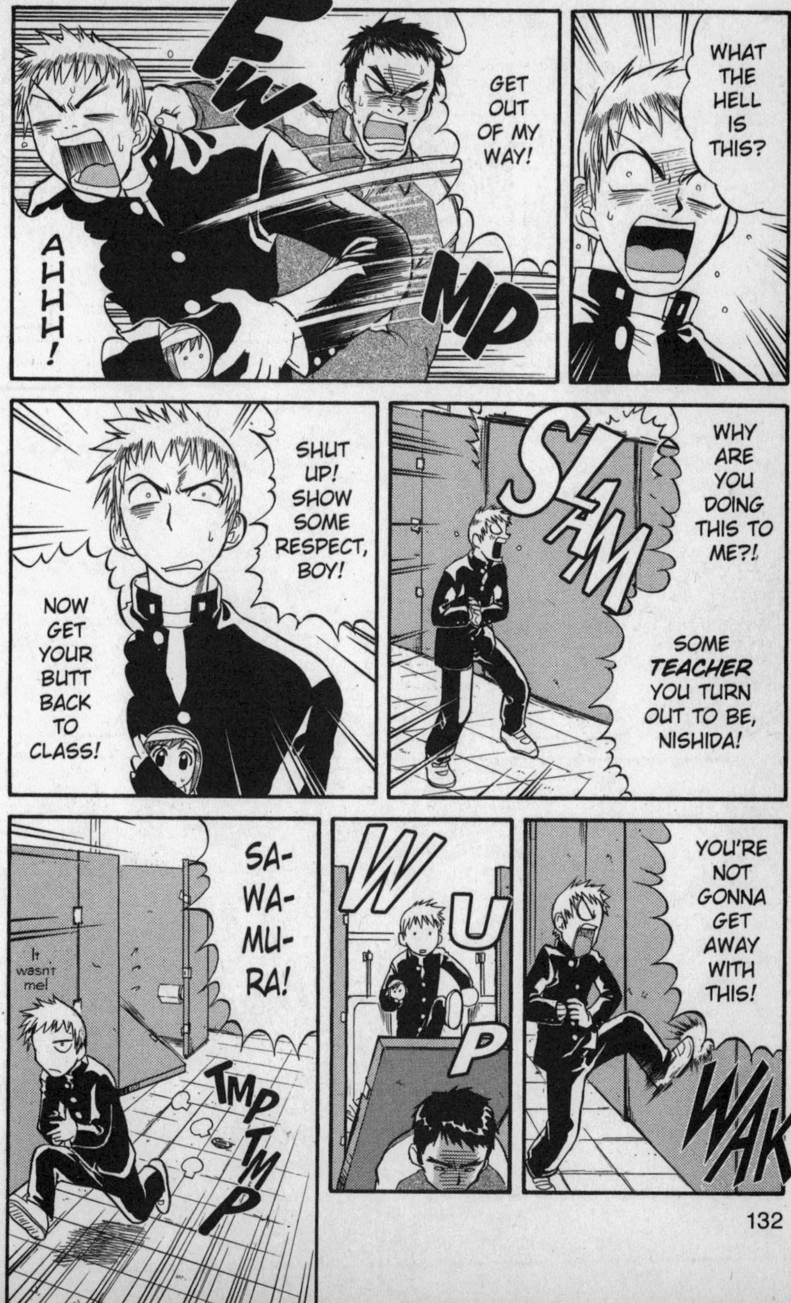
WHAT THE HELL IS THIS?
GET OUT OF MY WAY!
FW
MP
AHHH!
WHY ARE YOU DOING THIS TO ME?!
SLAM
SOME **TEACHER** YOU TURN OUT TO BE, NISHIDA!
SHUT UP! SHOW SOME RESPECT, BOY!
NOW GET YOUR BUTT BACK TO CLASS!
YOU'RE NOT GONNA GET AWAY WITH THIS!
WAK
WUP
SA-WA-MU-RA!
TMP TMP
It wasn't me!

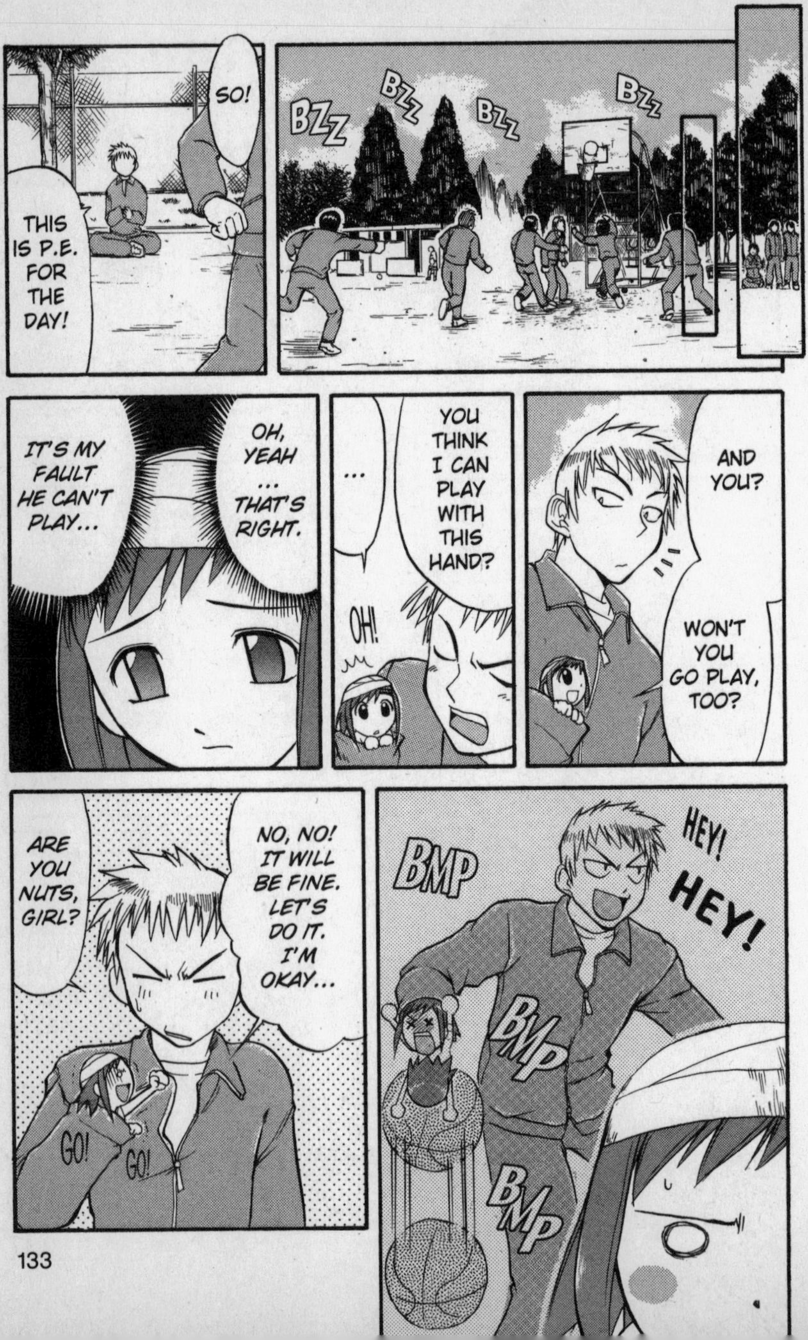
BZZ
BZZ
BZZ
BZZ
SO!
THIS IS P.E. FOR THE DAY!
AND YOU?
WON'T YOU GO PLAY, TOO?
YOU THINK I CAN PLAY WITH THIS HAND?
...
OH!
OH, YEAH ... THAT'S RIGHT.
IT'S MY FAULT HE CAN'T PLAY...
HEY!
HEY!
BMP
BMP
BMP
NO, NO! IT WILL BE FINE. LET'S DO IT. I'M OKAY...
ARE YOU NUTS, GIRL?
GO!
GO!

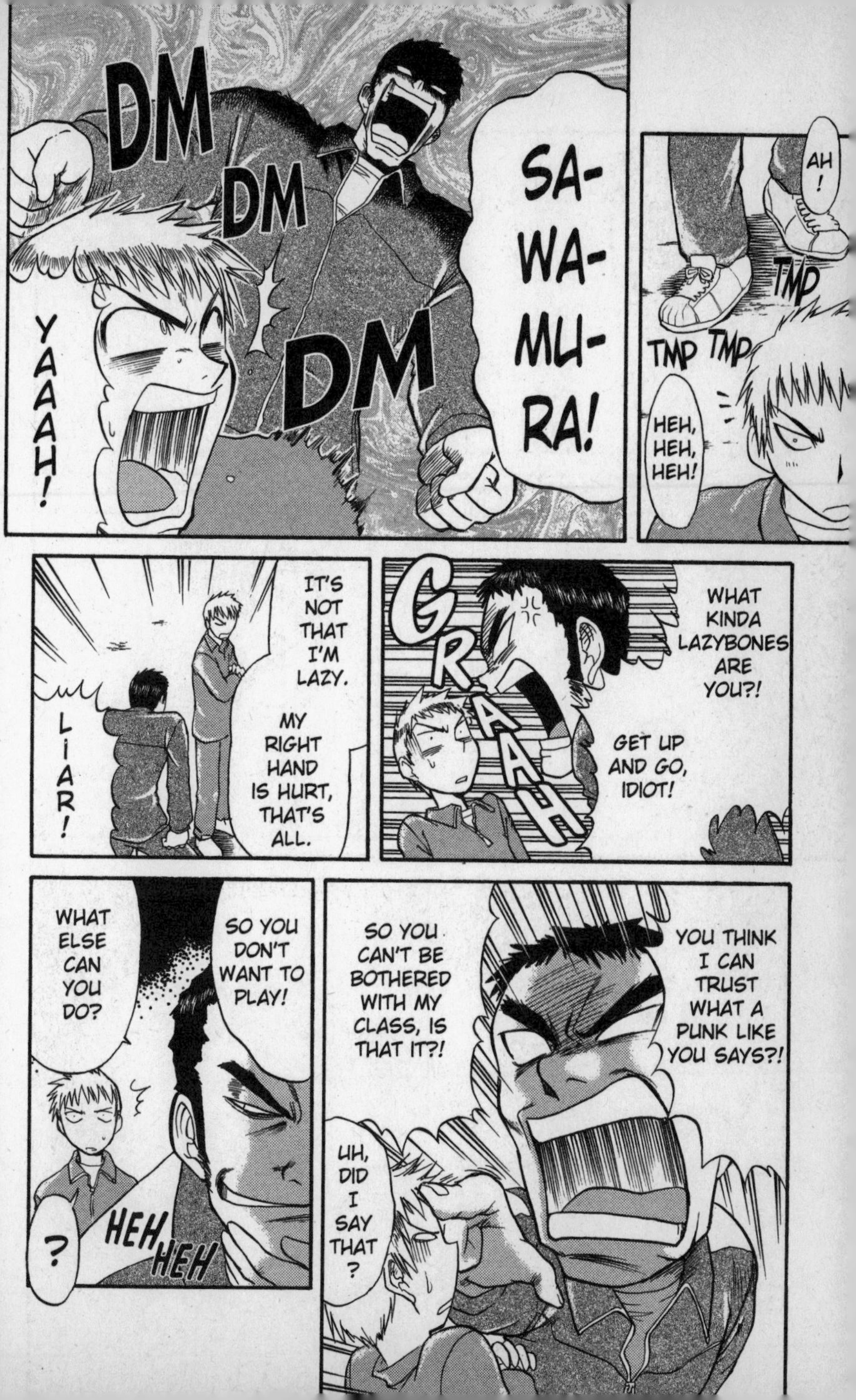
AH!
TMP
TMP TMP
HEH, HEH, HEH!
SA-WA-MU-RA!
DM
DM
DM
YAAAAH!
WHAT KINDA LAZYBONES ARE YOU?!
GET UP AND GO, IDIOT!
GRAAAH
IT'S NOT THAT I'M LAZY.
MY RIGHT HAND IS HURT, THAT'S ALL.
LIAR!
YOU THINK I CAN TRUST WHAT A PUNK LIKE YOU SAYS?!
SO YOU CAN'T BE BOTHERED WITH MY CLASS, IS THAT IT?!
UH, DID I SAY THAT?
SO YOU DON'T WANT TO PLAY!
WHAT ELSE CAN YOU DO?
HEH HEH
?

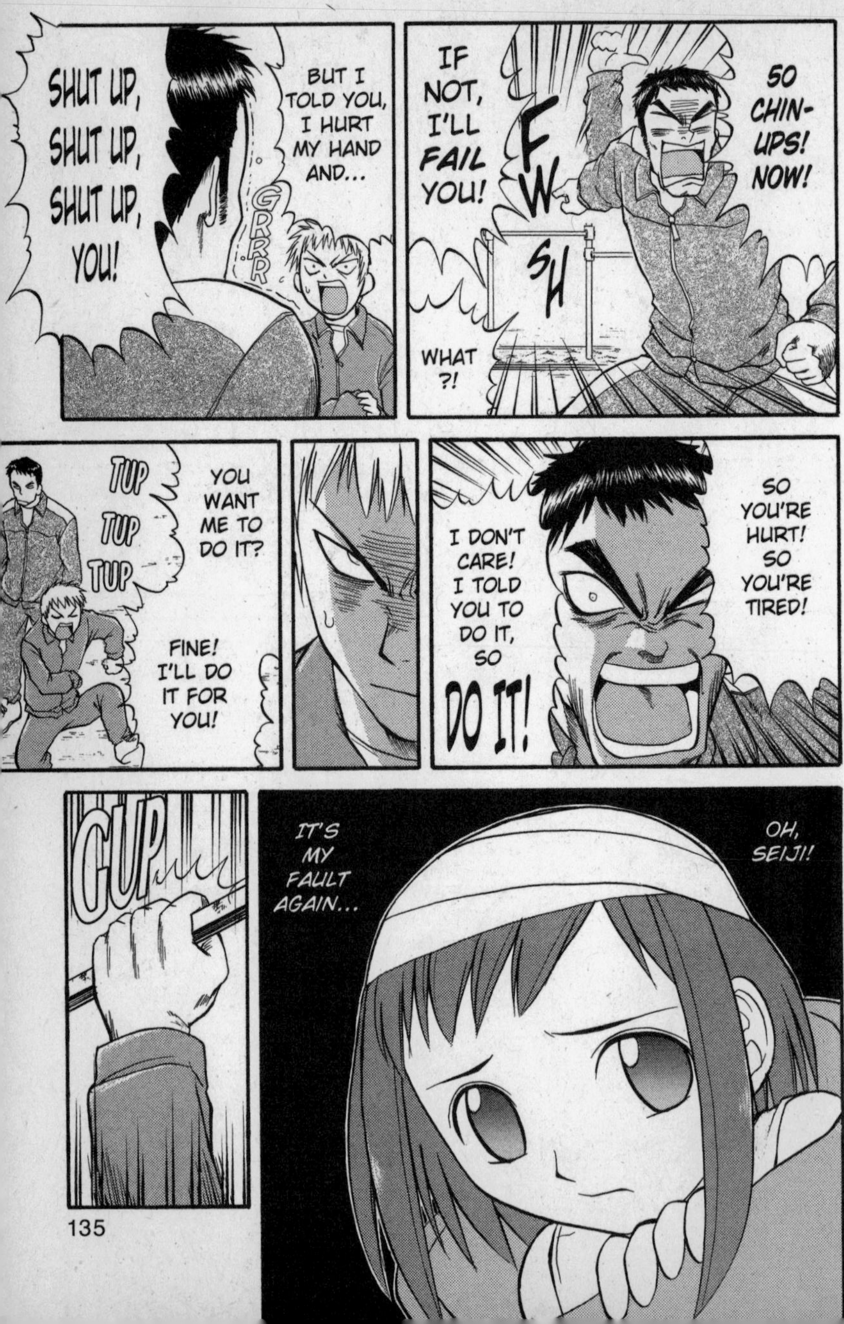

SO CHIN-UPS! NOW!
FWSH
IF NOT, I'LL FAIL YOU!
WHAT ?!
BUT I TOLD YOU, I HURT MY HAND AND...
GRRR
SHUT UP, SHUT UP, SHUT UP, YOU!
SO YOU'RE HURT! SO YOU'RE TIRED!
I DON'T CARE! I TOLD YOU TO DO IT, SO DO IT!
YOU WANT ME TO DO IT?
TUP TUP TUP
FINE! I'LL DO IT FOR YOU!
OH, SEIJI!
IT'S MY FAULT AGAIN...
CUP

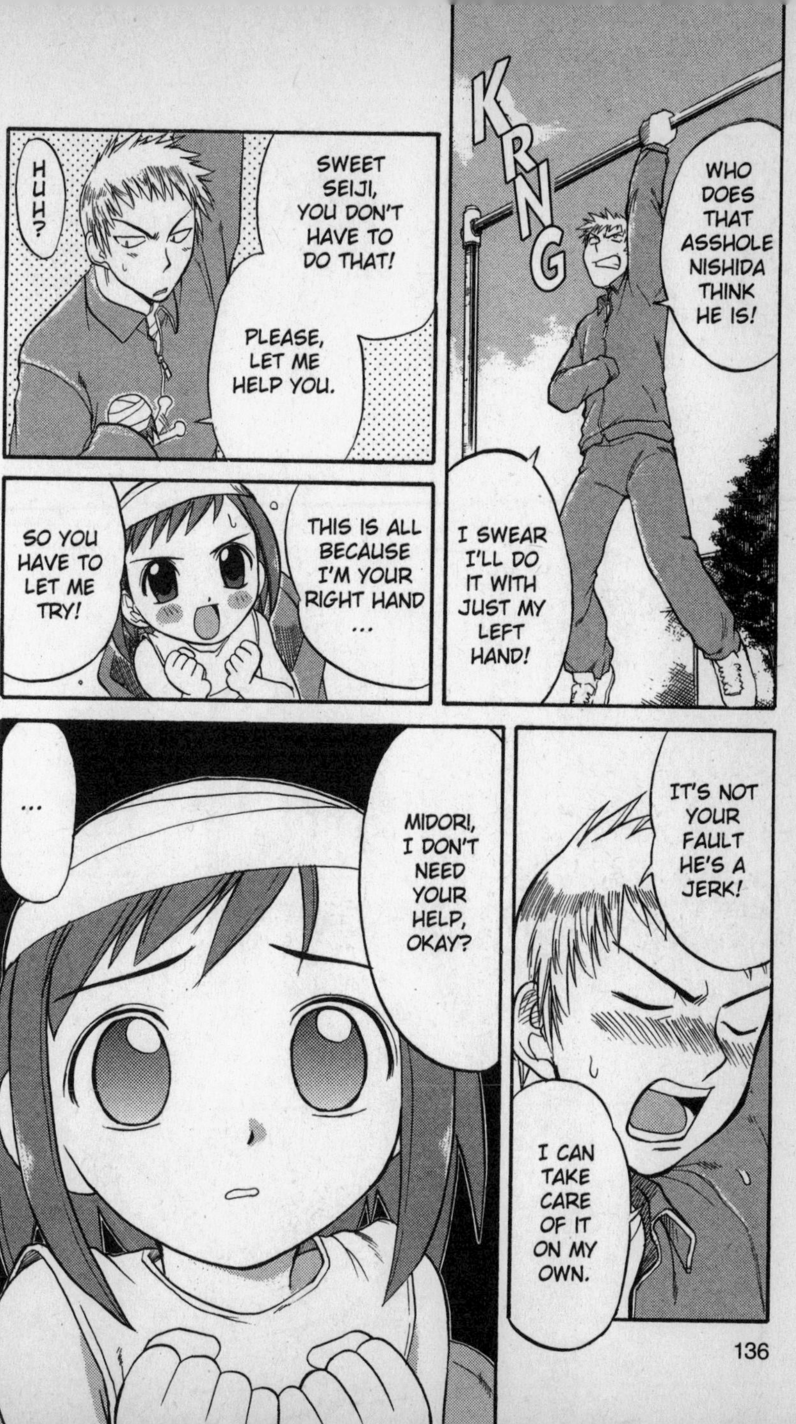
KRNG
WHO DOES THAT ASSHOLE NISHIDA THINK HE IS!
I SWEAR I'LL DO IT WITH JUST MY LEFT HAND!
SWEET SEIJI, YOU DON'T HAVE TO DO THAT!
PLEASE, LET ME HELP YOU.
HUH?
THIS IS ALL BECAUSE I'M YOUR RIGHT HAND ...
SO YOU HAVE TO LET ME TRY!
IT'S NOT YOUR FAULT HE'S A JERK!
I CAN TAKE CARE OF IT ON MY OWN.
MIDORI, I DON'T NEED YOUR HELP, OKAY?
...

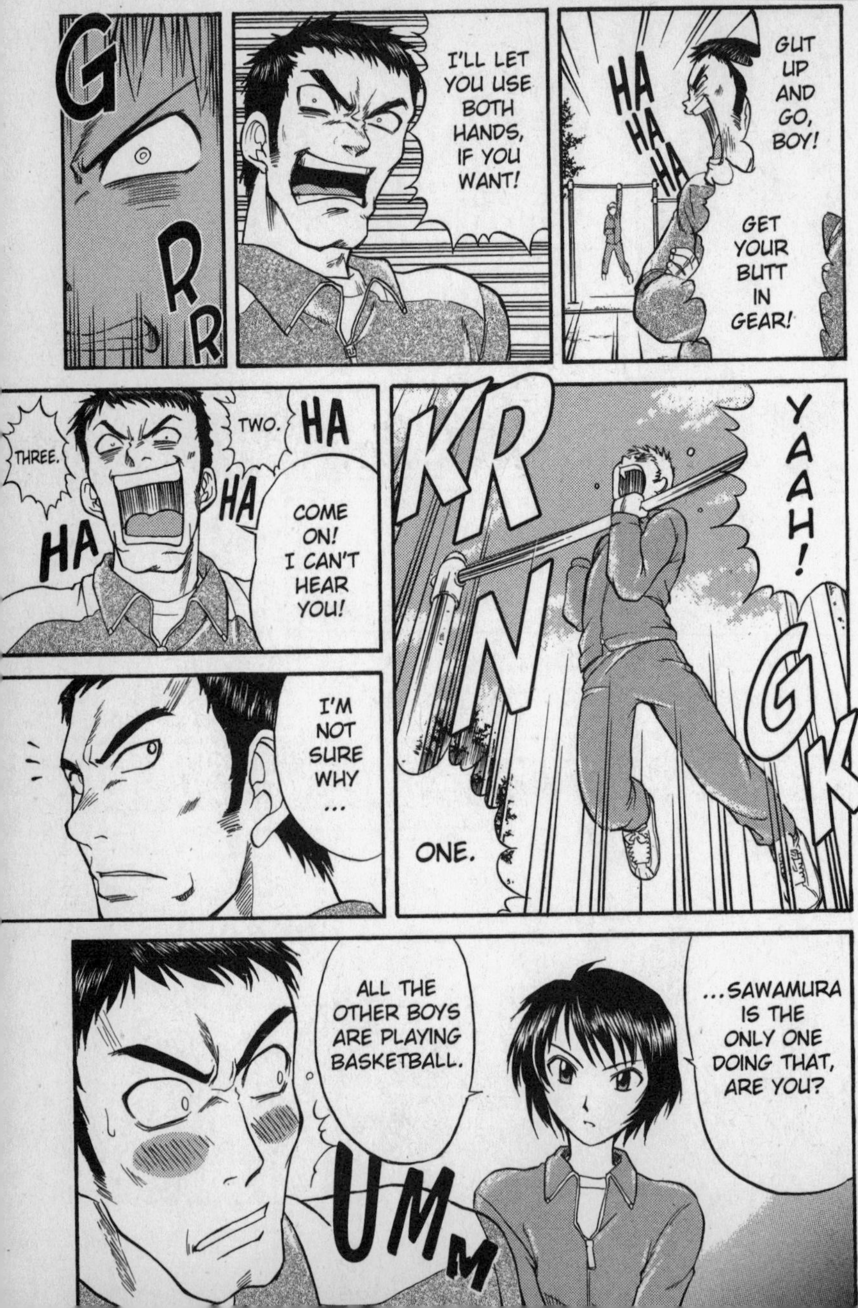
HA HA HA
GUT UP AND GO, BOY!
GET YOUR BUTT IN GEAR!
I'LL LET YOU USE BOTH HANDS, IF YOU WANT!
GRR
YAAH!
KRNNGK
ONE.
HA
TWO.
THREE.
HA
HA
COME ON! I CAN'T HEAR YOU!
I'M NOT SURE WHY ...
...SAWAMURA IS THE ONLY ONE DOING THAT, ARE YOU?
ALL THE OTHER BOYS ARE PLAYING BASKETBALL.
UMM

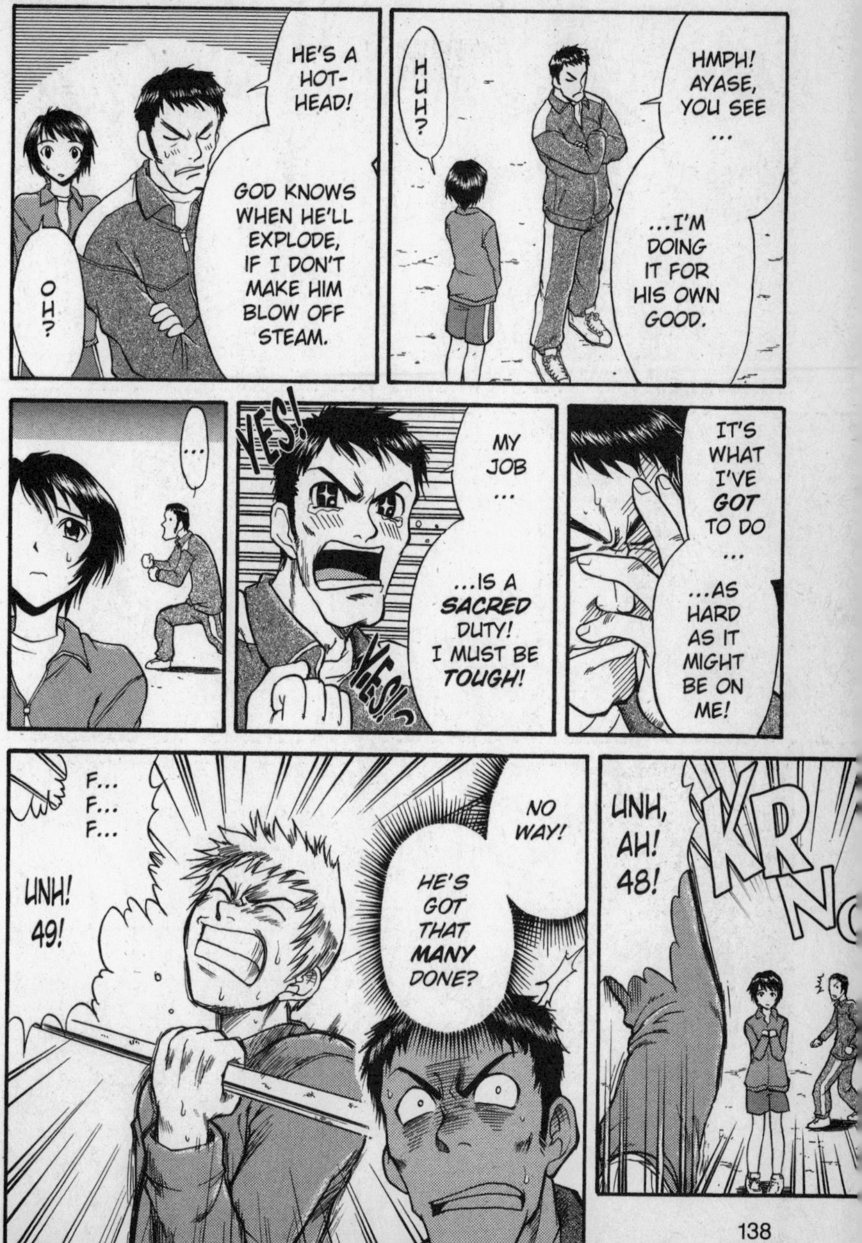

HMPH! AYASE, YOU SEE ...
...I'M DOING IT FOR HIS OWN GOOD.
HUH?
HE'S A HOT-HEAD!
GOD KNOWS WHEN HE'LL EXPLODE, IF I DON'T MAKE HIM BLOW OFF STEAM.
OH?
IT'S WHAT I'VE *GOT* TO DO ...
...AS HARD AS IT MIGHT BE ON ME!
YES!
MY JOB ...
...IS A *SACRED* DUTY! I MUST BE *TOUGH!*
YES!
...
KR
UNH, AH! 48!
NO WAY!
HE'S GOT THAT *MANY* DONE?
F... F... F...
UNH! 49!

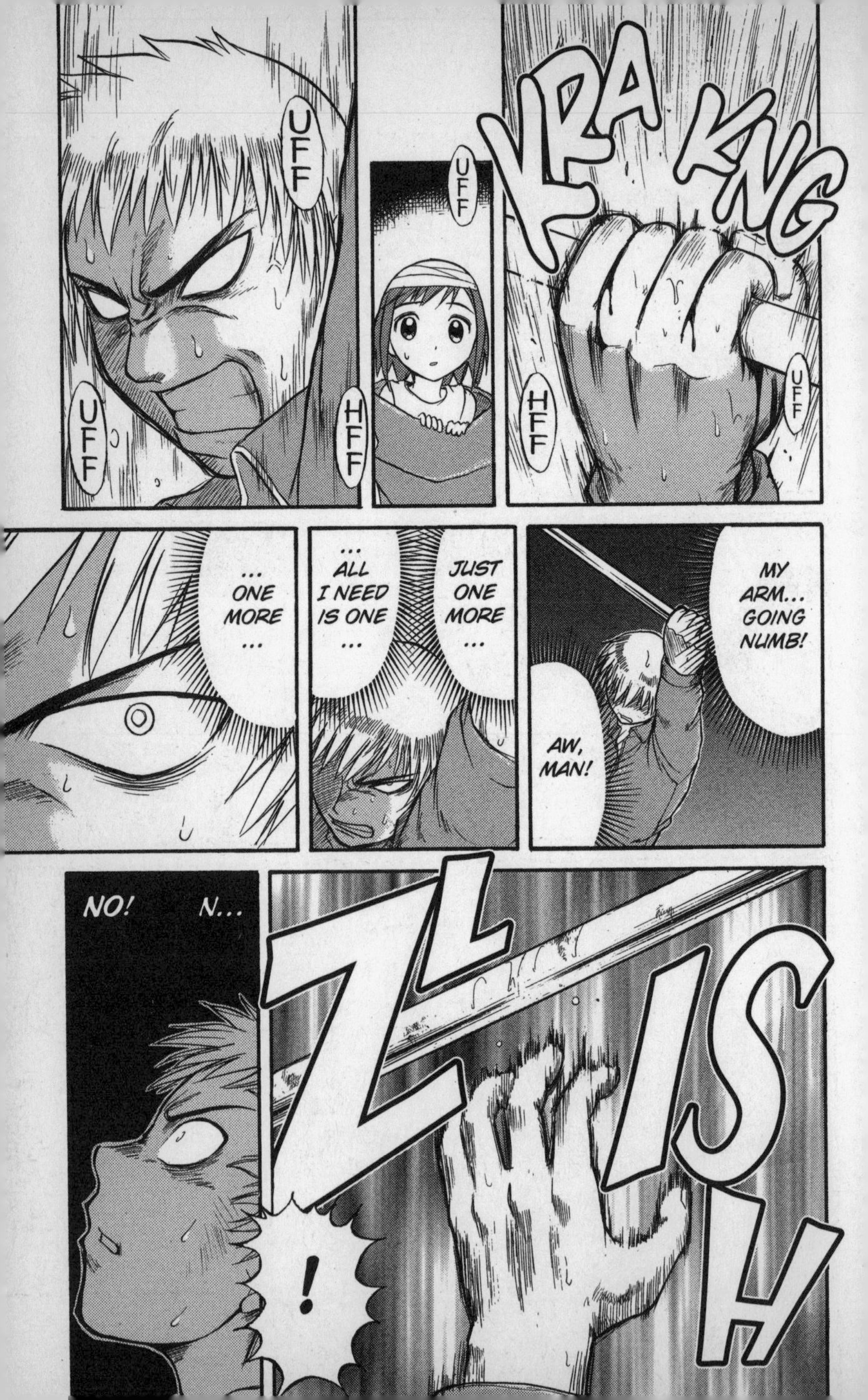
KRAKNG
UFF
HFF
UFF
HFF
UFF
UFF
MY ARM... GOING NUMB!
AW, MAN!
JUST ONE MORE ...
... ALL I NEED IS ONE ...
... ONE MORE ...
ZZISH
!
NO! N...

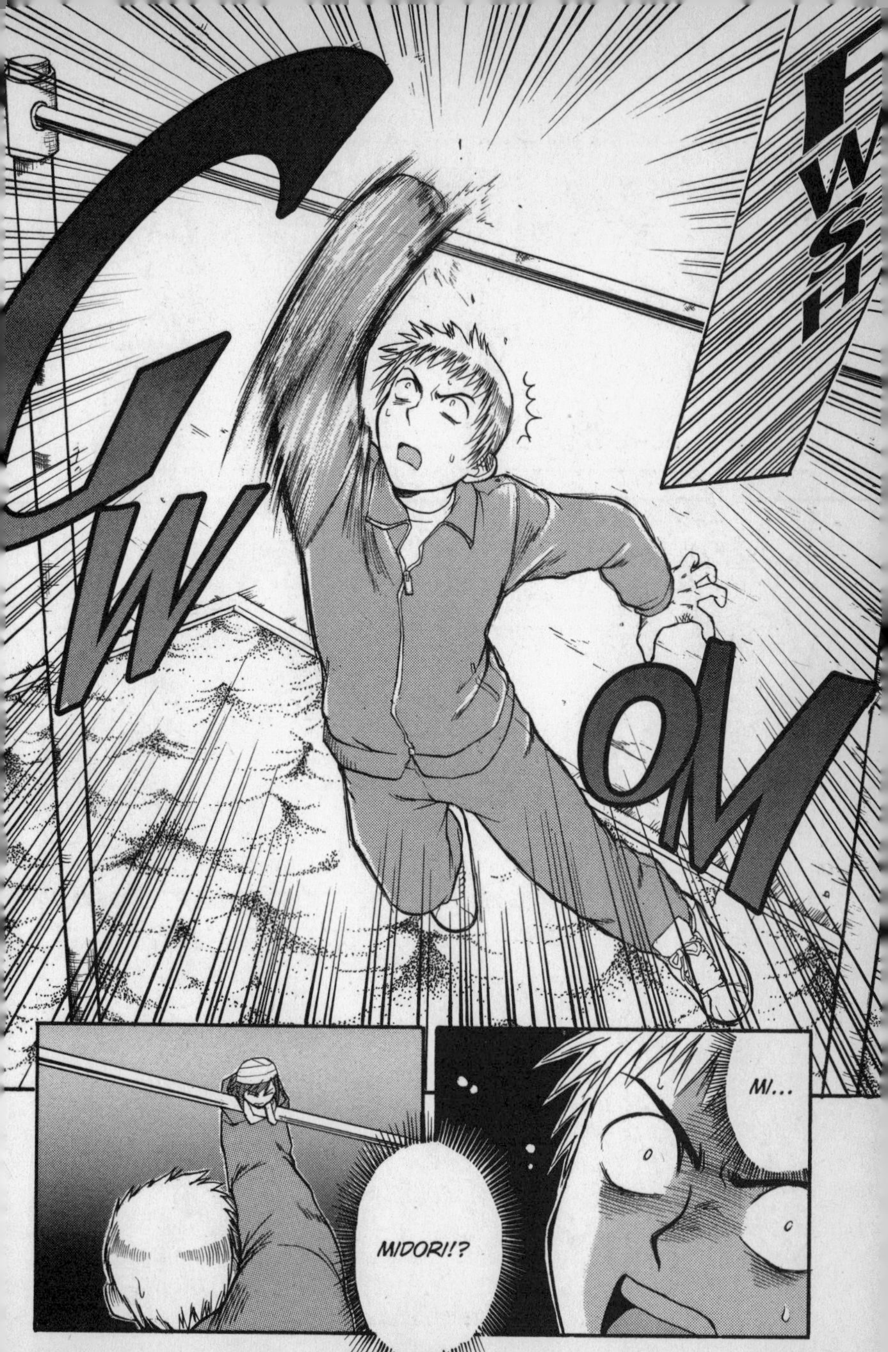
FWSH
MI...
MIDORI!?

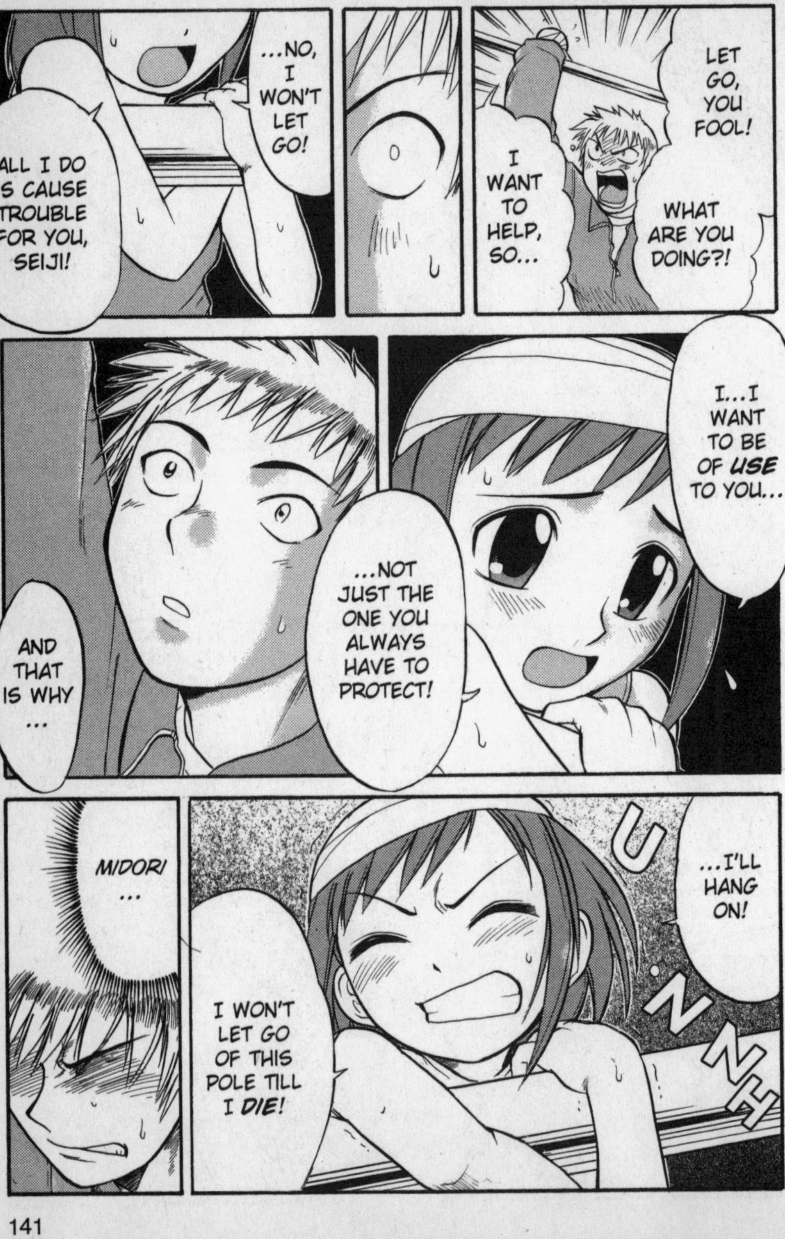
LET GO, YOU FOOL!
WHAT ARE YOU DOING?!
I WANT TO HELP, SO...
...NO, I WON'T LET GO!
ALL I DO IS CAUSE TROUBLE FOR YOU, SEIJI!
I...I WANT TO BE OF *USE* TO YOU...
...NOT JUST THE ONE YOU ALWAYS HAVE TO PROTECT!
AND THAT IS WHY ...
UNNNH
...I'LL HANG ON!
I WON'T LET GO OF THIS POLE TILL I *DIE*!
MIDORI ...

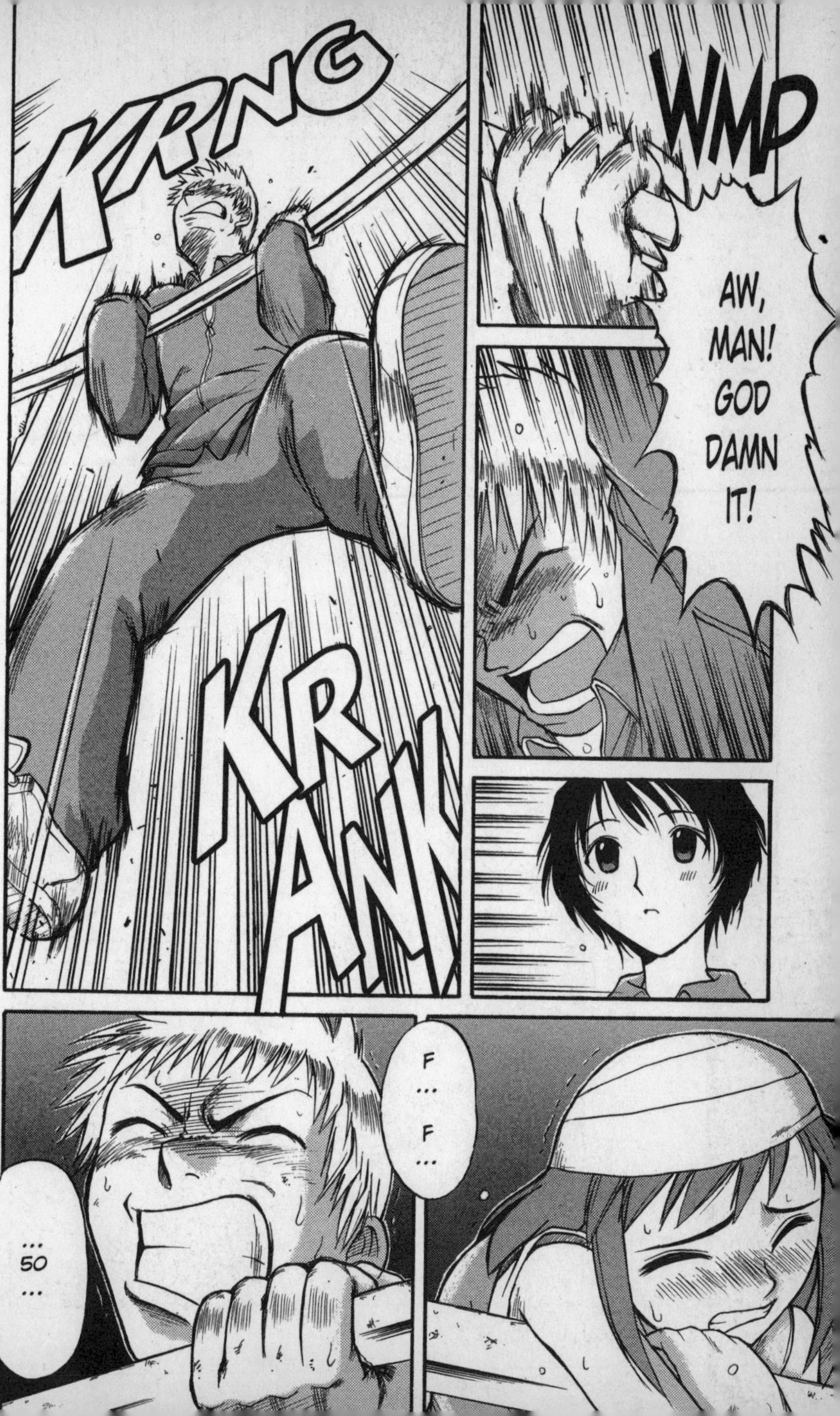
WMP
AW, MAN! GOD DAMN IT!
KRNG
KRANK
F... F...
...50...

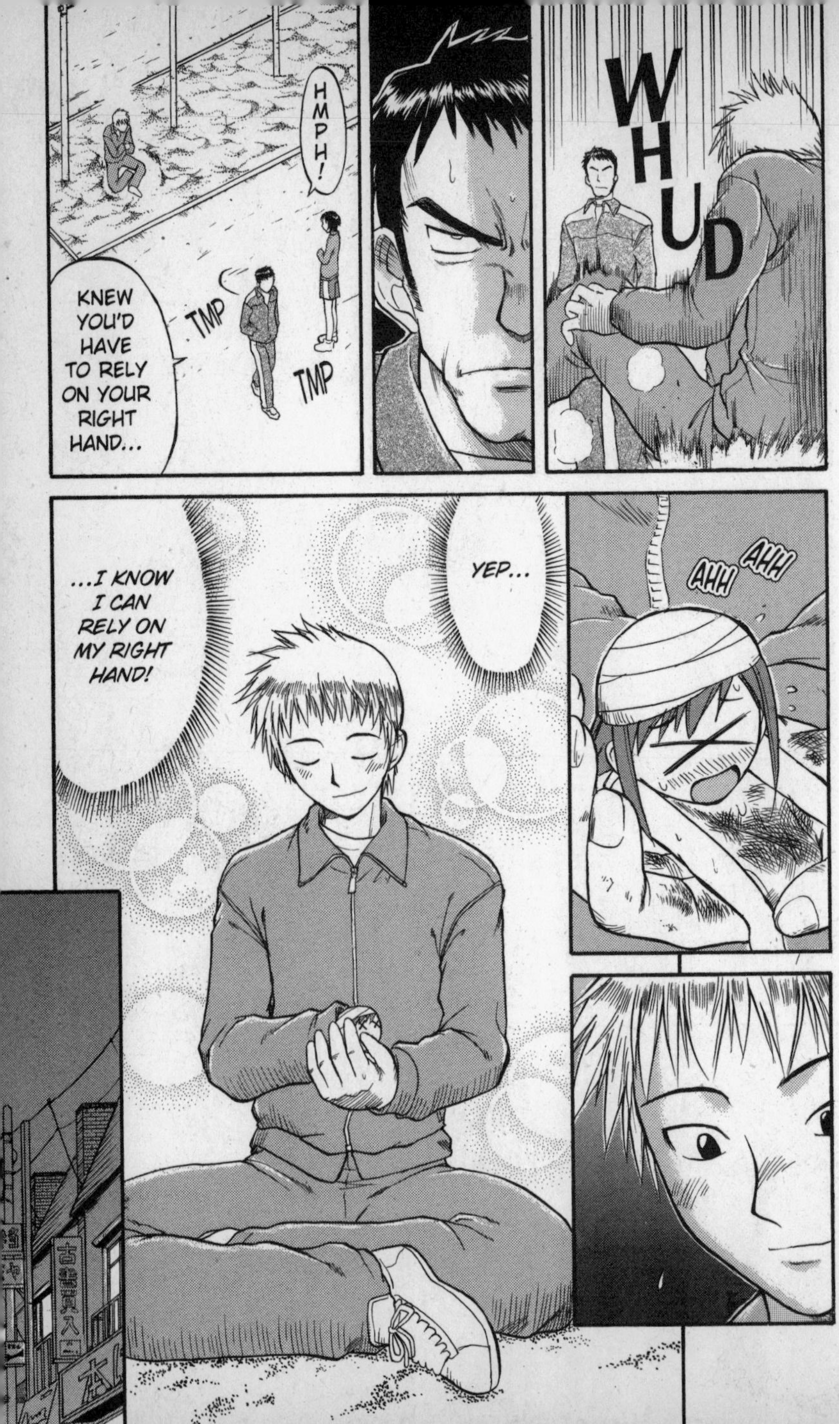
WHUD
HMPH!
KNEW YOU'D HAVE TO RELY ON YOUR RIGHT HAND...
TMP
TMP
AHH
AHH
YEP...
...I KNOW I CAN RELY ON MY RIGHT HAND!

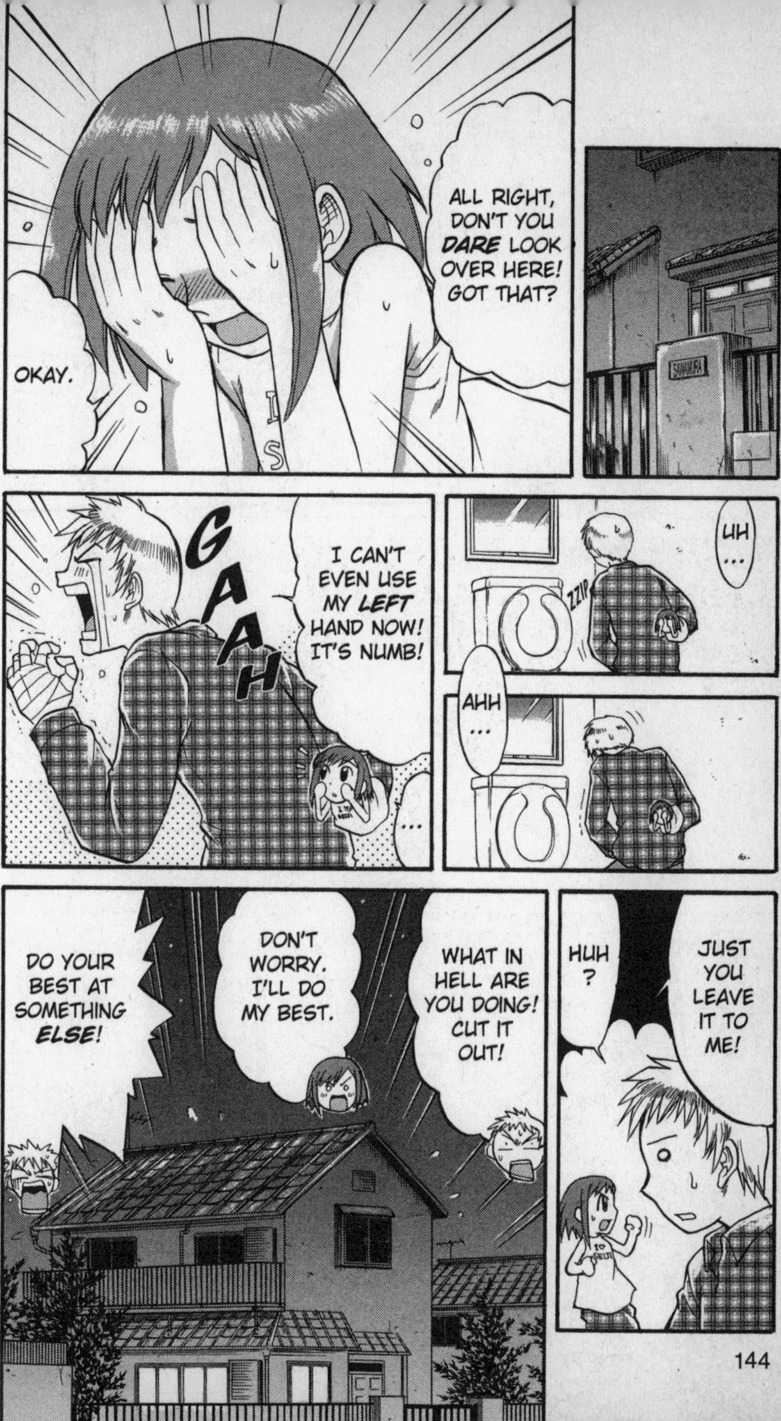
ALL RIGHT, DON'T YOU DARE LOOK OVER HERE! GOT THAT?
OKAY.
UH ...
ZZIP
AHH ...
I CAN'T EVEN USE MY LEFT HAND NOW! IT'S NUMB!
GAAH
...
JUST YOU LEAVE IT TO ME!
HUH ?
WHAT IN HELL ARE YOU DOING! CUT IT OUT!
DON'T WORRY. I'LL DO MY BEST.
DO YOUR BEST AT SOMETHING ELSE!

DAY 8 A PITIFUL MAN

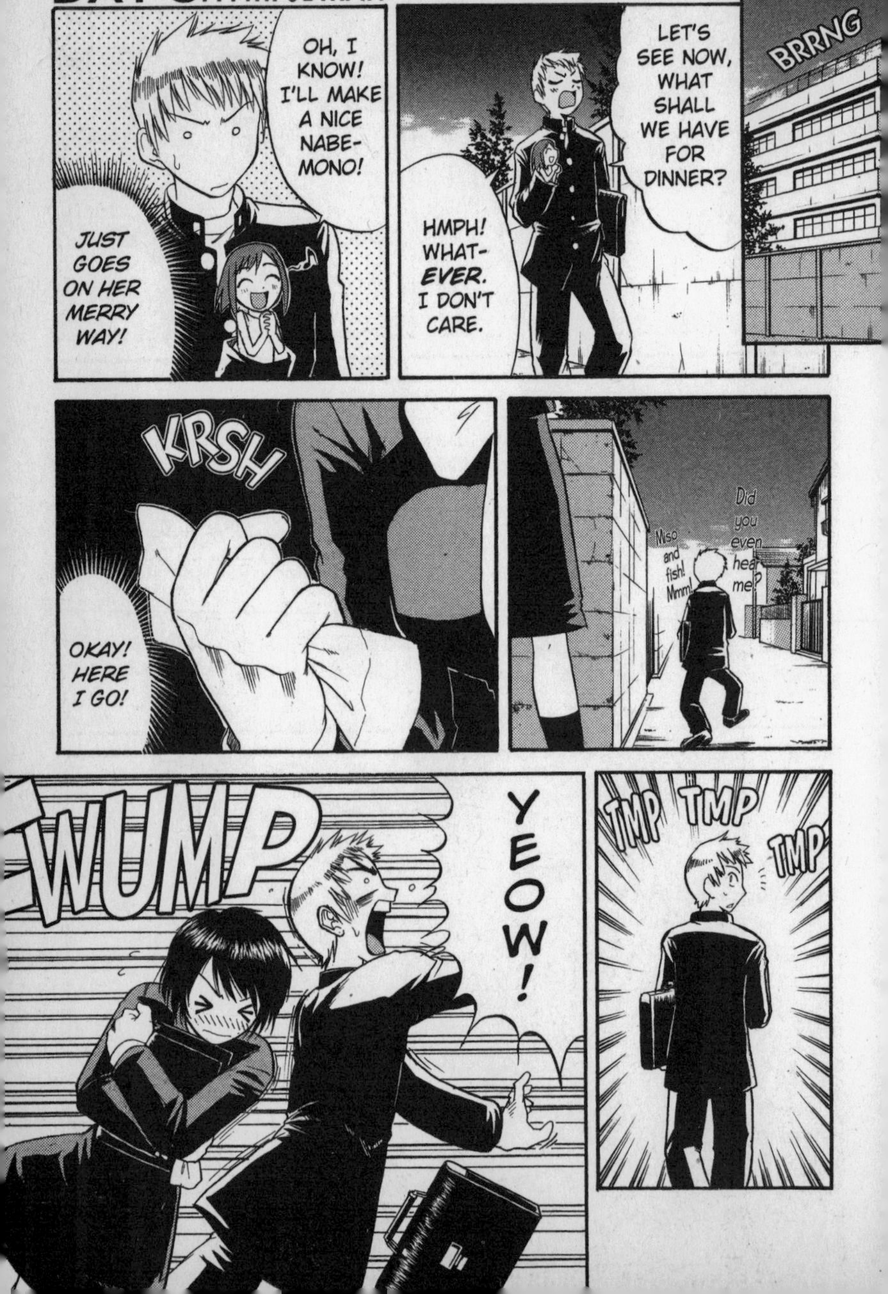
BRRNG
LET'S SEE NOW, WHAT SHALL WE HAVE FOR DINNER?
HMPH! WHAT-EVER. I DON'T CARE.
OH, I KNOW! I'LL MAKE A NICE NABE-MONO!
JUST GOES ON HER MERRY WAY!
Did you even hear me?
Miso and fish! Mmm!
KRSH
OKAY! HERE I GO!
TMP TMP TMP
WUMP
YEOW!

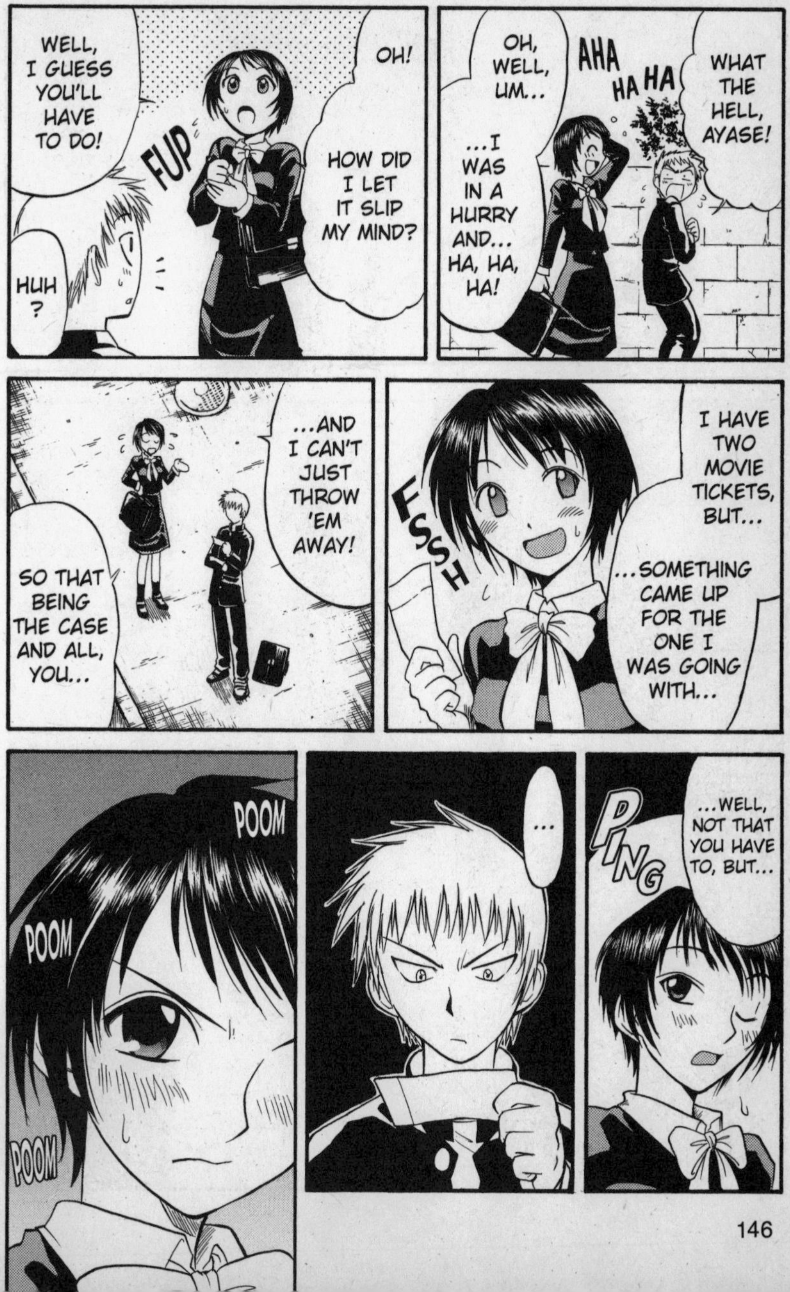
WHAT THE HELL, AYASE!
AHA HA HA
OH, WELL, UM...
...I WAS IN A HURRY AND... HA, HA, HA!
OH!
HOW DID I LET IT SLIP MY MIND?
FUP
WELL, I GUESS YOU'LL HAVE TO DO!
HUH?
I HAVE TWO MOVIE TICKETS, BUT...
...SOMETHING CAME UP FOR THE ONE I WAS GOING WITH...
FSSH
...AND I CAN'T JUST THROW 'EM AWAY!
SO THAT BEING THE CASE AND ALL, YOU...
PING
...WELL, NOT THAT YOU HAVE TO, BUT...
...
POOM
POOM
POOM

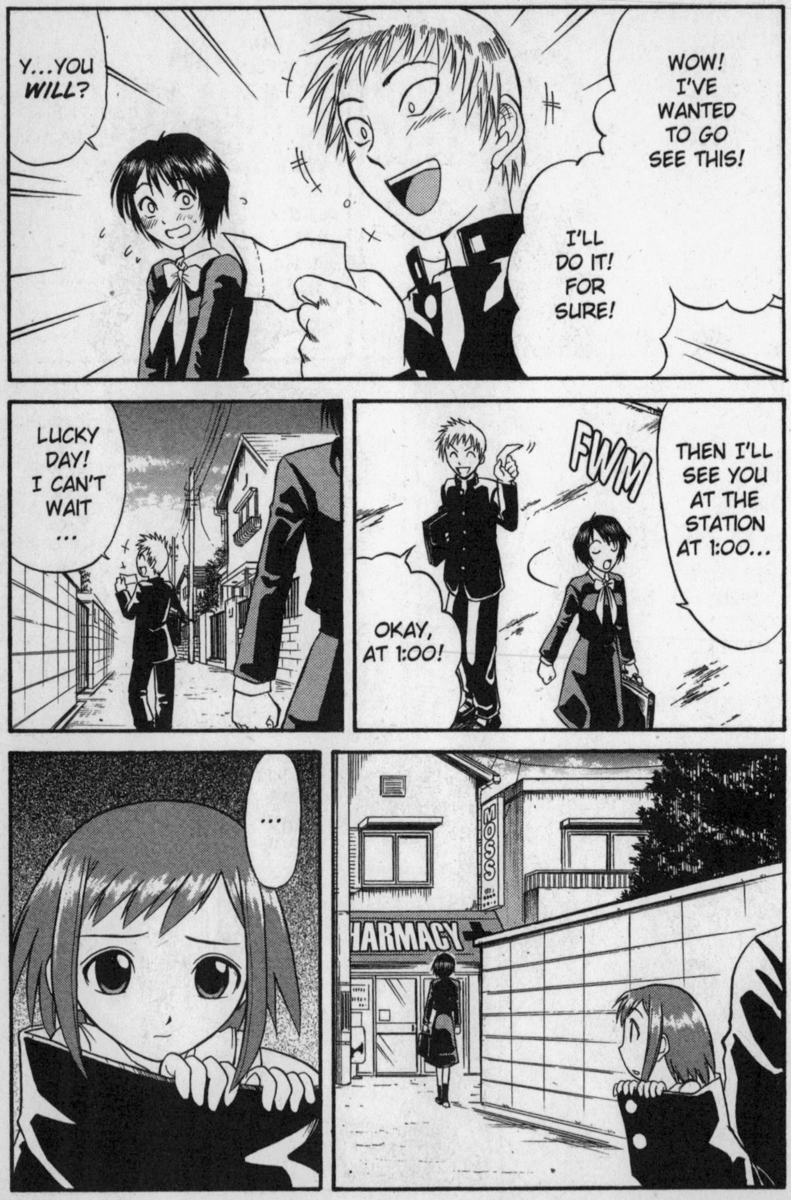
WOW! I'VE WANTED TO GO SEE THIS!
I'LL DO IT! FOR SURE!
Y...YOU *WILL*?
THEN I'LL SEE YOU AT THE STATION AT 1:00...
FWM
OKAY, AT 1:00!
LUCKY DAY! I CAN'T WAIT ...
MOSS
HARMACY
...

DAY 8
A PITIFUL MAN

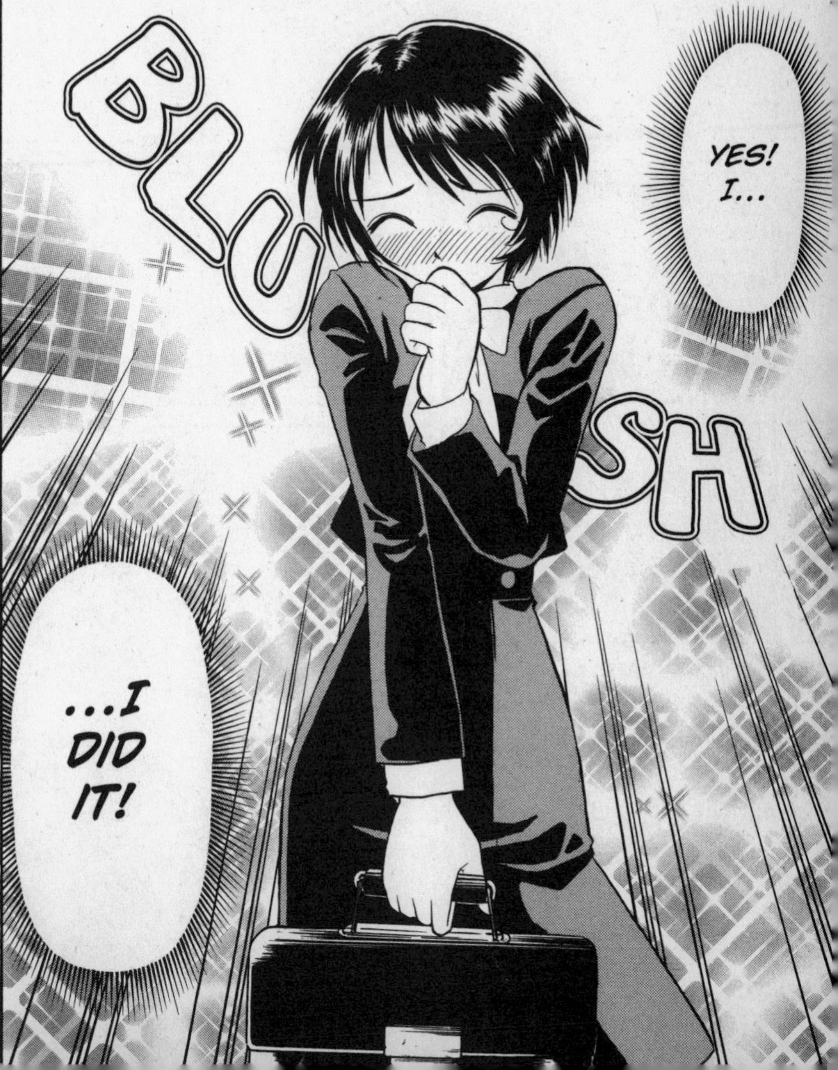
YES! I...
BLUSH
...I DID IT!

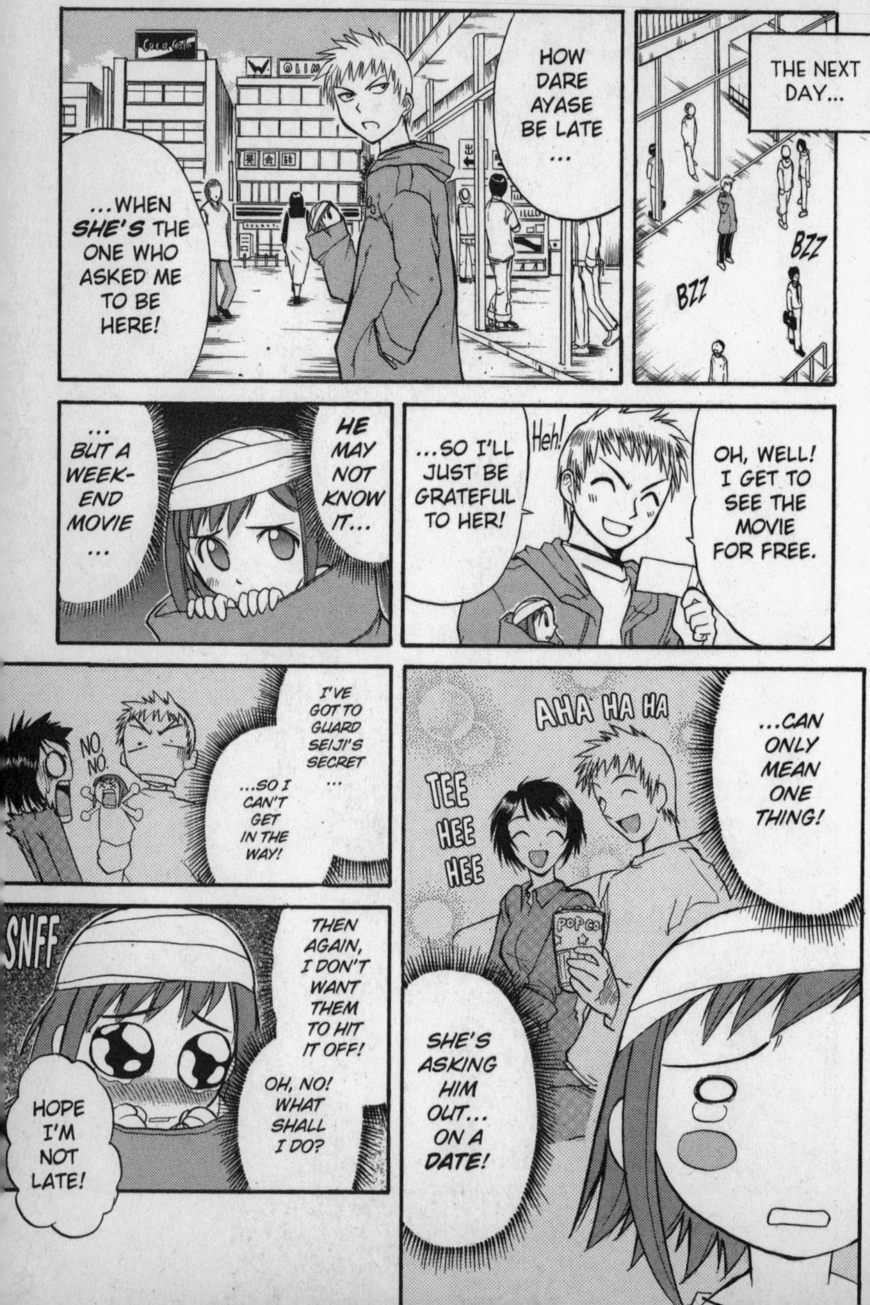
THE NEXT DAY...
BZZ
BZZ
HOW DARE AYASE BE LATE...
...WHEN SHE'S THE ONE WHO ASKED ME TO BE HERE!
OH, WELL! I GET TO SEE THE MOVIE FOR FREE.
Heh!
...SO I'LL JUST BE GRATEFUL TO HER!
HE MAY NOT KNOW IT...
...BUT A WEEK-END MOVIE...
...CAN ONLY MEAN ONE THING!
AHA HA HA
TEE HEE HEE
SHE'S ASKING HIM OUT... ON A DATE!
I'VE GOT TO GUARD SEIJI'S SECRET...
...SO I CAN'T GET IN THE WAY!
NO, NO.
THEN AGAIN, I DON'T WANT THEM TO HIT IT OFF!
OH, NO! WHAT SHALL I DO?
SNFF
HOPE I'M NOT LATE!

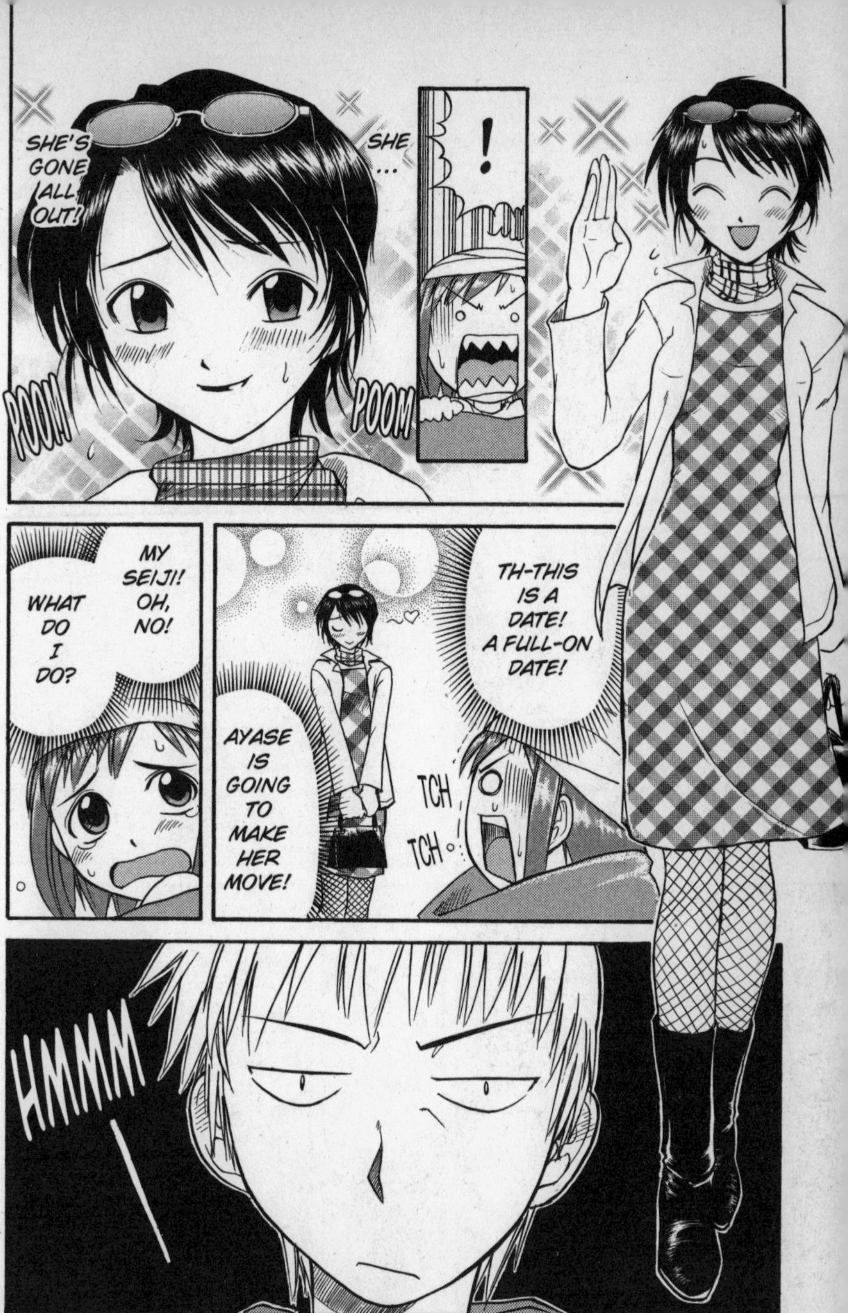
SHE ...
!
POOM
SHE'S GONE ALL OUT!
POOM
TH-THIS IS A DATE! A FULL-ON DATE!
AYASE IS GOING TO MAKE HER MOVE!
TCH
TCH
MY SEIJI! OH, NO!
WHAT DO I DO?
HMMM

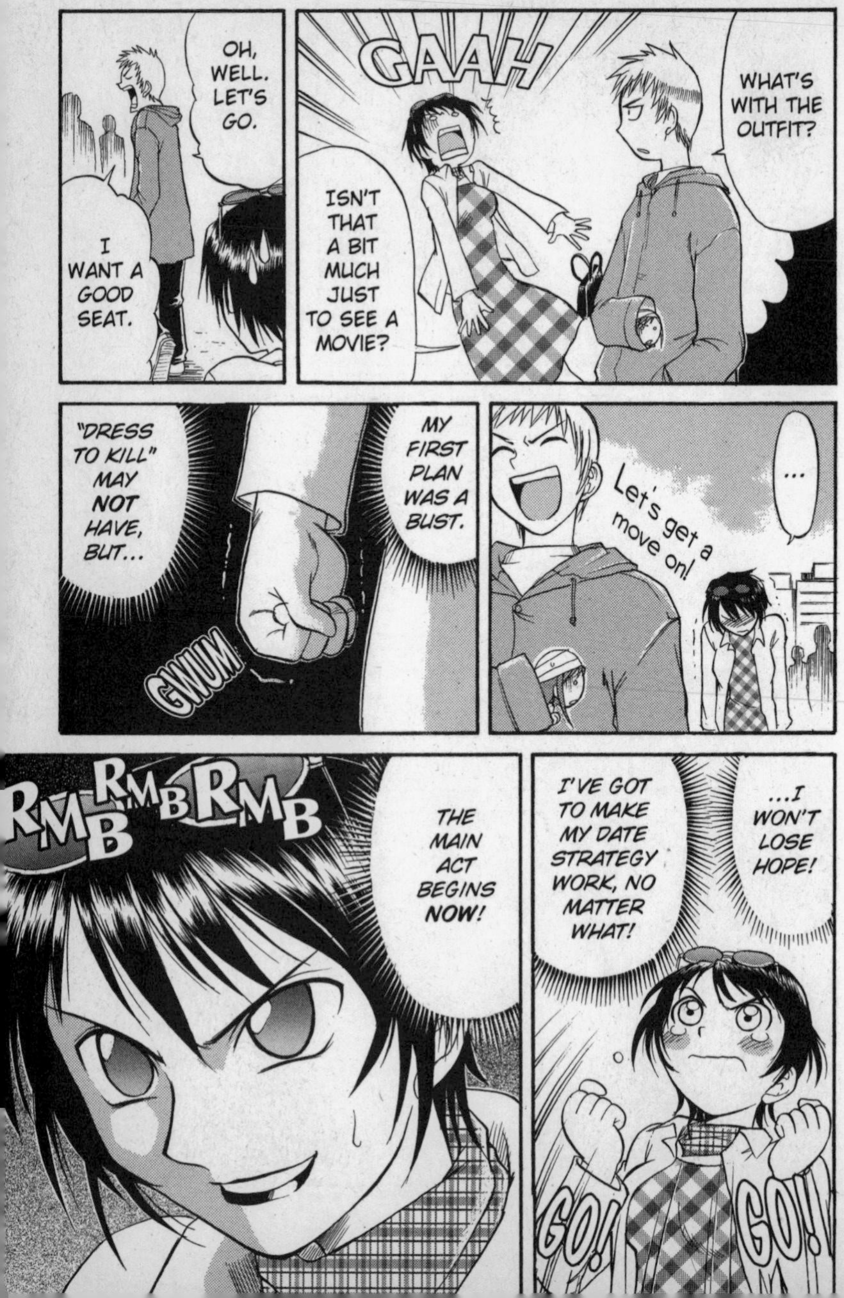
WHAT'S WITH THE OUTFIT?
GAAH
ISN'T THAT A BIT MUCH JUST TO SEE A MOVIE?
OH, WELL. LET'S GO.
I WANT A GOOD SEAT.
...
Let's get a move on!
MY FIRST PLAN WAS A BUST.
"DRESS TO KILL" MAY NOT HAVE, BUT...
GWUM
...I WON'T LOSE HOPE!
I'VE GOT TO MAKE MY DATE STRATEGY WORK, NO MATTER WHAT!
GO! GO!
THE MAIN ACT BEGINS NOW!
RMB RMB RMB

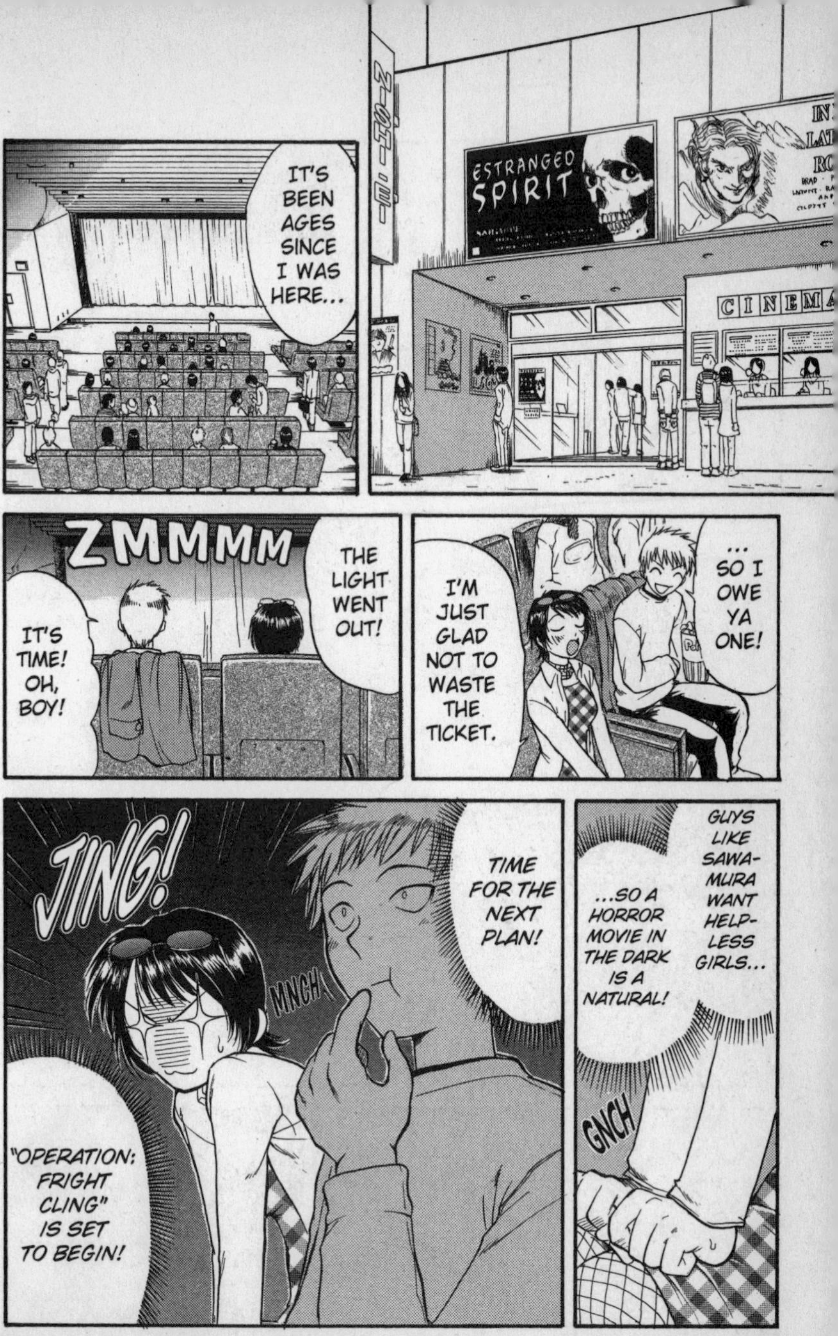
ESTRANGED SPIRIT
CINEMA
IT'S BEEN AGES SINCE I WAS HERE...
...SO I OWE YA ONE!
I'M JUST GLAD NOT TO WASTE THE TICKET.
THE LIGHT WENT OUT!
ZMMMMM
IT'S TIME! OH, BOY!
GUYS LIKE SAWAMURA WANT HELPLESS GIRLS...
...SO A HORROR MOVIE IN THE DARK IS A NATURAL!
GNCH
TIME FOR THE NEXT PLAN!
JING!
MNCH
"OPERATION: FRIGHT CLING" IS SET TO BEGIN!

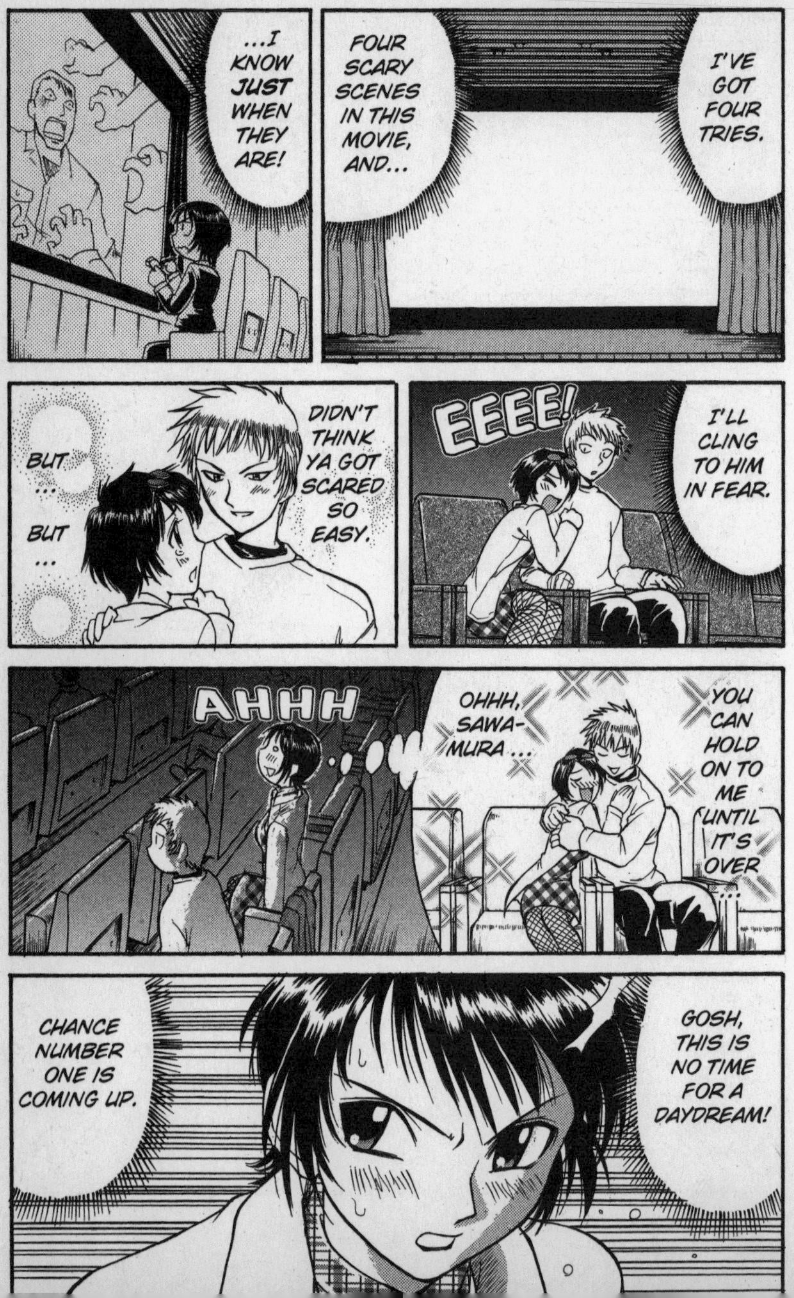
I'VE GOT FOUR TRIES.
FOUR SCARY SCENES IN THIS MOVIE, AND...
...I KNOW JUST WHEN THEY ARE!
I'LL CLING TO HIM IN FEAR.
EEEE!
DIDN'T THINK YA GOT SCARED SO EASY.
BUT... BUT...
YOU CAN HOLD ON TO ME UNTIL IT'S OVER...
OHHH, SAWAMURA...
AHHH
GOSH, THIS IS NO TIME FOR A DAYDREAM!
CHANCE NUMBER ONE IS COMING UP.

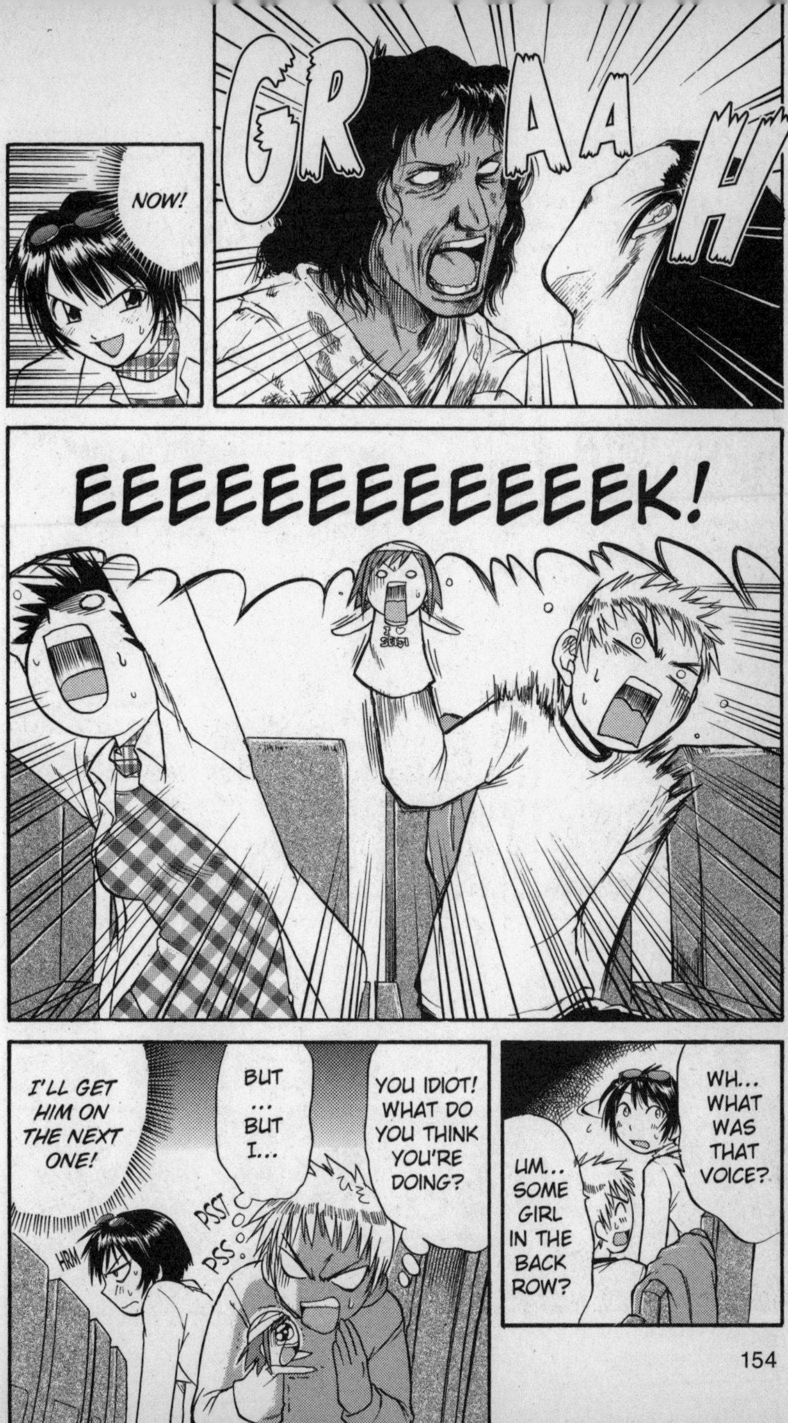
GRAAAH
NOW!
EEEEEEEEEEEEEK!
I ♥ SEIJI
WH... WHAT WAS THAT VOICE?
UM... SOME GIRL IN THE BACK ROW?
YOU IDIOT! WHAT DO YOU THINK YOU'RE DOING?
BUT ... BUT I...
PSST
PSS
I'LL GET HIM ON THE NEXT ONE!
HRM

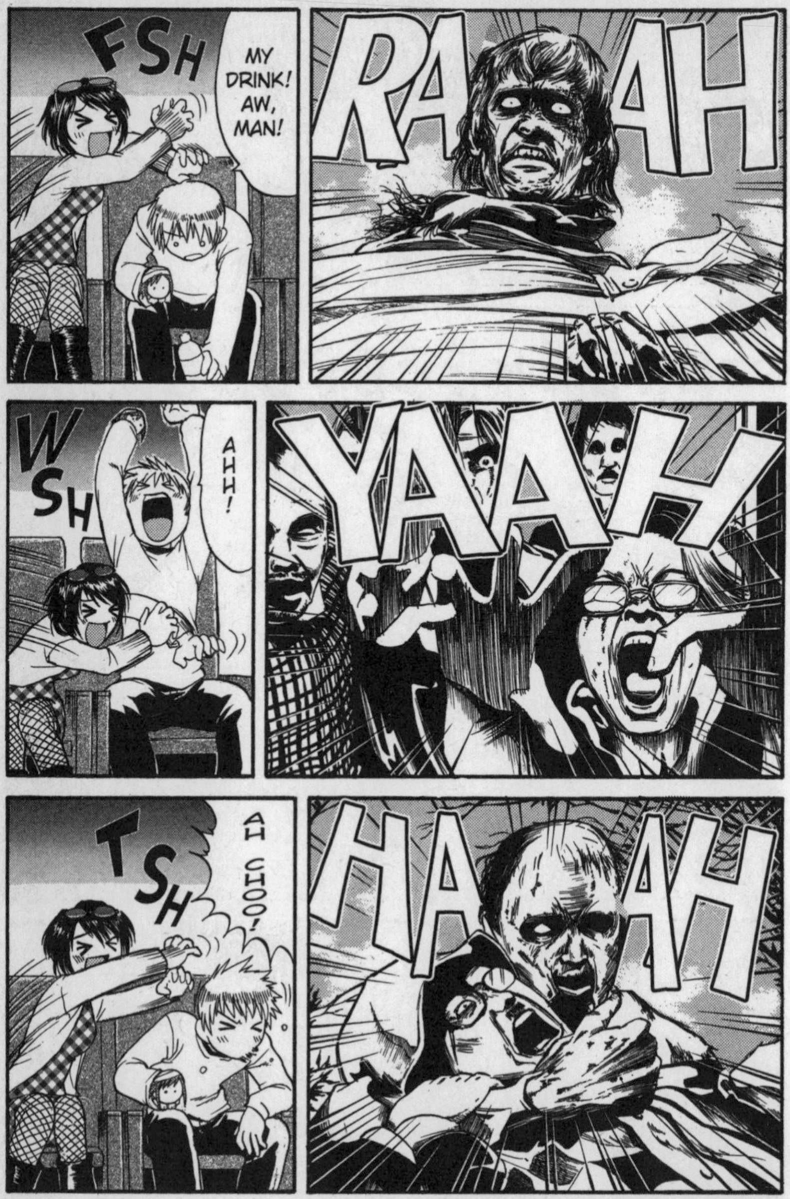
RAAH
FSH
MY DRINK! AW, MAN!
YAAH
WSH
AHH!
HAAH
TSH
AH CHOO!

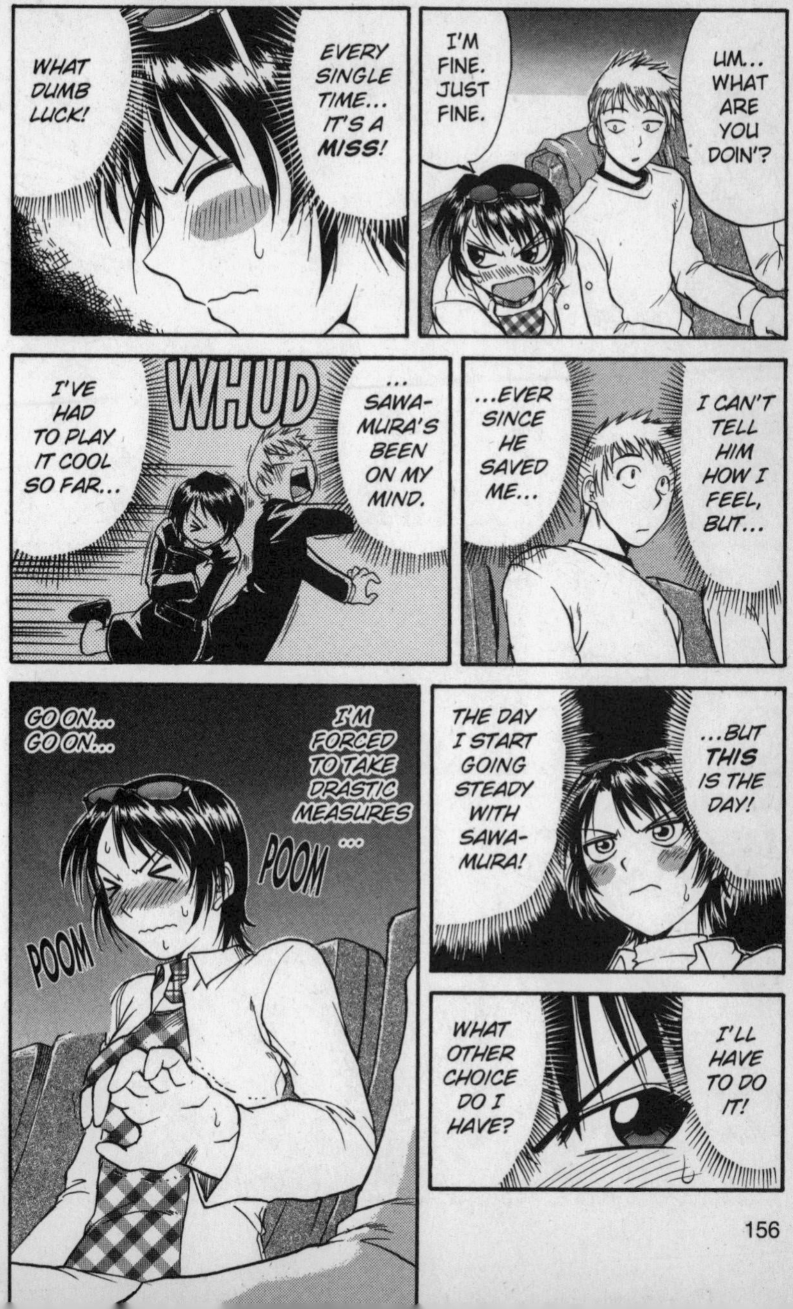
UM... WHAT ARE YOU DOIN'?
I'M FINE. JUST FINE.
EVERY SINGLE TIME... IT'S A MISS!
WHAT DUMB LUCK!
I CAN'T TELL HIM HOW I FEEL, BUT...
...EVER SINCE HE SAVED ME...
...SAWAMURA'S BEEN ON MY MIND.
WHUD
I'VE HAD TO PLAY IT COOL SO FAR...
...BUT THIS IS THE DAY!
THE DAY I START GOING STEADY WITH SAWAMURA!
I'LL HAVE TO DO IT!
WHAT OTHER CHOICE DO I HAVE?
I'M FORCED TO TAKE DRASTIC MEASURES...
POOM
GO ON... GO ON...
POOM

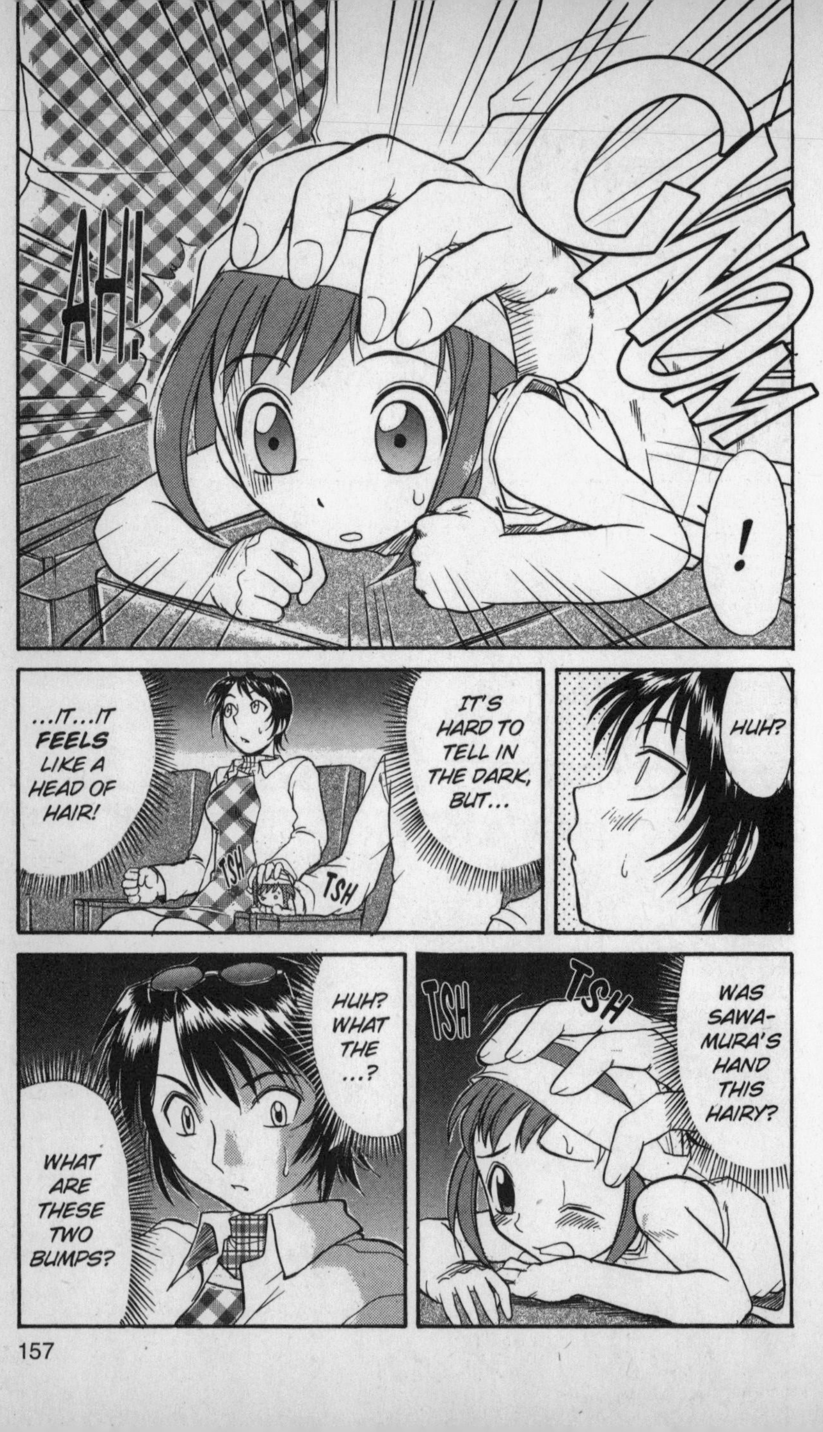
GMOM
AH!
!
HUH?
IT'S HARD TO TELL IN THE DARK, BUT...
...IT...IT FEELS LIKE A HEAD OF HAIR!
TSH
TSH
TSH
TSH
WAS SAWAMURA'S HAND THIS HAIRY?
HUH? WHAT THE ...?
WHAT ARE THESE TWO BUMPS?

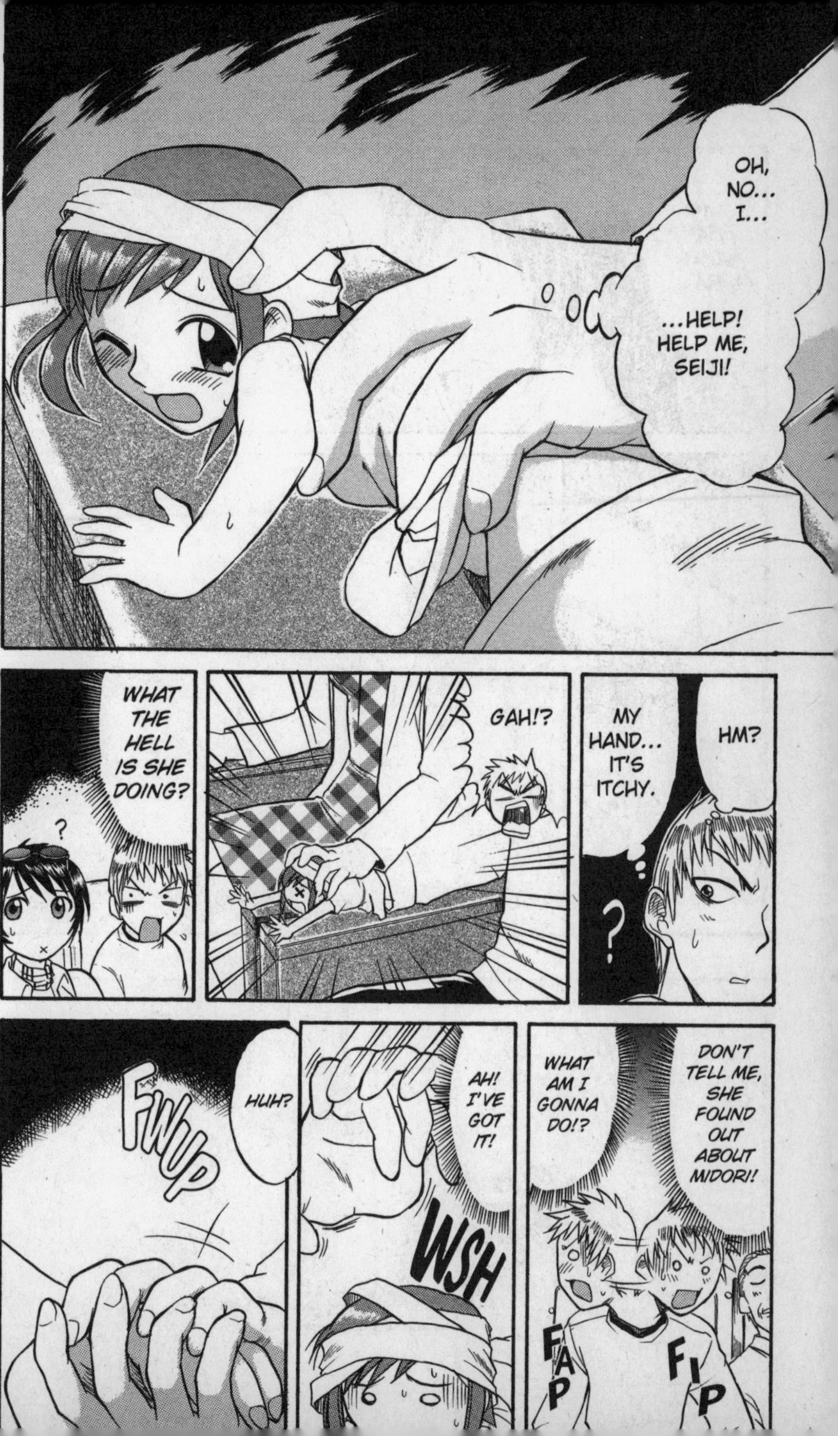
OH, NO... I...
...HELP! HELP ME, SEIJI!
HM?
MY HAND... IT'S ITCHY.
GAH!?
WHAT THE HELL IS SHE DOING?
DON'T TELL ME, SHE FOUND OUT ABOUT MIDORI!
WHAT AM I GONNA DO!?
FIP
FAP
AH! I'VE GOT IT!
WSH
HUH?
FWUP

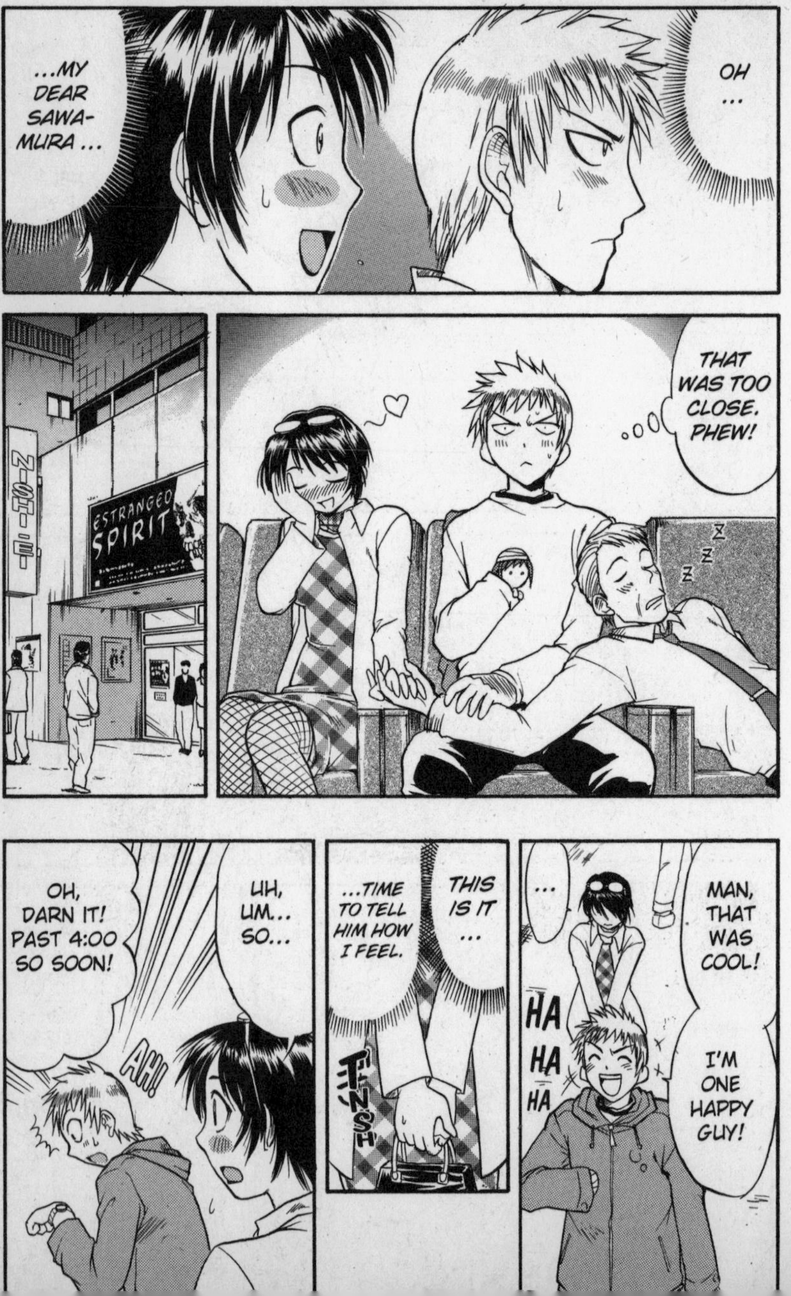
OH ...
...MY DEAR SAWAMURA ...
THAT WAS TOO CLOSE. PHEW!
Z Z Z
NISHI-EI
ESTRANGED SPIRIT
MAN, THAT WAS COOL!
...
HA HA HA
I'M ONE HAPPY GUY!
THIS IS IT ...
...TIME TO TELL HIM HOW I FEEL.
UH, UM... SO...
OH, DARN IT! PAST 4:00 SO SOON!
AH!

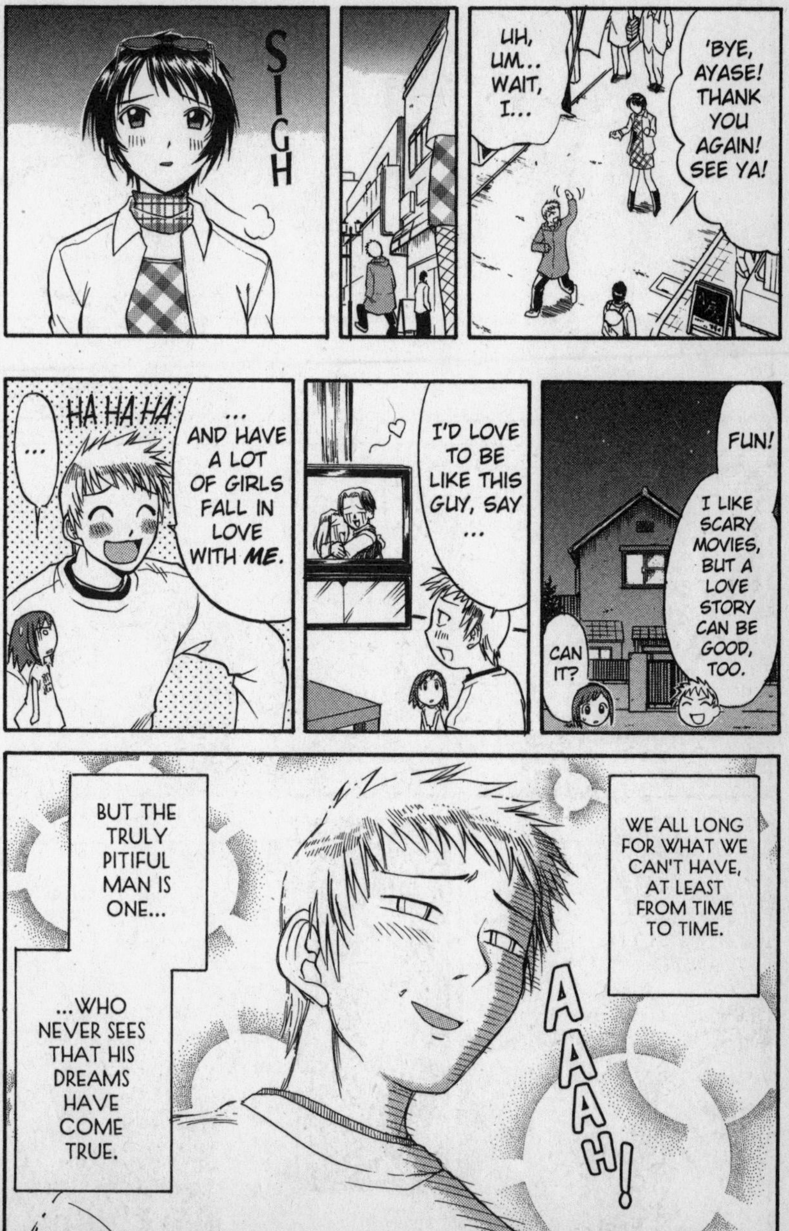
'BYE, AYASE! THANK YOU AGAIN! SEE YA!
UH, UM... WAIT, I...
SIGH
FUN!
I LIKE SCARY MOVIES, BUT A LOVE STORY CAN BE GOOD, TOO.
CAN IT?
I'D LOVE TO BE LIKE THIS GUY, SAY ...
... AND HAVE A LOT OF GIRLS FALL IN LOVE WITH *ME*.
HA HA HA
...
WE ALL LONG FOR WHAT WE CAN'T HAVE, AT LEAST FROM TIME TO TIME.
AAAAH!
BUT THE TRULY PITIFUL MAN IS ONE...
...WHO NEVER SEES THAT HIS DREAMS HAVE COME TRUE.

DAY 9 A QUIET DAY

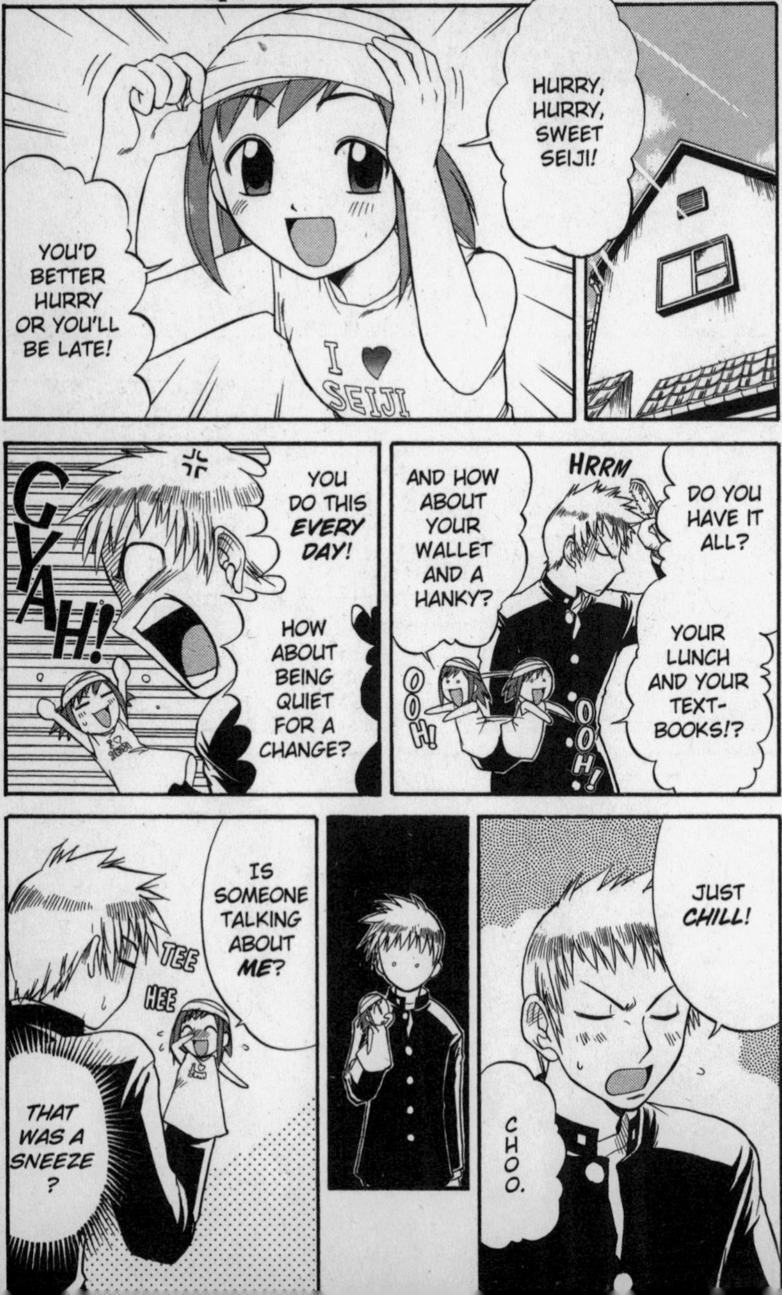
HURRY, HURRY, SWEET SEIJI!
YOU'D BETTER HURRY OR YOU'LL BE LATE!
I ♥ SEIJI
HRRM
DO YOU HAVE IT ALL?
AND HOW ABOUT YOUR WALLET AND A HANKY?
YOUR LUNCH AND YOUR TEXT-BOOKS!?
OOOH!
OOOH!
YOU DO THIS EVERY DAY!
GYAH!
HOW ABOUT BEING QUIET FOR A CHANGE?
JUST CHILL!
CHOO.
IS SOMEONE TALKING ABOUT ME?
TEE HEE
THAT WAS A SNEEZE?

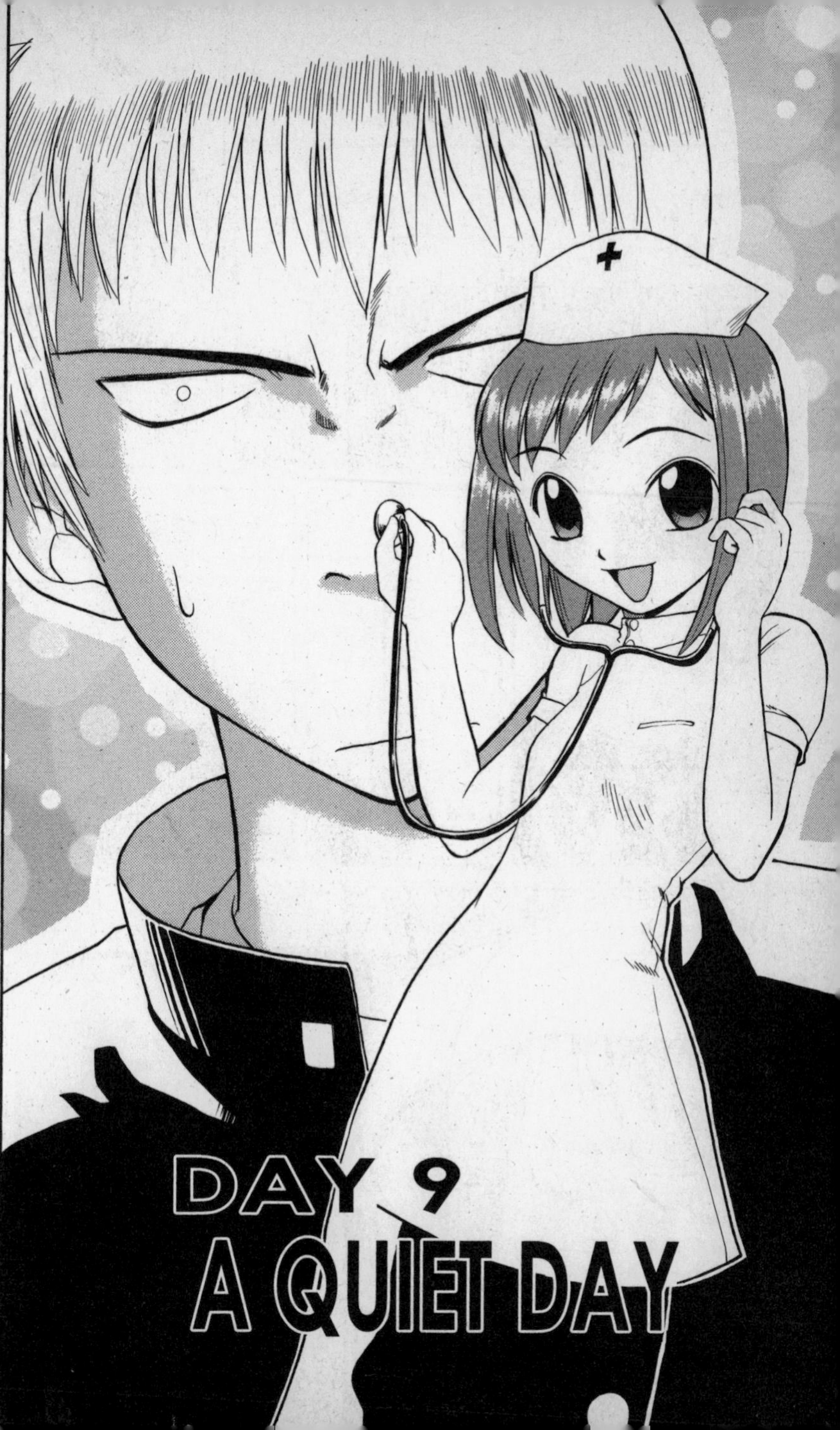
DAY 9
A QUIET DAY

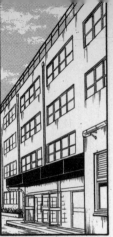

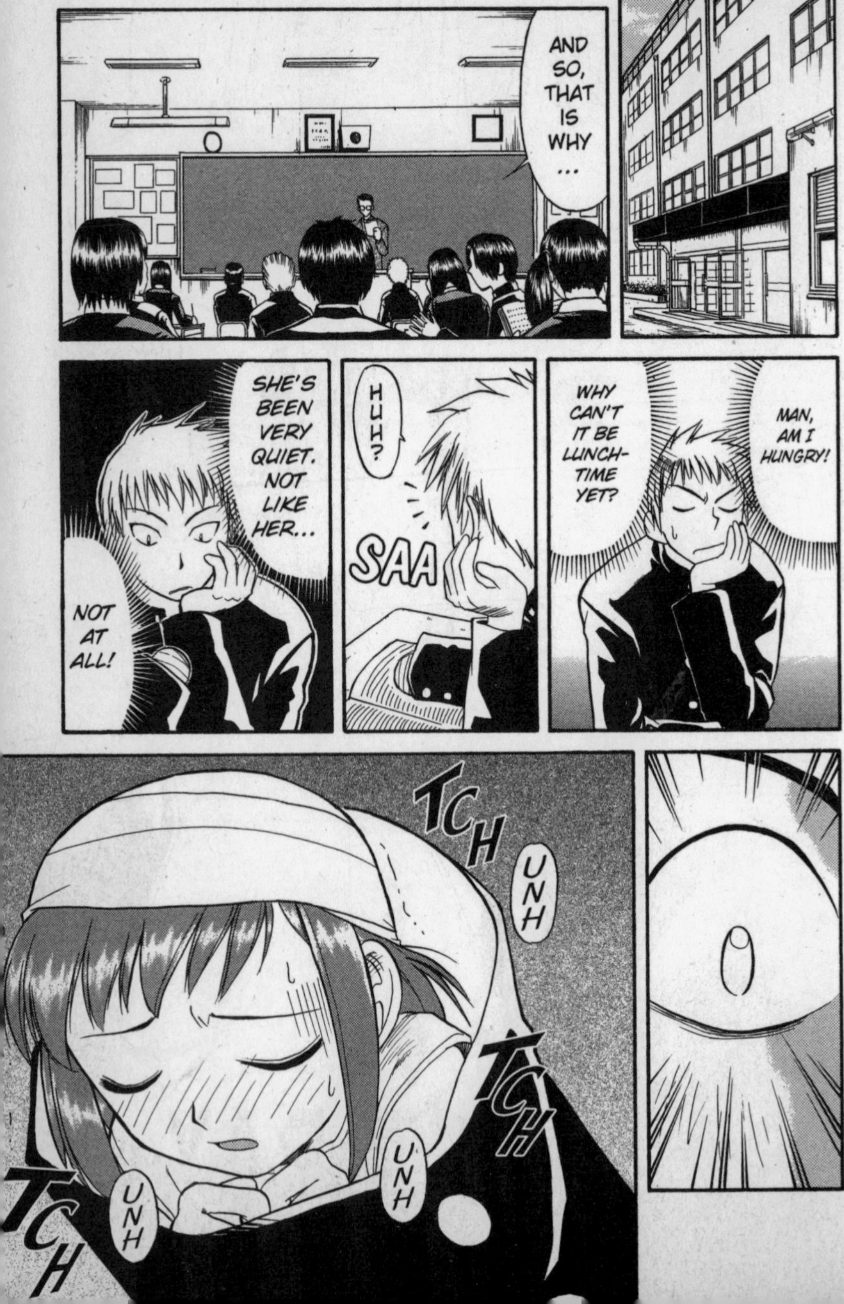
AND SO, THAT IS WHY ...
MAN, AM I HUNGRY!
WHY CAN'T IT BE LUNCH-TIME YET?
HUH?
SAA
SHE'S BEEN VERY QUIET. NOT LIKE HER...
NOT AT ALL!
TCH
UNH
TCH
UNH
UNH
TCH

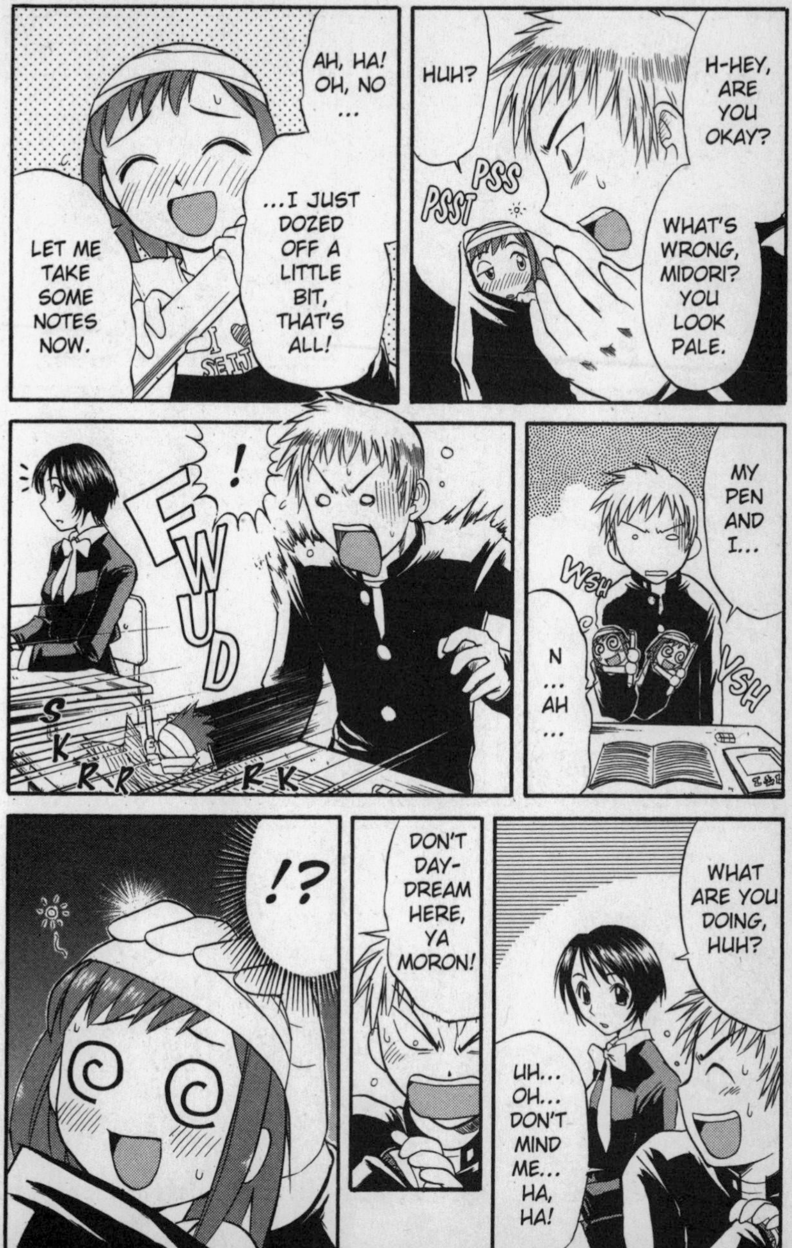
H-HEY, ARE YOU OKAY?
HUH?
PSS
PSST
WHAT'S WRONG, MIDORI? YOU LOOK PALE.
AH, HA! OH, NO ...
...I JUST DOZED OFF A LITTLE BIT, THAT'S ALL!
LET ME TAKE SOME NOTES NOW.
MY PEN AND I...
WSH
N ... AH ...
VSH
!
FWUD
SKRRRK
WHAT ARE YOU DOING, HUH?
UH... OH... DON'T MIND ME... HA, HA!
DON'T DAY-DREAM HERE, YA MORON!
!?

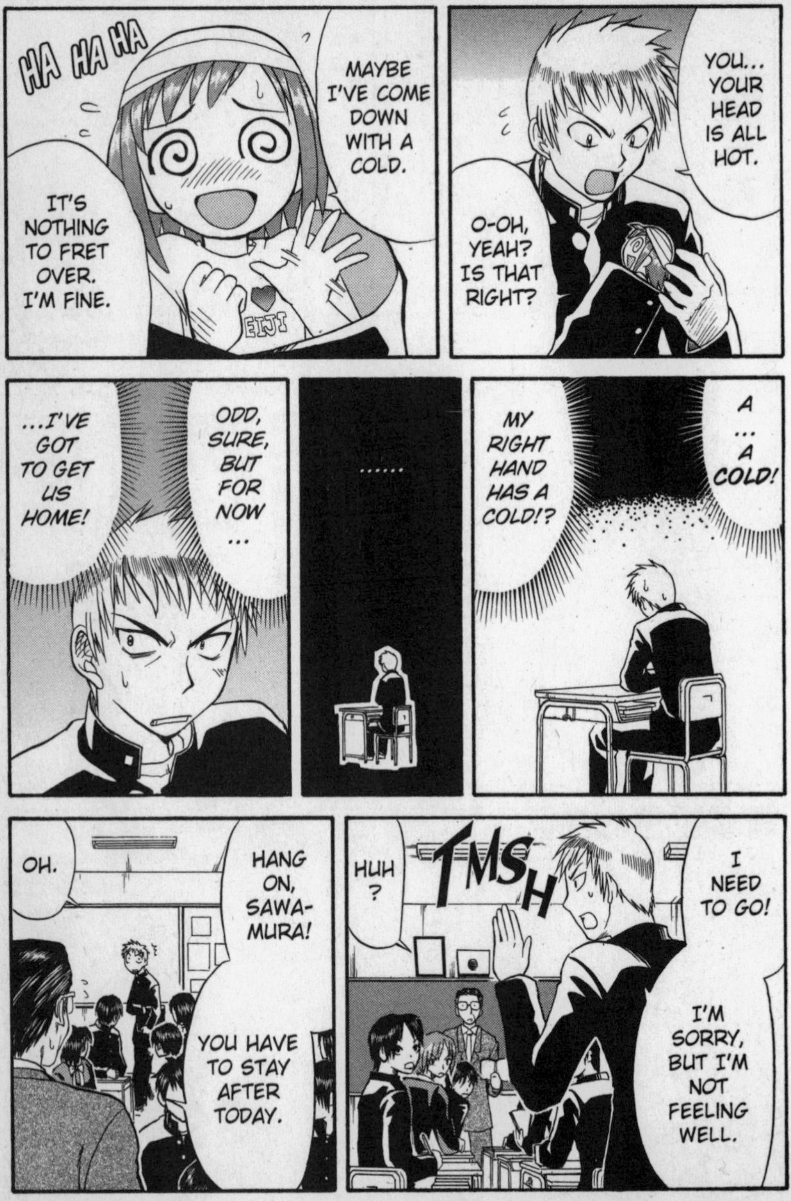
YOU... YOUR HEAD IS ALL HOT.
O-OH, YEAH? IS THAT RIGHT?
HA HA HA
MAYBE I'VE COME DOWN WITH A COLD.
EIJI
IT'S NOTHING TO FRET OVER. I'M FINE.
A ... A COLD!
MY RIGHT HAND HAS A COLD!?
......
ODD, SURE, BUT FOR NOW ...
...I'VE GOT TO GET US HOME!
I NEED TO GO!
TMSH
HUH ?
I'M SORRY, BUT I'M NOT FEELING WELL.
HANG ON, SAWAMURA!
OH.
YOU HAVE TO STAY AFTER TODAY.

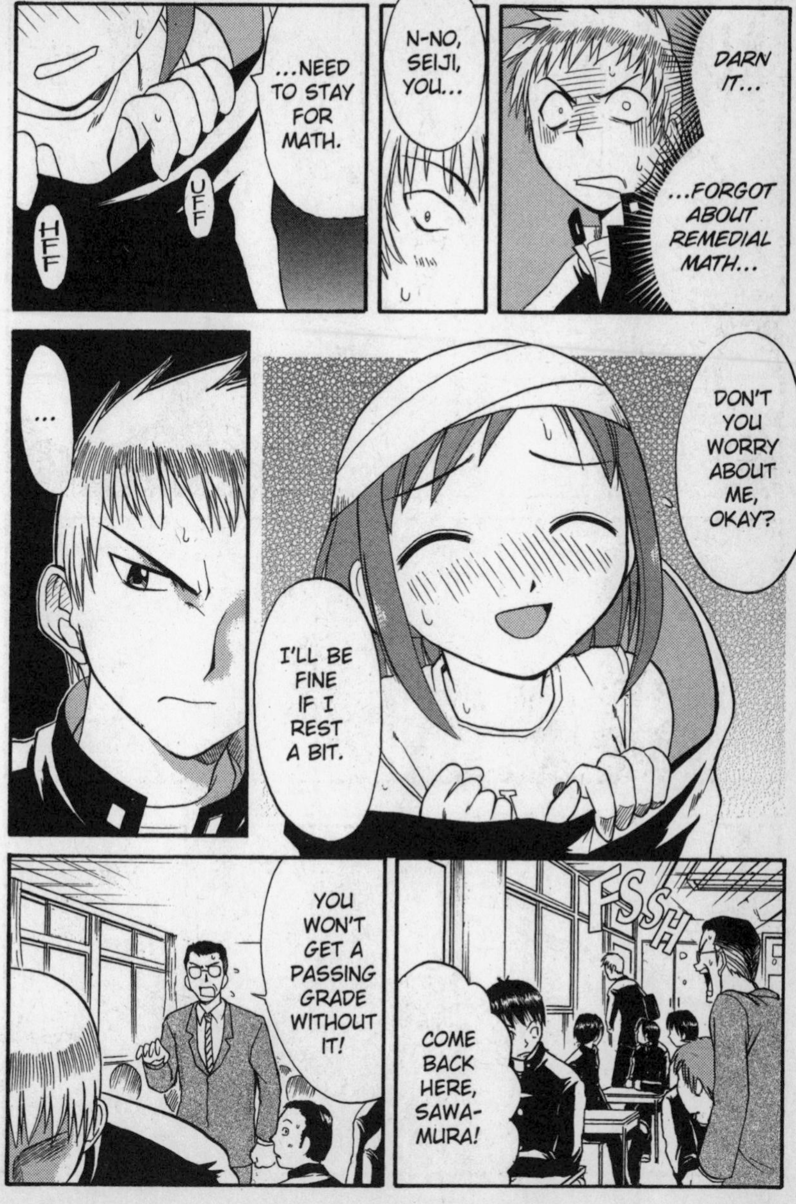
DARN IT...
...FORGOT ABOUT REMEDIAL MATH...
N-NO, SEIJI, YOU...
...NEED TO STAY FOR MATH.
UFF
HFF
DON'T YOU WORRY ABOUT ME, OKAY?
I'LL BE FINE IF I REST A BIT.
...
FSSH
COME BACK HERE, SAWAMURA!
YOU WON'T GET A PASSING GRADE WITHOUT IT!

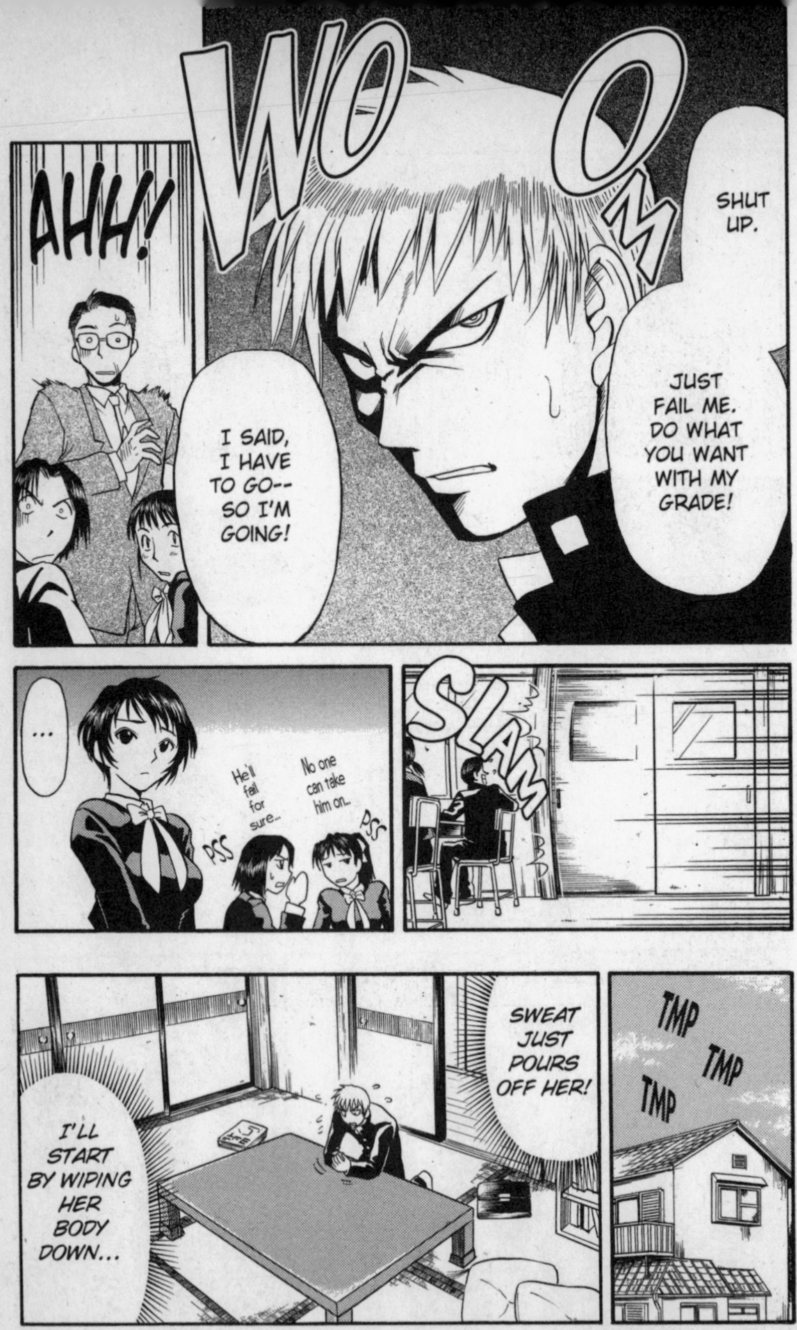
WOOM
SHUT UP.
JUST FAIL ME. DO WHAT YOU WANT WITH MY GRADE!
I SAID, I HAVE TO GO-- SO I'M GOING!
AHH!
SLAM
PSS
No one can take him on..
He'll fail for sure..
...
PSS
TMP TMP TMP
SWEAT JUST POURS OFF HER!
I'LL START BY WIPING HER BODY DOWN...

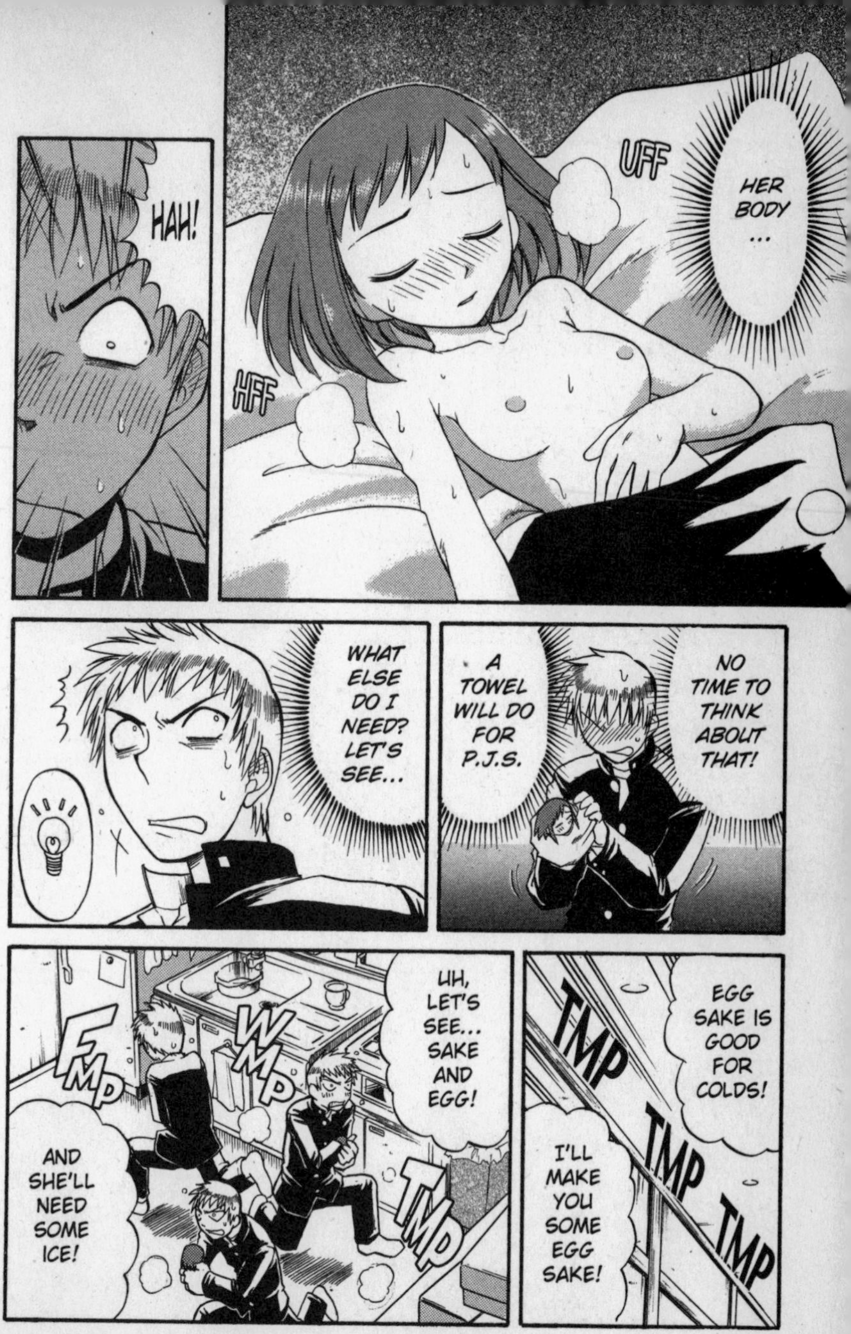
HER BODY ...
UFF
HFF
HAH!
NO TIME TO THINK ABOUT THAT!
A TOWEL WILL DO FOR P.J.S.
WHAT ELSE DO I NEED? LET'S SEE...
EGG SAKE IS GOOD FOR COLDS!
TMP
TMP
TMP
I'LL MAKE YOU SOME EGG SAKE!
UH, LET'S SEE... SAKE AND EGG!
WMP
FMP
TMP
AND SHE'LL NEED SOME ICE!

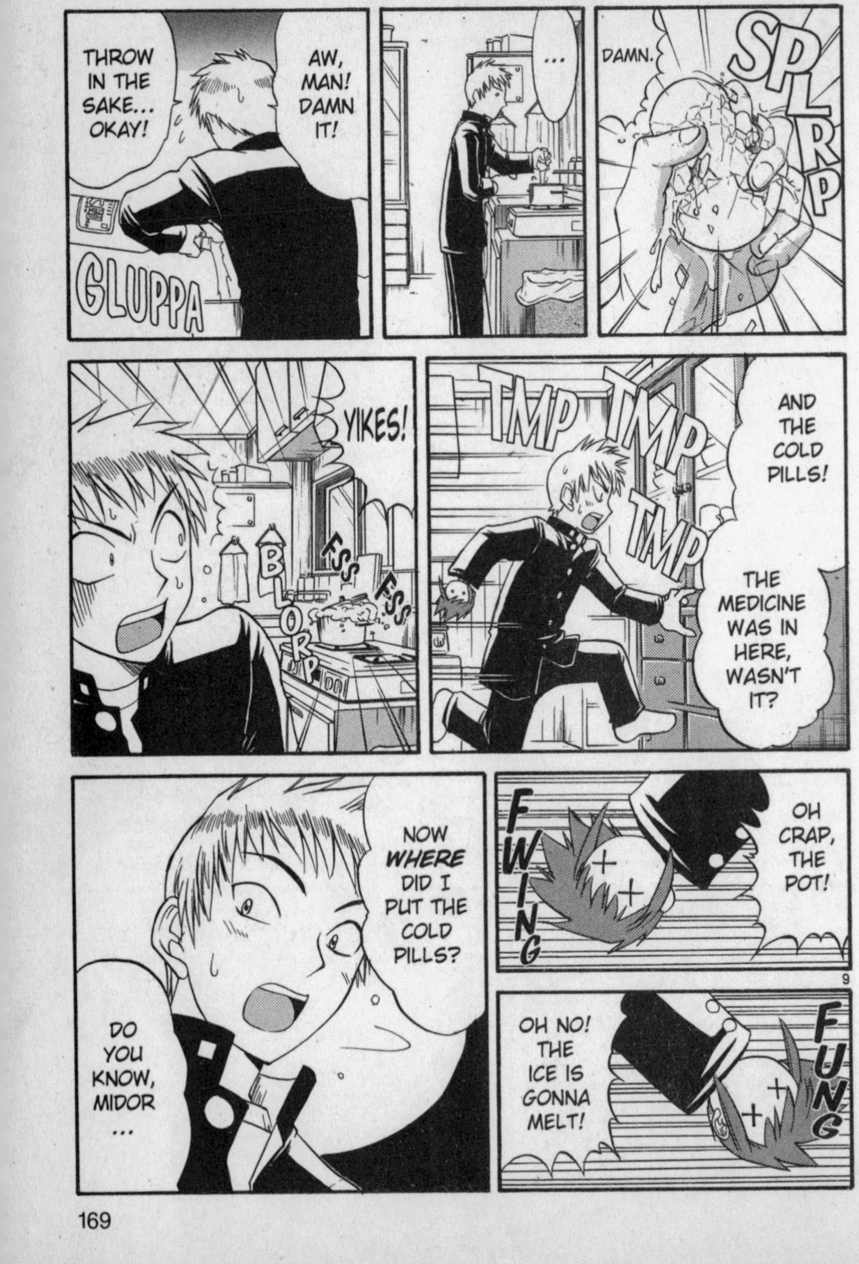
SPLRP
DAMN.
...
AW, MAN! DAMN IT!
THROW IN THE SAKE... OKAY!
GLUPPA
AND THE COLD PILLS!
TMP TMP TMP
THE MEDICINE WAS IN HERE, WASN'T IT?
YIKES!
FSS FSS
BLORP
OH CRAP, THE POT!
FWING
FUNG
OH NO! THE ICE IS GONNA MELT!
NOW *WHERE* DID I PUT THE COLD PILLS?
DO YOU KNOW, MIDOR ...

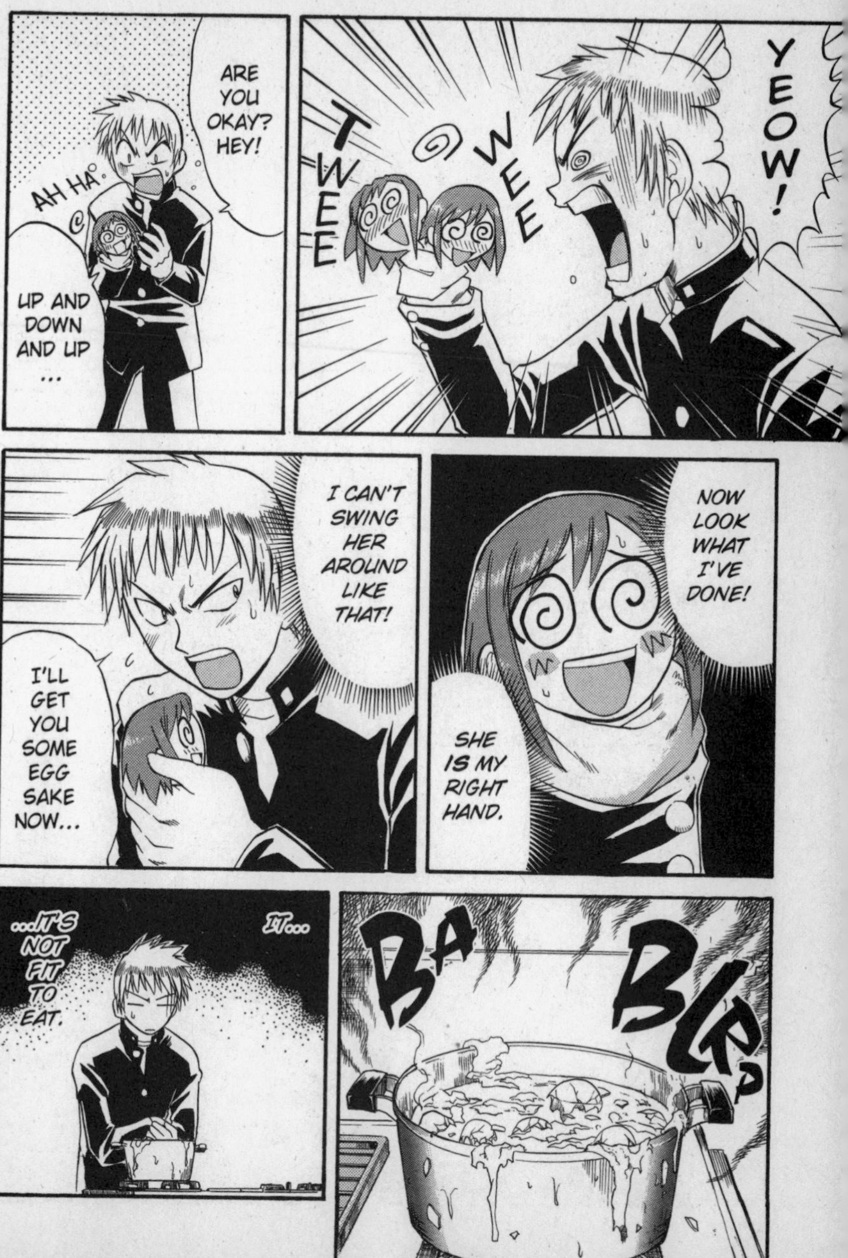
YEOW!
TWEE
WEE
ARE YOU OKAY? HEY!
AH HA
UP AND DOWN AND UP ...
NOW LOOK WHAT I'VE DONE!
SHE IS MY RIGHT HAND.
I CAN'T SWING HER AROUND LIKE THAT!
I'LL GET YOU SOME EGG SAKE NOW...
BA
BLRP
IT...
...IT'S NOT FIT TO EAT.

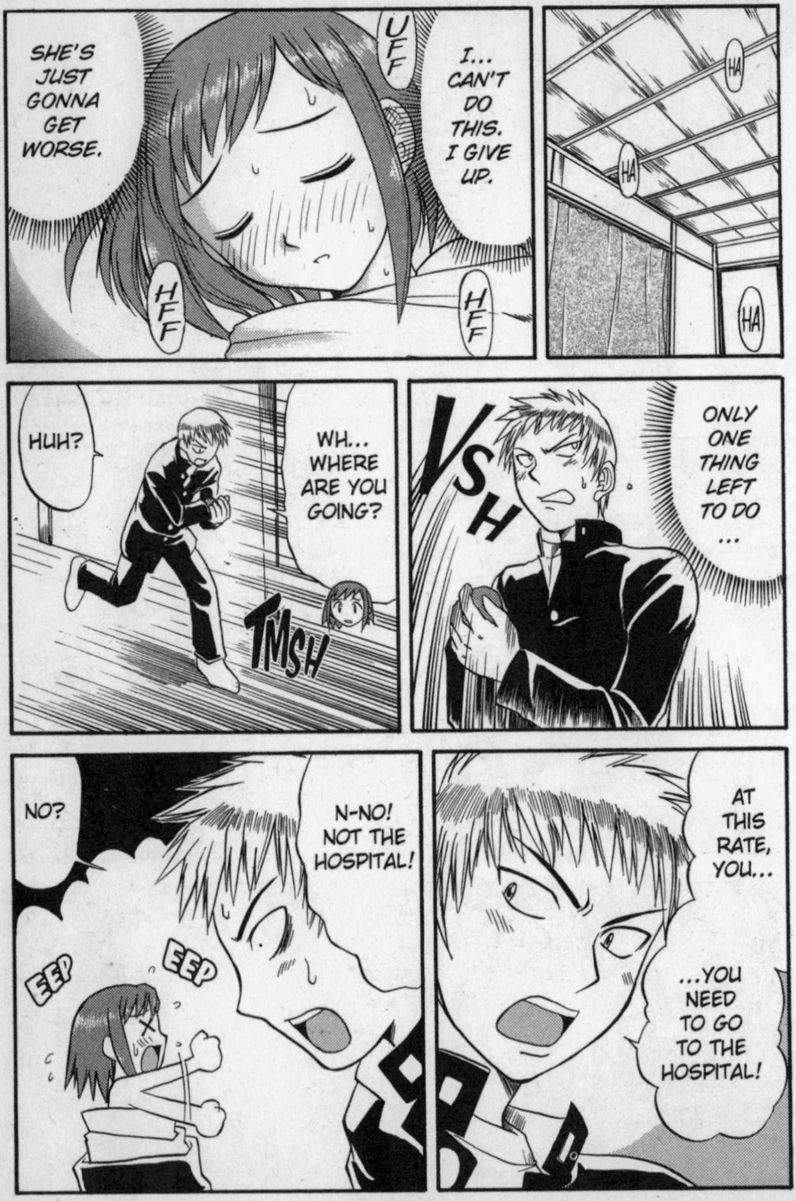
HA
HA
HA
UFF
I... CAN'T DO THIS. I GIVE UP.
SHE'S JUST GONNA GET WORSE.
HFF
HFF
ONLY ONE THING LEFT TO DO...
VSH
WH... WHERE ARE YOU GOING?
HUH?
TMSH
AT THIS RATE, YOU...
...YOU NEED TO GO TO THE HOSPITAL!
N-NO! NOT THE HOSPITAL!
NO?
EEP
EEP

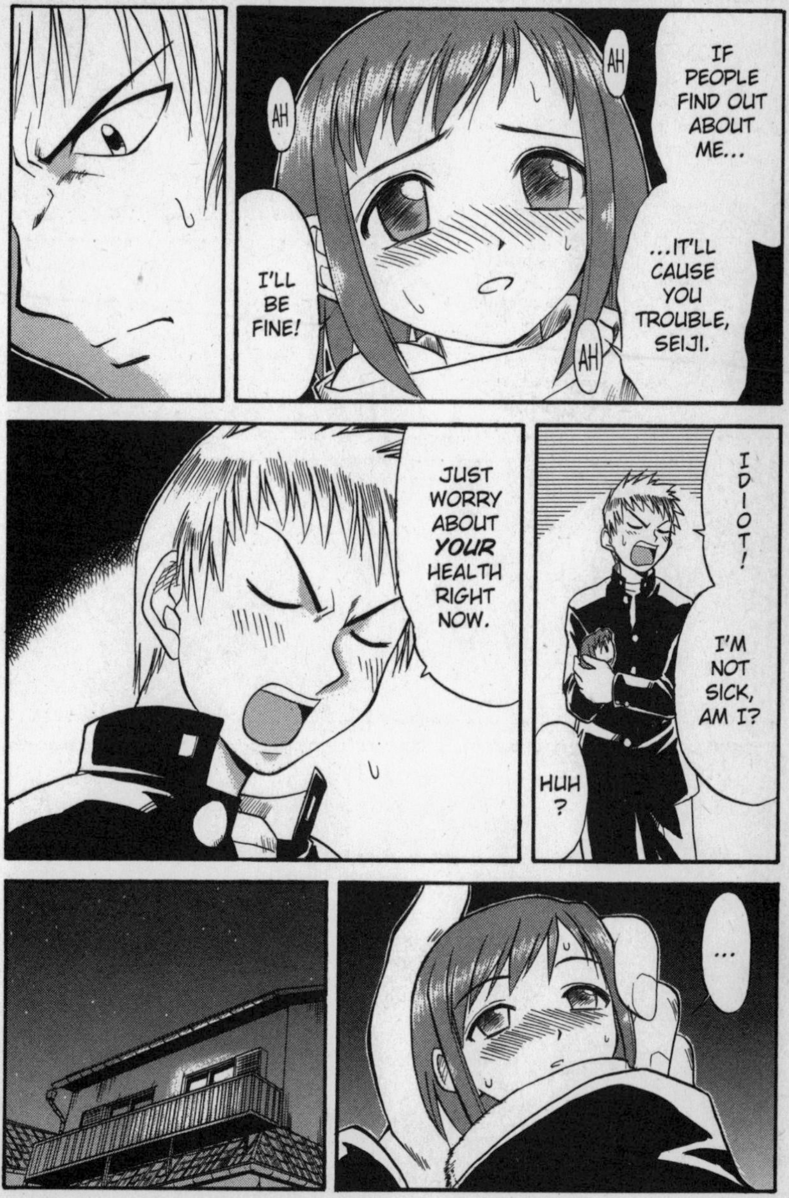
IF PEOPLE FIND OUT ABOUT ME...
AH
...IT'LL CAUSE YOU TROUBLE, SEIJI.
AH
AH
I'LL BE FINE!
IDIOT!
I'M NOT SICK, AM I?
HUH?
JUST WORRY ABOUT **YOUR** HEALTH RIGHT NOW.
...

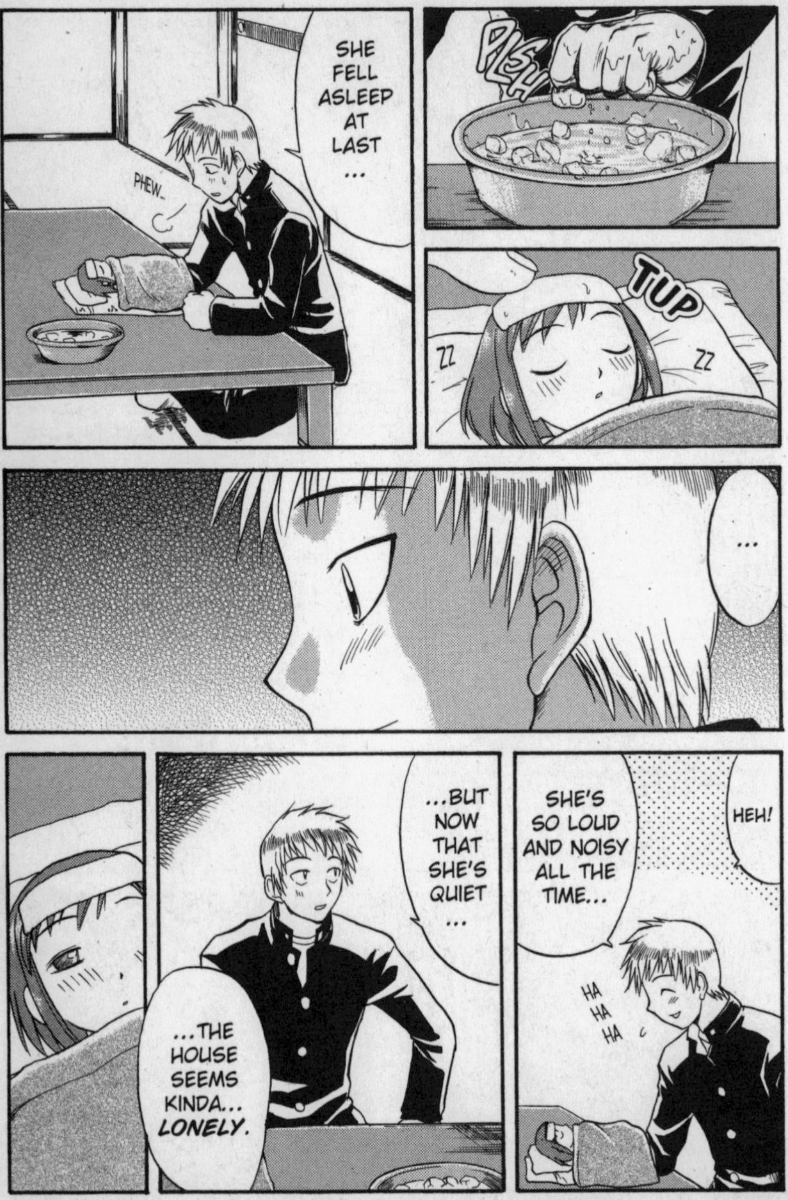
PLSH
TUP
ZZ
ZZ
SHE FELL ASLEEP AT LAST ...
PHEW...
...
HEH!
SHE'S SO LOUD AND NOISY ALL THE TIME...
HA HA HA
...BUT NOW THAT SHE'S QUIET ...
...THE HOUSE SEEMS KINDA... *LONELY*.

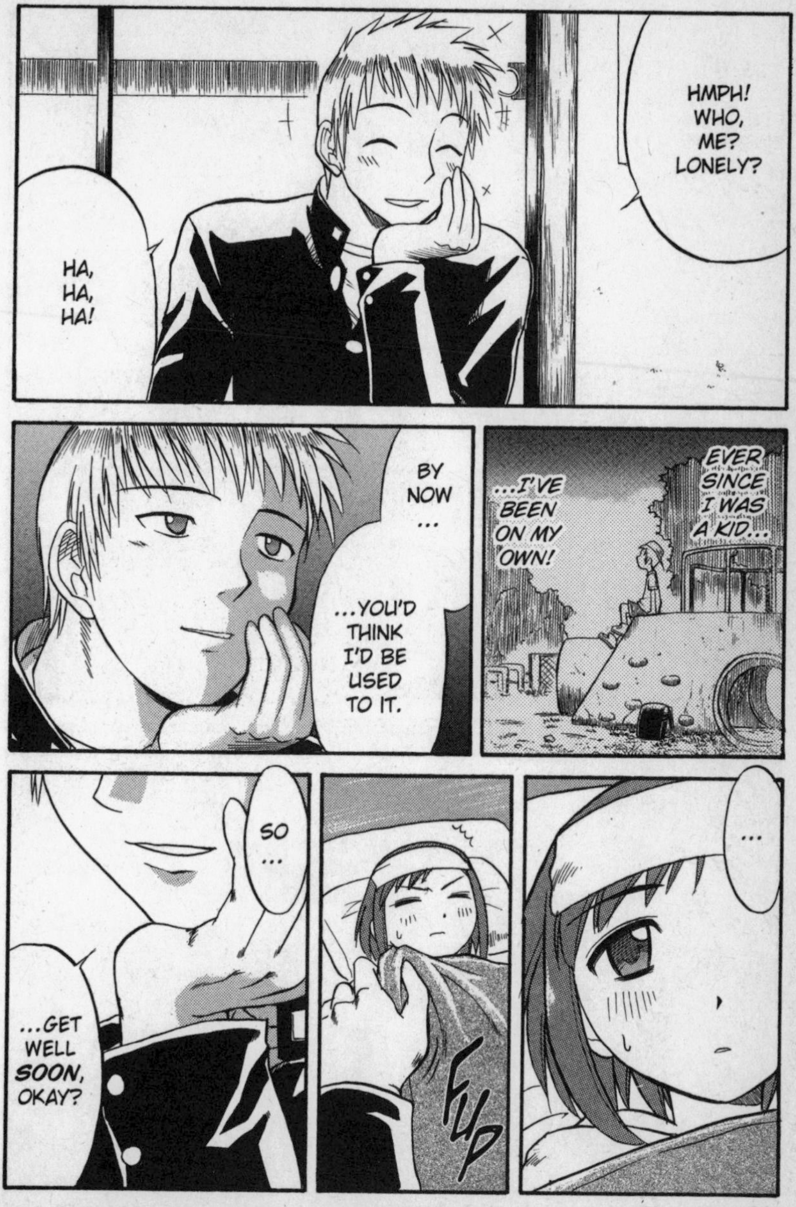
HMPH! WHO, ME? LONELY?
HA, HA, HA!
EVER SINCE I WAS A KID...
...I'VE BEEN ON MY OWN!
BY NOW ...
...YOU'D THINK I'D BE USED TO IT.
...
FLIP
SO ...
...GET WELL SOON, OKAY?

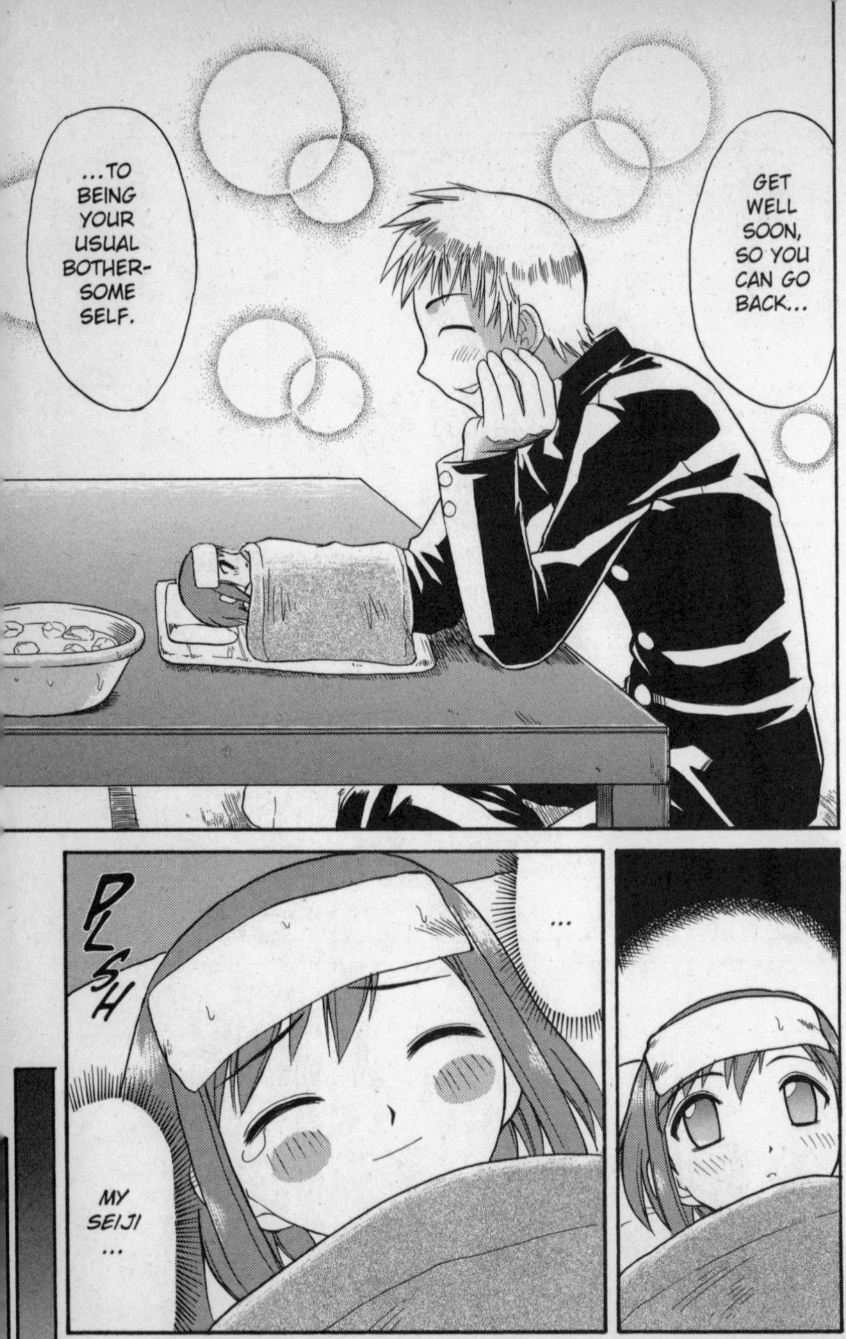
GET WELL SOON, SO YOU CAN GO BACK...
...TO BEING YOUR USUAL BOTHER-SOME SELF.
PLSH
...
MY SEIJI ...

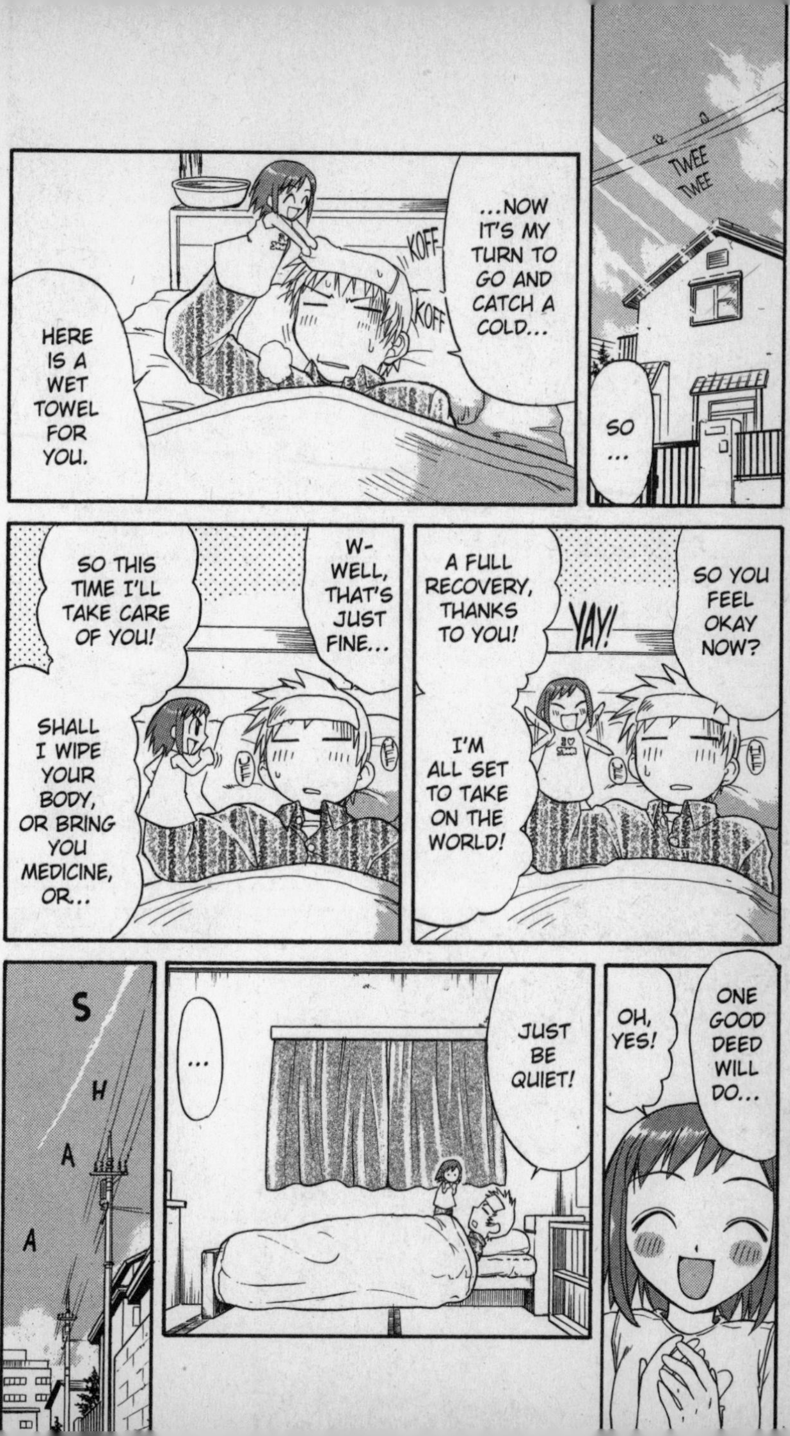
TWEE TWEE
SO ...
...NOW IT'S MY TURN TO GO AND CATCH A COLD...
KOFF
KOFF
HERE IS A WET TOWEL FOR YOU.
SO YOU FEEL OKAY NOW?
YAY!
A FULL RECOVERY, THANKS TO YOU!
I'M ALL SET TO TAKE ON THE WORLD!
W-WELL, THAT'S JUST FINE...
SO THIS TIME I'LL TAKE CARE OF YOU!
SHALL I WIPE YOUR BODY, OR BRING YOU MEDICINE, OR...
ONE GOOD DEED WILL DO...
OH, YES!
JUST BE QUIET!
...
SHAA

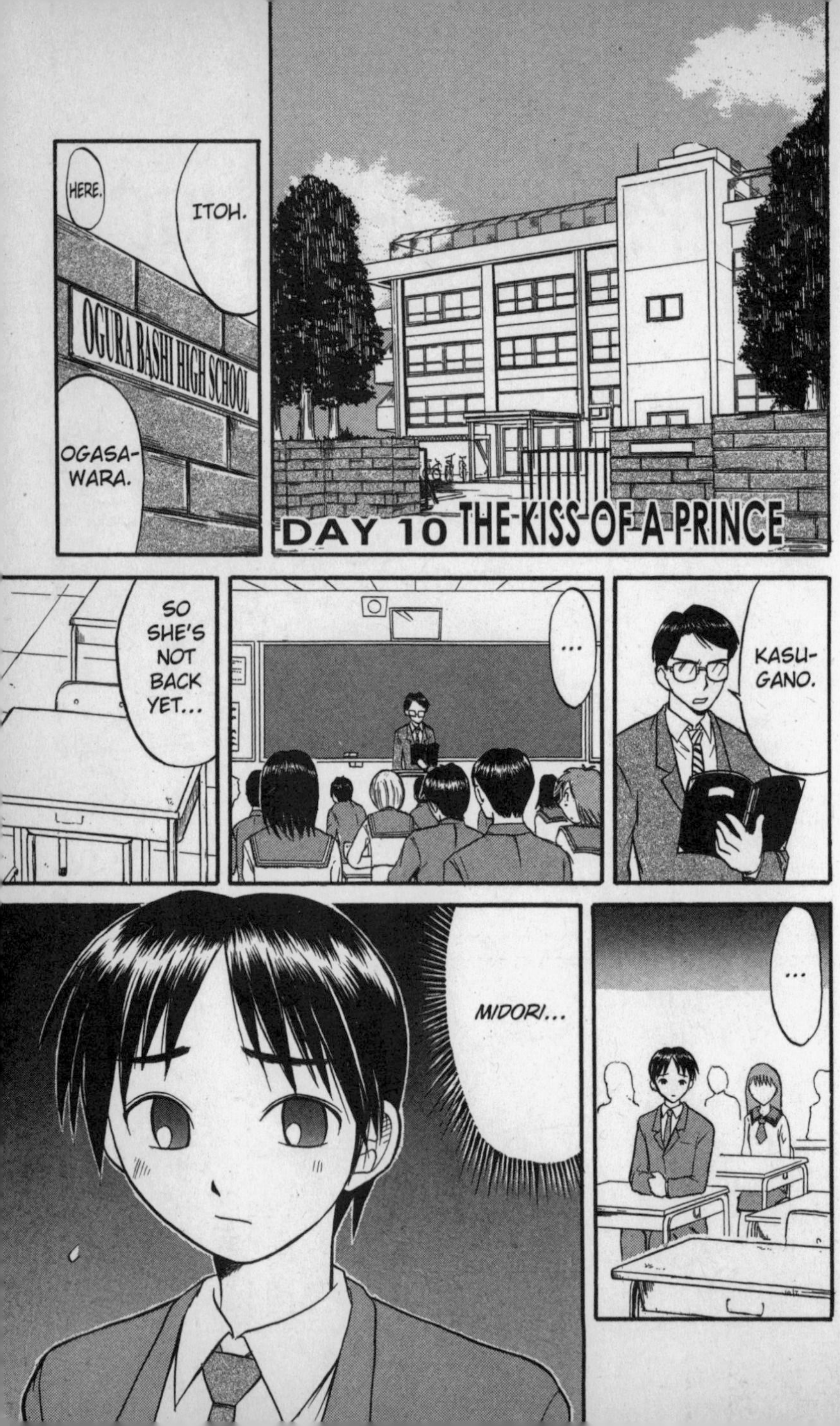
DAY 10 THE KISS OF A PRINCE
ITOH.
HERE.
OGURA BASHI HIGH SCHOOL
OGASA-WARA.
KASU-GANO.
...
SO SHE'S NOT BACK YET...
...
MIDORI...

DAY 10
THE KISS OF A PRINCE

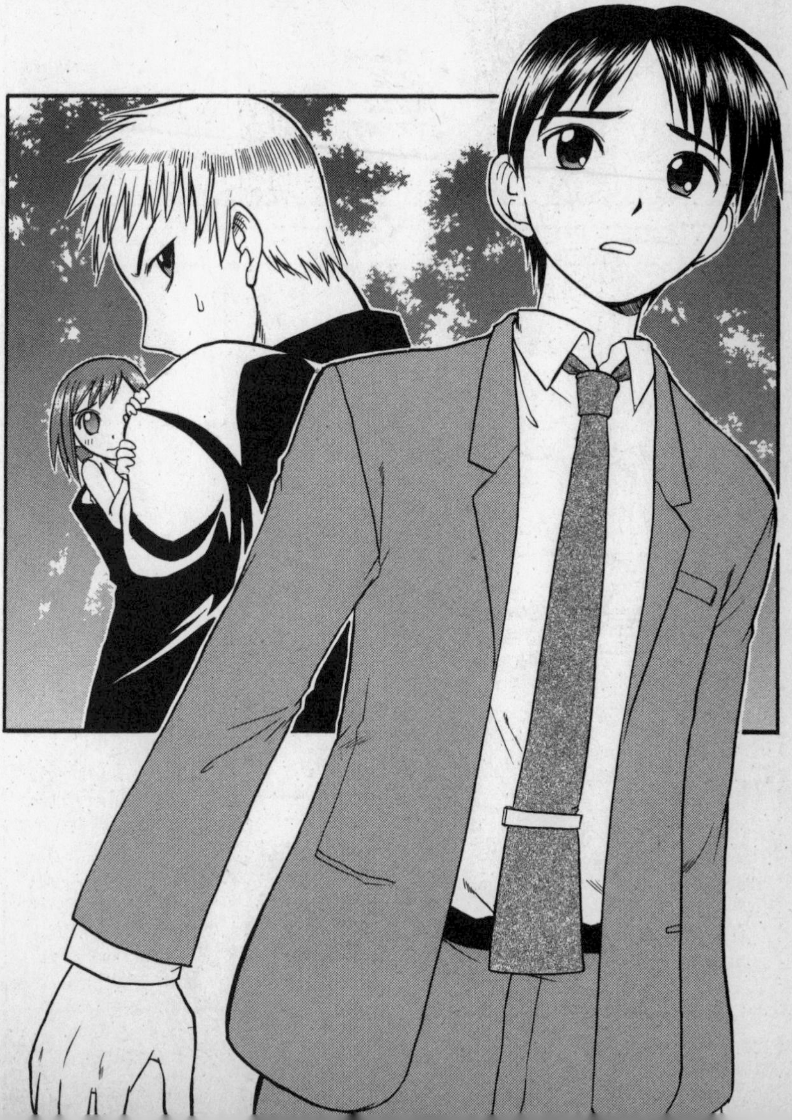

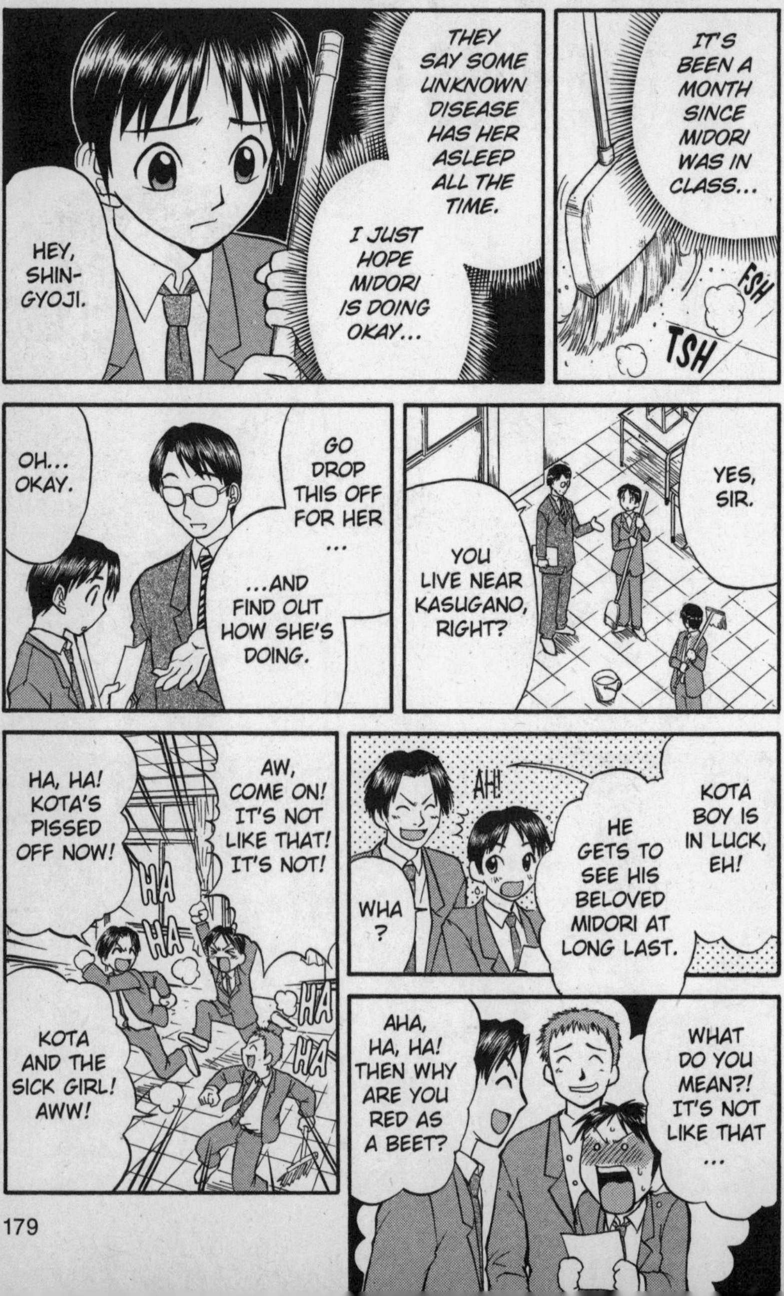
IT'S BEEN A MONTH SINCE MIDORI WAS IN CLASS...
FSH
TSH
THEY SAY SOME UNKNOWN DISEASE HAS HER ASLEEP ALL THE TIME.
I JUST HOPE MIDORI IS DOING OKAY...
HEY, SHIN-GYOJI.
YES, SIR.
YOU LIVE NEAR KASUGANO, RIGHT?
GO DROP THIS OFF FOR HER ...
...AND FIND OUT HOW SHE'S DOING.
OH... OKAY.
KOTA BOY IS IN LUCK, EH!
HE GETS TO SEE HIS BELOVED MIDORI AT LONG LAST.
AH!
WHA ?
WHAT DO YOU MEAN?! IT'S NOT LIKE THAT ...
AHA, HA, HA! THEN WHY ARE YOU RED AS A BEET?
AW, COME ON! IT'S NOT LIKE THAT! IT'S NOT!
HA, HA! KOTA'S PISSED OFF NOW!
HA
HA
HA
HA
KOTA AND THE SICK GIRL! AWW!

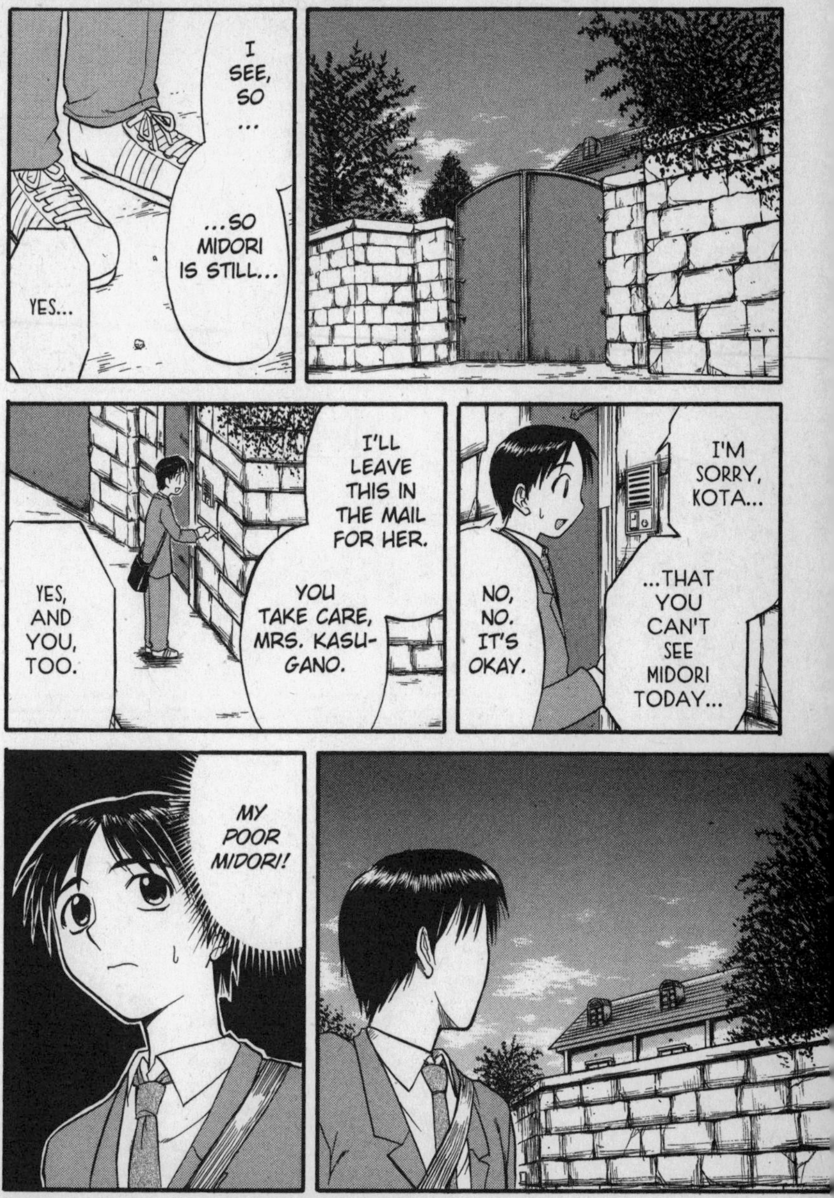
I SEE, SO ...
...SO MIDORI IS STILL...
YES...
I'M SORRY, KOTA...
...THAT YOU CAN'T SEE MIDORI TODAY...
NO, NO. IT'S OKAY.
I'LL LEAVE THIS IN THE MAIL FOR HER.
YOU TAKE CARE, MRS. KASU-GANO.
YES, AND YOU, TOO.
MY POOR MIDORI!

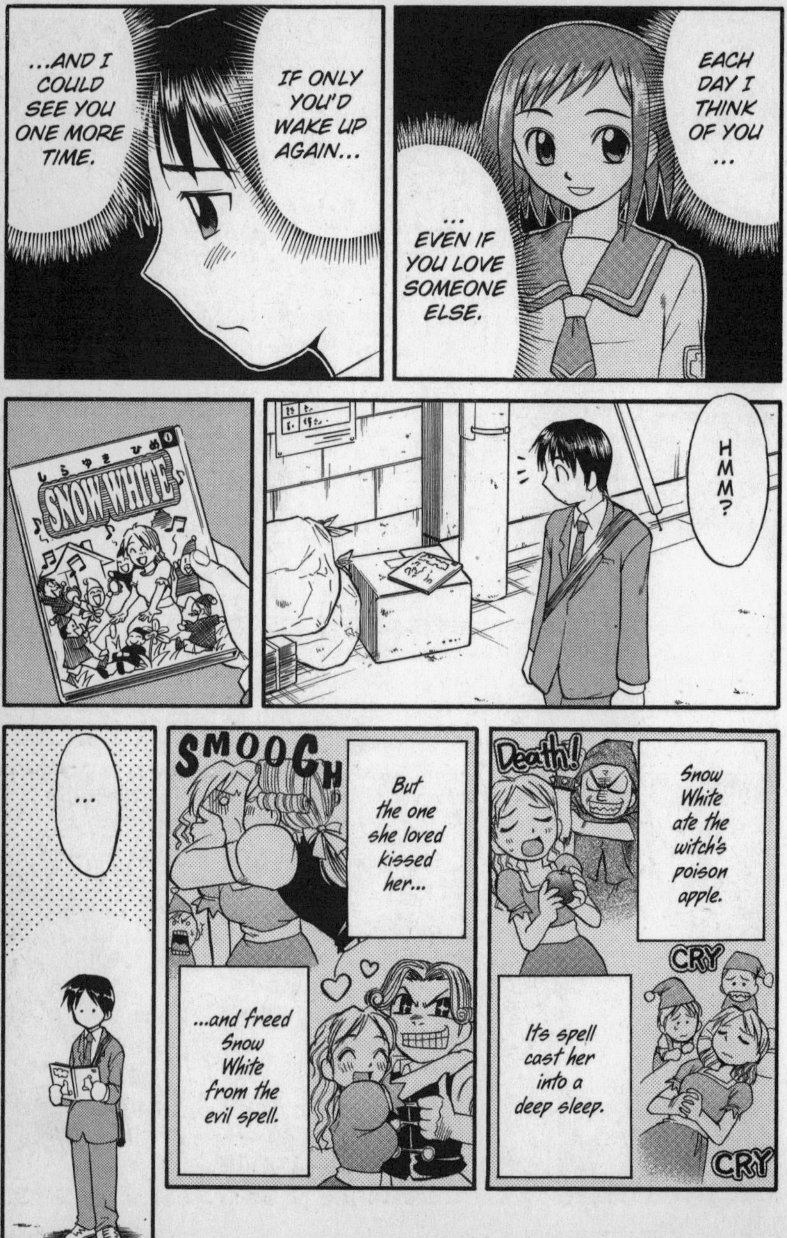
EACH DAY I THINK OF YOU ...
... EVEN IF YOU LOVE SOMEONE ELSE.
IF ONLY YOU'D WAKE UP AGAIN...
...AND I COULD SEE YOU ONE MORE TIME.
HMM?
しらゆきひめ
SNOW WHITE
Snow White ate the witch's poison apple.
Death!
CRY
Its spell cast her into a deep sleep.
CRY
SMOOCH
But the one she loved kissed her...
...and freed Snow White from the evil spell.
...

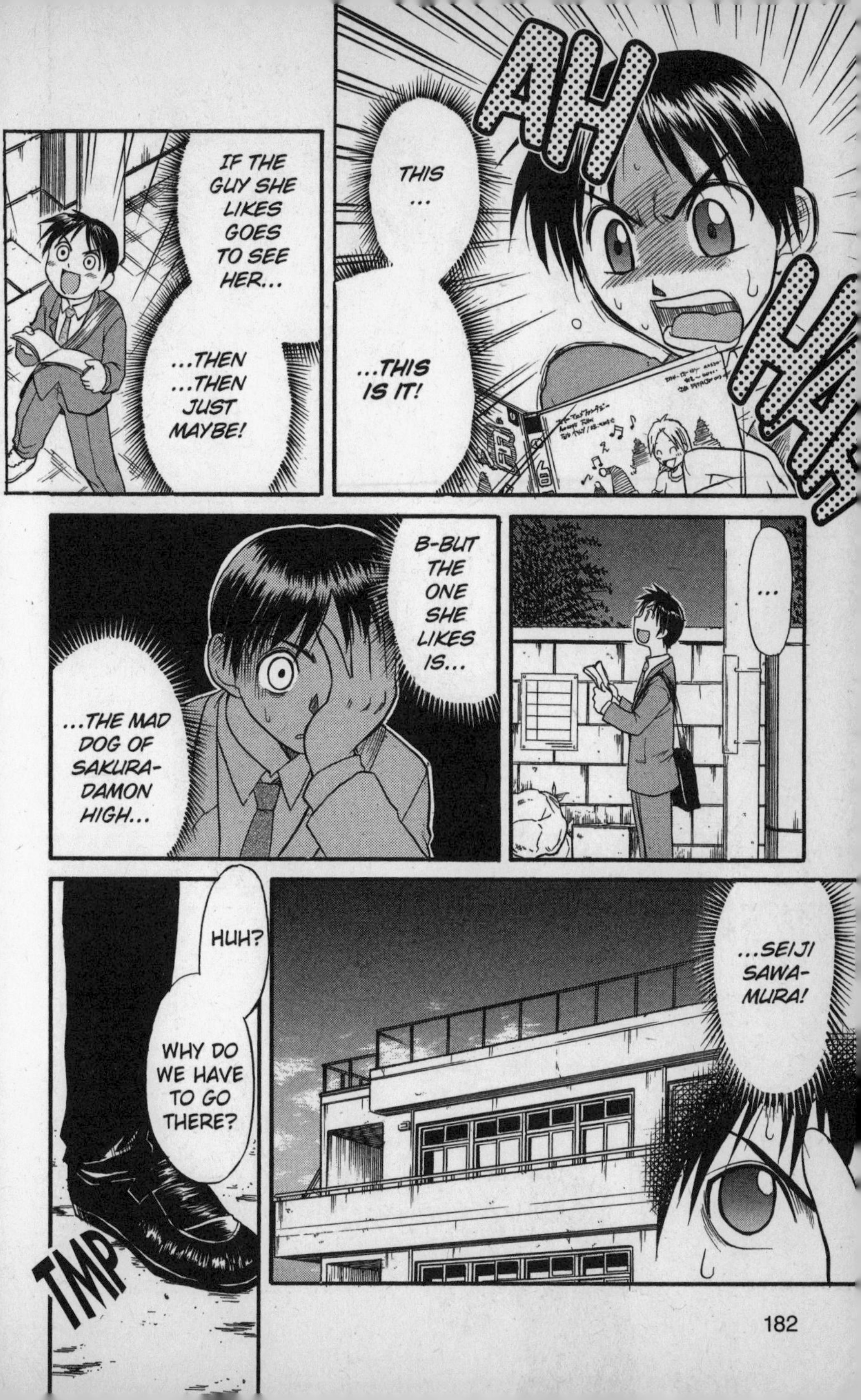
AH
HAH
THIS ...
...THIS IS IT!
IF THE GUY SHE LIKES GOES TO SEE HER...
...THEN ...THEN JUST MAYBE!
...
B-BUT THE ONE SHE LIKES IS...
...THE MAD DOG OF SAKURA-DAMON HIGH...
...SEIJI SAWAMURA!
HUH?
WHY DO WE HAVE TO GO THERE?
TMP

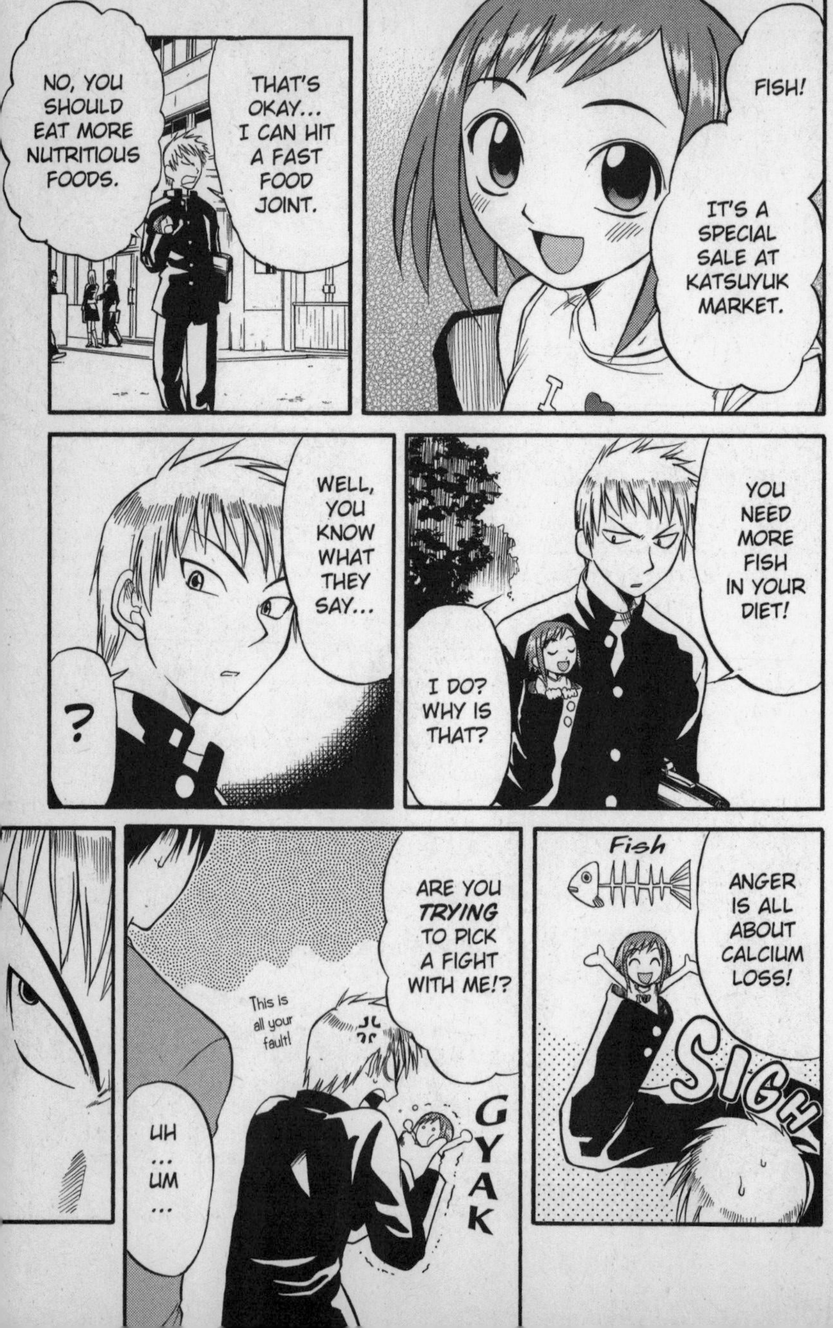
FISH!
IT'S A SPECIAL SALE AT KATSUYUK MARKET.
THAT'S OKAY... I CAN HIT A FAST FOOD JOINT.
NO, YOU SHOULD EAT MORE NUTRITIOUS FOODS.
YOU NEED MORE FISH IN YOUR DIET!
I DO? WHY IS THAT?
WELL, YOU KNOW WHAT THEY SAY...
?
Fish
ANGER IS ALL ABOUT CALCIUM LOSS!
SIGH
ARE YOU *TRYING* TO PICK A FIGHT WITH ME!?
This is all your fault!
GYAK
UH ... UM ...

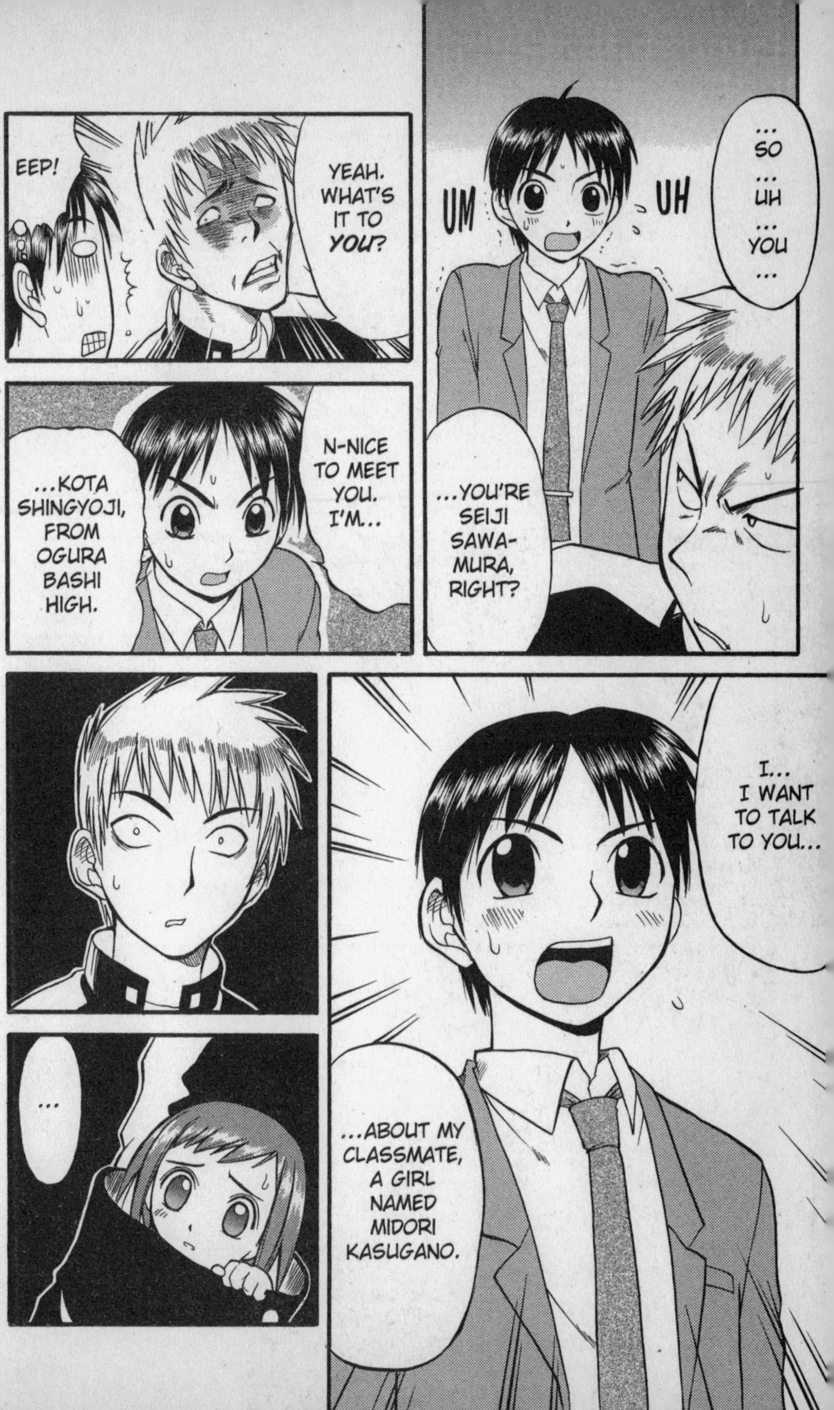

... SO ... UH ... YOU ...
UH
UM
...YOU'RE SEIJI SAWAMURA, RIGHT?
YEAH. WHAT'S IT TO *YOU*?
EEP!
N-NICE TO MEET YOU. I'M...
...KOTA SHINGYOJI, FROM OGURA BASHI HIGH.
I... I WANT TO TALK TO YOU...
...ABOUT MY CLASSMATE, A GIRL NAMED MIDORI KASUGANO.
...

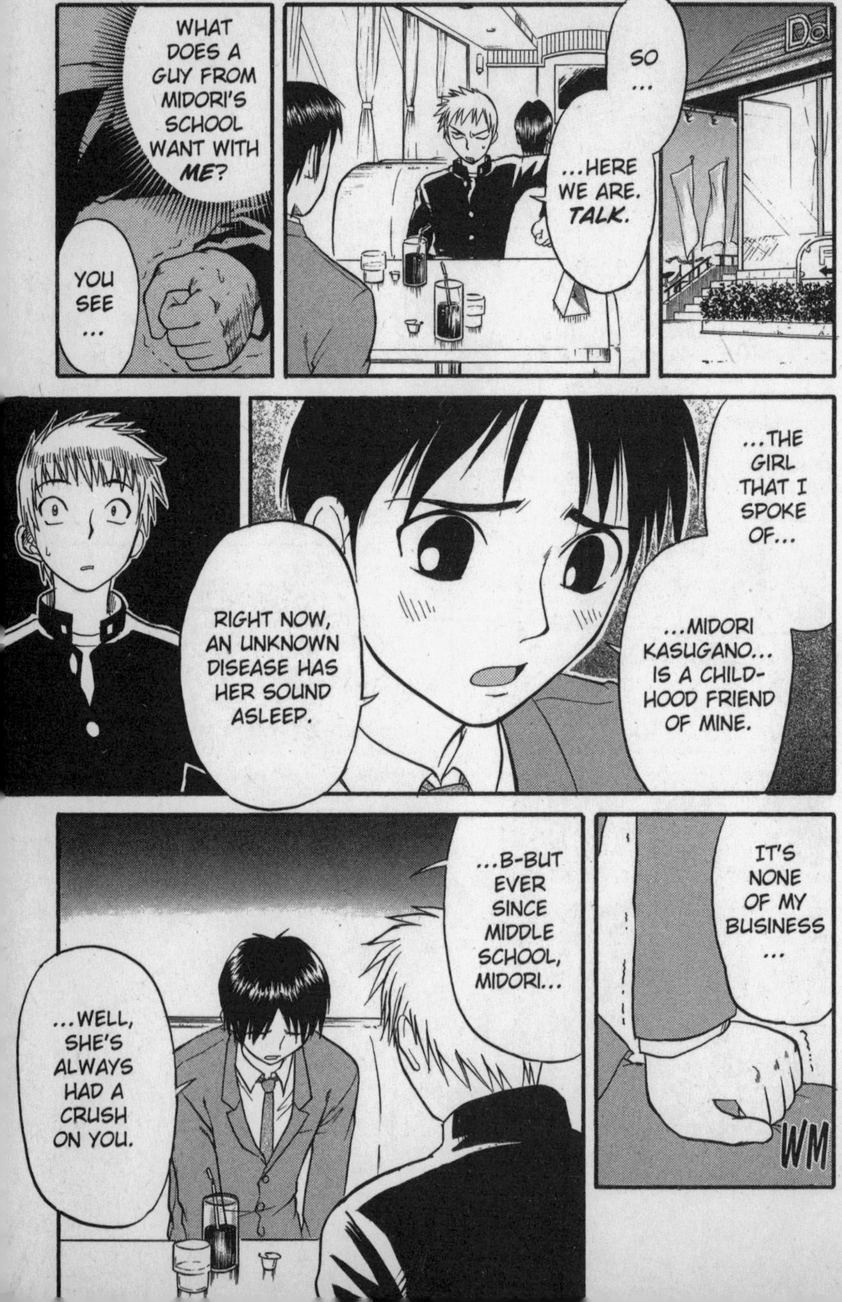
SO ...
...HERE WE ARE. *TALK.*
WHAT DOES A GUY FROM MIDORI'S SCHOOL WANT WITH *ME*?
YOU SEE ...
...THE GIRL THAT I SPOKE OF...
...MIDORI KASUGANO... IS A CHILD-HOOD FRIEND OF MINE.
RIGHT NOW, AN UNKNOWN DISEASE HAS HER SOUND ASLEEP.
IT'S NONE OF MY BUSINESS ...
WM
...B-BUT EVER SINCE MIDDLE SCHOOL, MIDORI...
...WELL, SHE'S ALWAYS HAD A CRUSH ON YOU.

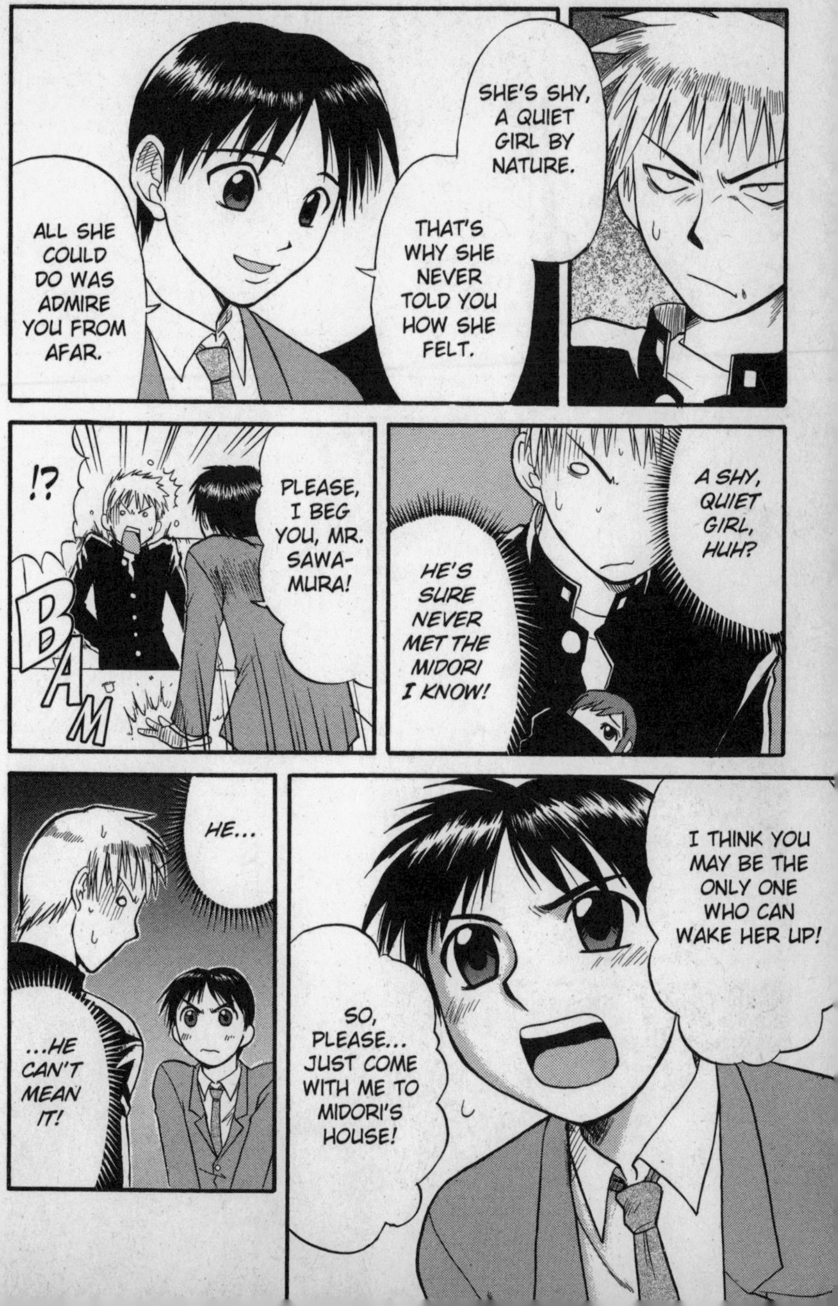
SHE'S SHY, A QUIET GIRL BY NATURE.
THAT'S WHY SHE NEVER TOLD YOU HOW SHE FELT.
ALL SHE COULD DO WAS ADMIRE YOU FROM AFAR.
A SHY, QUIET GIRL, HUH?
HE'S SURE NEVER MET THE MIDORI I KNOW!
PLEASE, I BEG YOU, MR. SAWA-MURA!
!?
BAM
I THINK YOU MAY BE THE ONLY ONE WHO CAN WAKE HER UP!
SO, PLEASE... JUST COME WITH ME TO MIDORI'S HOUSE!
HE...
...HE CAN'T MEAN IT!

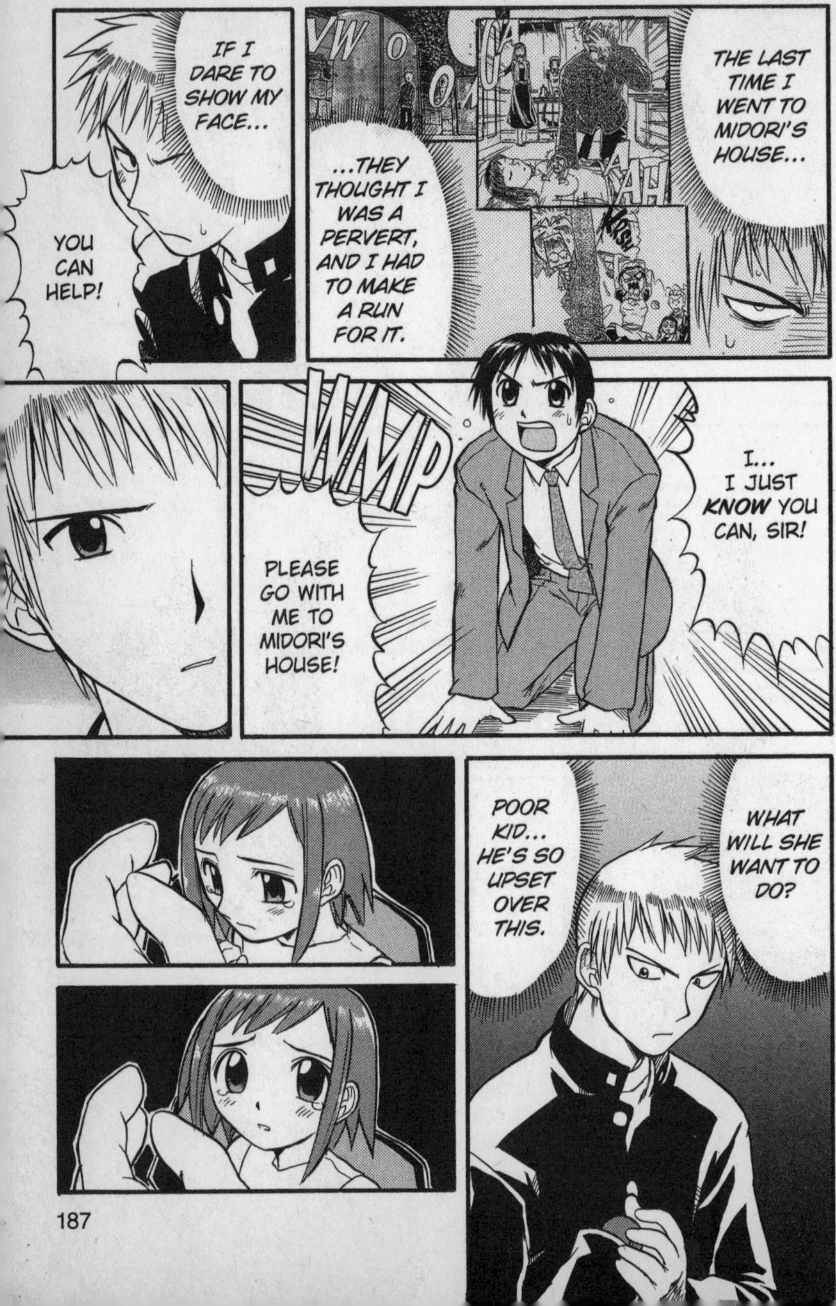
THE LAST TIME I WENT TO MIDORI'S HOUSE...
...THEY THOUGHT I WAS A PERVERT, AND I HAD TO MAKE A RUN FOR IT.
IF I DARE TO SHOW MY FACE...
YOU CAN HELP!
WMP
I... I JUST KNOW YOU CAN, SIR!
PLEASE GO WITH ME TO MIDORI'S HOUSE!
WHAT WILL SHE WANT TO DO?
POOR KID... HE'S SO UPSET OVER THIS.

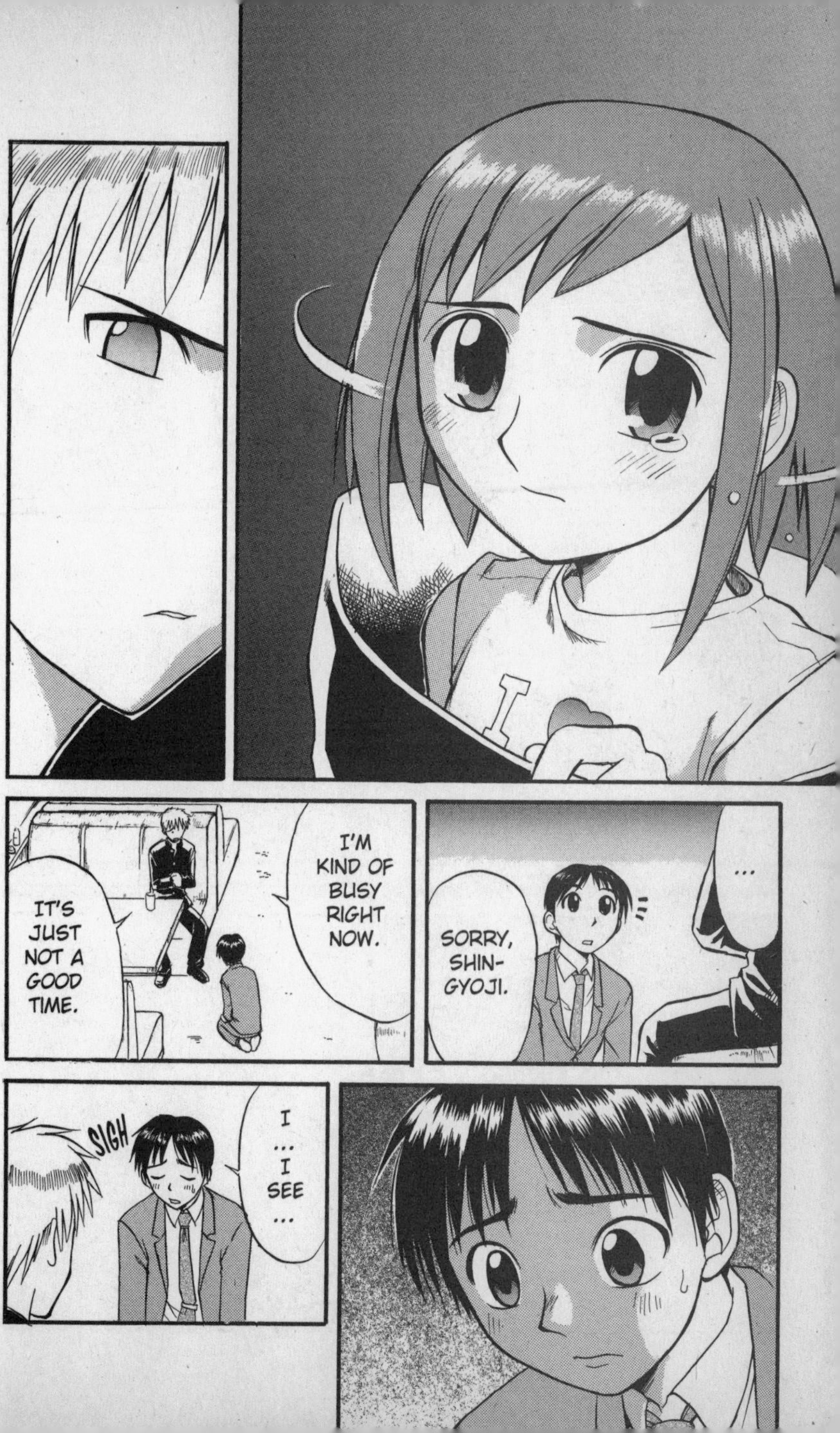
...
SORRY, SHIN-GYOJI.
I'M KIND OF BUSY RIGHT NOW.
IT'S JUST NOT A GOOD TIME.
I ... I SEE ...
SIGH

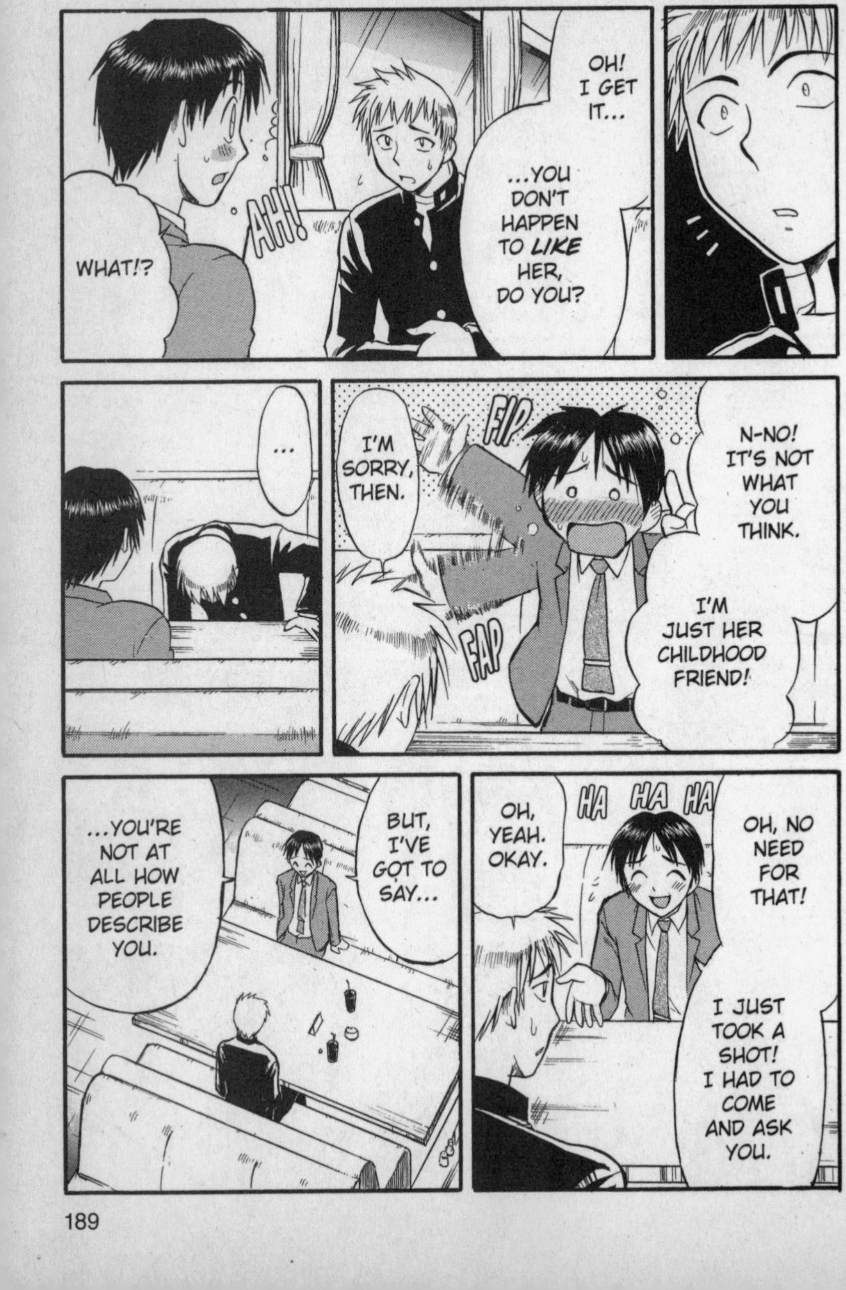
OH! I GET IT...
...YOU DON'T HAPPEN TO *LIKE* HER, DO YOU?
AH!
WHAT!?
N-NO! IT'S NOT WHAT YOU THINK.
I'M JUST HER CHILDHOOD FRIEND!
FIP
FAP
I'M SORRY, THEN.
...
HA HA HA
OH, NO NEED FOR THAT!
I JUST TOOK A SHOT! I HAD TO COME AND ASK YOU.
OH, YEAH. OKAY.
BUT, I'VE GOT TO SAY...
...YOU'RE NOT AT ALL HOW PEOPLE DESCRIBE YOU.

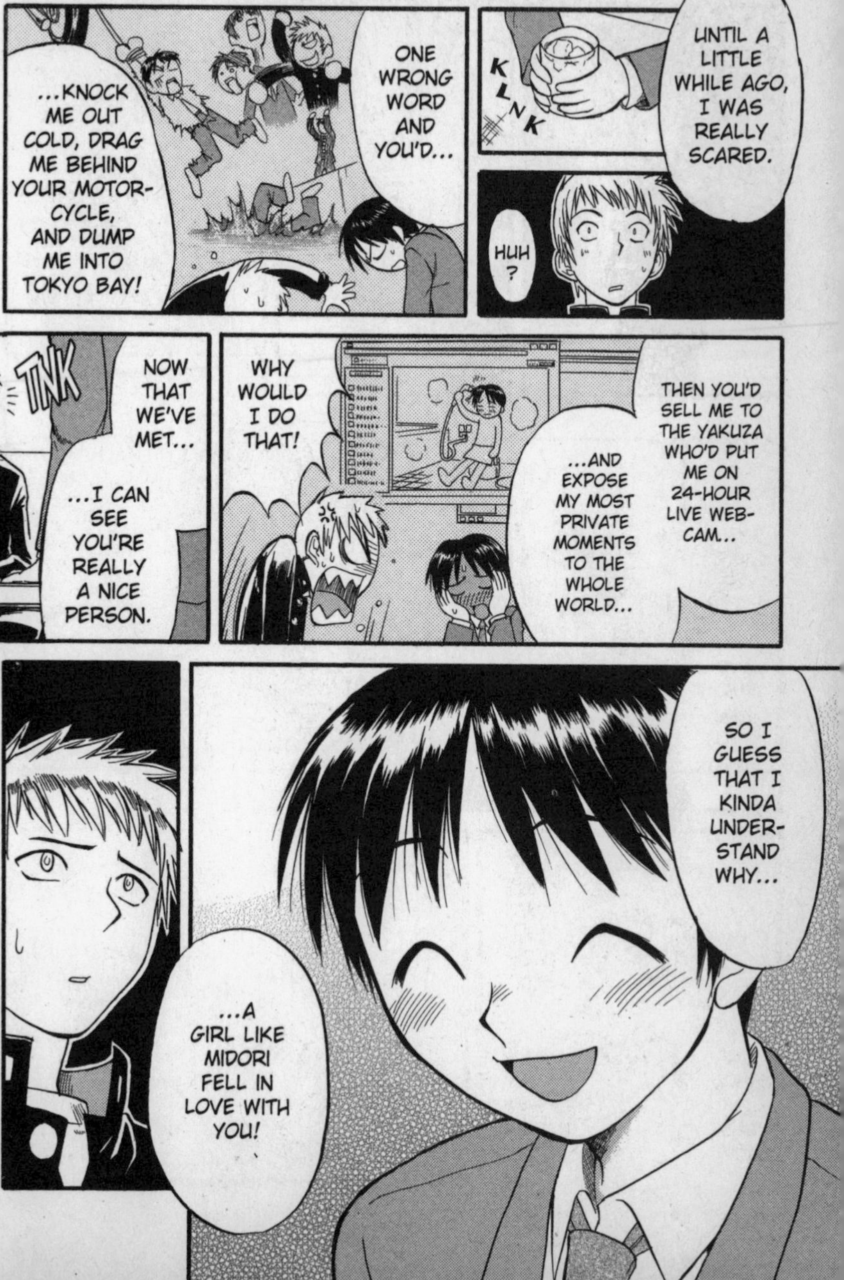
UNTIL A LITTLE WHILE AGO, I WAS REALLY SCARED.
KLNK
HUH?
ONE WRONG WORD AND YOU'D...
...KNOCK ME OUT COLD, DRAG ME BEHIND YOUR MOTOR-CYCLE, AND DUMP ME INTO TOKYO BAY!
THEN YOU'D SELL ME TO THE YAKUZA WHO'D PUT ME ON 24-HOUR LIVE WEB-CAM...
...AND EXPOSE MY MOST PRIVATE MOMENTS TO THE WHOLE WORLD...
WHY WOULD I DO THAT!
TNK
NOW THAT WE'VE MET...
...I CAN SEE YOU'RE REALLY A NICE PERSON.
SO I GUESS THAT I KINDA UNDER-STAND WHY...
...A GIRL LIKE MIDORI FELL IN LOVE WITH YOU!

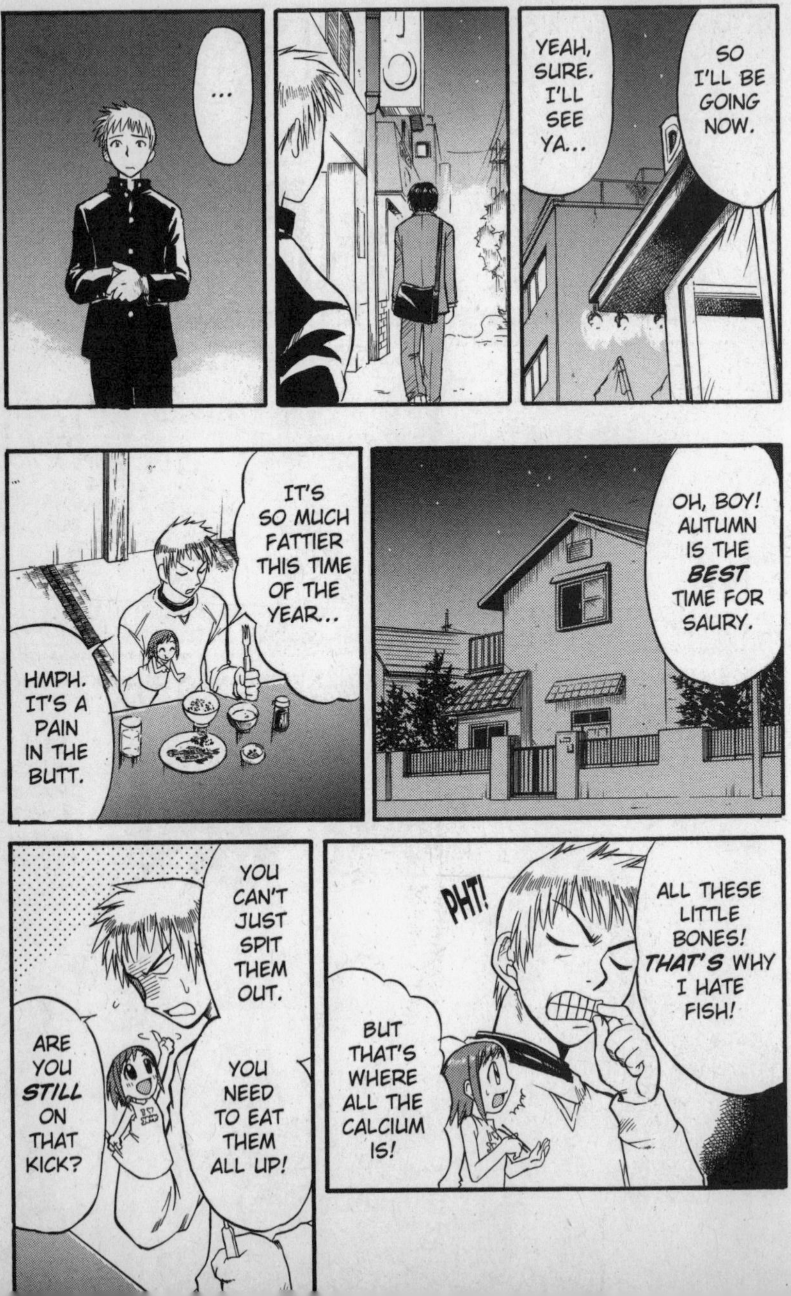
SO I'LL BE GOING NOW.
YEAH, SURE. I'LL SEE YA...
...
OH, BOY! AUTUMN IS THE BEST TIME FOR SAURY.
IT'S SO MUCH FATTIER THIS TIME OF THE YEAR...
HMPH. IT'S A PAIN IN THE BUTT.
ALL THESE LITTLE BONES! THAT'S WHY I HATE FISH!
PHT!
BUT THAT'S WHERE ALL THE CALCIUM IS!
YOU CAN'T JUST SPIT THEM OUT.
YOU NEED TO EAT THEM ALL UP!
ARE YOU STILL ON THAT KICK?

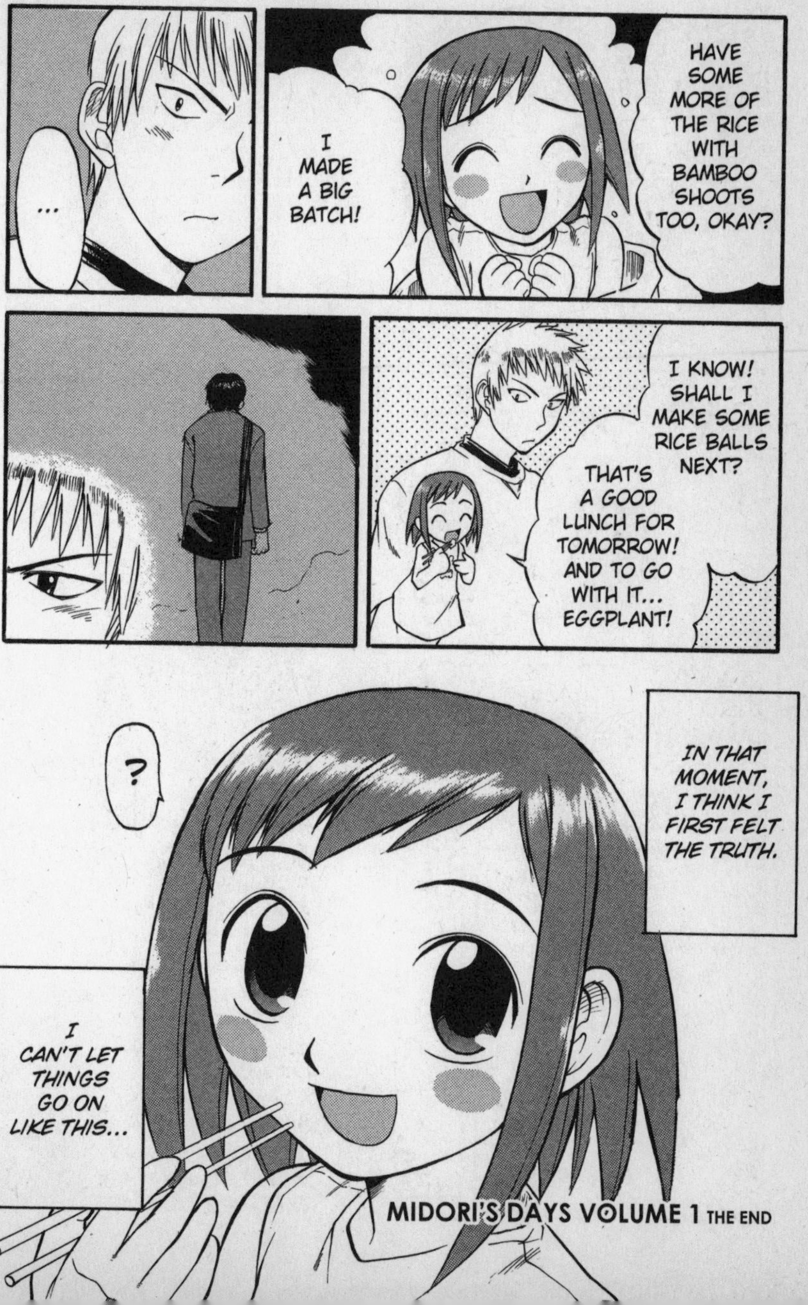
HAVE SOME MORE OF THE RICE WITH BAMBOO SHOOTS TOO, OKAY?
I MADE A BIG BATCH!
...
I KNOW! SHALL I MAKE SOME RICE BALLS NEXT?
THAT'S A GOOD LUNCH FOR TOMORROW! AND TO GO WITH IT... EGGPLANT!
IN THAT MOMENT, I THINK I FIRST FELT THE TRUTH.
?
I CAN'T LET THINGS GO ON LIKE THIS...
MIDORI'S DAYS VOLUME 1 THE END

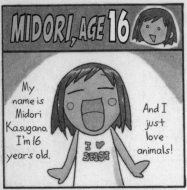

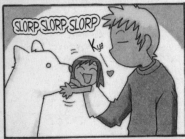

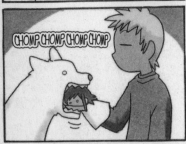

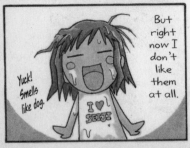

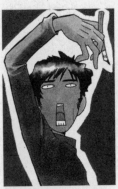

KAZUROU INOUE

Finally, the completion of the first volume! Excitement, anxiety and days and days of stress (with no time off) have resulted in this comic. I'm totally speechless! My cerebral CPU has gone up in flames! (What *is* that anyway?) This is a story filled with love and comedy, and I hope that you'll read it leisurely, without thinking too deeply about it.

MIDORI, AGE 16
My name is Midori Kasugano. I'm 16 years old.
And I just love animals!
I ♥ SEIJI
SLORP SLORP SLORP
Kya
CHOMP CHOMP CHOMP CHOMP
But right now I don't like them at all.
Yuck! Smells like dog.
I ♥ SEIJI

EDITOR'S RECOMMENDATIONS

More manga!
More manga!

If you enjoyed this volume of

MIDORI DAYS™

then here's some more manga you might be interested in.

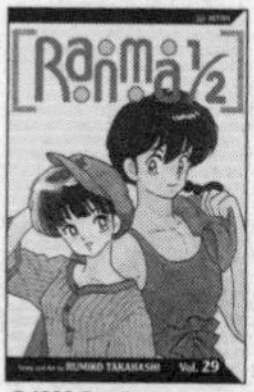
Ranma 1/2
RUMIKO TAKAHASHI
Vol. 29

©1988 Rumiko Takahashi/Shogakukan, Inc.

***Ranma* 1/2 by Rumiko Takahashi:**
RANMA 1/2 is a martial arts/teenage romance comedy like nothing you've ever seen! When Ranma and his father Genma get splashed with cold water, Dad transforms into a giant panda and male Ranma becomes a young girl!

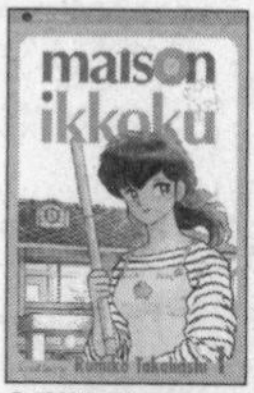
maison ikkoku

© 1984 Rumiko Takahashi/Shogakukan, Inc.

***Maison Ikkoku* by Rumiko Takahashi:**
When you're a poor college student who can barely pass his classes or make a decent living, and always have to fend off the nosiest neighbors in the shabbiest apartment ever, how are you supposed to win the woman of your dreams? Between romantic rivals, financial difficulties and hilarious misunderstandings, will it ever work out?

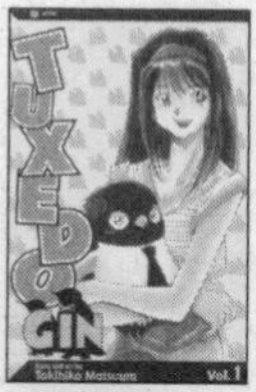
TUXEDO GIN
Vol. 1

© 1997 Tokihiko Matsuura/Shogakukan, Inc.

***Tuxedo Gin* by Tokihiko Matsuura:**
Seventeen-year old Ginji Kusanagi is on the eve of making his debut as a pro boxer. He's also just met Minako Sasebo, the girl of his dreams. Unfortunately, Ginji has an accident and dies...and is then reincarnated as a penguin! Will love be able to bloom between a boxing penguin and a beautiful girl!?

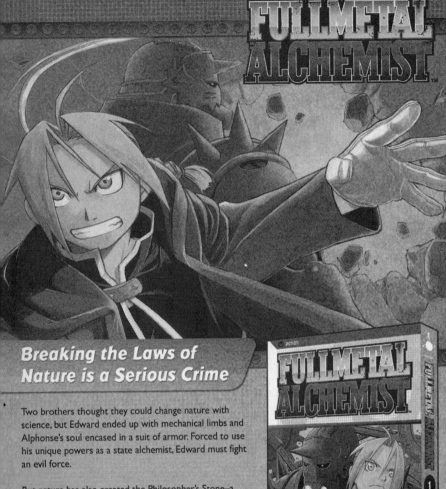
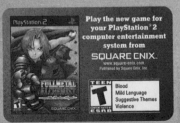

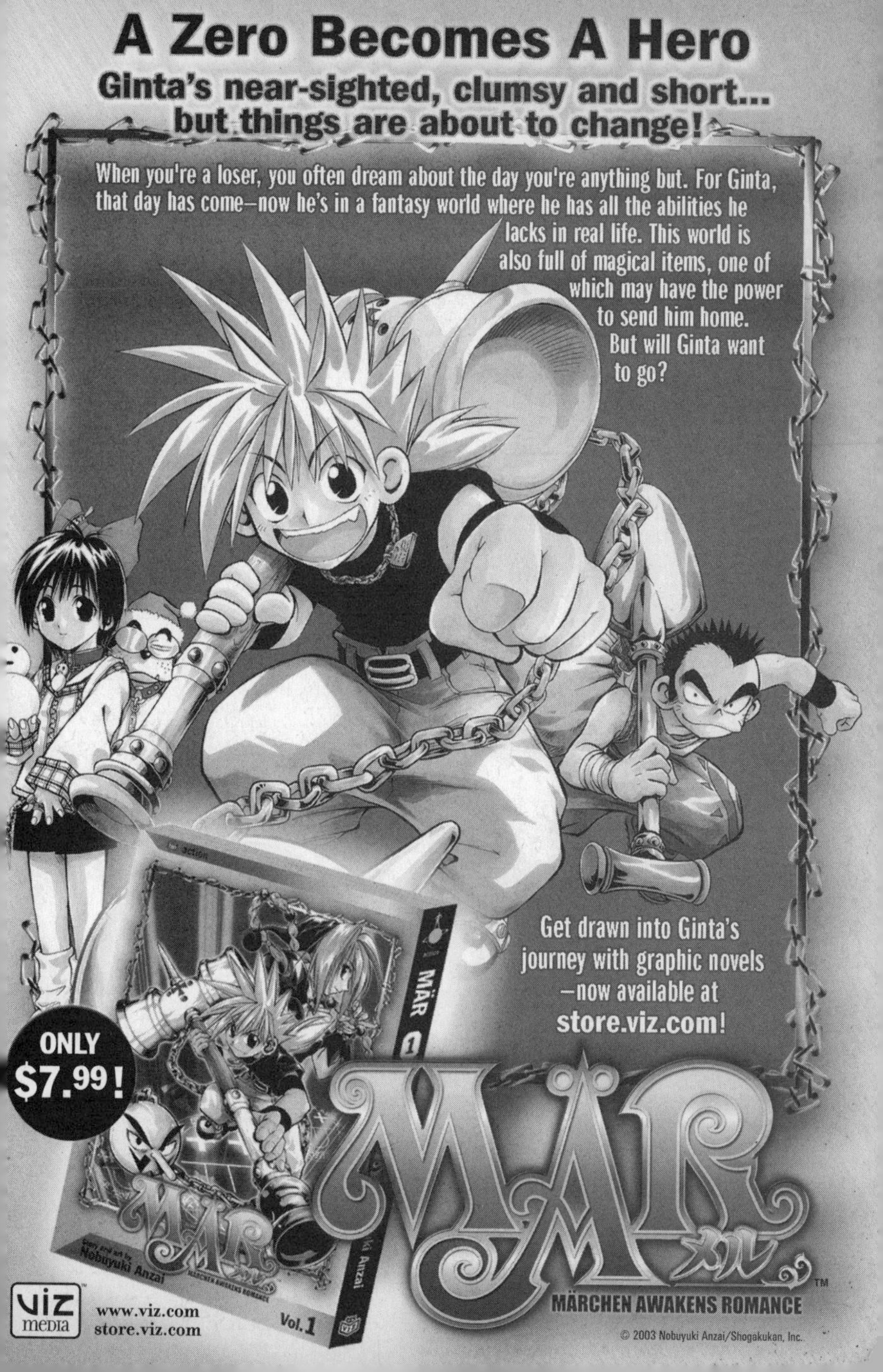
A Zero Becomes A Hero
Ginta's near-sighted, clumsy and short...
but things are about to change!
When you're a loser, you often dream about the day you're anything but. For Ginta, that day has come—now he's in a fantasy world where he has all the abilities he lacks in real life. This world is also full of magical items, one of which may have the power to send him home. But will Ginta want to go?
Get drawn into Ginta's journey with graphic novels —now available at store.viz.com!
ONLY $7.99!
MÄR
MÄRCHEN AWAKENS ROMANCE
Vol. 1
Nobuyuki Anzai
www.viz.com
store.viz.com
© 2003 Nobuyuki Anzai/Shogakukan, Inc.

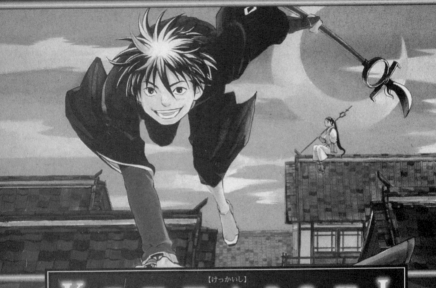
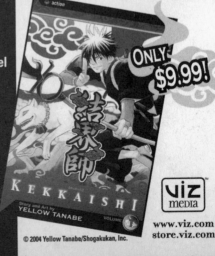

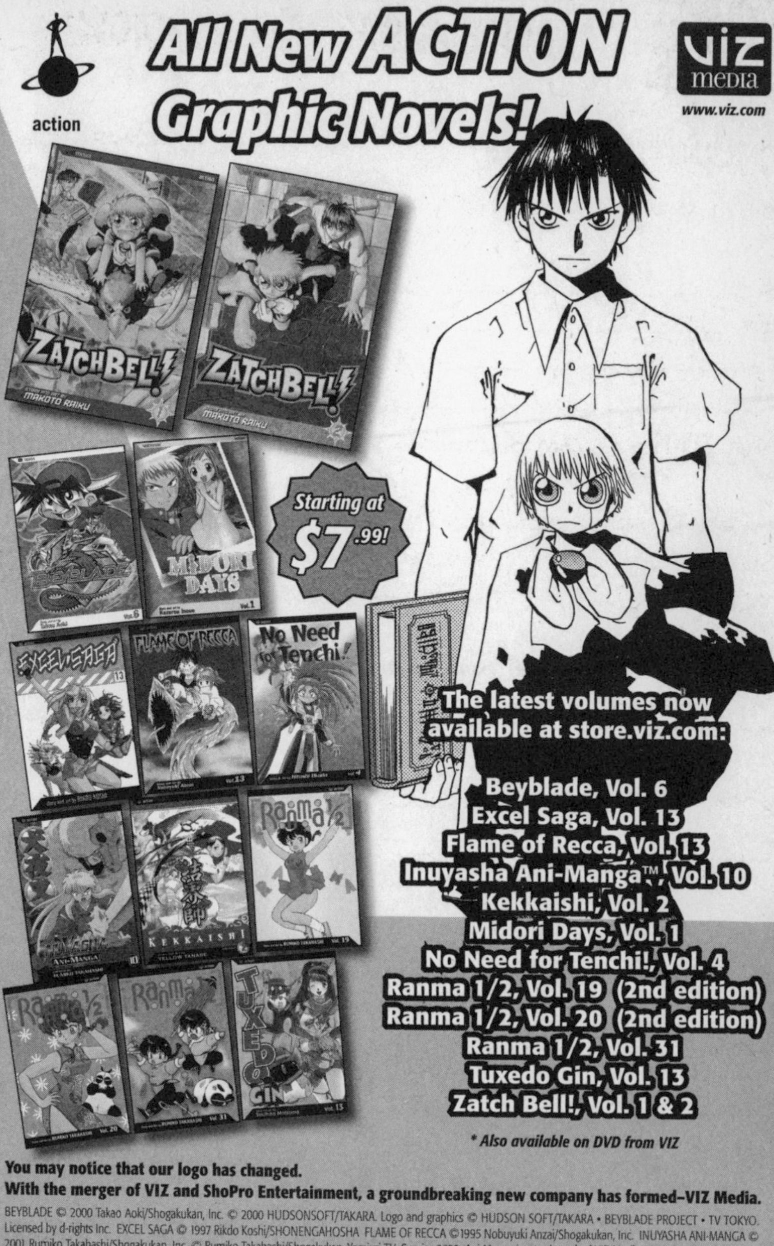
action
All New ACTION Graphic Novels!
VIZ media
www.viz.com
Starting at $7.99!
The latest volumes now available at store.viz.com:
Beyblade, Vol. 6
Excel Saga, Vol. 13
Flame of Recca, Vol. 13
Inuyasha Ani-Manga™, Vol. 10
Kekkaishi, Vol. 2
Midori Days, Vol. 1
No Need for Tenchi!, Vol. 4
Ranma 1/2, Vol. 19 (2nd edition)
Ranma 1/2, Vol. 20 (2nd edition)
Ranma 1/2, Vol. 31
Tuxedo Gin, Vol. 13
Zatch Bell!, Vol. 1 & 2
* Also available on DVD from VIZ
You may notice that our logo has changed.
With the merger of VIZ and ShoPro Entertainment, a groundbreaking new company has formed–VIZ Media.
BEYBLADE © 2000 Takao Aoki/Shogakukan, Inc. © 2000 HUDSONSOFT/TAKARA. Logo and graphics © HUDSON SOFT/TAKARA • BEYBLADE PROJECT • TV TOKYO. Licensed by d-rights Inc. EXCEL SAGA © 1997 Rikdo Koshi/SHONENGAHOSHA FLAME OF RECCA © 1995 Nobuyuki Anzai/Shogakukan, Inc. INUYASHA ANI-MANGA © 2001 Rumiko Takahashi/Shogakukan, Inc. © Rumiko Takahashi/Shogakukan, Yomiuri TV, Sunrise 2000 Ani-Manga is a trademark of VIZ Media, LLC. KEKKAISHI © 2004 Yellow Tanabe/Shogakukan, Inc. MIDORI DAYS © 2004 Kazurou Inoue/Shogakukan, Inc. NO NEED FOR TENCHI! © HITOSHI OKUDA 1996 © AIC/VAP • NTV RANMA1/2 © 1988 Rumiko Takahashi/Shogakukan, Inc. TUXEDO GIN © 1997 Tokihiko Matsuura/Shogakukan, Inc. ZATCH BELL! © 2001 Makoto Raiku/Shogakukan, Inc.

LOVE MANGA?   LET US KNOW!

☐ Please do NOT send me information about VIZ Media products, news and events, special offers, or other information.

☐ Please do NOT send me information from VIZ Media's trusted business partners.

Name: _____

Address: _____

City: _____ **State:** _____ **Zip:** _____

E-mail: _____

☐ Male ☐ Female   **Date of Birth** (mm/dd/yyyy): ___ / ___ / ___   (Under 13? Parental consent required)

What race/ethnicity do you consider yourself? (check all that apply)

☐ White/Caucasian   ☐ Black/African American   ☐ Hispanic/Latino

☐ Asian/Pacific Islander   ☐ Native American/Alaskan Native ☐ Other: _____

What VIZ title(s) did you purchase? (indicate title(s) purchased) _____

_____

What other VIZ titles do you own? _____

_____

Reason for purchase: (check all that apply)

☐ Special offer   ☐ Favorite title / author / artist / genre

☐ Gift   ☐ Recommendation   ☐ Collection

☐ Read excerpt in VIZ manga sampler   ☐ Other _____

Where did you make your purchase? (please check one)

☐ Comic store   ☐ Bookstore   ☐ Grocery Store

☐ Convention   ☐ Newsstand   ☐ Video Game Store

☐ Online (site:_____)   ☐ Other _____

How many manga titles have you purchased in the last year? How many were VIZ titles?
(please check one from each column)

MANGA	VIZ
☐ None	☐ None
☐ 1 – 4	☐ 1 – 4
☐ 5 – 10	☐ 5 – 10
☐ 11+	☐ 11+

How much influence do special promotions and gifts-with-purchase have on the titles you buy?
(please circle, with 5 being great influence and 1 being none)

1 2 3 4 5

Do you purchase every volume of your favorite series?

☐ Yes! Gotta have 'em as my own ☐ No. Please explain: ______________________

What kind of manga storylines do you most enjoy? **(check all that apply)**

☐ Action / Adventure
☐ Comedy
☐ Fighting
☐ Artistic / Alternative
☐ Science Fiction
☐ Romance (shojo)
☐ Sports
☐ Other ______________________
☐ Horror
☐ Fantasy (shojo)
☐ Historical

If you watch the anime or play a video or TCG game from a series, how likely are you to buy the manga? **(please circle, with 5 being very likely and 1 being unlikely)**

1 2 3 4 5

If unlikely, please explain: ______________________

Who are your favorite authors / artists? ______________________

____

What titles would like you translated and sold in English? ______________________

____

THANK YOU! Please send the completed form t

NJW Research
42 Catharine Street
Poughkeepsie, NY 12601

Your privacy is very important to us. Al **es only and will not be sold or otherwise divulged.**